The Language-Experience Approach to the Teaching of Reading

SECOND EDITION

Russell G. Stauffer
University of Delaware

HARPER & ROW, PUBLISHERS, New York
Cambridge, Hagerstown, Philadelphia, San Francisco,
London, Mexico City, São Paulo, Sydney

1817

Sponsoring Editor: George A. Middendorf
Project Editor: Pamela Landau
Production Manager: Jeanie Berke
Compositor: The Composing Room of Michigan, Inc.
Printer and Binder: The Murray Printing Company
Art Studio: J & R Technical Services Inc.

The Language-Experience
Approach
to the Teaching
of Reading
SECOND EDITION

Copyright © 1980 by Russell G. Stauffer

Library of Congress Cataloging in Publication Data

Stauffer, Russell G
    The language-experience approach to the teaching
of reading.

    Includes bibliographies and index.
    1. Reading (Elementary)—Language experience
approach.   I. Title.
LB1573.33.S72 1980   372.4'1   79-17805
ISBN 0-06-046409-7

Contents

Preface, vii

Chapter 1 Language-Experience Foundations, 1
Language and the Organization of Experience, 4
Experience and the Organization of Knowledge, 9
Actions and Interactions, 15
Conclusion, 17
Bibliography, 19

Chapter 2 Early Reading Instruction:
The Process of Personal Discovery, 22
Readiness for Learning, 25
Administrative Considerations, 27
Individual Differences, 29
What About Reading?, 31
Language Plays a Central Role, 37
Social and Emotional Adjustment, 54
Standardized Reading-Readiness Tests, 55

Conclusion, 56
Bibliography, 57

Chapter 3 Language-Experience Practice at the Primary Level, 59
Getting Started, 61
Developing Word Recognition Power, 69
Grouping as an Antecedent to Individualization, 79
Individual Dictation, 84
Stimulus Interest Areas, 90
Classroom Seating, 105
Conclusion, 107
Bibliography, 108

Chapter 4 Building a Word Bank, 109
How to Develop a Sight Vocabulary, 109
Word Banks, 113
Words, Words, Words, 117
Word Recognition Skill, 121
Conclusion, 124
Bibliography, 125

Chapter 5 Creative Writing, 126
Handwriting, 127
Getting Started, 131
Promoting Creative Writing, 137
Concept Development, 140
Initial Creative Writing Examples, 141
Other Ideas About Creative Achievement, 159
Conclusion, 162
Bibliography, 163

Chapter 6 The Library, 165
Some Reflections on School Libraries, 166
Classroom Libraries, 168
The School Library, 172
Conclusion, 182
Bibliography, 182

Chapter 7 Directed Reading-Thinking Activities, 184
The Directed Reading-Thinking Plan, 185
Directing the Basic DRTA Steps, 188
A Directed Listening-Thinking Activity, 194
A Directed Reading-Thinking Activity Illustration, 196
Conclusion, 212
Bibliography, 213

Chapter 8   Inquiry Reading I, 215
Alternating Instruction, 219
Instructional Procedures—First Grade, 220
A Language Actions Foundation, 226
Conclusion, 227
Bibliography, 228

Chapter 9   Inquiry Reading II, 229
Inquiry Reading: Next Stages, 233
Inquiry Reading: Its Extension and Refinement, 237
Skills Acquired in Inquiry Reading, 253
Conclusion, 258
Bibliography, 259

Chapter 10   Word Recognition, 261
Word Recognition Defined, 262
A Puzzling Circumstance, 262
Meaning Clues to Word Recognition, 263
Vowel Keys, 269
Structural Variations, 272
Dictionary Usage, 273
Roots in Action, 275
Concept Development, 277
Conclusion, 280
Bibliography, 281

Chapter 11   Spelling Instruction, 282
Spelling, 287
Conclusion, 292
Bibliography, 293

Chapter 12   The Universality of LEA, 295
Third Year and Beyond, 296
Special Uses of LEA, 302
Clinical Cases, 320
Conclusion, 325
Bibliography, 326

Appendix A   A Language-Experience Film, 329
Appendix B   Research in Language Experience, 331

Index, 335

Preface

This book is a revision of a text first written in 1967 and 1968 and raises the question, "Why revise?" The answer is simple indeed. Anyone should have grown and learned much over a 10-year period. That is what this revision is to reflect.

As a matter of fact, comparison will show this revision is at least 80 percent different from the 1970 edition. In fact, it might have been more fitting to publish this edition under a slightly changed title, *The Experience-Language Approach to the Teaching of Reading.*

In a recent biography of Samuel Johnson, Bates writes about how Johnson "stormed the maingates of experience" to acquire mastery.[1] Johnson's life and words illustrate the resilience of the will. That, in brief, is the purpose of this revision, to help teachers and pupils to storm the maingates of experience, to experiment and search for the truth, and to use children's language to instruct and communicate. All that is required is the natural curiosity of the children and their will to achieve. That is why, woven into the fabric of each chapter, there are many detailed accounts reflecting pragmatic idealism and cognitive-veneration.

[1]W. Jackson Bates, *Samuel Johnson* (New York: Harcourt Brace Jovanovich, 1977).

This is not an account created in an armchair utopia. Quite the contrary. The text reflects years of close firsthand experience with classroom teachers, supervisors, and school administrators. To learn, one must get to where the action is—the classroom.

The instructional procedures described in this text reflect clearly that for instruction and learning to be effective there must be much pupil–pupil and teacher–pupil contact. This must take place with respect for students' interests and tastes, ideas and speculations, freedom of choice, self-expression, and honesty. We cannot afford to use psychological sorting and labeling of children as an excuse for professional failure.

The activities described at all levels from preschool to adult have a common thread—the students are active participants in the learning process. The key words are *action* (pupil and teacher action), *interaction* (among pupils and pupils and teachers), and *transaction* (cognitively and affectively). Respect is shown not only for the experiences and language children bring with them to school, but also for their sociocultural heritage and their natural curiosity.

In the first edition the discussion on spelling appeared only as a subtopic. However, subsequent experience as a consultant to teachers and teaching graduate courses on Language-Experiences Approach (LEA) procedures indicated that it would be wise to have a short, separate chapter on spelling.

Attention is given to the development of reading interests and tastes and to critical reading-thinking skills. This is done by means of group type *directed reading-thinking activities* and by *inquiry reading*. The group DRTA's foster the interaction of minds and the inquiry reading provides for a broad range of activities in which the pursuit of knowledge taxes the dimensions of multimedia communication. As a result, the library, as a multimedia center, becomes the hub of the reading instruction program.

Extensive reading is initiated in first grade and develops as a major activity. Children read and read and read. Intensive reading is also done as children convert interests into tastes and as they prepare sharing reports. They learn that there are many ways to share but that each requires preparation. All these activities and abilities foster a favorable attitude toward reading and a regard for reading as a means of acquiring knowledge.

Again, innumerable people should be named as contributing to the refinement of ideas recorded in this text. But to name all the children, teachers, supervisors, and administrators is impossible. Even so I am indebted to all and to all I am indeed most grateful. Some few must be named even at the risk of offending others: Dr. Kenneth Madden, State Superintendent of Schools for Delaware and formerly Superintendent of Schools at Seaford, Delaware; Mrs. Mary Phillips, Reading Supervisor, Seaford, Delaware; Mrs. Evelyn Kay, Elementary Supervisor, Cecil

County, Maryland; Mrs. Naomi England, Principal, Rising Sun, Maryland; Dr. Richard Petre, State Supervisor of Reading for Maryland; Dr. Dorsey Hammond, former State Supervisor of Reading for Maryland; Mrs. Dorothy Nave, Elementary Supervisor, Dorchester County, Maryland; Dr. Stephen Camper, Principal, St. Clair Elementary School, Cambridge, Maryland; Dr. Ann Jameson, Director of Elementary Education, Charles County, Maryland; Mrs. Evelyn Winfield, Supervisor of Reading, Charles County, Maryland; Mrs. Ann Smith, former Principal, Friends Lower School, Wilmington, Delaware; Mr. Max Harrell, Principal, Friends Lower School, Wilmington, Delaware; Dr. Charles Hutton, former Headmaster, Friends School, Wilmington, Delaware; Mrs. Marlene Harrell, Reading Supervisor, Sterck School for the Deaf, Newark, Delaware; Mr. Donald Nelson, Director, University of Delaware Learning Resource Center and his staff.

The highest form of commendation a teacher can receive is to be called an "eclectic teacher," one who takes advantage of good practices whenever possible and regardless of their source. The best label that can be applied to the language-experience approach is the "eclectic approach to reading instruction." It embraces the best practices regardless of their source and does so in a functional, communication-oriented way.

Finally, I must remind the reader that preschool children learn language without knowing any of the rules that authorities have declared by hindsight. The reason children learn language so readily is because they do so in the course of using it to satisfy their own purposes. Intentions, or purposes, are the indispensable key to learning. If, as James Britton says, we see human beings as creatures who take up *enterprises* that are actualized by *intentions* and set up *expectations*, then we will use the language and experience wealth of children not as "gold in coffers but as capital expertly invested," enabling them to make fresh encounters nourished by refined powers of anticipation. We must remember that this is the era in which Charles Duke went hunting 240,000 miles away, left the Apollo lunar module, drove across Descartes Region to Plum Crater, and left Rover to collect samples of rocks.

R.G.S.

Chapter 1
Language-Experience
Foundations

INTRODUCTION

This opening chapter is designed to provide pedagogic foundations for the almost manual-like chapters that follow. Similar in nature to the first chapter in the first edition, this presentation is a reaffirmation of the basic tenet that people's actions are governed primarily by what they truly believe in. Accordingly, even though this chapter is brief and perhaps challenging, it will provide the fountainhead for the basics that follow.

Graduate students and experienced teachers may want to pursue even further the groundwork so briefly provided. For them the thirty some references provided in the bibliography will prove most helpful. Of special value are the writings of Roger Brown (6, 7), Jerome S. Bruner et al. (9), John Dewey (13), Herbert Klausmeier (20), and Jean Piaget (23, 24).

Undergraduates may prefer to start with Chapter 2 and become acquainted with the multiple instructional actions and learner interactions that are detailed in the following chapters. Then, with the insights thus provided, they may better appreciate the pedagogical foundations delineated in this chapter.

In may ways the label the *language-experience approach to the teaching of reading* is a more lucid, descriptive accounting of means to ends when expressed as the experience-language approach. It suggests that the experience and the language of children are being used for reading instruction purposes, because they represent the concrete richness that becoming involved in firsthand functional situations promoting verbal interactions can produce. When this occurs the instruction becomes an extension of children's preschool learning rhythms, in which they generate a system of language usage primarily in the course of using it *to satisfy their own purposes.* Thus the extension of this "natural process" is based on teacher-structured situations that promote cooperation between adult and child. The language production that results does so from an intention to say something and to do so with contextual support.

On the other hand, viewing the language-experience approach this way tends to limit interpretation of its scope to initial reading instruction. Such an interpretation overlooks the model of language as an expressive art that is seen developmentally as a matrix from which innumerable uses are achieved in all areas of the curriculum and over a wide range of tasks. In this regard it may be more fitting to use the label *communication arts* because of the complementary provisions this broad term includes. Reading, writing, listening, and speaking are the *verbal arts.* When they are coupled with the *iconic arts* of sketching, painting, recording, and the like, they embrace the concept of *total communication.* Total communication includes the full spectrum of communication modes. It also suggests clearly the involvement of people interacting freely and purposefully with people. Thus reading instruction is based on and grows out of rich and vast experiences springing out of human interactions achieved developmentally by a process of progressive differentiation. By using the symbolic arts as a means of getting something done and documenting experiences a wide range of activities is covered.

The twin pillars of experience and language suggest features that some people tend to build into a dichotomized construct of language and experience. This is unfortunate because it narrows instructional expectations and thwarts our enterprises. We must therefore choose an alternative that acknowledges the wide range of the communication arts. It seems that a more comprehensive way of framing the concept of language and experience is to hyphenate the word and unify the concept. This way of perceiving and interpreting provides a paradigm by which to justify the interpretation chosen. Thus "experience and language" becomes the language-experience framework relevant to teaching and learning. We need a theory that utilizes the human use of language (concepts) based on experience (perceptions) and in quest of understanding (cognition) in order to reflect and to communicate. Because the human being is "essentially a symbol-using animal" (10, p. 47), all his significant actions are influenced by language. It thus creates a storehouse of representations that are selective. Furthermore, because language is only one of a number of ways by which we represent the world, and because symbolizing does not occur in an experience vacuum, any representation becomes a language-experience construct. Thus the compound is based on a sound semantic relationship.

The functional dynamism of the composite language-experience concept has other implications that make it dynamic. *Experience* and *experiment* are so closely associated in meaning that they are sometimes confused.

> Both terms denote a practical as opposed to a speculative way of finding out about a thing... facts that are not obvious or outwardly eivdent. Experience implies direct personal knowledge through immediate observation, actual practice, or conscious subjection... it especially implies knowledge which comes as a result of one's normal way of life, one's particular environment, or one's character or training. *Experience* is applicable not only to an individual's way of finding out facts, but to a group's way, as that of a class, a people, a race, or the like [35, p. 317].

Experiment, on the other hand, adds the dimensions of "trying or trial, testing or test, proving or proof, demonstrating or demonstration" (ibid.). In turn, language is the prime means for storing experiences, for generalizing from visual modes, for documenting and classifying, and above all for setting up expectations. Teacher-structured experiences or experiments and teacher inventiveness in creating situations forge the links that can give experiences rich language instructional import.

The language-experience approach (LEA) to learning to read is developed in this book as an eclectic, global approach or as a *concept-percept*-based approach. It is as all-embracing a concept in the world of education as the concept of time-space and the theory of relativity is in the world of science. The practices and procedures of LEA can be as influential in education in general, and in the teaching of reading and writing in particular, as symbolic logic has been in the world of the scientist. It should replace, in the design of educational processes, the false interpretations and polarizations of the *synthetic* and *analytical* methods. Both are based on a faulty empiricism and a haphazard analysis of the communication process. Both dichotomized extremes represent a cancer of pedagogical narrowness whose effects are readily seen. They fail to stand up under scrutiny, either theoretically or in practical situations, both inside and outside the schools.

LANGUAGE AND THE ORGANIZATION OF EXPERIENCE

A study of the evolution of language involves two tenets. First, language as a means of communication is ordinarily thought of as being directed from person to person. Language belongs to human beings as members of a social community. Second, it is a means by which persons encode and decode meanings with signals or symbols. As such, language has the fineness of clear and repeated accuracy needed to make a code. In brief, language is a code that represents the learned behavior of a social community.

To think of communication and language in the person-to-person sense or in the social sense is to think of them functionally. The *function* of language is to communicate, and that is its primary purpose. If language usage—either oral or written—is to be taught effectively, the teaching must be based on the functional use of language. This means, in brief, instruction accomplished in functional situations and not with kits, skill books, and apparatus.

In addition, because language provides a means for classifying experiences and making hierarchical distinctions, it provides a useful strategy for thinking. In fact, it may be generally agreed "(a) that higher processes of thinking are normally achieved by the interaction of a child's language behavior with his other mental and perceptual powers; and (b) that language behavior represents the aspect of his thought processes most accessible to outside influences, including that of the teacher" (10, p. 49).

Human interest in language appears to be innate. Babies, if left alone, will make attempts at speech. A community of people out of contact with other groups emerges with an unmistakable language. The impulse to use some kind of language is apparently intense, both psychoneurologically and socially (7).

Speech is a human activity and a learned activity. Whatever the mode of speech acquired by a social community, it is a particular language that has to be learned in each special instance. Each example of language—dialect, vernacular, jargon, and slang—represents humanity's freedom and ability to use any pronounceable sound code for some meaning or other and to pass on this code from generation to generation.

Speech is sometimes regarded as humanity's greatest achievement. It permits humans to attach significance to sounds, to retain and use a huge repertoire of codified sounds, and to form complex relationships among experiences, phonemes, and morphemes.

There seems to be a critical period during which speech is learned most readily. Between the ages of one and five, children are particularly adept at learning not only the language of their community, but other languages as well. In fact, if speech is not learned at the proper time, the entire social aspect of an individual may be affected.

Most children are responsive to the continuous stream of language influences in the world about them. This means that they are alive to what is happening phonologically and linguistically in their world and that they are participating in a continual development of symbols (language and signs) and their exchange. As a matter of fact, because of the arbitrary nature of language, it is almost more a process than a means of storage. This is because language is constantly meeting the demands of the time. New words are added, old words are dropped or adapted to new meanings, and new idea structures are formulated.

The infant who learns to make the sound *da-da* and learns to associate it with the adults about her has learned from repeated experience to use sound to produce a response. As she matures, the number and frequency of experiences needed to learn to use a sound, or set of sounds, to symbolize a concept, decreases, varies, quickens, and exacts. It does so in response to many influencing variables of a personal and social nature. Nevertheless, the learning pattern has been established, and the principles of phonology, syntax, and semantics that she acquires remain functional throughout her life. This is so whether or not patterns are learned by the child on her own or are taught by someone else.

Language is not only a means for constructing representations but also a means for combining words into continuous speech or writing and for grasping lexical and semantic relationships. L. H. Vigotsky points out that when a concept is embodied in a word, it represents an act of generalization. At first the generalization is primitive and associations are made on the basis of vague general impressions of similarity. Thus "bow-wow" is applied to a series of objects that from an adult point of view are quite disparate (34, p. 83). These potential concepts play a part in the formation of genuine concepts and are formed in the sphere of enactive perceptual or practical action-bound circumstances. This may be illustrated by the discrepancy between childrens' ability to form concepts and their ability to define them. Jean Piaget asked seven-to eight-year-olds the meaning of the word *because* in the sentence, "I won't go to school tomorrow because I am sick." Most of the children said it meant "he is sick" or "he won't go to school," and seemingly based their definitions on enactive meanings of what can be done. They did not realize that the question did not refer to separate facts of sickness and of school absence but to their connection. Yet they grasped the meaning of the sentence (ibid., p. 87). This illustrates, too, a distinction between concepts spontaneously formed by children and what might result when concepts are deliberately taught. Nevertheless, words play an integral part in the developing process.

By the time children connect two words such as "Da-Da come" and then adapt the expression to call their pet dog and say, "Bo Bo come," they are usually between the ages of 15 and 24 months. These expressions, sometimes labeled *telegraph language*, carry the essential information of what they had heard and how they may be imitating or speaking and creating for themselves or both. This functionally correct order of noun-verb or subject-predicate or object and action on object shows how the genesis of thought and of syntax unify and function in a practical situation. When someone expands the contraction and says, "Yes, Daddy is coming home," the child tends to imitate and use not only adjectives and adverbs but also connectives (8). But imitation is only part of the story. Children's inventiveness in the use of language reflects the discovery not only of its communication scope but also of its morphological regularities, a discovery they may refine for the rest of their lives. The home becomes as James Britton put it "a language workshop in which the child serves an eager apprenticeship" (6, p. 13). In this regard one must take into account (teachers particularly) that there are differences in language environment between socioeconomic groups and within groups.

For the LEA-schooled teacher it is of utmost importance to make the instructional environment an "experience-language workshop" and do so in such a way that the children continue to be eager apprentices. This can be accomplished if another aspect of language production is taken into account, "the intention to say so-and-so," because intention plays a vital role (28). Teaching must be done in such a way that "discovery learning" through firsthand experiences and experiments becomes the key mode accompanied by pupil intention both to learn and to communicate what has been discovered. In this way the verbal actions and interactions are initiated and sustained largely by pupil motivation. Then, as Britton says, "when the rhythms of learning that attend a learner's initiative are free to operate, there are real breakthroughs in learning and language development" (6, p. 15).

Another interesting aspect of thought and language development is a comparison of the almost building-blocklike emergence of a syntactical system, on the one hand, and the generalization of a system of concepts as if from the top down from superordinate concepts to the implied existence of subordinate concepts, on the other. *Syntactically* the child proceeds word by word, differentiating and unifying, as in "Daddy come" to "Daddy come soon" to "Daddy come home soon," proceeding from the concrete noun (thing) and verb (action on) to adverb and adjective (modifiers) qualifiers. *Conceptually*, as Vigotsky describes, a child learns a word like *flower* (a superordinate concept) and then learns the word *rose* (a subordinate concept). For a long time the two labels are interchanged, but once flower becomes generalized, then other subordinate concepts (*tulip*, *petunia*) also crystallize and a system begins to take shape (34, 92–93). Thus it might be said that syntactically children proceed from the part to the whole as they apply its organizing power to their own experiences and conceptually they proceed from whole to part as the rudiments of systematization are acquired.

All this is of utmost importance to school instruction because of the relationship between development and instruction. "The former creates the potentialities; the latter realizes them" (34, p. 94). The measure of a child's level of development is how he thinks about subjects, and the measure of instruction is how he can transfer what has been learned to new media or new situations. It stands to reason that as children develop, the formal disciplines of awareness, abstraction, and control play an increasingly more important role than in the more elementary, spontaneous processes.

> To sum up, then, we have to generalize from particular representations of past experiences in order to apply them to new ones, and language helps us to do this by providing a ready means of classifying these experiences. The important thing to remember is that as long as every event is experienced as unique and different from all other events we cannot set up expectations regarding the future. It is by recognizing recurrences that we learn from experiences]10, p. 48].

Constance Kamii described this succinctly when she wrote about how a child after one or two falls begins to anticipate a descent and adjusts accordingly. This anticipation or expectation becomes a part of adaptation. Then before long the child can anticipate running up and down a stairway without actually doing so. Thus knowledge is created progressively out of adaptive actions (19). This seems to account, too, for the reason that all peoples have developed language. Language helps them to organize their experiences and in turn their mental powers. Children are indeed born learners.

It has been estimated that by the time children are of school age, the size of their functional speaking vocabulary ranges from about 2,500 words (30) to 12,000 words (26, 31). A recent study (32) of the number of different words used by first-grade children in dictated stories yielded a count of 3331. With both extremes in mind, it seems reasonably safe to estimate the number of words known to six-year-olds at about 7500. (11, p. 32)

It is, thus, readily apparent that six-year-olds bring with them to school a functional speaking vocabulary of almost unlimited wealth. The number of different morphemes (words) they can use is large and far exceeds the number of words usually presented in a first-year basic reader program (about 400). This makes the magnitude of the ratio of the difference strikingly apparent: 4/75. Even if the least adequately prepared child has a vocabulary of only 1000 words, the contrast to a first-year basic reader vocabulary is still striking: 2/5. The teaching and vocabulary circumstance is not materially altered when a co-basal is used (32) or when parallel readers or transitional readers are foisted on pupils (33). The vocabulary poverty of basic readers, singly and in groups, puts schoolchildren at a serious disadvantage when only basic readers represent "the reading program," as they have been doing for too long now in more than 90 percent of the nation's schools (2).

It is talk "that makes the world his apple, and forces him to eat" (6, p. 16). Children do and will talk and talk and talk unless of course silenced as they are in so many schools where instructors do not know how to turn pupil talk or pupil curiosity or pupil anticipation into natural instructional actions. "Pupil talk makes individual learning overt; by its means a good teacher is better able to engage in the dialogue that constitutes good teaching... pupil talk will in the end establish the learner as the chief protagonist in his own learning processes" (6, pp. 16–17).

Learning derives from actions. Whatever children can demonstrate or explain or interpret extends the "natural" way children learn when on their own. Teachers are quick to confess a most paradoxical revelation, by confessing that when they started teaching or explaining to students they began to understand. That is the way of the learner "to explain to others" and this makes the admonition to teachers "you talk too much" the toughest to acknowledge. Furthermore, when children demonstrate or interpret, they are very likely to use a full spectrum of culturally important commmunication modes: gestures, illustrations, pictures, recordings, and amplifications, including talk.

Because this process of demonstrating, explaining, interpreting is a social process, not only is the presenter the chief protagonist in his own learning, but also a chief protagonist in the learning of others in the group. The context of the presenter and those attending or the speaker-listener must set up expectations and active interactions so that the spectators become participants.

Linguists tell us that by the time children have acquired functional speaking vocabularies of the sizes previously referred to, they will also have acquired expert phonological skill. When the sound vibrations of speech hit the air and then the inner ear and its connection with the cerebral center, the circuit has been completed and the raw material of language—sound—is serving its purpose. Phonemes are the distinctive basic sound elements of language and have no referential function, but they make up the component parts of the signs of language (morphemes), which do have referential meaning and grammatical functions. Infants learning to use the language of their community need to differentiate the varieties of sounds that occur in the language. In addition, they must learn that the sounds function as signs only as they represent form differences of communicative value. Because these phoneme– morpheme sign systems represent a high degree of sound complexity, talking six-year-olds have accomplished a most impressive feat. At the same time, their knowledge includes appropriate reaction to the gestures, facial expressions, stresses, intonations, and junctures that ordinarily accompany speech behavior.

All these responses to sound that children are capable of do not qualify them as phoneticians, however. Even a linguist, to become a phonetician must become an expert in the science of speech sounds (phonetics) and be able to *describe* the varieties of sound that occur. To learn to read, children do not need to be phoneticians. What they do need is an opportunity to use the vast knowledge of sound that they already possess when they learn that print is a representation of speech.

Impressive as this record of the knowledge of sound is, however, it is an accounting of only a part of children's wealth. Words used to communicate are arranged into acceptable sequences, as in a sentence, and these arrangements are known as syntax, or the grammar of the language. It is claimed that by the time children of normal intelligence are six years old, they know practically all the essential grammatical structures of their language. All this language knowhow is acquired without formal teaching or structuring or programming and forces us to view grammar for what it really is, "a system of relationships that makes language possible" (5, p. 132). The secret teaching ingredient is *functional* (purposeful or intentional) *communication*. Children learn to listen and talk and use oral language to serve themselves as they operate in the environs of their sociocultural world.

Most six-year-olds possess a wealth of language that is as astounding as the facts provided here indicate. Of course, there are children who have neurological disabilities, speech or hearing disabilities, and the like, but they are the exception. Furthermore, they can usually be readily identified and given appropriate instruction. It remains, then, for teachers of beginning reading to capitalize appropriately on children's language opulence.

EXPERIENCE AND THE ORGANIZATION OF KNOWLEDGE

The age of wisdom has been described as being between six and sixteen. At six, children can ask every conceivable question, and at sixteen they can answer all questions. This ask-all-questions age encompasses the concept we are concerned with here. Asking children have inquiring minds that ferret out the attributes, relationships, and hierarchies in their perceptual and conceptual worlds.

The experiences of six-year-olds are as numerous as the stars and many recur so frequently that they become dangerously familiar. Others are unique, and so receive attention. Whatever the circumstances, the sensible universe—sight, sound, smell, touch, taste—activates numerous pathways to the central nervous system, where experience is stored and classified.

Current research in child development, as collated and interpreted in the Russell Sage Foundation's *Review of Child Development Research* (17), can help sensitize teachers to the range of child behavior at different ages and in different settings. The diverse stimuli of the physical and social world are gradually identified by children and grouped into some orderly schema. Thus they adapt to and function appropriately toward many objects, events, and people in their environment. From this they develop a system of concepts that functions, as Irving Sigel says (27, p. 209), "as an adaptive mechanism through which we cope with reality."

In his classic *Experience and Education* John Dewey said that it is not enough to insist on the necessity of experience to education but that everything depends on the *quality* of the experience. He stated (14, p. 17), "The more definitely and sincerely it is held that education is a development within, by, and for experience, the more important it is that there shall be clear conceptions of what experience is." Experiences must be more than immediately enjoyable; they must promote fruitful and creative subsequent experience. Educationally, this must be done in such a way that each pupil's power of judgment and capacity to act intelligently in new situations are in harmony with the principles of growth. This is the theory of the continuity of experience, which means that (14, p. 27) "every experience both takes up something from those which have gone before and modifies in some way the quality of those which come after." This is principally what differentiates civilization from savagery, and, to a considerable degree, the curiosity and creativity of the normally developing child from the overindulged or the mentally or emotionally handicapped child.

In the years before school, the developing child acquires a complex set of learnings based on perception, discrimination, transposition, and generalization. He acquires concepts—the "crucial links between the environment and the individual" (27, p. 209)—and a set of appropriate behaviors that may become a more or less fixed way of doing things. Concepts and habits enable children to cope with their environment, to meet and respond to the physical and social conditions of living, and to form emotional and intellectual attitudes. This developmental process gradually frees them from domination by the perceptual and sensory aspects of the environment and enables them, through language, to approach it conceptually.

The stages of intellectual development as described by Jean Piaget (16) provide a schematic description of developmental changes that occur through time. His stages are sufficiently open-ended to allow for the fact that children show different levels of ability, knowledge, and skills as a function of the rate and quality of the learning experience they encounter. The first two years of life are described as the *sensorimotor period.* Infants, using the inherent reflexes of their biological endowment, interact with their environment. The interplay of internal and external conditions through stimulation and response characterizes the normal development of infants. From the maze of undifferentiated, unreflective, and unspecified experiences, the child gradually attains rudimentary knowledge. As Sigel says (27, p. 215), to accomplish this, the child "establishes a differentiation of himself from objects; he localizes himself in space; he establishes a beginning awareness of cause and effect, or time and space." By the time they are 8 to 12 months old, most children have shown intention or goal-directed activity. Purpose or the intentionality of purpose now begins to influence a child's interactions. This is a big stride intellectually, as awareness of means-end relationships help children cope with the physical and social complexities of their world. By the end of this stage children are well on the way to dealing with their environment inventively, symbolically, and conceptually. They can already invent solutions in their minds and are no longer required to act them out by trial and error.

It is apparent, then, that in the first two years of life children live in a concrete world and in numerous series of situations. The interaction that is going on between children and their physical and social world permits them to separate themselves from the environment as well as to realize that the environment has certain properties of space, location, permanence, and causality. They are increasingly able to operate symbolically by classes or groups. They can tell that Rover is a member of the dog family even though they cannot deal with the category *animal.*

The next five years of life Piaget describes as the *preoperational phase* (16, pp. 150–163). In this phase language plays an increasingly important role as children acquire concepts through a complex set of processes. To attain concepts they have to become increasingly sensitive to objects in the concrete world. They have to learn not only that they exist but also that they have many characteristics and attributes. In addition, children see that diverse items can be organized into classes or categories (Rover, collie, dog, animal, vertebrate) and that language can facilitate as well as direct the process of conceptualization.

The third stage, or *operational stage,* is described as taking place roughly between ages 7 and 11. Because symbols and language play an increasingly significant role in the intellectual functioning of a child, the second and third stages have on occasion been treated together (7, p. 218). Roger Brown does this because, as he says, in general the same problems have been used to study both periods. At the preoperational stage, children perform less adequately than at the operational stage. It is the development and use of language, though, that suggests the grouping of the two stages together.

However, Piaget not only declares that there are two stages but further breaks the preoperational stage into two periods. The first occurs between ages two and four, the time when the child learns, in Brown's language (7, p. 218), to "name things, to ask questions, issue commands, and assert propositions." During the sensorimotor period, the child makes a giant intellectual stride as he is influenced by intention or purpose, and the sensing of means-end relationships. At this stage an equally significant stride is made as the sensorimotor infant becomes, through symbolic functioning, a manipulator of representations. The act of symbolic functioning is the result of the generalized capacity to differentiate between signifiers (symbols that stand for something) and significates (the objects). This representational intelligence, through its possession of symbolic functioning, sets the stage for the upper limits of cognition and the manipulation of reality.

At this stage, though, conceptualization is dominated by the world of percepts. To a large degree, the potency of physical attributes determines the concepts formed. Piaget calls this the *preconcept period*, because children primarily grasp first-level concepts. They can grasp the fact that peaches and pears are food but cannot distinguish between different pears. Or they can recognize that certain very different things belong together: Daddy's watch, Daddy's chair, Daddy's hat.

Between four and seven years of age, the *intuitive period*, increased symbolic functioning is possible. Piaget discriminates between symbols and signs as signifiers. Symbols are of the dream-symbol variety or of deferred imitation or of representational play. They are private non-codified signifiers. Signs—linguistic signs—are acquired from the social surroundings and are shared socially. Words are the commonest signs of a codified and socially shared linguistic system.

The use of private signifiers or symbols and the early use of linguistic signs provide the focus for Piaget's statement that children are egocentric. They generally lack the ability to take the role of another person and to treat their own thought processes as the object of thought. Over and over again Piaget indicates that it is in the context of *social interaction* as a member of a learning group that children, forced to become increasingly cognizant of their own thoughts and their reliability and validity, emerge as sociocentric objective scholars.

In addition to grasping images and signs as signifiers, children learn to use them as anticipative mediators of future actions. Starting with imitative images that serve as anticipative schema, children begin to direct future action. They begin to evoke acts and deeds in thought rather than actually carrying them out in reality. This ability to anticipate, to conjecture, to speculate, to invent, leads to the ability to hypothesize, to deal with variants and covariants, to test logically. In the life of a learner, this is an advance of the utmost importance. It is the pattern of inquiry that George Kneller (22, p. 42) defines as the ability to "analyze the problem and to consider ways of dealing with it—that is, to set up hypotheses." Learners are now becoming more reflective and less impulsive. They are beginning to want proof, to suspend judgment, to think of information as tentative and relative. Rather than seizing on the first idea that occurs to them, they now pause, suspend judgment, to notice whether or not there are better ways or other alternatives.

Another cognitive advance that occurs at this stage is the ability to use numbers, not only to order things in terms of quantity but also to see that relationships can exist on a numerical basis. In the dimensions of concept attainment as defined by Herbert Klausmeier (21), this is referred to as the ability to deal with formal properties. When *formal* is compared with *intrinsic* and *functional,* its meaning can be grasped more quickly.

Intrinsic properties are observable properties, experienced directly through the sense organs. The common elements—an object or event— are observable. *Functional properties* are classifications of objects based on use. For example, a hammer, a pulley, and a slide rule are all tools, classified by their functional properties. *Formal properties* are products wholly of man's mental processes, such as number systems and alphabets. Number systems, for example, have properties too, in this case formal properties that are agreed on by mathematicians. The child who can combine two quantities to produce a sum $(2 + 2 = 4)$ deals with an abstraction based on formal properties of mathematics.

The latter part of the preoperational stage of the *intuitive stage* finds children making judgments largely on the basis of partial and immediate perceptions or on the basis of objective similarity. They judge by the way things look and usually in terms of just one of a number of relevant dimensions. Even so, three fundamental operations occur. They can think in terms of classes: When presented with circles and squares, they can classify them on the basis of roundness. They can think in terms of relationships: Mr. Jones is the father of Ralph, Mr. Jones is bigger than Ralph, and Ralph is the oldest of three children. They can think in terms of quantity or by handling number concepts.

In the *concrete operations period,* the thought of children aged 7 through 11 is more like that of the adult, in that they think more in logical terms. *Operations* is used by Piaget to refer to mental acts or imminent acts of an internalized nature taking place in the mind. These mental acts represent a process of interaction and development whereby new syntheses are formed *by discovery.* Attributes are noted, objects classified, and categories determined. The syntheses are real in the sense that they not only have a location in time and space but also take place in the mind. In the process of cognitive growth through making discoveries and syntheses, the individual is merely the neural medium in the resynthesis of cultural elements.

Three significant operations described by Piaget are *reversibility*, as in arithmetic (2 + 3 = 5, or 5 − 3 = 2), *classification*, or the organization of objects into classes (desk, chair, table = furniture), and *seriation*, or arranging ideas along a spectrum of increasing values (2, 4, 8, 16, 32). In brief, at this stage the child is able to treat objects as alike (desk-chair, furniture) even though different, to note that they can be in more than one class and that some classes can be subordinate to others, and to count one item as first and another as second.

In addition, the child understands the concept of *conservation*. In other words, he can see that certain properties of objects, such as quantity, can remain invariant even in the face of certain changes. For instance, two circles each with a diameter of 6 inches remain the same even though one is cut into quarters and the other is cut into thirds. Cutting a circle does not alter the amount or quantity of the circle.

To arrange items in a series along a continuum, a child must grasp the principle of *transitivity*. He must understand the sort of ordering whereby if A is larger than B, and B is larger than C, then A is larger than C.

Interestingly enough, it is reported that understanding conservation and transitivity occurs sometime between the ages of five and seven (4, 20, 23, 27, 29). Almy conducted an "excellent psychopedological" study (1) of a cross-sectional and longitudinal nature to determine the validity of Piaget's account of the principle of conservation and to determine the relevance of such understanding to children's progress in kindergarten and first and second grade. The results underscored the importance of maturational factors and "more generally . . . the transition from thought that is intuitive and perceptually dominated to thought that is systematic, or, in Piaget's terms 'operational.'" The results also supported Piaget's findings on conservation and highlighted the role of experience.

In addition, Almy and her colleagues investigated the processes of children of various socioeconomic backgrounds and the relationships with measures of intellectual functioning, readiness, and achievement. They found that the sequential development of children in lower-class schools, although similar to that of children in middle-class schools, was at a much slower pace. Moreover, children who did better on tests of mental ability, readiness, and achievement generally grasped conservation at an earlier age. To this must be added the findings and interpretation reported by Jerome Bruner and his co-workers (9). They state that invariance, or conservation of various forms of quantity across transformations in appearance, can be grasped by very young children as reflected by their actions. The "do" rather than "tell" features of the Bruner et al. work apparently provides less impediment in learning conservation as a tool of thought.

In the concrete operations stage, the children's thoughts, even though they may be logical and systematic, are limited to the direct experiences they have had. When they have no direct experience, they tend to reason by analogy to something they have experienced. In this regard, verbal ability, as well as physical activity and social interactions with verbal ability, may be crucial in acting as a support to help a child overcome the influence of visual perceptions. Although training designed to increase vocabulary may facilitate the development of logical thinking and help resolve the perceptual-cognitive conflict, it is "equilibration" or self-regulation that takes on greatest significance. To permit a child "to learn an appropriate answer without making certain that he can retrace his steps, or arrive at the same result in another way, is to encourage the erection of a verbal superstructure that may crumble under even minimal cognitive stress" (1, p. 132).

The fourth stage, the *formal operations stage*, is the time when abstract thinking develops, at about the beginning of adolescence. Now children begin to deal with the possible without reference to the actual. They begin to grasp the complexity of human knowledge by learning how to construct theories and make logical deductions about their consequences without the need for empirical evidence. As Hunt puts it (18, p. 355), "instead of observation directing thought . . . the adolescent's thought directs his observing." In all this, language, or representational thought, plays an important role, but Piaget is of the opinion that ability to use language to express logic is an outcome of activity and that attempts to improve children's logic by instructing them in the use of language are not apt to be very successful.

ACTIONS AND INTERACTIONS

In essence, the idea of activity—a child's need to reach by his own efforts an understanding of the world in which he lives and the experiences in which he participates—represents Piaget's first critical variable in the teaching-learning experience. A child may accommodate his thoughts to those of others, but only when *he tries out* the ideas of others to see how they function and retraces the ideas can he assimilate the ideas and make them his own. For the teacher this means that each child's readiness to make a discovery or to acquire a new idea must be determined and then instruction must be so paced that the child has both the required knowledge and the cognitive abilities needed to make or acquire it. Almy says that, for curriculum makers and teachers,

in the early childhood period activity and language need close association. For example, in the case of the socially disadvantaged child, no adequate comparison of quantities can be made by a child who does not understand the terms "more" and "less," or "most" and "least." But comprehension of those terms may not be developed through words alone, but rather through a combination of manipulation and verbalization [1, p. 138].

Piaget, in summing up a talk on development and learning, said that all his remarks represented the child and the learning subject as active: "Learning is possible only when there is active assimilation" (24, p. 18). He had said earlier that, if the development of knowledge is to be understood, we must grasp the idea that to him is central—the idea of an operation:

> Knowledge is not a copy of reality. To know an object, to know an event, is not simply to look at it and make a mental copy, or image, of it. To know an object is to act on it. To know is to modify, to transform the object, and to understand the process of this transformation, and as a consequence to understand the way the object is constructed. An operation is thus the essence of knowledge; it is an interiorized action which modifies the object of knowledge [24, p. 18].

An operation is an interiorized action that is reversible and never isolated or is always a part of structure: "Knowledge is not drawn from objects but it is drawn by the actions effected upon the objects" (24, p. 12). Piaget is saying, in other words, that learning is subordinate to development.

When challenged, Piaget says he always has three questions: (1) Is the learning lasting, or what remains two weeks or a month or a year later? (2) Can the learning be used for generalization or the transfer of a generalization? (3) What was the *operational* level of the learner before the learning experience and what more complex structures has he achieved through this learning? He asks this because all development consists of momentary conflicts and incompatibilities that must be overcome if a higher level of equilibrium is to be reached (24, pp. 17–19).

With respect to the point made by question 3, Almy and her colleagues say (1, p. 136), "We can think of no better safeguard against meaningless verbalization and rote memorization than a teacher who is able both to appraise the difficulty of the concepts and to assess the children's comprehension of them." Nancy Bayley, writing on the growth of intelligence, has said (3, p. 807): "Intelligence appears to me . . . to be a dynamic succession of developing functions, with the more advanced and complex functions in the hierarchy depending on the prior maturing of earlier simpler ones."

It seems, then, that language development as a part of maturation or all-round mental capacity influences much of a child's progress from thought that is predominantly perceptual and intuitive to thought that is conceptual and logical. A child's verbal accommodation to a learning experience is helpful, but it will produce lasting effects only if, through further self-regulation, generalization to other tasks has resulted. It is not enought just to have had an experience, even verbally, unless it affects a child's way of organizing experiences.

Social interaction, or sharing by pupils, represents the second critical variable in a teaching-learning experience, according to Piaget. Children must be given the freedom and opportunity to reveal and share their thoughts. Social exchange with their peers may help children learn from each other, overcome their egocentric view of things, and lead to a critical frame of mind: "Cooperation is indeed co-operation" (15, p. 4).

Finally, as Piaget has declared, transition from one level of thought to the next involves principally maturation, social interaction, physical activity, and, most importnat, the process of equilibration or self-regulation. As Hunt says, in view of the technological developments in Western culture that demand high ability to manipulate such organizational structures as schemata, operations, and concepts in the solution of problems, the

> hope of increasing the average level of intelligence by proper manipulation of children's developmental encounters with their environment, a hope which becomes reasonable with the evidence surveyed here and with relinquishing the assumptions of fixed intelligence and predetermined development, provides a challenge of the first order [18, p. 346].

CONCLUSION

The purpose of this chapter is to show how the experience-language-cognitive wealth that children bring with them to school at ages five and six provides a sound, all-embracing foundation on which to construct and develop reading ability. The size of their functional speaking vocabularies is much larger than is usually believed by unsophisticated teachers and parents, and it is more encompassing than is allowed for by basic reader programs, with their numerous preprimers and primers. A child's experience wealth is proportionately equal in opulence (even though varied) to his social-cultural-economic background. The all-round maturation characteristic of the preoperational and operational stages is cognitively a source of neuropsychological affluence with tremendous implications for learning and reading instruction.

It is not the purpose of this chapter to deal with the vexing linguistic relation between language and thought. This has been done by others—notably Chomsky (12), John Carroll (11), Roger Brown (7), and James Britton (5). Language and thought are discussed in this chapter in some detail to show that both represent processes. These processes can serve individuals as they manipulate ideas to either communicate with others directly and intellectually, or to satisfy individual desires indirectly or autistically. Intelligence, as it undergoes maturation and a gradual process of socialization, increasingly uses concepts through the bond established between thoughts, words, and deeds. Directed thought is controlled more and more by the laws of language, experience, and logic, and it is influenced enormously by the need to communicate thoughts to others.

Carroll says, in speaking of different languages (11, p. 111), that "there are more similarities than differences in the way language codes symbolize concepts, because these concepts are the result of the transactions of human societies with a physical and social environment that has many uniformities over the world." He also says

> Thinking is the conscious or unconscious manipulation of internal processes for oneself, usually in some particular direction such as the solution of a problem. Communication, whether through language or through other means ... is behavior in which the initiator of the communication seeks ... to arouse certain internal processes in the recipient of the communication and possibly to secure certain overt responses on his part [11, p. 10].

In reporting on studies in cognitive growth, Bruner discusses how certain features of human development and growth are culture bound. He compares Wolof children with Western children and concludes (9, p. 323), "The difference lies, at the very least, in the extent to which and the manner in which children learn to use language as an implement of thought." When language is used to convey the content of experience and action, there is (9, p. 322) "more often than not a requirement of developing correspondence between what we do, what we see, and what we say. It is this correspondence that is most strikingly involved in reading and writing, in school learning, and in other abstract pursuits."

The bond between word and action and thought, between language and experience, between reading and writing and communication, is of enormous importance. What educationally significant conclusions can we draw from these facts? It would seem that the most functional way to show children that reading is no more than speech written down is to do a great deal more than we do about using their language-experience wealth or their concept-percept wealth to share each other's intellectual life. Piaget writes (25, p. 64), "The mere fact, then, of telling one's thought, of telling it to others, or of keeping silence and telling it only to oneself must be of enormous importance to the fundamental structure and functioning of thought in general, and of child logic in particular."

What is important is that language and experience, examined experience, play an enormously important role not only in the way reading ability develops into critical comprehension but also in the way logical thinking develops. We need not speculate any longer about the experiential and maturational factors that may be most influential or the instructional factors that have most utility value. We must give attention to the most effective ways of challenging the thinking of children, capitalize on their curiosity and individual differences, encourage intellectual exploration, and above all avoid ritualizing instruction through memorization and rote learning. Philip Coombs said (13, p. 167), "Nobel prizes are won in science for challenging and upsetting old truths and discovering new ones. The same wholesome irreverence for 'time honored truths' must somehow be instilled into the enterprise that is supposed to breed Nobel Prize winners."

Finally, in the view of the Bullock Committee certain inferences are to be drawn from a study of the relationship between language and learning (10, p. 50):

1. all genuine learning involves discovery, and it is as ridiculous to suppose that teaching begins and ends with 'instruction' as it is to suppose that 'learning by discovery' means leaving children to their own resources;
2. language has a heuristic function; that is to say a child can learn by talking and writing as certainly as he can by listening and reading;
3. to exploit the process of discovery through language in all its uses is the surest means of enabling a child to master his mother tongue.

It remains in the following chapters to see how the language-experience (concept-percept) approach to initial reading instruction in particular and to all reading instruction in general is an effective means of accomplishing the high cognitive and communicative skills alluded to in this chapter. Numerous examples and details are provided for those who wish to use the approach.

Bibliography

1. Almy, Millie, Edward Chittenden, and Paula Miller, *Young Children's Thinking*. New York: Teachers College, Columbia University, 1966.
2. Austin, Mary, and Coleman Morrison, *The Torch Lighters, Tomorrow's Teachers of Reading*. Cambridge, Mass.: Harvard University Press, 1961.
3. Bayley, Nancy, "On the Growth of Intelligence," *The American Psychologist*, 10 (December, 1955), 805–818.
4. Braine, M. S., "Piaget on Reasoning: A Methodological Critique and Alternative Proposals." In W. Kessen and Clementina Kuhlman (eds.), "Thought in the Young Child," *Monographs of the Society for Research in Child Development*, 27 (whole no. 83, 1962), 41–64.
5. Britton, James, *Language and Learning*. Baltimore: Penquin Books, 1970.
6. Britton, James, "Language and the Nature of Learning: An Individual Perspective." In James R. Squire (ed.), *The Teaching of English*, The Seventy-sixth Yearbook of the National Society for the Study of Education, Part I. Chicago, Ill,: University of Chicago Press, 1977, pp. 1–38.
7. Brown, Roger, *Social Psychology*. New York: Free Press, 1965.
8. Brown, Roger, and Ursula Bellugi, "The Three Processes in the Child's Acquisition of Syntax," *Harvard Educational Review*, 34 (Spring, 1964), 133–151.
9. Bruner, Jerome S., Rose R. Olver, and Patricia M. Greenfield, *Studies in Cognitive Growth*. New York: Wiley, 1966.
10. Bullock, Sir Alan, *A Language for Life, Report of the Committee of Inquiry Appointed by the Secretary of State for Education and Science* (England). London: Her Majesty's Stationery Office, 1975.

11. Carroll, John B., *Language and Thought*. Englewood Cliffs, N.J.: Prentice-Hall, 1964.
12. Chomsky, Noam, "Language and the Mind." In C. Laird and R. M. Gorrell (eds.), *Reading About Language*. New York: Harcourt Brace Jovanovich, 1971.
13. Coombs, Philip, *The World Educational Crisis: A Systems Analysis*. New York: Oxford University Press, 1968.
14. Dewey, John, *Experience and Education*. New York: Macmillan, 1938.
15. Duckworth, Eleanor, "Piaget Rediscovered." In Richard E. Ripple and Verne N. Rockcastle (eds.), *Piaget Rediscovered*, A Report of the Conference on Cognitive Studies and Curriculum Development (March, 1964). Ithaca, N.Y.: School of Education, Cornell University, 1964.
16. Flavell, John H., *The Developmental Psychology of Jean Piaget*. New York: Van Nostrand, 1963.
17. Hoffman, Martin L., and Lois Wladis Hoffman (eds.), *Review of Child Development Research*, Vol. I. New York: Russell Sage Foundation, 1964.
18. Hunt, J. McV., *Intelligence and Experience*. New York: Ronald Press, 1961.
19. Kamii, Constance, "An Application of Piaget's Theory to the Conceptualization of a Preschool Curriculum." Paper presented at City University of New York, May, 1970.
20. Kessen, W., and Clementina Kuhlman (eds.), "Thought in the Young Child," *Monographs of the Society for Research in Child Development*, 27 (whole no. 83; 1962).
21. Klausmeier, Herbert J., *Concept Learning and Problem Solving: A Bibliography, 1950–1964*. Technical Report No. 1. Madison: Research and Development Center for Learning and Education, University of Wisconsin, 1965.
22. Kneller, George F., *Logic and Language of Education*. New York: Wiley, 1966.
23. Kooistra, W. H., "Developmental Trends in the Attainment of Conservation, Transitivity, and Relativism in the Thinking of Children: A Replication and Extension of Piaget's Ontogenetic Formulations." Unpublished doctoral dissertation, Wayne State University, Detroit, 1963.
24. Piaget, Jean. "Development and Learning." In Richard E. Ripple and Verne N. Rockcastle (eds.), *Piaget Rediscovered*. A Report of the Conference on Cognitive Studies and Curriculum Development (March, 1964). Ithaca, N.Y.: School of Education, Cornell University, 1964.
25. Piaget, Jean, *The Language and Thought of the Child*. New York: Harcourt Brace Jovanovich, 1965.
26. Seashore, Robert. H., "The Importance of Vocabulary in Learning Language Skills," *Elementary English*, 25 (March, 1948), 137–152.
27. Sigel, Irving E., "The Attainment of Concepts." In Martin L. Hoffman and Lois Wladis Hoffman (eds.), *Review of Child Developmental Research*. New York: Russell Sage Foundation, 1964.
28. Slobin, Dan I., and C. A. Welsh, "Elicited Imitation as a Research Tool in Developmental Psycholinguistics." In C. S. Lavatelli (ed.), *Language Training in Early Childhood Education*. Urbana, Ill.: University of Illinois Press for ERIC Clearing House on Early Childhood Education, 1971, pp. 170–185.

29. Smedslund J., "Transitivity of Preference Patterns as Seen by Pre-School Children," *Scandinavian Journal of Psychology*, 1 (1960), 49–54.

30. Smith, Madorah E., "An Investigation of the Development of the Sentence and the Extent of Vocabulary in Young Children," *Studies in Child Welfare*, Vol. 3. Iowa City: State University of Iowa, 1926.

31. Smith, Mary Katherine, "Measurement of the Size of General English Vocabulary Through the Elementary Grades and High School," *Genetic Psychology Monographs*, 24 (1941), 311–345.

32. Stauffer, Russell G., "A Vocabulary Study Comparing Reading, Arithmetic, Health and Science Texts," *The Reading Teacher*, 20 (November, 1966), 141–147.

33. Strickland, Ruth B., *The Contribution of Structural Linguistics to the Teaching of Reading, Writing, and Grammar in the Elementary School*, Bulletin of the School of Education, 40 (January, 1964). Bloomington: University of Indiana.

34. Vygotsky, L. S., *Thought and Language*. New York: Wiley, 1962.

35. *Webster's Dictionary of Synonyms*. Springfield, Mass.: Merriam, 1942.

Chapter 2
Early Reading Instruction:
THE PROCESS OF PERSONAL DISCOVERY

Pupil actions, interactions, and transactions are basic to learning. "To learn to think, we must accordingly exercise our limbs, our senses, and our bodily organs, for these are the tools of the intellect." This is a passage from Jean Jacques Rousseau that John Dewey quotes in writing about education and development in his 1915 book *Schools of Tomorrow* (8, p. 11). Rousseau saw that the actions are a "part of the apparatus of action by which we adjust ourselves to our environment" (ibid., p. 12). Measure, count, weigh, compare, and guide the natural growth of children through the "slow and sure process of personal discovery." If this were true in Rousseau's day and Dewey's day, it is much more certain that the scientific and psychological advances of today have made absurd any education that forces on children exercises of parroting and chanting or other types of superficiality. The natural processes of learning the relation between themselves and things (a kind of experimental physics), in order to make judgments and exercise the senses, is the natural way the developing child learns, and begins long before a child reaches kindergarten age.

Prior to about 1965, preprimary-level education was viewed as helpful but not critical. Kindergarten programs were meagerly supported.

Early childhood education was indeed sporadic and fragmented and limited by and large to parent cooperatives and public and private nursery schools. Since 1965 various federally sponsored programs in particular have shown that planned learning programs reaching into the early years are not only acceptable but essential for children's optimal development.

Two short statements from the Plowden report (so named for the chairwoman of the preparing committee, Lady Bridget Plowden) provide, in brief, guidelines for education in general and preprimary and primary education in particular: "At the heart of the educational process lies the child" (6, p. 7) and, "The child must come first" (6, p. 138). Both statements focus on individual differences and the liabilities of lockstep instructional practices. Although it is generally conceded that primary-level teachers excel in the opportunities they provide and the stress they put on individual learning, preprimary education has brought into even sharper focus the need for instructional practices that provide a wide range of opportunities and programs for the wide diversity of children. As a result some children are reaching first grade with improved perceptual, cognitive, and language skills and with better ego and interpersonal development. They are acquiring a balanced education without undue emphasis on learning to read, write, and count.

Because of this the whole concept of readiness, particularly reading readiness, needs to be reexamined. Readiness skill books, with their lockstep practices, are clearly not the answer. The recent works of scholars such a Chomsky (4), Carroll (3), and Bugelski (1), to name a few, have strong implications for radical departures from these kinds of activities. A program of learning activities that provide play and talk; that build around the concepts of action, interaction, and transaction; and that provide numerous encounters with the variety and depth of language is needed. These ideas have their roots in John Dewey's thoughts about experience and nature (7). The interpretation here is not precisely that which Dewey made when he wrote as a philosopher rather than as a scientific inquirer into nature and experience. Nevertheless, the general features of his thesis seem to fit here.

The first concept of action is self-action. This designates the kind of action whereby a person acts on his own power. Since a person does not act in a void, which is particularly true in an instructional environment, a primary function of the learning environment is to provide the medium through which action is to be expressed. It is apparent that a prerequisite for self-action in the medium of a structured learning environment is *freedom to act*. The instructional environment is made up of the learning situations that a teacher structures, or, as Jean Piaget labeled them, provoked situations. In these planned and structured situations children perform operations of a sensorimotor, overt nature and of an intellectual, decision-making, covert nature. The freedom to act in the academic sense means primarily that the pupil is permitted and required by the structure of a situation to make decisions and to exercise judgment.

Cooperative planning between pupils and teachers constitutes a big step toward attaining the skill of self-action. The planning periods, though, must allow the children to plan in a real sense. The activities planned must include uninterrupted periods permitting some to act on an activity over several days and others to move from activity to activity. Children may act with and on graded puzzles, form boards, bead stringing, nuts-and-bolts boards, blocks, puppets, "dress-up" materials, weather charts, water and sand, and so on. The perceptual, cognitive, linguistic, and emotional key is pupil action.

Dewey viewed the concept of interaction as the leading concept of his philosophy, as does Piaget. Dewey saw learning in all its forms and at its different levels of complexity as a dynamic interplay of interrelated and interdependent elements in which deeds and decisions are functional and changing rather than fixed and static. In brief, experience is realistic and dynamic; it is an active process. In other words, a learning experience is purposive behavior unified by the fact that the learner sets out with a problem and seeks a solution. The child is viewed as a naturally curious, active explorer, and the teacher is to guide this exploratory activity.

Not only do children interact with elements in a situation, such as planting and caring for seeds in a window box, watching them grow, visiting a nursery, identifying the parts of a flower, noting the effect of sunlight, and so on (that is, dealing with concepts that are within their comprehension), they do so within the social character of the school. In brief, children learn how to interact with the members of the group to which they belong. Again, as both Dewey and Piaget point out, Children learn that cooperation is largely co-operation, whereby members of a group are jointly (co-) operating on the elements of a situation. Thus a child may note that others may view the same changes differently. L. Susan Stebbing, discussing "point of view" by using as illustrations mountains and a Holbein painting, says,

> a "point of view" emphasizes the fact that we see things differently in so far as we are different one from another. Fortunately, people's points of view often overlap. Otherwise, there could be no communication one with another. Sometimes one person can bring about a considerable alteration in another's point of view with regard to some topic [24, p. 38].

By sharing, by working together along common lines, with common aims, and in a common spirit, children learn to respect each other and to maintain and develop a self-regulatory spirit.

The third concept of action is transaction. Dewey makes subtle distinctions between physicochemical transactions (or those investigated by the physical sciences), psychophysical transactions (or grasping the greater complexity of natural transactions), and the level of mind and human experience. It is the last that is the most useful here because its distinguishing feature is humanity's ability to use language, which helps in discerning the complexity, function, and consequence of transactions. Language helps children to objectify an experience, to internalize it, to abstract from an immediate experience, and to note the qualitative ends of an action and the emergence of unexpected and unpredictable qualities. Language helps children to select a problem and to inquire into its conditions and consequences. Language helps pupils not only to objectify a transaction for increased understanding but to communicate the transaction as well. In communication there is a sharing of attitudes, emotions, desires, norms, and ends in view as well as a sharing of cognitive or rational experience. As a result of sharing, meanings are enhanced, deepened, and solidified.

For instance, children may germinate beans on moist cotton between glass panels and see how the plants begin to grow and how the roots and leaves form. They may then contrast this by planting fast-growing radish seeds. Predictions can be made, observations recorded, and accounts kept; above all, knowledge gained can be shared with others by language, by illustration, and by firsthand demonstrations. Teachers aid transactions by helping children to develop guiding questions and to think about possibilities, by sequencing activities, by looking for relationships, by noting cause and effect, by generalizing, and by arranging participating-type experiences that lead to discoveries. In brief, transactions represent the use of language to internalize actions and interactions, to objectify and obtain quality responses, and to communicate or share with others.

READINESS FOR LEARNING

When kindergartens were first established they were thought of as an adjunct to the formal instructional years that begin in the first grade. Opposition was voiced to requiring children five and younger to attend school. Support was obtained on the grounds that what would be done would be a readiness-for-learning program rather than a formal program (21). From this notion developed the idea of readiness for reading, a concept that received sanction on the national scene with the publication of the Twenty-fourth Yearbook of the National Society for the Study of Education (19). Section B of Chapter III was devoted to "Experience and Training Which Prepare Pupils for Reading," and Section C of the same chapter dealt with "Classification of First-Grade Children." If both of these sections are studied, one can gain a certain perspective on readiness as it is used today. The purpose of Section C was to point out the wide differences among pupils entering the first grade. Those pupils who came fully prepared for instruction in reading were said to come from homes or kindergartens in which they had been prepared. Those who were not adequately prepared for reading instruction needed training similar to that outlined for kindergarten children. This training would "extend their experience, develop habits of good thinking, improve their use of oral English, increase their vocabularies, improve and refine their enunciation and pronunciation, and stimulate keen interest in reading" (19, p. 31). In addition, the yearbook stated that "conscious attention at home and in the kindergarten to the six types of training which have been enumerated promotes growth that makes reading a natural and desirable activity in the first grade" (19, p. 27).

Studies on individual differences and human growth and development, along with experience in trying to teach readiness, led educators to see that home influence and kindergarten training might make a difference, although they were not a substitute for maturation. Increasing numbers of reading failures continued to occur. Gradually the concept of reading readiness changed to readiness for reading, and from readiness for reading at the beginning reading stages to readiness at all levels. This was the interpretation given by W. S. Gray in the Thirty-sixth Yearbook of the National Society for the Study of Education (13). In essence this change in interpretation gave recognition to the principle of continuity and interaction of experience (7, p. 27). To Dewey "continuity of experience means that every experience both takes up something from those which have gone before and modifies in some way the quality of those which come after" whereas interaction "assigns equal rights to both factors in experience—objective and internal conditions" (7, pp. 38–39).

In fact, it might be wise to drop the readiness idea and substitute for it the concept of *maturity*. Maturity in reading, then, implies some basic hypotheses concerning human growth and development and certain assumptions concerning the attitudes, interests, and skills involved in reading. Maturity is recognized as a process and is not thought of as a level of achievement. W. S. Gray and B. Rogers discuss six characteristics of mature citizens in a democracy: (1) feelings of security and adequacy; (2) understanding of self and others; (3) recognition of democratic values and goals; (4) problem-solving attitudes and methods; (5) self-discipline, responsibility, and freedom; and (6) constructive attitudes toward change (14, p. 49). If to these characteristics are added improvement of vocabularies and use of language, then the seven characteristics point directly to goals to be reached at all stages of progress toward the highest order of maturity in reading as well as citizenship. The maturing citizen as well as the maturing reader is acquiring attitudes that encourage growth and responsibility rather than merely seeking a level. Learning to read is accomplished not only in school but also throughout life. Goethe is quoted as saying, "The dear people do not know how long it takes to learn to read. I have been at it all my life and I cannot yet say I have reached the goal" (quoted in 14, p. 56). Maturity, then, is more an attitude toward reading and a willingness to keep trying than it is a level of competency. It is, in short, an ongoing process.

The real issue is not readiness for reading or readiness for learning as much as a matter of doing that which can be most productive at different levels of maturity. Undoubtedly skill acquisition has age-dependent determinants.

ADMINISTRATIVE CONSIDERATIONS

Long before a child reaches age four or five he has been acting, thinking, talking, and learning. The Plowden report states the case clearly and briefly:

> Long before a child is five he is already using words and is often familiar with books, toys and music. The issue is not whether he should be "educated" before he reaches school age because that is happening anyway. What has to be decided is whether his education is to take place in increasing association with other children and under the supervision of skilled people, as well as of parents, in the right conditions and with the right equipment [6, p. 118].

The findings and conclusions presented in two separate reports regarding preprimary education are timely and relevant. One report is the Plowden report, done in England (6); the other, performed pursuant to a contract with the U.S. Office of Education, is the Colman report (5). Both merit careful study by all school personnel associated with primary and preprimary education.

Some of the conclusions reached in the Plowden report and relevant to this discussion are as follows:

a. It [pre-primary education] should be part-time rather than whole time because young children should not be separated for long from their mothers. Attendance need not be for a whole half-day session and in the earlier stages only one, two or three days a week will often be desirable. In the words of Susan Isaacs, "the nursery school is not a substitute for a good home: its prime function . . . is to supplement the normal services which the home renders to its children and to make a link between the natural and indispensable fostering of the child in the home and social life of the world at large.

b. A minority of children will, however, need full-time nursery education for a variety of reasons [6, p. 121].

Recommendations
   (i) There should be a large expansion of nursery education and a start would be made as soon as possible.
   (ii) Nursery education should be available to children at any time after the beginning of the school year after which they reach the age of three until they reach the age of compulsory schooling.

(iii) Nursery education should be available either for a morning or afternoon session for five days a week except that over the country as a whole provision should be made for 15 percent of children to attend both a morning and afternoon session. . . .

(vi) Children should be introduced gradually to nursery education. . . .

(ix) All nursery groups should be under the ultimate supervision of a qualified teacher in the ratio of one qualified teacher to 60 places. The main day to day work of the groups should be undertaken by two year trained nursery assistants in the ratio of a minimum of one to every ten children. There should be at least one experienced nursery assistant in each group and where no teacher is always on the premises, one assistant able to cope with accidents and safety risks. Experienced assistants should be able to qualify on merit for a responsibility allowance. . . .

(xii) Ideally, all services, including nursery, for the care of young children should be grouped together and placed near the children's homes and the primary schools. The planning of new areas and the rebuilding of old should take account of nursery education [6, pp. 132–133].

(i) As soon as there is nursery provision for all children whose parents wish it, for a year before starting school, the normal time by which a child should go to school should be defined as the September term following the fifth birthday. . . .

(ii) There should be a three year course in the first (at present the infant) school. . . .

(iv) There should be flexibility in entry to school and in transfer between the stages of education to allow for the circumstances of individual pupils [6, pp. 151–152].

In the American report the concern was with maximal development of children—intellectually, socially, emotionally, and physically. More attention to and greater investment in preprimary education was urged because of the following factors:

The greater malleability of children under six; their rapid potential rate of development; the greater opportunity in early years to counteract the debilitating effects of poverty and thus to narrow or erase the widening gap of intellectual achievement between the poor and the non-poor; and the growing knowledge of how to establish and maintain programs for early childhood learning. [5, p. vi]

Presented here are some of the recommendations of the Preprimary Education report.

1. Group preschool participation (full-day or half-day . . .) for all four and five year old children from families with incomes below the designated poverty level and preferably for all children from families with incomes of $6,900 or below, with provision for payment for others earning higher salaries on a sliding scale basis. Staffing patterns for kindergartens should move toward an adult-child ratio of 1:10; for day care centers of 1:7. . . .

2. Planned education components built into day care programs . . .
3. Parent education programs for parents of children from birth through age three.
4. Provision for all secondary schools and colleges of child development programs to give students the understanding and skills necessary as future parents . . . .
5. Development and broadcast of television and other media programs, such as Sesame Street, as supplements to home or school based programs, to serve both children and parents. [5, pp. xii–xiii]

Other recommendations in this report aimed at individualization of instruction, heterogeneity of enrollment, continuity of learning experiences, parent involvement, a satisfactory ratio of adult-child contact, availability of consulting services, and recognition that the home is the principal education base for the child. Throughout the report, emphasis is given to planned learning experiences (actions) in a group setting (interactions). Much emphasis is also given to improvement of skills of parents as teachers.

INDIVIDUAL DIFFERENCES

Individual differences are both the boon and the bonds of classroom instruction. The range of differences in capacity, creativity, curiosity, social and emotional adjustment, physical stamina, and experiences and knowledge is what makes the wheels of society go around. These differences make a classroom a vital, exciting, and stimulating environment and can make instruction and learning functional and profitable. This is why John B. Watson said that by the time children go to school they are graduate students in terms of learned responses. Each pupil represents a tremendous reservoir of potential that can be put to good use by any teacher.

The bonds are largely of our making. We are the ones who make of learning a Procrustean bed. We try to rob children of their tremendous wealth, and to a good degree we succeed. Procrustes shortened or stretched the legs of his victims until all were a uniform length to fit the bed and all were dead. All too often, reading is taught in the Procrustean tradition, so that a love and need for reading are equally short-lived and equally dead. John I. Goodlad and Robert H. Anderson say:

Certain time-honored practices of pupil classification, while perhaps not lethal, trap school-age travelers in much the same fashion as Procrustes' bed trapped the unwary. These practices are concomitants of our graded system of school organization. First, a certain amount of progress is held to be standard for a year's work. Then, the content of the work is laid out within the grade, to be "covered" and, to a degree "mastered." The slow are pulled and stretched to fit the grade. In time, they learn to adapt to a pace that is slower than their natural one [12, p. 1].

Every teacher knows that children are different and that the differences exist at the preprimary level. The range of performance differences even at this level is a spread of about five years. Every teacher knows too that good teaching increases individual differences. Some know that changes in an individual pupil over a period of time can be greater than interpupil differences.

Strangely, as pointed out earlier, teachers seem more attentive to individual differences among preprimary children than at any subsequent level. It could be because the various stages of maturity (or immaturity) compel teacher recognition of differences. It could be also that by the time the children are eight and nine years old, teachers are more concerned about pupils acquiring certain skills in arithmetic, science, and so on; therefore, teachers become more preoccupied with so-called skill acquisition than with the curiosity, aptitude, security, and rate of learning of individual pupils.

At the preprimary level parents seem concerned about their children's transition from home to school and how they will adjust to the change. This attentiveness in turn can result in timely parent-teacher or home-school contacts. Home visits by teachers are more likely at this level than at any other. Open days, when it is possible to see the school at work can be quite helpful. Evening sessions can also be planned so that fathers can attend. As a result, individual pupil differences are given more attention and recognition than would otherwise be the case.

Increased understanding of individual differences in rates of maturing has resulted in the notion of developmental age as opposed to chronological age. The former refers to the degree to which a child has advanced toward full maturity. Common measures used are bone age, motor development, emotional development, and intellectual development. Readily identifiable are the excessively early and late developers.

At all stages of the learning process, neuromotor, perceptual, emotional, and intellectual operations are closely bound together; however, this is especially true in the early stages. A child's success on entering school is closely bound up with the satisfactory relationship with adults about him and with his emotional development. The development of behavior is a continuous process. Approval or disapproval, deprivation or punishment represent powerful motives for emotional and other learning both at home and at school. Consistency is extremely important in helping the child to find his way through the maze of do's and don'ts.

Sound practices must be built on certain truths about individual differences. First, differences among children of the same age are great and require individual and special attention. Second, it is unwise to try to teach a particular step forward if a child is not ready for it. Third, boys and girls develop at different rates and in different ways. Fourth, teachers must take account of children's developmental age as they grow up intellectually, emotionally, and physically.

WHAT ABOUT READING?

There is no question that children from birth to age six are highly plastic and responsive to stimulation and learning. From the sensorimotor through the preoperational phase an immense amount of intellectual development occurs. Because of this there is little question but that early stimulation and appropriate learning opportunities can vastly influence children's later learning and development.

"Reading can be viewed as the culmination of a series of learning experiences that begin at the time the child starts to speak, some 4½ years before he enters the first grade" (5, p. 21). This is a timely statement, but it might be qualified as Goethe did a similar statement by pointing out that refinement of reading and thinking skills is a lifelong activity. Nevertheless, the position taken places in sharp focus the interrelatedness between the developing language communication skills of children and the significance of suitable and related early perceptual, linguistic, and cognitive activities for learning to read.

To learn to read a child needs many opportunities to see the world about him (perceptual: to see, hear, feel, smell, taste), to talk about the things and events in his life (linguistic: to acquire labels and concepts), and to act on them (cognitive: to note how things are created, work, and are interrelated). As already noted, all this is best accomplished in a group situation where 8 or 10 children are under the instructional supervision of at least one adult who is prepared to teach and direct the interaction and transaction process.

Linguistic Opportunities

A group of seven carpenters recently put up the studding and siding for the first floor of a one-story country home. Among the group were two teenage boys, ages 15 and 16. They were working along with their father and three other experienced relatives. The younger lad did an expert job cutting and assembling a header for a window. A friendly, thoughtful workmanlike atmosphere prevailed. The two boys were serving a well-timed and productive apprenticeship, learning and being instructed through vital firsthand experience.

Learning and instruction at all levels seem best achieved in such an apprenticeship-type setting. The adults were firm about their demands, fair in their requests, and humorous about it all. It might be said that these three elements are the crux for instruction settings: to be firm, fair, and humorous. Undoubtedly children need to be oriented to classroom living and learning in such a fashion if instruction is to occur.

As was previously pointed out, children at ages four and five possess in varying degree the needed foundation skills essential to learning to communicate by means of printed language. A most essential foundation is the functional use of oral language. Not only do the majority of four- and five-year-olds have sizable listening and speaking vocabularies (see Chapter 1), they know all the essential grammatical structures of their language (form classes, constructions, and grammatical processes). Furthermore, they have also developed a storehouse of concepts and "meanings" that can function in any language context and transfer from one context to another.

This oral language power has been acquired in social situations where the reinforcement is both personal and social and where the need for the use of language is a part of the individual's environment or is firsthand. The functional use of oral language (that is, to communicate either by listening or by speaking) stresses the social aspect, and in so doing emphasizes the purpose of language, which is to communicate. This in turn evokes meaning or a meaningful use. Speakers program their language into syntactical order so that they may convey intent to a listener. The speakers' purpose determines the nature of their language usage, and their language power determines the quality of their programming.

In Chapter 1 the point was made that instruction in reading should be founded on the language and thought power that children possess, because language and thought are linked with actions and interactions in continuous reciprocity. This clearly suggests that instruction should avoid the use of substandard language materials produced by adults, artificial rewards (tokens are no substitute for communication success), rote memorization, and lockstep parroting of words and phonic elements.

Reading instruction can be fruitfully initiated among most four- and five-year-olds if the instruction is predicated on the fact that reading (and writing) is a system of communication that has a close relationship to oral language. The material to be read is the spoken language of the children written down. Thus the style and structure of the language are those of the children and not some artificial substandard usage. Furthermore, by converting the oral language of the children into print, attention is being given to the sound system of their language and the possible effects on the structure both phonologically and syntactically. Speech behavior cannot be measured solely in words; it must also be measured through the sounds that compose the words as well as by the speaker's gestures and expressions. Each of these psychophysiological processes aids recognition, recall, transfer, and use of recorded dictations.

The following dictation by a group of preprimary children is illustrative:

The Fire Engine
David said, "I see a fire engine." Mae said, "A
fire engine is red." Lee said, "A fire engine is
green too." Betty said, "A man stands on the
back." Sam said, "A fire engine can go very

fast." Lois said, "They help us." John said, "My
daddy is a fireman."

The children had seen a city fire engine drive up to the school and give a
brief demonstration (perceptual stimulation). They had talked about the
truck with each other, with the fireman, and with the teacher (social oral
language usage). They had thought about the truck and dictated
(cognitive-linguistic interaction). They had seen their spoken words written down (their sound system conventionalized in print).

It is evident that in this situation experience came first. Language
was created and used in a concrete, firsthand situation. Meaning and
communication (the purpose of language) provided the base for subsequent phonic analysis. Listening was done. Reading and rereading was
done through teacher pacing. In addition, each child drew a picture of a
fire engine, which established another form of symbolization. This provided clues to each child's drawing skill and dexterity and to the attributes
of the fire engine that was illustrated.

One illustration of how a learning episode based on communication
action and interaction can be used to introduce written language (reading)
is not sufficient. Even so, it is evident that the entire episode was structured and had a purpose and that it capitalized on the interrelatedness of
such events. Dealing with suitable experiences relates actions in continuous interrelated processes. In order to structure such processes wisely, it
is useful to examine them discretely.

Perceptual Opportunities

The first step in the world of percepts is to examine the familiar. This
should help children: to perceive more than one relationship at a time
(shapes, sizes, forms); to ask and respond to questions; to discover what is
known and what is not known; to hear and use words appropriate to
communication; and to order ideas by talking about them.

Impressions are acquired through sight and allow children to judge
shades of color and differences in size, shape, and speed. Children can
find and cut out red or green or blue items from magazines, newspapers,
and the like. They can study the colors of flowers or leaves or stones. They
can compare seashells, leaves, hands, cars, and so on. Rates of movement
of trains, buses, horses, dogs, people, grasshoppers, birds, and many
other things can be compared.

Sounds can be attended to (for example, high-low, loud-soft, long-
short) and human voice resonances and variations can be noted. Have
children listen to bird songs, rustling leaves, a meandering brook, road
and air traffic noises, music, breaking glass, and the like.

Smell impressions can be vivid and timely. The smell of toast, tea, overripe apples, mushroom centers, fresh lemon, freshly cut grass, spices, air pollutants, and so on, can be experienced.

Children can taste different ice creams, grapefruits, peanut butters, and so forth. Testing contests in which students are blindfolded are stimulating activities that promote attention.

Touch and feelings provide still another source of reaction and impetus to decision making. The familiar practice of putting one hand in cold water and one in warm water is excellent for studying feelings. Children can feel the wind, the rain, snow, fog, smooth and rough surfaces, and so on. They can also tell how they feel: tired, sleepy, happy, too hot, and so forth.

All these impressions can be translated into words: blue, yellow, orange, egg white, square, circle, triangle, large, small, medium, fast, slow, very slow, roses, violets, pansies, petunias, sugar maple, red oak, tulip poplar, locust, oyster shell, baby hands, my hands, foreign car, Chevrolet, Duster, loud, soft, peaceful, quiet, noisy, rippling, sweet, sour, rancid, hot, cold, warm.

Many of these impressions can be converted into actions, motions, pantomines, or dramatizations; above all, however, they can become a means of expressing experience. Oral sharing is the significant step insofar as reading actions are concerned. It is important for children to translate the reactions described into language. They can do this by sharing with each other extemporaneously and informally as well as through planned formal sharing. One group tells about bird songs they have heard; another tells about leaves they have collected and examined. Discussions among pupils and between teacher and pupil or with a guest specialist, a zoo attendant, or a school nurse are excellent ways to promote oral language usage. To this can be added a group-dictated account such as "The Fire Engine," and one can readily see how perceptually activated meaningful experiences provide foundation sources for dealing with print.

Cognitive Opportunities

Structured procedures planned for use with all children in general and preprimary-level children in particular are designed to develop both the language and thought of the child. Language is used not only to communicate but also to think. As D. G. Hennings and B. Grant point out clearly and in commendable detail, some oral and written accounts are simply a reflection of the world as perceived by an observer (15, p. 89). Others deal with relationships that already exist or might be created in the world. The former deals with the way a child describes his perceptions, reports on happenings, itemizes procedures, retells something he has heard, or summarizes what he has seen or dealt with. The latter deals with relationships perceived through comparisons, contrasts, classifying, analysis by quality and by sequence, and explanations based on cause and effect, supporting principles, interlocking generalizations, and rational intent. Add to this those perceptions that are created or felt and the overview of possibilities is far-reaching.

E. Paul Torrence stated that "creative imagination seems to reach a peak between four and four-and-a-half years" (25). The use of children's ability to create contributes not only to their language and thought development but also to their personal and social development. Children can create by using blocks, toys, puzzles, holiday gifts, room decorations, fruit, cards for Christmas or Valentine's Day, boxes, and designs; by mixing colors; by listening; by taking part in creative dramatics, dances, and rhymes; by using clay and rhythm sticks; by playing stories to music, by playing with puppets; and so on. The opportunities are as numerous as they are varied.

Celia Stendler Lavatelli's superb book, *Piaget's Theory Applied to an Early Childhood Curriculum*, describes curriculum activities designed to help the child of four to seven years make steady progress in the development of logical intelligence (18). The program proposes combining short, structured periods utilizing the designed activities along with directed play activities that provide reinforcement and help "ensure that more children have the thinking skills essential for problem-solving" (18, p. 145).

The activities are empirically, psychologically, and philosophically based on Piaget, and language usage plays an important part in the training. "The child is continually called upon to explain what he is doing and why" (18, p. 144). The activities are structured to promote language and intellectual competence. The latter is accomplished through the development of classification operations, number measurement and space operations, and seriation operations.

Once again it is apparent that dissecting experiences linguistically, perceptually, and cognitively is a scholar's trick. In reality every experience fosters interactions and transactions. Certain aspects of an experience can be stressed and enlarged on and deliberately planned and structured for just such a purpose. Nevertheless, it is timely here to look briefly at other kinds of experiences planned to provide resources for dealing with printed language.

The world of books and stories requires special mention in this regard. Every nursery and/or kindergarten area should have a library filled with easily reached books, magazines, and papers. Shelves and tables should be set up in such a way that the area is inviting and so that items are readily accessible. Different-sized chairs (including a number of rocking chairs), stand-up reading places, reading mats, and the like, should be available.

The book selection should be well balanced and should include well-illustrated books like winners of the Caldecott medal; folk tales and fairy tales; books about holidays and seasons; books of poetry; factual books about science, social science, nature, health, safety, inventions; encyclopedias like *Childcraft;* paperbacks and hardbacks; catalogues of seeds, furniture, clothing, sports equipment, general merchandise, and antiques. In addition, there should be a bulletin board.

Everyone knows the magic of a story hour. Stories well told capture and entrance the most active of youngsters, and poems well read have the same magic. The charm of story dramatization can hardly be measured. Even impromptu stories are a delight and involve children in a rewarding way.

Above all, however, the world of books provides stimulation perceptually, linguistically, and cognitively. It provides a marvelous ready source for promoting oral language conversion into print. The omnipresent availability of books means that no teacher is ever left without a prop for listening, talking, dictating, illustrating, sharing, sound discrimination training, recognition of printed words, and introduction of phoneme-grapheme relationships.

Room furnishings and the playground are as ready sources for experience as the library. In most classrooms a wide variety of materials and supplies are available to be acted with and on, to be examined and compared, to be talked about (for example, workbench equipment, playhouse equipment, blocks and accessories, art activities, manipulative equipment, rest-time equipment, audiovisual equipment, and so on). On the playground are trees, sliding boards, ladders, platforms, bridges, boats, balance rails, swings, monkey bars, hoops, balls, bean bags, and the like.

In many ways the most useful activities for children under six are the science experiences. They are so numerous that once again a teacher must learn to choose. At no time is the world of possible teaching-learning experiences barren.

The animal world of turtles, frogs, birds, nests, shelters, aquariums, hatcheries, caterpillars, cocoons, beetles, zoo, circus, horses, cows, sheep, hogs, rabbits, chickens, deer, fox, dogs, and cats provides enough opportunities for almost every hour of the school day. Add to this the plant world of flowers, seeds, trees, shrubs, field crops. In addition, there is the physical world of seasons, sounds, earth, moon, stars, magnetism, air pressures—all of physical science. And, of course, there are human beings. The list is endless.

Nor can one overlook the social sciences. Special holidays, brithdays, congressional hearings, elections, blast-off ceremonies, parades, parks, families, relatives—all fit into the scheme of things and take children's social and cultural environment into account. Properly used the experiences can help children learn not only how to read but how to live.

Not only are all the teaching-learning structures described thus far useful and beneficial for all children, but they are especially vital to the disadvantaged. The importance of early childhood education is voiced clearly and poignantly in the Colman report, referred to earlier.

> Studies have shown that, while intellectual deprivation begins to reveal itself in ever widening gaps as children mature, infants of poor families do not differ greatly from children in middle-class families in intellectual functioning. By the age of 18 months, however, children of poverty begin to differ from middle-class toddlers in language development and ability to make sense of the world. If the deprived condition exists into later years, the effects are likely to become permanent [5, pp. 1–3].

Early learning experiences as described thus far are conducive to learning on the part of all children and are particularly valuable among the disadvantaged if the effort is continuous. All children learn with or without special instruction, but there is no substitute for a beneficial, enriched environment to advance their learning. Broad educational services and home, school, community, and structured learning activities geared to individual learning rates and potentials are needed.

LANGUAGE PLAYS A CENTRAL ROLE

The development of language power through perceptually and cognitively examined experiences is indeed central to the learning-to-read process. Vocabulary size, sentence power, phonetic skill in articulating sounds, and concepts provide the foundation for the recognition of language converted to print. Printed language, like oral language, is used to communicate as well as to think, and it should be used in this way from the very beginning.

Again at the risk of oversimplification, it can be stated that instruction in language and thought (reading) can begin with the very first phase of language and thought development. E. Claparede, in his introduction to Piaget's *The Language and Thought of the Child,* uses an interesting analogy when he says that the child's mind is woven on two different looms, one above the other. The first, or lower, loom crystallizes about a child's wants and actions; the second is built up little by little by the social environment (20).

Whatever is done, therefore, during the formative years from infancy on readies a child to deal with the printed facet of language. Acts and deeds in the home are indeed influential in shaping later pedagogical achievement, which is of course not news to educators. Edmund B. Huey, in his 1913 book *The Psychology and Pedagogy of Reading* (17), devotes an entire chapter to the home and its influence. He discusses a wide range of factors from the child's "endless questionings" and his learning the alphabet and how to avoid "merely pronouncing words" to the assertion that the "secret of it all lies in parents' reading aloud to and with the child" (17, p. 332). A key comment in the same chapter is, "The natural method of learning to read is just the same as that of learning to talk" (17, p. 330). Roma Gans's chapter concerning the influence of the home in her book *Common Sense in Teaching Reading* (9) also stresses the importance of a child's early interactions with language, ideas, and varying experiences.

More recently, experiences with Head Start, Sesame Street, early childhood education, and the like, have reconfirmed what educators like Friedrich Froebel, Huey, and others have said. Development is a continuous interaction between a child and his environment, and the quality and quantity of experiences encountered affects development. Preschool programs are best when aimed at giving children a wide range of experiences, both individual and group, in which they have opportunities to share with others through work and play, to enjoy and appreciate the fund of circumstances in the world about them, to extend their creative powers, and to use language freely, frequently, and informally.

The research available, such as it is, does not provide conclusive evidence with regard to practices or procedures to be used to develop that language and thought power that will best facilitate each individual's achievement. The overwhelming evidence, though, of experienced scholars favors developing language usage that is rich and wide-ranging. This development should be done by means of vocabulary conceptualized through attribute and function recognition and serving as a tool for categorization. Thus since development in language usage and communication begins in the early years, it behooves us to provide the richest experiences possible as early as possible and on a continuous basis.

It seems apparent that in a language arts sense, instruction in reading should be inaugurated with the first use of language in which a child is active and creates the structures himself in order to satisfy a need. It is the total coordination of actions, or joining things together, of ordering things, of experimenting, of manipulating things and symbols, of posing questions and discovering answers, of comparing findings with those of others, of eliminating contradictions, incompatibilities, and conflicts, of dealing with probabilities as well as certainties—it is these mental functions that serve to promote (cognitive and linguistic) maturity in reading. It is a comprehensive developmental process augmented in the classroom by provoked situations as opposed to spontaneous ones. In other words, these are the fundamental social, linguistic, intellectual, and educational factors.

The general bases on which the use of the multimethod experience-language approach stand are sound and comprehensive. Even so, classroom teaching practices across the country do vary according to teacher differences and the degree to which teachers grasp the underlying theories. Nevertheless, certain practices are common to LEA procedures regardless of the degree to which they are exercised.

The following teaching-learning practices are not to be thought of as listed in rank order. In each procedure the student is the pivotal point of instruction that is based on the dynamic present. In each, instruction is directed in such a way that the student is given maximum opportunity to gain understanding from active and purposeful participation in the processes.

Dictation

DEVELOPMENTAL CLASSROOM

There will be a progression from dictated accounts of experiences that have just occurred and in which pupils have participated, to accounts of experiences observed or heard about, and on to created stories, providing numerous opportunities for children to see, react, think, speak, listen, read, and share. The dictations provide not only an opportunity to use language but also many opportunities to categorize objects, events, and people.

Whole-class accounts serve as a base for getting started. Obviously not all children dictate well-formulated ideas each time, but over a period of time all are given the opportunity to contribute. At the very least, all are interacting members of a group. The following dictation is illustrative:

The Frog
Karen said, "That frog is big and fat." Jamie said, "He stuck his tongue out." Susan said, "He likes me." Bobbie said, "He jumped out of my hand." Chris said, "The frog jumped off my desk." Lisa said, "He jumps on my arm."

Although language-experience instructional procedures are elaborated on in later chapters, there are certain learnings that are activated here that warrant recognition. First, the children participated actively in a firsthand experience (observing and handling the frog). Second, they talked as they acted (language and concepts developed and used socially to communicate and personally to think). Third, they related ideas and saw them recorded (oral language converted to print). Fourth, the teacher, Mrs. Chandler pronounced each word as she wrote it, and she read the entire selection after it was finished (printed language reconverted into oral language). Fifth, she pointed to each word as she proceeded from left to right (word perception and left-to-right progression). Sixth, the teacher paced the children as they read the story in unison (recognizing printed words and speaking them in an established syntactical order). Seventh, four of the children recognized their names—Karen,

Jamie, Chris, and Lisa (recognizing isolated words). Eighth, the same four read the word *frog* and found each use of the three usages in the story (recognizing and transferring to different idea contexts). Ninth, each child drew a frog (using a different symbol system, identifying frog attributes, and clarifying the concept of a frog).

The same dictation was reread on two successive days. Each time the teacher read the story first. Then she paced the class through the story. Again children found their names and the word *frog*. Each showed his drawing of the frog. Each drawing was labeled by the teacher, who had printed the words *The Frog* on a tape and then glued a printed copy at an appropriate place on each child's paper.

All this involved a firsthand experience, recording of oral language, paced rereading of printed language, and recognition of single words. Illustrating was done at a pace in keeping with the children's learning tempo. No undue pressures were brought to bear. No one was hurried. At the very minimum, all read in unison and could identify the words *The Frog*.

At regular time intervals of three to five days, new experiences were planned and new dictations obtained. The resulting charts were posted at eye level for the children and were available constantly. Children went to the chart stand individually and in small-group clusters to examine the charts. Each chart also had an illustration, which helped pupils to identify the story.

On a different occasion a police officer visited the class and talked with the children. This was another firsthand experience that provided action and interactions, conversation and questions, perceptions and attribute analysis, listening and sharing. The following story resulted:

Policeman
Jo said, "Steve got handcuffed." Tom said, "He had bullets and a club." Lisa said, "He had stripes on his pants." Kelly said, "He had stripes on his shirt." Jerry said, "He blew his whistle."

The dictations used thus far were obtained in a so-called inner-city school in a district with a predominantly black population of over 85,000. The kindergarten teacher was using this approach for the first time and doing an outstanding job. These illustrations were selected for use here because they show what can be done even by so-called disadvantaged children when experiences are within their grasp and are firsthand.

Individually dictated accounts are especially practical and useful. At times they are more difficult to obtain at this level, but if a teacher moves gradually from whole-class dictations to individual dictations the transition can be accomplished. The following is an example of an individually dictated account.

The Snow
I would play in the snow. I play with my friends. I
play all day. Michael comes and plays with me. I
would eat hot dogs and hamburgers.
The End
David

The likelihood of word recognition increases with individual dictation. The reasons seem obvious: a personal account, the language flow,
oral memory recall, individual illustration, the intimacy of individual dictation.

My Pet
My dog is Paddy. In the day he runs. I play with
him. Paddy plays with me. I feed him. I love dogs.
I pet him.
Eddie

Teachers who use the linguistic-cognitive (language) power of children as well as their perceptual-cognitive (experience) power and do so
under planned and structured learning schemes soon discover that this
practice fosters individual pupil growth and development. Not only are
the bright and gifted able to develop at a pace in keeping with their
potential, the slow and less able can do likewise. Both populations are
doing the same kinds of action, interaction, transaction activities, and
neither group is harnessed to the other. All participate in structured
experiences, all talk and share, all dictate and read, all obtain word recognition skill training. In brief, individual differences are recognized and
instruction is differentiated.

BILINGUAL CHILDREN
What has been said about practices with the disadvantaged applies
equally well to bilingual children. Experienced teachers testify that it is of
great help to speak the language of the children and to know about their
families, traditions, customs, and their habits of worship. The culture of
bilingual children can enrich the school and improve other children's
appreciations as well as teach these other children a different language.
Overcoming the language barrier is less of a problem for preprimary
children than for older ones. They acquire a relatively good command in a
short time and when they do, they learn to read with the methods described here.
The following dictations were obtained from six-year-olds who had
school opportunity to learn English and thus become bilingual.

Once there was a lost porcupine. He went to a
cactus. He asked, "Is that you, Mother?" And it
was her. So they went home.
Carlo

I saw a rattlesnake. He was very poisonous. He
had big fangs. He had a sharp tail.

                                        Maria

I like the desert. There is lots of plants. It is bright,
too. I love the desert.

                                        Jamie

On a visit to Las Cruces, New Mexico, in early January 1973, Mrs. Hayes visited bilingual classrooms in Mercedes. The children were at first- and second-grade level and represented a mixed population of native Spanish-speaking and English-speaking children. In this case, as in other visits, the demonstrator, Mrs. Hayes, was asked to work with the slowest achiever, in this instance a Spanish-speaking child seven years old. Team teaching was being done, and the four people involved assured her the boy, Eddie, had thus far failed to read a word although he spoke English with some fluency. Eddie and Mrs. Hayes sat down at a table and soon were surrounded by the teachers involved plus two others from adjoining areas. Mrs. Hayes asked Eddie about his Christmas gifts and then about his favorite gift. At first, under the stress of the situation, her newness, and the nearby observers, she had to talk with him through the Spanish-speaking teacher. His favorite gift was a pony named Jordi. Eddie dictated the following in English and she recorded:

Jordi
Jordi is white. Jordi has a spot on his cheek. I
rode Jordi when Christmas.

                                        Eddie

I read back his dictation, then we read it together. I then asked him to point to the word *Jordi*, and he pointed to the title. Next I asked him to find the word some other place, and he found the other three uses. He seemed obviously pleased with his ability, and his teachers beamed. Encouraged by this, I asked him to find *Christmas*. He hesitated for a moment, studied the writing, and then pointed to the word. I selected *Christmas* because of its interest and its location in the dictation. Becoming bolder, I asked him to locate the word *white*. This he did rather readily. Then I asked him to find the word *spot*. I had noted that he had spoken this part with considerable expression. At first Eddie seemed puzzled but he started searching from the beginning of the story and did locate the word. Then I wrote the word *Jordi* at the bottom of the page and asked him what word I had written; he readily replied, "Jordi."

Now it was recess time and of course Eddie wanted to join the others. After recess, Eddie and I sat down together again, and to the astonishment of the teachers gathered about he remembered and located each of the four words.

This episode is related here, even though Eddie was not preprimary in the usual sense, because in pedagogical ways he almost fits such a classification. It also shows the efficacy of meaning, of using firsthand experiences, of using a child's oral language even though in this instance it was a recently acquired second language, and of proceeding with the instruction at a pace in keeping with the circumstances. Eddie read his dictation orally with steady supportive pacing. He located four words I had spoken. He located four different locations of the word *Jordi*. He recognized the word *Jordi* in isolation and without oral prompting. He remembered the four words for at least a half hour, with recess and play intervening.

EARLY ACHIEVEMENT
The following accounts were obtained from a nursery school and from a kindergarten teacher in an independent school (Mrs. Sarah Yearsley, Mrs. Nancy Woodward, and Mrs. Patricia Slingwine, Sanford School, Hockessin, Delaware). The three teachers involved are intimately familiar with using children's oral language to make the transition to printed language.

Jill was three in March, and in September she entered nursery school. In the spring she dictated the following accounts and illustrated them. Most important she could read them.

My Daddy
My Daddy works in duPont. Daddy works on the machinery. Daddy gets his ring caught in the machinery.

My Mommy and Daddy
My Mommy works in the hospital. And my Mommy gives some shots. And my Mommy and my Daddy are doing good.

My Dog
My dog jumps on me. And when he gets his dinner I think he gets excited. And he gets excited when I get home.

In the academic year during which Jill turned five, she dictated accounts as follows:

My Grandmom's   9-19
I went up to my Grandmom's. I helped my Grandmom move. The moving men carried all the stuff up the stairs. And we got the bed in the middle room.

My Daddy Went Away   2-1
My Daddy went away to the airport. And he is going to come back. He got on the airplane. Then the plane went.

My Fish Died   4–3
My fish died. And one day Mommy and I buried
him. And we found a worm. And I said, "Mommy
does worms like mud and water?" And she said,
"Yes."

Carolyn came to kindergarten in September. She had turned five the previous May. Carolyn could read quite well when she entered school, and she could read back dictated accounts with ease. She readily grasped phoneme-grapheme relationships when taught them. As a result, she was introduced to creative writing. On September 13th she wrote:

Carolyns Mithr ad FAthER R AT A PRTE.

On April 16 Carolyn wrote:

ThE Things AT SlooLE
    (like)
I LiED ThE things at aloolE. I liEK My
(friends)
Frins. I liEK MicHELLE I liEK TO BE a Pig.
        (costume)
I ware a Pig Costum.

Later in April she wrote the following:

Signs of Spring
I saw a rebin on the door. I Plae out wieth My
franes in spring. My DaD saw a rabat Hoping. My
Dad CallD My Mom. My Mom Cam runing.

Marcus came to kindergarten in September at age five and turned six in January. On September 11 he dictated and illustrated the following:

When I Was Going to Maryland
I went on a bus by myself. I found some money
on the bus. A car came and picked me up. It took
me to Maryland.

On May 1 he dictated as follows:

Philadelphia Zoo
We went to the zoo and we saw seals. We saw
elephants. We fed peanuts to the elephants. The
elephant squirted water at us. The baby elephant
sneezed dirt at us. We petted the lambs. We saw
the polar bears. We saw the lions. We saw the
black panther. We saw a Chinese leopard. The
hippopotamus ate an apple. The polar bear was
dancing.

On May 28 he wrote the following creative paragraph. It should be remembered that the children who write creatively do their own encoding (spelling). Most of them encode (morpheme-grapheme relationships) by sound and depend largely on auditory-visual perception. Some children, however, seem more dependent on visual configurations or perceptions.

Rain
Rain is GooD. It is bad to. We can not
   (outside) (because)
Go oat said beCaic we can not Go oat
But you can Have Fan. We cannot Have a
(picnic)   (flowers)
PakNak. Rain can Halp the Folwrs. I
love Rain.

Marcus wrote creatively on May 23:

Signs of Spring
     (because)   (robins)
I lak Spring BayKas the RoBans
(came) (back)   (bloom) (in)
Kam Bak. The FlawRS Blawm An
      (time)
the SPring Tat.

On November 6 he had dictated the following:

Swimming Pool
I got a new swimming pool at my apartment in
Florida. One day it was being worked on. I had to
go to the beach. When I came back the swiming
pool was done.

On February 11 David listened to a tape named "The Eagle Has Landed." Then he examined the book of the same title and the three accounts in an encyclopedia on planets, rockets, and satellites. Next he prepared two scenes by drawings and cutouts. One showed the Eagle landing on the moon and planets in outer space. The other showed the Eagle at splashdown and a helicopter and destroyer coming to the rescue. All this done, requiring hours of steadfast creative devotion pursuing a scheme of his design, he wrote his own account to accompany the large 4-x-7-foot display.

The sps men wr at the rct sashn. 10-9 ignshn
8-7-6-5-4-3-2-1-0 Blst Off. The rct 1st the frst
sdag. 100 fet up in sps the scnt sdag fl off. The
eagle Landed on the moon.

It might be helpful to take a look at a class as a whole and show samples of productions across a year. First is a set of dictations resulting from a sequence of events that provoked much pupil action, physically and emotionally, much pupil interaction and transaction through the use of oral language, the introduction of new concepts, and an extension of vocabulary. The children visited an orchard, picked and ate apples, climbed ladders, and so on. The following is a class dictation that resulted.

The Apple Orchard
Leslie Anne said, "We went to the apple
orchard." Chris said, "We picked apples." Anita
said, "We climbed up the ladder." Steven said,
"We put the apples in the basket." Jennifer said,
"We ate apples." Douglas said, "It was cold at
the apple orchard."

Applesauce
Brian said, "We washed the apples." Lenny said,
"We cut the apples." Steven said, "We cooked
the apples." Kristen said, "We mashed the
apples." Jennifer said, "We put in cinnamon and
sugar." Trippi said, "We stirred up the
applesauce." Lenny said, "We ate it."

Note how the events are related in an order of occurrence and reflect pupil response to experiences in which they participated. The experiences were a source of efficient action and of happiness, and involved development of the mind directly dependent on the use of body muscles and the senses. As Rousseau said, "Childhood has its own ways of thinking, seeing, and feeling." Learning is indeed a "necessary incident of dealing with real situations" for our real teachers are "experience and emotion."

From these two dictations more than half the class learned the words, *apple, orchard, basket, applesauce, we, said,* and 12 pupil names—a total of 19 words from a total of 92 running words and a total of 39 different words.

In January of the same year they visited the nearby community fire station and the following dictation resulted.

The Fire Station
Kenny said, "I liked the fire engines." Steven
said, "I saw the pumper truck." Anita said, "We
saw the bandages in the ambulance." Allison
said, "We saw the ladders on the fire trucks."
Douglas said, "We learned that different fire
trucks carried different amounts of water." Jimmy
said, "I liked the fire hats." Neil said, "I liked the
ambulances." Leslie Anne said, "I liked the
stretcher." Lenny said, "I enjoyed the fire coats."

In March a visit to a radio station produced the following dictation:

The Radio Station
Brian said, "We went to the radio station." Renee
said, "We played the record player." Jennifer
said, "We heard Bill talk on the radio." Vivek
said, "I liked all the records." Trippie said, "I liked

Porky Pig at the end." Kristen said, "We all said
good-bye on the radio."

By this time, March of the school year, the children could read all
the words and do so with ease.

Most nursery and infant teachers recognize that when young children are
involved in some activity the talk that accompanies it becomes an important
instrument for learning. Talk is a means by which they learn to work and live
with one another. It enables them to gather information and build into their
own experience the experience of others. . . . Talk of this kind is a consolidating activity, a way of re-ordering experience to make it acceptable. Into this
context of purposeful, sociable and consolidating talk, the infant teacher
introduces the written language [2, pp. 62–63].

The following is illustrative of the writing creations produced by
about two-thirds of the class after a visit to the zoo in May. Some of the
children are now six years old.

Dar Mr rozin barge
Thak you For soing us
your zoo and hop you Can find
anaf mony To keep the zoo opend.
                                        Love Neil

Later in the month the class examined dried tobacco leaves that a
visitor had brought from a Tobacco Auction house in La Platta, Maryland.
Seventeen children wrote about the experience and the discussion.
Stacey's written account was one of the better ones.

Smoking
Smoking is Bad for yor lugs. Toebako levs also
gros in the sowth. The toebako is dri wen thay
mushs it up. They Haing From Hooks. They cant
use it wile its green. The ues it For Cgrets. The
uset to snef it up.

Another group dictated the following account, which was recorded
on 3-x-5-inch oaktag. (Newsprint serves adequately, too, but oaktag is
more substantial for posting and handling.) At the top of the account two
of the children drew a large-sized tobacco leaf showing the veins.

Tobacco Leaves
The tobacco leaves smell good. They grow in the
south. The leaves grow on a plant. The leaves
were green but then they hung them up and they
dried. The leaves look old and dry and they feel
crumbly. They look very big.

In another independent school, Friends School of Wilmington, Delaware, superb instruction is being done by Frances Altmaier and Jerry
Drysdale in the nursery and kindergarten program, which also includes a

so-called pre–first grade. The latter is a local label applied to a group that varies considerably in its structure from very bright four- and five-year-olds to some bright five- to six-year-olds that are not as settled to "school" constraints. Even so their creative and productive activities do motivate them to pursue their own interests, linked up with social interests and experiences and express themselves through drawing and the like, dramatizations and oral language. The results are very similar to those described. The spacious facility of the classroom is filled with action-type things (easels and brushes, clay molding, construction blocks, puzzles, costume fitting, musical instruments, magnets, microscopes) and with innumerable dictations and creative writings. In the following dictation note the quality of the language syntactically and grammatically and the sequence of ideas.

Three Nests
Meegan brought a bird's nest in a kettle from her shed and two mouse nests. In the bird's nest there is a feather. Hudson thought the mouse nests stunk. Linda said it was funny the mouse nests were different. One nest was made of sticks and the other had soft stuff in it. The two mouse nests were in a box. The nests are empty because the mice moved.

In November a group of eight children prepared a booklet entitled The Pilgrim Story." The booklet had 18 pages. Each page was approximately 8 x 5 inches. Two-thirds of each page contained a pupil-prepared illustration. At the bottom of each page three or four lines were typed from pupils' dictation. Of course the booklet had a title page. Some of the dictation account was as follows:

Page 1: The King wanted the Pilgrims to go to his church.
Page 2: They went to Holland and couldn't understand their children. They were speaking Dutch.
Page 3: They went to America on the Mayflower. They left on Pete's birthday, August 5th, 1620.
Page 4: Two boys got in trouble. They lit a rope and got it close to a barrel of gunpowder.
Page 5: They got off the boat at Cape Cod and washed their clothes and themselves.
Page 6: Then they went to Plymouth Rock. They built a fort. Then it was winter.

[and so on]

Another booklet, fittingly bound, using and prepared on 9-x-12-inch oaktag was titled "The Adventures of Slowpoke," the story of a turtle. The book was dictated and illustrated by 17 children and was dated May 24. Again two-thirds of each page was devoted to illustrations.

Page 1: M. R. found a box turtle in a chicken coop.

Page 2: He gave it to Meagan who named it Slowpoke and brought it to school in a box.

Page 3: Slowpoke does not like a lot of noise. He keeps his head in his shell when we talk too loudly.

Page 4: When we go to the zoo tomorrow Slowpoke might get out of his box and explore the school.

Page 5: When we're away he might feel braver.

[and so on to the last page]

Last Page: Slowpoke now lives in the woods behind Friends School.

Another dictated account prepared by seven children is an example of a midyear experience and the language it evoked.

The Candle Factory
We melted wax in big juice cans. We took a wick and we dipped it in the hot wax. We had red and blue and green wax. Then we walked around a table to let the candle cool off. Then we came back and dip again. We dip it a lot of times so the candle can get thicker.

In each group, the kindergarten group and the pre-first grade group, there were either 17 or 18 children. As stated earlier, many of the teacher structured experiences involved the entire group.

When dictation is done at this level two clear-cut variations seem to occur whether the school population is inner city, suburban, or rural. I have visited in classrooms, demonstrated with four- to six-year-olds in a variety of situations from large population centers like Chester, Pennsylvania; Wilmington, Delaware; cities like Boise, Idaho, and Santa Fe, New Mexico; rural areas like Dorchester and Charles Counties, Maryland; and university communities like Stark, Mississippi; and Las Cruces, New Mexico; and talked with teachers and find that generally preschoolers are best instructed in group situations of five to seven members or in situations where only one or two are together and produce almost entirely individually. On the other hand, among six-year-olds and in first grade both groupings are used, and one is as effective as the other. Thus the children can be shifted about readily.

The writing of accounts at the kindergarten level usually begins late in the school year, or from about April on. First graders are usually ready to begin creative writing by November and sometimes October. Here are two creative writing accounts produced by kindergarten children in May.

5-77

We saw a black billy goat from mark phipps farm.
Its name was jack.

Arlene

We Went to see Jack the billy goat the billy goat was blak. They cut of His horns So he wood Not But The children Now it is Safe

Scott

Both of these children, even though only five years old, read fluently. Arlene had been reading since she was three. Both contributed to "The Pilgrim Story" and to "The Adventure of Slowpoke." Both enjoyed writing and doing the encoding on their own. Arlene, as is apparent, produced the accepted letter order (correct spelling) in each instance. Sometimes very bright children will limit their writing to words they can produce and they are reluctant to encode phonologically. One can account for this only by conjecture, but there seems a consensus among discerning teachers that some of the very bright are reluctant to proceed phonologically because they "see" that what they produce does not look like the visual image of the word as they remember it. It seems that in these instances the strong visual imprint of the word dominates their action but is not sufficiently established to permit them to recall and produce the accepted letter order. This may constrain their writing production, but once they feel the independent and self-realized spirit of creative writing, they overcome this concern and produce lengthy writings using phonological encodings. This results because they learn to edit a production. They then feel free to write.

On the other hand, some like Scott will freely encode phonologically. When this happens the written production is a marvelous evidence of achievement. First, it shows creative young minds eager to write and produce. Second, it provides evidence of phonic (phoneme-grapheme) ability. It also shows where further instruction is needed. Scott's encoding of *blak* for *black* shows a considerable grasp of phoneme-grapheme relationships (the *bl* blend, the medial short vowel *a*, the ending *k*) and the need for clarification of *ck* endings as in bla*ck*, ba*ck*, and Ja*ck*. The latter was encoded appropriately. Because *Jack* is correct it provides a good starting point for establishing the *ck* encoding.

The examples provided here are representative of typical preprimary-level children, of so-called disadvantaged children, or bilingual children, and of early maturing children. In each case the results are similar because the language and experience of the children, regardless of their classification or labeling, served as the foundation on which to develop the ability to read. Meaningful oral language usage provided the semantic-conceptual base for transfer to the use of printed symbols. It is evident that individual differences exist even at the preprimary level and that good teaching increases the range of differences and does not force the children into lockstep.

That bright children, regardless of their ethnic group or culture, learn to write creatively at age five should not astound anyone. Some of these samples are produced by black children and some by white children. These children not only acquired considerable skill in making letters but also, and vastly more important, acquired facility in noting phoneme-grapheme relationships. The instruction is described below and is detailed in a later chapter. The important point is that instruction was paced and geared to the different rates of development of abilities of children.

Auditory Discrimination Training

Long before the child enters school he has learned to discriminate between vocal sounds sufficiently to differentiate one word from another and to obtain understanding. Seldom, however, is the preschool child able to identify syllable sound units that are alike and are heard in different words. It is extremely unwise to assume that a child who hears and understands words is also able to tell how words are alike or different by sound elements alone. This skill, which forms the foundation for phonetic analysis, needs to be carefully developed.

Nursery school and kindergarten children need experience with nursery rhymes and television commercial jingles to develop sensitivity to rhyming words. In doing so they also acquire some sensitivity to rhythm and time. The general awareness of the uniform recurrence of a beat, an accent, or rhyming words readies a child to identify words that have similar sound units and can be used in a rhyme. The ability to perceive differences as well as likenesses is essential to auditory discrimination. The ability to recognize sound units that agree or do not agree with a rhyme pattern is necessary if children are to use the more penetrating skills in phonetic analysis.

At all times one must be careful not to distort a word by exaggerating a sound. The quality of a sound unit is determined by an almost imperceptible blending of sounds. For all purposes of phonetic (phonic) analysis, sounds should always assume their conventional qualities as an interacting part of the sound unit of which they are a member. There is no *tee* sound in *cat*. It is useful to know that the sound represented by the letter *t* is part of the total sound unit *cat*, which is similar to *bat*, *hat*, *fat*, and so on.

Just as rhyme helps children hear words that sound alike, *alliteration* will help them to become sensitive to words that begin with the same sound. Alliterative effect is evident, for example, in *tip, tap, toe.*

The ability to recognize that spoken words can begin with the same consonant sound is essential to the sound analysis (phonetic analysis) of printed words. Therefore, in developing skill at recognizing initial consonant sounds, one needs to provide activities that permit frequent and varied repetition and that capture as much rhythmic movement as alliteration and voice modulation can give. Some children find it difficult to perceive the rhythmic pattern of alliteration and need frequent hearing opportunities. Once the pattern is acquired, they are ready to deal with the reason that words agree with one another—that is, because they begin with the same sound. The following suggestions are useful:

1. Play a sound discrimination game. Let one child cover his eyes. Choose another child to make different sounds (tap on glass, rap on a desk, beat a drum, start a fan, clap erasers, clap hands, strike a high note on the piano). Allow the child with eyes hidden 10 seconds to identify the sound. Let the rest of the class see the noisemaker in action.

2. Place a screen in front of the piano. Have one pupil behind the screen use the loud or the soft pedal; strike a high or a low note; strike a key and hold it for a long sound, or release it immediately for a short sound. The other pupils will decide whether they heard a loud or soft note; a high or low note; a long or short note.

3. (a) Have the children make rhymes using the names of people and rhyming them with the names of food or other items, such as:

I saw Sam.　　I see Mabel.
Eat a ham.　　Clean the table.

I see Anna.　　I saw Paul.
Eat a banana.　Paint the wall.

(b) Play a picture-name matching game. Place different pictures along the board in the chalk tray. One pupil names one of the pictures (cat) and another finds a picture whose name rhymes (hat). This might be timed to add interest.

4. Present orally some simple phrases that use two words whose initial sounds are to be compared, such as, "I saw a boy. He had a _____." Then present two pictures, one of a baseball bat and one of a glove. The pupils will decide that *bat* and *boy* begin with the same sound. Sometimes children need much practice with activities like this in which they select one of two words. Be certain that the two words represented by the pictures have strikingly different beginning sounds.

5. Some of the verses written by Laura Richards are interesting and

have alliterative patterns. The chorus in "Master Jack's Song" (p. 111) in her book *Tirra Lirra,** is particularly useful:

> Where the jam-pots grow!
> Where the jam-pots grow!
> Where the jelly jolly, jelly jolly jam-pots grow
> The fairest spot to me
> On the land or on the sea
> Is the charming little cupboard where the jam-pots grow.

Also useful are "The Baby Goes to Boston" (pp. 123–124); "Was She a Witch?" (p. 145); and "Eletelephony" (p. 31), which appear in the same book.

6. The teacher might proceed as follows: "I am going to say two words. Listen carefully so that you can tell whether or not the two words begin with the same sound.

soda—some	far—fat
sand—sing	feet—fence
say—boy	pet—down
fan—see	do—door

Sometimes children grasp the sound difference well during a training period, only to have great difficulty a day later. Such pupils need frequent experience at spaced intervals.

Most useful, of course, are the words and the language of the children as recorded in their dictations. Rhymes can be developed such as: "I see a *frog* sitting on a log." "He jumped out of my *hand* into the sand." "He jumped on my *arm* when I was on the *farm*." "I know *Jo*, she is on the go." "I like to *play* on every *day*."

Alliteration can be done as follows: "*T*im, *T*om, *t*able all begin alike; *T*im, *T*om, *b*ox do not." "*P*lay, *p*lease, *p*lant; *p*lease, *p*lay, *t*ree;" "*D*avid, *d*oor, *d*og; *D*avid, *d*oor, *m*an." This can be continued, narrowing the selection to two words: *D*avid, *D*arwin; *T*om; *B*ill.

Auditory-visual or phoneme-grapheme or sound-letter training can be started by writing the word *frog* on the chalkboard and then having the children decide whether or not the following spoken words begin like *frog: from, free, fry, freeze, Tom, French, friend, fresh, sun,* and so on. It is wise to use three or more confirming instances before introducing a negative instance. When a different beginning sound is used it is helpful to use one that is distinctly different, as *T*om and *s*un.

*Laura Richards, *Tirra Lirra*. Boston: Little Brown, 1932.

Visual Discrimination

Noting likenesses and differences in form, shape, size, and so on, as described earlier in this chapter, provides the perceptual-cognitive maturity for noting likenesses and differences in words. An important fact to remember is that the children actually compare and contrast items and by so doing acquire some functional dimension by which to make perceptual decisions.

When Eddie, the bilingual boy, located the word *Jordi* he was doing so on the basis of configuration clues and the features that distinguished that word from the other 13 words. When he located the word in the four different locations, each time he was reinforcing the perceptual clues he was using for decision making, and he was transferring his perceptual know-how to new situations.

The demonstrator had supported the visual perception recognition by linking them with auditory perception. She spoke (oral-auditory) the word *Jordi* and asked Eddie to find the printed symbol. Such linking of sound and sight (phoneme-grapheme) is both wise and timely.

Every dictated account provides an instructor with innumerable opportunities for developing visual perception skills appropriately linked with auditory skills. In fact, each time a teacher or the pupils point to a word as the oral rereading of a chart proceeds, they are being attentive to the visual-perceptual differences in each word.

Additional training can be provided by giving children a copy of a word in a chart and asking them to go to the chart and match the word. Phrases may be used similarly, or, in some instances, entire sentences may be used.

Each piece of creative writing provides evidence not only of a grasp of phoneme-grapheme relationships, but also of the configuration of words. Many words are produced with the accepted letter order (correct spelling) because of the influence of a well-established visual-perceptual imprint. They are words that can be read with ease and as a result have established a clear impression.

In brief, the language of the children can be used functionally to develop needed perceptual skills so essential for independent word recognition. Actions can be activated as described here and repeated frequently.

SOCIAL AND EMOTIONAL ADJUSTMENT

Good mental hygiene within a peer group is essential to learning. Security, self-confidence, acceptance, tolerance, and a sense of belonging are the foundation for attitudes that encourage fair play, free expression, emotional poise, and participation in effective learning experiences. Approaches to learning that take into account social and emotional factors emphasize the necessity for planning with and for the children in terms of everyday, overall growth.

Early school experiences are important ones. Maintaining happy, relaxed, stimulating relationships within the group as a whole and between each child and the teacher promotes personality growth that in turn advances achievement. The stimulating situations that are provided should foster individual creativity and exploration and at the same time help to fix learning where needed. In such situations some competition is recognized, and mistakes are considered as attempts and accepted as ways of learning. "Try, try again" or "Your were almost right," says the more experienced person (the teacher) in the classroom to the less experienced one (the pupil).

STANDARDIZED READING-READINESS TESTS

Standardized tests of reading readiness, combined with the judgment of able teachers, provide a measure of pupil achievement. The general purpose of such tests is to predict a child's ability to learn to read.

The tests usually have subsections designed to check on different aspects of reading readiness, such as the ability to make visual discriminations of objects, symbols, letters, and word forms; to make auditory discriminations; to name letters; and to understand vocabulary. They also provide information on the student's learning rate, ability to perceive relationships, ability to interpret feelings and make inferences, and so on. None of the standardized tests measure all these areas. The range and completeness of subtests vary considerably. For example, one of the widely used tests—the Lee-Clark Reading Readiness Test—has four subtests measuring recognition of likenesses, discrimination of differences, experiential background, including understanding of vocabulary, and ability to discriminate among similar but different letter and word forms. The test requires only 15 to 20 minutes. The Harrison-Stroud Reading Readiness Profile has seven parts: using symbols, making visual discriminations (two parts), using the context, making auditory discriminations, using context and auditory clues, and giving the names of letters. It is recommended that the tests be administered in three sessions, and the testing time is estimated at 80 to 90 minutes.

As Helen M. Robinson points out in her review of the American School Reading Readiness Test, usually only 6 to 10 items are used in the subtests, and this number is too small to provide reliable information. When the sample size is so small, there is considerable doubt about the predictive value of the scores obtained. In this regard, this particular test is no different from others on the market. In addition, manual directions accompanying such tests usually indicate that each subtest contains both easy and difficult items, which increases the burden of predictive value placed on subtests (21, p. 773).

James R. Hobson reviewed the Lee-Clark Tests and voiced the kind of caution that might be exercised in using any standardized reading-readiness test.

> Neither the test itself nor any of the technical data presented in the manual would appear to support the rather elaborate normative and interpretative tables. These are attractive and logical enough; but in the absence of any experimental support or statistical verification, it must be assumed that they have been more or less subjectively derived and that their validity for such exact and detailed analysis is in question [16, p. 777].

Nila Banton Smith, in her thorough article on readiness for reading indicates that the relationship between intelligence test results and reading-readiness tests has led to a number of conclusions:

1. When intelligence tests are used in conjunction with other tests, intelligence is one of the most significant indices in predicting readiness for beginning reading. . . .
2. Intelligence is a major factor in reading success at any level. . . .
3. Too many bright children are failing at all levels. . . .
4. A mental age of from 6 to 6½ is considered by many investigators to be essential for success in beginning reading. . . .
5. No one mental age is a guarantee of beginning reading success. [22, p. 15]

Other studies (10, 11, 23) also indicate that no one mental age is a guarantee of success in learning to read. Furthermore, they give support to the idea that a *constellation of factors* determines readiness for reading and that these factors differ from individual to individual.

Standardized reading-readiness tests do provide information that can be useful in determining the range and level of achievement children have attained by the time they are required to enter school. However, standardized reading-readiness tests do not provide information about the wealth of child's experiences, his depth and variety of language understanding and usage both syntactically and semantically, and his cognitive powers. If the results are used in conjunction with other sources of information, such as intelligence tests and informal reading-readiness tests and especially teacher observations, a substantial picture of each child may be obtained. The end result of such study should be a program of instruction in reading that can be paced by each pupil's potential.

CONCLUSION

Marked individual differences are evident among three- and four-year-olds and need to be dealt with on a differentiated instruction basis. At no time should they be fitted into lockstep procedures. In addition, the language and perceptual power overtly and covertly evidence on cognitive-affective levels should be used to best advantage. This is done by involving the children in actions, interactions, and transactions that are carefully planned and coordinated. At the preprimary level it is just as imprudent to set a fixed age limit for activating reading instruction as it is at a later age. Children are different and must be taught accordingly.

Bibliography

1. Bugelski, R., "Learning Theory and the Reading Process." In D. L. Cleland and P. E. Stanton (eds.), *Psychological and Physiological Aspects of Reading: A Report of the 24th Annual Conference and Course on Reading*. Pittsburgh: School of Education, University of Pittsburgh, 1968, pp. 36–54.
2. Bullock, Sir Alan, *A Language for Life, Report of the Committee of Inquiry Appointed by the Secretary of State for Education and Science* (England). London: Her Majesty's Stationery Office, 1975.
3. Carroll, John, "The Analysis of Reading Instruction: Perspectives from Psychology and Linguistics." In E. R. Hilgard (ed.), *Theories of Learning and Instruction*. Chicago: National Society for the Study of Education, University of Chicago Press, 1964, pp. 336–353.
4. Chomsky, C. A., "Stages in Language Development and Reading Exposure," *Harvard Review of Education*, 42 (1972), 1–33.
5. Colman, Joseph C., and Corazan Sandocal, *Pre-Primary Education: Needs, Alternatives and Costs, 1971–1980*. Washington, D.C.: U.S. Department of Health, Education and Welfare, Office of Education (OEC-0-71-2747), 1971.
6. Department of Education and Science, *Children and Their Primary Schools, A Report of the Central Advisory Council for Education* (England), Vol. 1. London: Her Majesty's Stationery Office, 1967.
7. Dewey, John, *Experience and Education*. New York: Macmillan, 1938.
8. Dewey, John, and Evelyn Dewey, *Schools of Tomorrow*. New York: Dutton, 1915.
9. Gans, Roma, *Common Sense in Teaching Reading*. Indianapolis: Bobbs-Merrill, 1963.
10. Gates, Arthur I., "The Necessary Mental Age for Beginning Reading," *Elementary School Journal*, 37 (March, 1937) 487–508.
11. Gates, Arthur I., and Guy L. Bond, "Reading Readiness: A Study of Factors Determining Success and Failure in Beginning Reading," *Teachers College Record*, 37 (May, 1936), 679–685.
12. Goodlad, John I., and Robert H. Anderson, *The Nongraded Elementary School*. New York: Harcourt Brace Jovanovich, 1959.
13. Gray, William S., "The Nature and Organization of Basic Instruction in Reading." In *The Teaching of Reading: A Second Report*, Thirty-sixth Yearbook of the National Society for the Study of Education, Part I. Bloomington, Ill.: Public School Publishing, 1937.
14. Gray, William S., and Bernice Rogers, *Maturity in Reading: Its Nature and Appraisal*. Chicago: University of Chicago Press, 1956.
15. Hennings, Dorothy G., and Barbara Brant, *Content and Craft: Written Ex-*

pression in the Elementary School. Englewood Cliffs, N.J.: Prentice-Hall, 1973.

16. Hobson, James R., "Lee-Clark Reading Readiness Test, 1951 Revision," in Otto Krisen Buros (ed.), *The Fifth Measurement Yearbook.* Highland Park, N.J.: Gryphon, 1959, pp 777–778.

17. Huey, Edmund D., *The Psychology and Pedagogy of Reading.* New York: Macmillan, 1913.

18. Lavatelli, Celia S., *Piaget's Theory Applied to an Early Childhood Curriculum.* Cambridge, Mass.: American Science and Engineering, 1970.

19. National Society for the Study of Education, *Report of the National Committee on Reading,* Twenty-fourth Yearbook of the National Society for the Study of Education, Part I. Bloomington, Ill.: Public School Publishing, 1925.

20. Piaget, Jean, *The Language and Thought of the Child.* New York: Harcourt Brace Jovanovich, 1965.

21. Robinson, Helen M., "Tests and Reviews: Reading-Readiness." In Otto K. Buros (ed.), *The Fifth Mental Measurement Yearbook.* Highland Park, N.J.: Gryphon, 1959.

22. Smith, Nila B., "Readiness for Reading," *Readiness for Reading and Related Language Arts,* NCRE Research Bulletin. Chicago: National Council of Teachers of English, 1950.

23. Stauffer, Russell G., and John Pikulski, "A Comparison and Measure of Oral Language Growth Among Six Year Olds," *Elementary English,* 51 (November, 1974), 1151–1155.

24. Stebbing, L. Susan, *Thinking to Some Purpose.* London: The White Friars Press, Ltd., 1939.

25. Torrance, E. Paul, "Adventuring in Creativity," *Childhood Education,* 39 (October, 1963), 98–112.

Chapter 3
Language-Experience
Practice at the Primary
Level

Most educators and even outsiders seem to agree that there is no one way to teach all children. This generalization appears to be a faulty inversion of the Lincolnish commonplace that "you cannot fool all of the people all of the time." There are also reading specialists and reading teachers who repeat the same platitude. When asked to explain, they seldom get beyond the grossly misunderstood polarizations labeled by G. Stanley Hall as the "synthetic" and the "analytic" methods, or the "look-say" and the "phonic" method, or Worcester's the "whole word" method (1828), and the "ABC dearian" methods (fifteenth century). For those teachers who are largely journeymen the defense becomes by and large an excuse for ignorance. For the publishers and authors who proclaim their materials as either the "natural" or "new" or "logical" way, such claims may become huge sources of revenue. After a brief statement about this, the Bullock report concludes

> We believe than an improvement in the teaching of reading will not come from the acceptance of simplistic statements about phonics or any other single aspect of reading, but from a comprehensive study of all the factors at work and the influence that can be exerted upon them [3, p. 78].

It is in this respect that the experience-language approach as described in this text reflects a global approach. It represents an integration of instructional conditions, both immediate and long term, that are rightly a part of the total search for instructional truth. As has already been discussed in Chapters 1 and 2, the *language* portion, perhaps better referred to as the *language arts* and best as the *communication arts,* encompasses the four facets of communication and is founded on the purposeful social-personal use of language. *Experience* encompasses an individual's perceptual and conceptual world, his interests and curiosities, his creativity, his culture, his capacity to adjust, to learn, to use, and above all his extraordinary flexibility.

Other conditions warrant repeating and reestablishing even though some of them may appear to be commonplace. *First* is the fact that among typical six-year-olds the range of individual differences and/or maturity is at least five years. This means that if instruction in the reading process is to be paced even in part by ability grouping, the nature, range, and frequency of pupil distribution must be considered.

Second, reading is not only to be thought of as a thinking process primarily and a communication process generally but is to be taught that way. Comprehension and communication, not parroting and repeating, are the incontrovertible issues. Reading is a process of self-sustaining and text-generated action. Before we can read we must know the nature and purpose of our actions. We cannot comprehend without knowing our aim and the means to achieve it. To become scholars we must think and make choices.

Third, instruction must be individualized to foster the art of inquiry. Inquiry is native to the mind. Even as an infant each child is busy gathering data from the environment to symbolize and conceptualize it (14). As children grow older their search for, collecting, and processing of data become broader and more complex and take on more of the character of invention and research. Therefore, children who are being instructed to reorganize their conceptual systems must be given innumerable opportunities to try out their own stores of conceptual models by using them to raise questions and make predictions, to gather data, and to resolve predictions or questions or cognitive conflicts (15).

Fourth, materials must be soundly structured and designed. "Breaking the code" must mean comprehending a well-written passage and artificiality must be avoided. No excuse can justify the false conflicts or unnecessary tensions resulting when the syntactic structures are disconnected and forced and far removed from anything the child, or anyone for that matter, ever hears in real life. Furthermore, the library should always be the principal source of materials, and abridgements of any kind should be avoided.

Fifth, the vocabulary, concepts and cognitive processes that children have developed for oral communication should be fully utilized and augmented.

Sixth, word attack skills must be taught as an *auxiliary* aid to comprehension. Words must be introduced in a communication context. Meaning clues to recognition and comprehension based on interpolation (closure) or extrapolation (predicting) can then be the functional source of help that only context can provide. Similarly, phoneme-grapheme or letter-sound relations are best learned in the context of a whole word or in brief in the *sound context in which they occur.* Thus the question is not whether or not to teach phonics; the question is how and when to do it so that it becomes an aid to meaning and not an end in itself.

Seventh, pupil interests must be utilized and expanded, their experiences extended, refined, and vivified, their curiosities livened and magnified, their concepts examined and refined. Above all, these must be utilized as a basic source of printed material.

Eighth, the basic skills of comprehension and versatility must be taught and paced in such a way that they can over a period of years be assimilated and utilized. Possibly the greatest liability of even the most intelligent readers is their inability to adapt their rate of reading to the nature and difficulty of the material.

Ninth, the laws of learning must be observed. It is not only repetition but repetition in a new context, not only memory but functional use in meaningful circumstances, not only decision making but decision making in response to self-declared problems, not only an assimilation of facts but more so a utilization of the value of the facts, not only a matter of grinding out consequences, but a coping with consequences.

Tenth, the freedoms and responsibilities of self-selection must be activated from the earliest. The librarian and the library must become the most important source of help. It is essential though that the library be viewed as a multimedia center. Not all knowledge is stored in books.

Eleventh, above all a love of and appreciation for what reading can do for people must be fostered. Reading not only can change attitudes and practices but can be put to practical uses to solve a variety of problems. Reading not only can entertain but can be helpful in understanding oneself and others (19).

GETTING STARTED

This portion of the text may seem strangely out of place to the reader who has carefully read Chapter 2. However, because the differentiation of instruction continues to be largely a matter of talk rather than of practice and because a distorted notion of "readiness" continues to prevail in all too many instances, reading instruction continues to be activated largely in first grade.

As Goodlad says, this is no way to face either the present or the future

... the common expectation and demonstrated function of our schools are coverage of tasks and materials that have been predetermined for specific grades and period of time.... This... denies our growing awareness of individual differences in learning and the probability that what children learn has more to do with the subject matter they are exposed to rather than our genius in the grade placement of children and content [7, p. 36].

This is truly the "can of worms." We are, as Goodlad goes on to say, "locked into outworn, inadequate strategies." Because this is so, I enlarge here on the "how" aspects in the context of "grades" rather than in the context of "preschool, kindergarten and grades" and the broad concept of individual differences and differentiation of instruction.

By the time children are about six most of them are eager to read. This eagerness stems from the culture as well as from maturity. Of course, some come to school able to read after a fashion and eager to show that they can. Others are eager to show that they want to try. This is why an immediate "reading" start should be made. If the object of the start is to show children how their talk can be recorded and read, then the beginnings become personalized, suggestive, and enterprising.

The way to accomplish this is by means of a pupil-dictated account of a firsthand experience. Arrange to have available some item that will capture and hold pupil interest. Select an item that the children can "act" on by employing as many as possible of the sensory gateways and that they can "interact" about. The more active and involved the children become, the better. One teacher, on the second day of school, began in a most advantageous way. She had brought into the room a white mouse and when she introduced it to the class, it immediately evoked reactions and stimulated talk. Many other similar ideas could have been used: a puppy, chick, mouse, box turtle, a novel toy, to name but a few.

The teacher placed the mouse cage on a pupil-level viewing table. The children gathered around and watched the mouse move about, nibble on greens, and sniff at water. Then she took the mouse out of the cage and allowed it to move about on the table. She showed no concern about handling it and her confidence and poise influenced the class. The children exclaimed, "Look, he's standing up!" "He nibbles!" They talked to each other about him. The teacher further underlined their reactions by asking attention-focusing questions that caused them to attend even more carefully. She pushed the "experience" into the "examined experience" category. "What color are his eyes?" "How does he feel?" "How long do you think his tail is?" and so on. The questions caused them to look each time with a different and specific set.

"What should we name him?" asked the teacher. This evoked a number of responses such as "Whitey," "Snow White," "Pink Eyes." Of the different names given, the class preferred Snow White. The choice was made by a show of hands, which allowed all to participate, express an opinion, and operate in a democratic atmosphere. Group cohesion as *esprit de corps* was being developed.

The teacher put the mouse back into the cage, covered the cage and set it aside, and then gathered the class around an easel on which she had tacked a large piece of lined newsprint approximately 2 x 3 inches in size. After printing the mouse's new name, Snow White, on the top line, she invited the class to tell about the mouse, indicating that she would print what they said, just as she had recorded the name.

Dick said, "Snow White scratched around in his cage." Jane added, "Snow White has pink eyes." Alice said, "He stood up on his hind legs and looked at us." And so on.

As different children offered an idea, the teacher recorded it, saying each word as she printed it. After each idea had been recorded, she read it back to the group in general and to the pupil dictating in particular. Thus she proceeded, recording the ideas of six different pupils and completely filling the newsprint sheet. All this took but a few minutes; the pupils were fascinated by the performance and were eagerly attentive. The account when she finished read as follows:

Snow White
Dick said, "Snow White scratched around in his cage." Alice said, "He stood up on his hind legs and looked at us." Jane said, "Snow White has pink eyes." Jerry said, "His tail is two feet long." Bill said, "Snow White ran around on the table." Nancy said, "Snow White is soft and furry."

Now the teacher read the entire story to the class. As she read, she pointed quickly and briefly to each word. Then all the class read the story together. The teacher pointed to each word as they proceeded, saying each word and the pupils saying it with her. Even though the pointing and the repeating after by the pupils made for some arrhythm, a surprisingly even-paced performance resulted. The tone and intent of the teacher's voice helped bridge the slightly arrhythmical gaps.

Then she had Dick stand by and she paced him through the account. Dick recognized *Snow White* each time it occurred and each word he had contributed. Jane recognized *Snow White* and each word Dick had dictated and what she had added. Jerry did not recognize any of the words, not even *Snow White*. Bill, on the other hand, recognized every word, or 56 running words and 37 different words.

Next she gave each pupil a large sheet of white paper and asked them to make a drawing of Snow White. While the children were drawing, she went about the room, printing the words *Snow White* at the top of each paper. The drawings or illustrations provided the teacher with a Goodenough-Harris type drawing that could be analyzed much as the Man drawing test (6). In brief, this helped her gain insight into likely mental maturity, dexterity, and art ability of each child. By placing the title "Snow White" above the child's drawing the two symbol systems were junctured, thus aiding pupil recognition and retention of the two words.

Some of the results of this experience can be itemized as follows:

1. Pupils saw that reading is no more than talk written down.
2. They saw that the teacher could read back all the story or just parts of it.
3. They saw that some of the class members could read some of the words and that Bill had read all of them.
4. They noted how the teacher paced the reading and helped each child, especially Jerry.
5. They followed the reading process from left to right.
6. They made return sweeps from the end of one line on the right to the beginning of the next line on the left.
7. They saw that different letters are made differently. Some were capitals. *Snow White* always started with capital letters.
8. They saw the use of punctuation in a meaningful language context.
9. They experienced the thrill of "reading" as they read with the teacher.
10. Some of the pupils saw their names in writing and their ideas in writing.
11. They had displayed *curiosity* as they watched and examined the mouse and *creativity* as they told about their reactions.
12. They were stimulated to oral language usage as they reacted to seeing the mouse.
13. Ideas were shared in the dynamics of a class situation and in response to an immediate experience.
14. The teacher's questions had caused them to observe more carefully.
15. Each had opportunities to listen to others speak, to hear their ideas, and to discover how others reacted to the same circumstances.
16. Each had an opportunity to vote and express preference for a name for the mouse and to learn how to accept the decision of the majority.
17. Each had an opportunity to make his own drawing and show the attributes of the mouse that he recognized, recalled, and produced.
18. The title "Snow White" written on each drawing gave pupils an opportunity to link two different symbols for one referent: a printed name and a picture.

In addition, the teacher had had an excellent opportunity to discover some things about her class:

1. their curiosity about the mouse
2. their concern or lack of concern about seeing the mouse out of the cage and on the table and their reluctance or readiness to touch it
3. their willingness to move about the table and among each other
4. their oral language usage and, particularly, their choice of words
5. their attention span, persistence, and cooperativeness
6. the ability of some to read (as the story was being read back by the class, some pupils read ahead)
7. their dexterity with crayons and ability to illustrate ideas.

For all concerned, this was a profitable experience. The parents heard about the event. They also heard that reading had been done. "I read a story about Snow White," said one girl to her mother. "Oh," was the pleased reply, "You read about Snow White and the seven dwarfs." "No, Mother, we read about a white mouse. We named him Snow White. See, here's his name on my picture. He's standing up looking at us."

The next day the teacher gathered the children about the dictated account. Then she read it again pointing to each word as she read it. After this, she invited other children to come forward and she paced them through the material. These children, not being contributors to the account, were required to read entirely what others had written and thus they assumed in good part a typical reader-author relationship. The group also took a look-see at each others illustrations.

•*Word Recognition.* In addition, the teacher wrote some words from the story in isolation on the chalkboard to find out if the children could recognize them when they were not in the context of the story. These were the words she had noticed some of the children "reading" without her assistance as they were paced through the story. She chose words like *Snow White, Dick,* other children's names, and *cage, tail, table.* It is to be noted that in the context of this story these words are all nouns. The recognition of nouns is more likely to occur because nouns are names of persons, places, or things; their attributes or characteristics can be readily identified; and strong bonds can be formed with the names. The children had seen and examined *Snow White,* had illustrated *Snow White,* and had spoken about *Snow White.* Similarly, they knew *Bill,* they had heard him read, and this promoted strong, immediate, and varied associations. They had seen the *cage,* handled it, and talked about it.

In addition, the teacher wrote the word *furry* in isolation on the chalkboard. *Furry* had certain association clues to facilitate recall and recognition; it was the last word in the account, and was a vivid adjective supplied by one of the children. This word recognition skill training activity was soundly based on meaning and a functional use of language. That is why this paragraph was introduced with the words *word recognition*. This heading will be used throughout this chapter to indicate examples that show how readily skill training activities can be structured functionally, based on a meaningful setting and how they differ from artificially contrived skill activities.

•*Word Recognition.* On this second contact with the dictated account the teacher had also placed on a classroom library table (see Chapter 6) a book about Snow White and the seven dwarfs and two volumes of an encyclopedia. One volume was open to the section on snow and the other to the section on cages. The book, *Snow*,[1] and preprimers containing some of the pupil's names, Bill, Dick, and so on, were also there. She had the children gather around the table and introduced them to another superb word recognition skill training activity—locating and recognizing words in a different context. The teacher was using (functionally) probably the most basic law of learning—*the transfer of knowledge to a new situation.* The children were delighted and exclaimed whenever they located a word. One child found the word *snowman* and read it. Another found the word *snowy* and said, "I have found the word *snow* but it has a tail on it." locating the word *snow* in *snowy* was a marvelous use of *configuration* or *visual discrimination* clues and *semantic* or *meaning* clues. One girl had brought with her from home a copy of *Jack and Jill* magazine, in which, in a story with a winter setting, the word *snow* appeared a number of times.

By this time the pupils all had their names on their desk tops. Posted in the room was a roster of class members, so the children could locate their names on the roster either by immediate full recognition or by matching the name on the desk with the roster. Wherever possible the teacher had pupils locate their names in a book, magazine, newspaper or the like. To read a pupil name was just as much an act of reading as to read any other word.

Not only did the children locate words in different contexts but they did so without questioning the fact that in reality the words looked different. When the teacher wrote the word on the chalkboard the configuration was in large manuscript. In the books, however, the words appeared in different typefaces and type sizes and in upper and lower case letters.

•*Word Recognition.* By the following day the teacher had reproduced the "Snow White" dictation and had a copy available for each pupil. She had reproduced it exactly as the words appeared in the original chart. This helped some of the children orient themselves to words they had learned to identify in part by their position on the chart or by the geography of the

---

[1]John Burningham, *Snow*, N.Y.: Thomas Y. Corwell Co., 1975.

chart. She urged each child to point to each word in their desk copies while she read and pointed to the word in the original chart. Then she permitted them to just pore over the dictation while she went from child to child. In this person-to-person contact she underlined for the children each word that they recognized on their own. Some had only the title underlined; some, like Alice, had eleven words underlined, including each pupil's name; Bill had every word underlined. In addition, the teacher wrote the date at the bottom of the reproduction as well as the pupil's name if he or she was unable to do so. Each pupil's copy was placed in a booklet. In addition extra copies of the dictation were available to take home.

Each child was supplied with a notebook. In this book were placed the dictated accounts. An account was placed on the right-hand side of facing pages and an illustration by the pupil on the left-hand side. Each entry was numbered and dated. This provided a numerical-chronological accounting. The booklet was constantly in the child's possession and could be turned to at appropriate times. The booklet was a ready source of reading material.

In the meantime the teacher had found time to accomplish all the other pupil-getting-acquainted activities that are a part of the first days in school; recognizing names and name cards; locating seats and desks, closets, and lavatories; meeting the teacher next door, the school nurse, the principal; and so on. She read to the children daily, told stories, had them listen to music, and soon had them settled into the business of school life.

A number of momentous instructional transactions took place during this triple contact cycle with the "Snow White" dictation. For the pupils, the following assertions are particularly noteworthy:

1. The children had opportunities to interact in group and whole-class situations as well as to act on their own.
2. They responded to teacher pacing, as members of a group and privately.
3. They could "read" either in concert with a group or individually.
4. They could study and restudy the private copy now entered in their own booklet.
5. They could show their parents a copy of the account and "read" for them. Everyone could at least read the title.
6. They listened to class members read and recognize words. Some read only a word or two but some, like Bill, read each word, thus recognizing 37 different words.
7. They were continually reinforcing the concept that reading is communication of ideas—not an exercise in saying meaningless isolated words or sounds.

8. *Visual discrimination* of words was done each time pupils read a word either in context or in isolation. The recognition was done without drawing shadow boxes or framing a word with hands. Such techniques are futile.

9. *Auditory-visual* discrimination was done each time the teacher spoke a word (oral-auditory) and a pupil or pupils located the word (visual discrimination). Thus, basic phoneme (phonic)-grapheme (print) skills were activated and developed. Pupils were being taught how deliberately to set about making more precise discriminations, and by doing so were learning some of the fundamental transactions by which scholars acquit themselves.

In many respects the teacher was reaffirming that "all good teaching is diagnostic." In this instructional time span she had been making an informal inventory of pupil abilities and achievements. This assessment of developmental status and continuous reevaluation was based on a vigorously dynamic and enduring commitment to evaluate pupil behaviors on both an immediate and long-term basis. It was done within the classroom instructional environment in an effort to keep at a minimum pupil failures and to maximize pupil successes. When this type of assessment, with its daily feedback, is coupled with a diagnostic team of specialized experts and cooperating agencies, it can be said that a concerted effort is being made to have children develop their full potential.

The following are other whole-class participating dictations obtained either on the second or third day of school, in other classrooms. The first account was dictated in response to a white rabbit stimulus and the second in response to a box turtle. Again the children experienced an examined experience, an event rooted in the here and now, and done under the guidance of the teacher.

Snowball
Garry said, "He is eating a carrot." Larry said, "His ears are long." Melody said, "The rabbit nibbles his food." Carol said, "He likes to eat his food." Danny said, "The rabbit is white." Stephanie and Mark said, "He has red eyes." Tina said, "He hopped up on me."

The Box Turtle
Reginald said, "He lives in a shell." Jeffrey said, "When you pick him up his head goes into the shell." James said, "He can swim." Charisse said, "He is green and yellow." Regina said, "He likes living in his box shell." Darren said, "He has two eyes and four feet." Lisa said, "His tail is short." Tyrone said, "He crawls around in his box."

It is hoped that by this time the reader of this text understands that the children in the third illustration had had the opportunity to observe, feel, and talk about a box turtle before dictating. The use of stimuli such as the mouse, the rabbit, and the turtle provides excellent opportunities for pupils to *act on* an experience, to *interact* with the group about the experience, and to *transact* or objectify and internalize an experience. The number of items that could be used as stimuli is enormous and they exist, as Russell Conwell said, in "an acre of diamonds in your own back yard." No matter where you live and teach you will be surrounded with items to use or things that children can do. The problem becomes which ones to select from the many available.

It is suggested, however, that the early experiences used to stimulate oral language usage and dictated accounts involve some type of concrete object the children can act upon through some physical contact such as those used for the preceding dictations. Other stimuli that have been successfully used are various types of toys and puppets. Action-oriented activities such as science experiments, short trips to various parts of the school, musical instrument and marching games, cooking, making things with clay or paper bag puppets are among the numerous ones that lend themselves to much pupil action, interaction, and language usage.

DEVELOPING WORD RECOGNITION POWER

Context Clues to Word Recognition

Word recognition ability involves the use of context or meaning clues by means of closure or extrapolation, phonic or sound clues by use of phoneme-grapheme relationships, and structure or sight clues provided usually by syllables (sound units) or prefixes and suffixes. If one needed to place these three capabilities in rank order, the best arrangement would be as given: (1) context, (2) phonics, (3) structure clues.

Context clues to recognition place a premium on meaning or comprehension, and this is always of first-order importance. Context clues are based on the psychological principles of closure and of extrapolation. Both refer to closing a gap and doing so by obtaining from the context relevant information. This promotes and depends on a fruitful and relentless search for meaning.

Pupil dictations are superb means for developing context clue abilities. When pupils read a whole-class dictated chart they benefit from a series of meaning clues. Meaning is derived from the title, the illustrations, the spaced pupil names, the idea flow or sequence of the account, and the syntax. If a pupil contributed to the chart, he may recognize each word he dictated because his name helps him locate and recall what he said. When he reads what others dictated, he may grasp a word because "it makes sense."

When he has progressed to individual charts the opportunities for context clue usage abound. Because he is the author of all that is recorded he may fill in any unrecognized gap by doing a bit of reflection and remembering what he said.

It is not sufficient though to limit context clue training to this level. Pupils must be taught how to read what others have written and how, when doing so, to use context clues effectively. Such instruction can be done first by using group-dictated accounts and, later, by reading the individual dictations of others. Each provides a ready source of instructional opportunities and skill practice.

Systematic instruction in the use of context clues can be started early in the year by using group-dictated accounts. The teacher can deliberately pick a word in a story that she thinks the children do *not* know but that is in such a rich context that the semantic and syntactic clues clearly suggest what the word should be. For example, in the "Snowball" story she may choose the word *food* in the sentence, "The rabbit nibbles his food," or the word *up* in the "Box Turtle" story in the sentence, "When you pick him up. . . . " This she does by printing the word in isolation on the chalkboard. Then she asks the children to find it in the story (visual discrimination). She then has them read the story with her until they come to that word, at which time she stops reading and has them read on alone. She then reinforces the recognition of the word by referring to it as printed on the chalkboard and having the children speak the word. Later, as the children master phonics they learn to utilize sound clues in conjunction with semantic and syntactic clues to recognition. The teacher is continually alert to circumstances in the dictations that lend themselves to such instruction and has many such teaching sessions.

This traning may be augmented by other very pointed analysis. This can be done by providing closure-type sentences such as the following. These sentences are naturally taken from the dictated stories.

The turtle _____ around in his house.   (walks)
His _____ are open.   (eyes)
He walks around very _____.   (slow)
I have a _____ and a dog.   (cat)
I sleep in my _____.   (bedroom)
My baby brother has a broken _____.   (collar bone)
I brush my _____ very day.   (teeth)

Closure-type training activities can be varied and made increasingly more complex. The preceding sentences provide the key word and simplify the filling-in procedure. A next step is to provide two words and require the pupil to make a decision "The turtle _____ around in his home." (walks, shell) Another procedure is to provide a sentence but not provide a word, and so on.

Auditory Discrimination

Each dictation is also an "acre of diamonds" as a source for auditory word recognition skill training. *Audition* is hearing sound, and "the study of oral sounds used in communication is known as phonetics" (18, p. 3). The study of sounds as they are related to reading is called *phonics* (4, p. vii). The fact that *phonetics* and *phonics* are often used interchangeably does not alter their original meanings. Since language is a tool of society, it is important to know how the two terms are interchanged.

Discrimination means noting likenesses and differences. Auditory discrimination means noting likenesses and differences among sounds one hears. In brief, because *auditory* means sound and *sound* means phonetics (or phonics), auditory discrimination is in essence phonetic (or phonic) discrimination. In this context phonic analysis is the label that best describes what is being done.

Teachers and parents frequently ask when instruction in phonics should begin. The most acceptable answer is that it should begin at the very beginning of a child's reading instruction.

In Chapter 1 much was said about the phonological wealth of children entering school. Children who can speak provide, almost regardless of other circumstances, ample evidence that they have an ear for sound. Children display an astounding blending of auditory-speech-meaning capabilities when, as so often happens, they hear a word new to them spoken only once and then, maybe a day or so later, use it, speaking it correctly and in a proper context without having heard it in the meantime. This feat occurs again and again in the preschool years. It prompted Otto Jespersen to say that in his whole life, man achieves nothing so great as when he learns to talk (11, p. 103).

It is truly remarkable how well children observe sounds, how they learn to correct their own speech errors and those of others, and how they constantly add to their word wealth. The sound wealth children bring with them to school is fabulous. Even the poorest is wealthy.

Auditory discrimination instruction capitalizes on this phonological wealth and proceeds to make the *children articulate about it,* and learn how to analyze and refine it and use it deliberately. The way to start is to use words they know and to keep the decisions they must make simple and within their power.

RHYMING

Some training can be initiated on the very first day of school. Use a pupil's name, particularly one that has a distinct ending sound like Bill, or Jane, or Tom, or Ann. Say to the class, "I'm going to say a word and you tell me if it sounds like Bill or if it does not." Then ask Bill to stand up so that all eyes will be focused on Bill and say without distortion, the word *hill*. Some youngsters will always recognize that *Bill* and *hill* sound very much alike and will say so. This gives the teacher an excellent opportunity to say, "Yes, *Bill* and *hill* sound alike."

This can be repeated with other words: *pill, fill, book, will, door, mill,* and so on. Notice that the first two words are like *Bill* but that the third is distinctly different. Then the next word is like *Bill,* and so the sounds go, back and forth from like to different, with only one discrimination decision to be made.

The next day another pupil's name can be used in the same way. Auditory training has thus been started, and it can be continued at a pace in keeping with the children's responses. The decision making has been kept simple: "*Yes,* it is" and "*No,* it is not."

A way to increase the challenge and the number of decisions is to present two words at a time. The key word may be *Ann.* Two other words spoken by the teacher may be *can* and *sit.* The decision that must be made is now to select the word that sounds like *Ann.* This type of activity can be repeated as frequently as desired or needed.

In each instance the words that sound alike are rhyme words, which direct auditory attention to the vowel sounds. To implement this training, reading poetry aloud is most advisable; some reading can be done every day. In addition, the reading and repeating of common nursery rhymes helps sharpen the ear.

ALLITERATION

Alliteration, or noting the likeness and differences of readily heard beginning sounds, is equally as important as the hearing of rhyming elements. Perhaps it should be said that alliteration is of first-order importance because when a pupil attacks a word that he does not recognize at sight he invariably proceeds from left to right or from the beginning of the word.

Alliteration is not as readily grasped by some children as is rhyming. However, when three words are grouped together in a singsong fashion a beat and a rhythm can be established that helps facilitate beginning sound discrimination. Thus three words that begin with a single consonant, such as big, bad, Bill, or ding, dong, day, or look, lady, look, or see, Sam, sit, or Mary, makes, money, can be said by the teacher and then repeated by the class or an individual. In each instance beginning sounds can be stressed by giving them, so to speak, the beat. It must be remembered that this is all auditory. It must be remembered, too, that daily repetition of alliteration phrases will help children grasp what is meant by "beginning sounds."

It is apparent that by this time much practical sound training has been given. By starting with the rhyme of words or word endings, attention was focused on vowels, and this was helpful because they represent dominant sound carriers. Auditory vowel readiness was being established.

When the switch was made to the beginning sounds and alliteration (tip, tap, toe), attention was directed to consonants. When people attack words they do not recognize at sight in American English they invariably do so from left to right. This means they deal with beginning sounds first, and since most of the beginning sounds are represented by consonants, the approach being taught is in keeping with the demands of most of American English word circumstances.

It is evident by now, too, that there is an order for teaching sound knowledge and for combining it with slight knowledge. The order for teaching is a pragmatic, functional arrangement of sounds. The system for teaching is based on a practical application of the psychology of learning, which requires action (auditory) and decision making on the part of the learner.

Once children grasp alliteration as described, the very essential next step is to have them note whether two words either begin alike or do not begin alike. This type of decision making causes children to focus more sharply on the beginning sound and thereby recognize the phonic utility value of a sound. For example, children can be asked to decide whether or not the following pairs of words begin the same:

boy—bear
boy—run
bear—man
sit—boy
toy—table
Bill—time
fun—sun
man—can
mat—man

Note that some of the words also rhyme. This requires the listener to be increasingly more attentive to the beginning sound. In brief, another element of complexity has been added and the decision making becomes a bit more demanding.

Other types of auditory discrimination exercises for beginning sounds should also be used. For example, three words such as *Bill, boy, mother* or *Bill, my, make* are pronounced and the child decides which of the three words does not have the same beginning sound as the others. Or the teacher may say a word such a *Bill* and then ask the children to determine which of the two words pronounced next (*my, boat*) has the same beginning sound. Variations of these kinds of activities are numerous. The important thing is that the child learns to discriminate auditorily between beginning sounds of words. This ability is necessary so that the child can develop sound phoneme-grapheme relationships.

Auditory-Visual Discrimination

The functional use of language to relate an experience and dictate an account creates a circumstance in which communication prevents discrete introduction to phonic skills. Letters are not divorced from the service they render as *units* to represent sounds in a word; words are not isolated but represent *classes* as they function in a semantic or sentence context; the *relations* of words, as they are joined by syntactical order, serve functionally in continuous communication.

Even though language usage is discursive and does not allow diverse events to be presented in their coincidence, our thinking processes allow for astounding coincidence; as a result, analyzing such events sequentially, as first, second, third is fallacious. Although knowledge of sounds and the letters that represent them is helpful, analysis by breaking up coherent wholes or semantic units into so-called phonetic elements divorces the value of words and sounds from their communication purpose. So it is not surprising at all that the many so-called phonic systems and so-called linguistic systems show lack of agreement. The processes they are trying to analyze are those in which sounds communicate meaning but they are interpreted to be those in which sounds are broken into incoherent units. Effective teaching of phonics, therefore, must avoid discrete artificial phonic analysis of word encoding processes and keep teaching-learning focused on coherent sound units, discursive communication and semantics. As a matter of fact, the most fitting theme for phonic analysis skill training is "never in isolation."

As previously stated (see p. 69), word recognition involves the ability to use context or meaning clues, phonic or sound clues, and structure or sight clues. If this makes learning to read seem difficult, how is it that year after year many children learn to read on their own? Their success implies three things. First, the skills of word recognition cannot be too complex or else these preschoolers would not be able to work out their own quite reliable systems. Second, there must be some pattern to the development of these skills or else the children would develop as many different systems as the well-meaning adult phoneticians have done. Third, there must be a tremendous latent power that facilitates recognition residing in meaning and communication or else the words would remain unknown.

Compare a reading performance in which immediate word recognition fails with one in which no difficulty is encountered. Recognition becomes the act of simultaneously seeing the word and identifying its meaning. Meaning directs the entire process.

Because meaning plays a dominant role in both situations—dealing with words that are not immediately recognized at sight and words that are—it is unquestionably the most functional key to word recognition. This is the position taken throughout this book, because *meaning* emphasizes *comprehension* and *communication*, to which all other aids are subordinate. One deals with the phonic elements not merely to say a word but as an aid in grasping its meaning.

Accordingly, one does not develop a sight vocabulary by using words in isolation, one at a time, or by illogical repetition of words with the notion that frequency of contact is an aid to retention ("Run, Dick, run, run, run,") or by warped discursive and semantic elements assembled in the name of linguistic uniformity ("Can Dan fan Pan?"). Quite the contrary, words whose sounds and usages are known by children are used by them to present semantically functional ideas. From a communication context, words become identifiable in print because of their primacy in context (*Snow White*), their attributes as parts of speech (*White*, noun; *run*, action verb; *furry*, qualifying adjective), their position in context (title, last word in story), their functional repetition (four different uses of *Snow White*), their discursive usage to communicate (declarative, imperative, interrogative sentences), or the general semantics of denotation and connotation (*snow, box, Snow White, snowy*).

One does not first teach sounds or letter names or a sight vocabulary in isolation. One does not teach all the possible auditory discrimination skills first, and then, weeks later, try to link them with a sight vocabulary acquired in isolation. Quite the contrary, auditory discrimination is linked with visual discrimination from the very beginning of the unified reading-to-learn, learning-to-read program. Both consist of construction of relationships resting upon empirically controlled activities.

In brief, as soon as *one word* is recognized in print, as soon as it becomes a *sight word*, it can be used for auditory-visual discrimination training. If all or many of the children, for example, recognize "turtle" at sight, the word can be written on the chalkboard underlining the begining letter, t. Now, while all eyes focus on the word, the teacher proceeds to audition by saying a word like *time* and asking the class or a member of the class to decide whether it begins like "turtle" or not. Then words like *talk, town, boy, take, took, touch, walk,* and so on, are spoken as stimulus words. The children can also be asked to identify the name of the letter with which the word *turtle* begins and then as each word is pronounced by the teacher either say it begins like *turtle* or it begins with the letter t or not. Throughout these exercises *eyes* are *focused* on a printed word and *ears* are *tuned* to a spoken word. In the all-auditory approach it was suggested that a pupil's name be used and that he or she stand so that all eyes could focus on him or her. The parallel here may readily be seen.

As more words are learned by sight recognition, they become available for auditory-visual discrimination exercises. After the children worked on the "Snow White" story, *cage* and *table* were recognized readily by many. Then in other reading, words like *rabbit, food, box,* and, of course, the names of the children were recognized. It is not necessary to wait until 50 or more words have been learned, as was recommended once.

Every day, some training in auditory discrimination and in auditory-visual discrimination *must* be done. The more proficient the children become, the more apt they are to transfer the skill and unlock other words in their own dictated stories, in those of their classmates, and in other reading materials.

It is a simple psychological matter to increase the complexity of sound-letter learning. If two words are used, pupils must be increasingly more attentive. For instance, *box* and *turtle* can be printed on the chalkboard and the children asked to select which of the two words has the same beginning sound as a word pronounced by the teacher. One-syllable words beginning with a single consonant such as *take, boy, book, toy, big, ten,* can be used. Notice that the first sound in each spoken word agrees with one or the other of the two words printed on the chalkboard. Much practice of this kind should be done daily. Then three or even four words can be used, thus sharply increasing the complexity of the task.

A good next step, after two or three known words have been set up in a column for selection and discrimination, is to ask the children to underline the letter that represents the beginning sound. The words *turtle, box,* and *furry* may be presented in a column as a list of sight words (visual discrimination). Then words like *toy, fun,* and *bat* may be used as the teacher-spoken word or auditory stimulus word (auditory discrimination).

toy	*fun*	*bat*
turtle	turtle	turtle
box	box	box
furry	furry	furry

Now the children are learning a sound-letter or phoneme-grapheme combination while the specific letter being studied remains in a semantic (word) and phonic (syllable) unit. Thus again, one is carefully avoiding letter isolation from either a meaning or sound context. By this time most of the children will know the alphabet and this type of letter recognition reaffirms that knowledge. Always be sure that *auditory training* is done first and frequently. The children must be able to hear sounds selectively if they are to apply discriminate sound knowledge to letters in words.

Letter Substitution, or Word Families

The old game of building word families is just as captivating and beneficial today as it was a century and more ago. The label "word families" seems more appropriate and arouses more emotional warmth than any other label such as "letter substitution," "consonant substitution," or "linguistic substitution." Whatever you call it, the practice has tremendous utility and promotes a great deal of interest. One of the best summations of it was made by a six-year-old, who said, "Gee, I got eight words from one word." Thereafter, in that room the children would talk about a five-word word or a nine-word word, and so on, and were constantly making words. One stimulus, for example, might be *run*, from which can be derived *s*un, *f*un, *b*un, *g*un, *n*un, *p*un.

The procedure is simple and puts psychological learning principles to work. The words are always placed in columns and each word can readily be compared with a word above or below it. Transfer of knowledge occurs. Skill in blending sounds is enhanced. Letter order or spelling consciousness is fostered. Nonsense words are made from time to time, and they require a more independent sound-blending skill and are a bigger challenge. Furthermore, such blending abilities and training will prove helpful when children later deal with polysyllabic words.

Start with a word known by the class such as *Bill;* have the children identify it and then place the word *hill* directly below it; have the children note that the endings are the same and that the new word, *hill*, will therefore rhyme with the known word, *Bill*. If they seem to have difficulty dealing with the beginning sound, the teacher may write on the chalkboard known words such as *hat* or *house* and have the children identify them and note their beginning sound. Then the teacher may have the children note that the unknown word, *hill*, begins like *hat* and *house* and ends like *Bill*. Usually this is all that is necessary and once the principle is understood few difficulties are encountered with such lists as:

Bill	boy	make	go	like
hill	toy	take	so	bike
will	joy	lake	no	Mike
mill	Roy	rake		dike

Children should not be asked merely to list words or to do such activities as making words with an ending such as -ay by substituting the letters *s, m, b, l,* and so on. No thinking or decision making is involved and often the children have just written words and cannot say them.

After the children understand the word family idea they can either be given key words by the teacher or choose words from their word banks (see pp. 121–124) to use. If they make lists of meaningful words as shown above, however, they should have an opportunity to share these orally with others. Another way in which they can develop skill in consonant substitution is to first have the children make their own alphabet key using words from their own word bank. For example, Bill's key may be as follows: *B*ill, *c*age, *D*ick, *f*ort, and so on. Then using the alphabet key each child sets up a chart such as the following:

(key word: *like*)

Nonsense Words   *Words*

cike   bike
fike   dike
gike   hike
jike   like
                Mike, etc.

While making such a chart Bill must decide whether each sound unit produced by substituting the various consonants is meaningful or not. By proceeding this way, the children get more words and do more blending, and if they can identify the "words" produced as being either meaningful or nonsense words one can feel confident that they have grasped the basic principle.

One should not be hesitant about changes in word endings. They also fit the comprehensive-family plan. When the children show some proficiency with beginning-consonant substitution, switch to consonants at the ends of words:

can	*sat*	*his*	*big*
cat	sad	him	bit
cap	Sam	hit	bin
cab	sap	hip	Bill

As blends and digraphs are introduced they, too, may be added to the "key" and used in the same manner.

Dick	*cap*	*down*
brick	lap	town
slick	rap	frown
Shick	slap	clown
chick	trap	brown
spick	flap	crown
trick	tap	drown
click	snap	
kick	strap	
lick	clap	
pick		
thick		

Making words through word families is a useful activity for the rest of the year. It does many things for the child, and it proves particularly helpful when children are involved with creative writing and encoding becomes more demanding. Many a word can be encoded (spelled) by means of the family-association plan.

GROUPING AS AN ANTECEDENT TO INDIVIDUALIZATION

Not all the time during the first weeks in September should be devoted to settling in and getting acquainted; neither should all the time be devoted to reading instruction. This is so even though the latter includes examined experiences, oral language usage, group and class interactions, auditory and visual-auditory discrimination skill training, the accumulation of a sight vocabulary, locating known words in a variety of materials, classroom library reading and overviewing of materials, illustrating dictated accounts, listening to poetry and prose, and viewing films, filmstrips, and the like. The school librarian should stop by to talk about books and perhaps tell a story. Second and third graders might stop in, too, to do a puppet show or similar activities.

By the end of the first three weeks a teacher will have acquired much understanding concerning the experiences, the language facility, the interests and tastes, the intellectual maturity, the cultural heritage, and the social-personal poise of each pupil. Now to differentiate instruction and pace the learning more carefully a class can be organized into three groups. This plan has many instructional advantages:

1. More children can contribute to dictated accounts. Instead of one whole class chart with five or six pupils dictating, there will now be three versions—one by each group and with 18 or more pupils contributing.
2. Within each group there will be increased opportunity for active pupil participation and for increased group interaction.
3. The members of one group can read and respond to the dictated accounts of the other two groups.
4. Because each group dictates about the same stimulus, a certain nomenclature relative to the experience (box turtle) will very likely appear in each version and can be identified. Thus transfer of knowledge (word recognition) to a new situation is facilitated.
5. Comprehending accounts of others is a major step in developing basic comprehension skills. Indeed, the experience and dictation serve much as an *advance organizer.*
6. Because the syntax will vary even though all three are dictations about the same interest, the children can note how others organized and expressed their ideas about the same topic. Thus they can forge new connections, generate a growing language system, and expand their own outputs.

7. While the teacher is busy with one group, the members of the other two groups must learn how to be studious either as individuals or as a group. During the first three weeks the teacher posts a list of activities a pupil or pupils can engage in such as:

(a) illustrate an account
(b) underline known words
(c) reread previous dictations
(d) buddy up and read a dictation to another
(e) buddy up and compare sight words
(f) find known words in another group's account
(g) find known words in other places such as books, magazines newspapers
(h) buddy up and do auditory discrimination and/or
(i) visual-auditory discrimination activities
(j) do word bank activities (see pp. 114–115)
(k) view a filmstrip
(l) listen to a tape; or above all
(m) go to the classroom library.

Children learn to select two or three activities and learn what to do when those are accomplished. All of these activities are monitored by the teacher but the teacher is also moving the children along the way toward being their own chief protagonists in the learning experience.

The groups should be formed randomly at first so that each may contain pupils with a range of capabilities. Thus each group might contain a Bill, a lad who already has a sizable reading vocabulary, and a Jerry, one who recognizes only a word or two. Everyone in a class soon knows that Bill is the "best" reader and that Jerry is not. Bill knows this and so does Jerry. Their parents may know. What is of utmost importance is to maintain a climate in the classroom marked by enthusiasm for each one's success, good will, and self-reliance. Jerry must not be labeled and cast aside; he must be helped, his spirit must be buoyed, his interests capitalized on and extended.

Here are two accounts dictated by two groups. Note that the first account has 52 running words and 33 different words; this represents a typical relationship between the number of different words and running words. About two-thirds the total number of words are different words. In the second version of the guinea pig account there are 54 running words and 36 different words, and again a two-thirds ratio appears. This kind of spread promotes an increase in sight vocabulary and range of word usage, and avoids idle repetition.

Note, too, that 14 different words appeared in both accounts. This is an overlap of almost 50 percent of the different words, thus providing excellent opportunities for transfer of recognition power. In addition, comparisons can be made between *eat* in story 2 and *eating* in story 1, and between *can, cannot,* and *can't.* Each form of the word can be entered into the word banks (p. 115). When other similar forms appear, fruitful comparisons can be made.

Two Guinea Pigs

Gary said, "Whitie and Brownie are two guinea pigs." Rodney said, "They are eating carrots." Mark said, "They are eating rabbit food." Rose said, "They were drinking water and spilled it." Tina said, "They cannot climb." Valerie said, "They can't run fast." Cleo said, "They have short ears."

Guinea Pigs

Tanya said, "Two guinea pigs eat carrots." Sandra said, "They eat biscuits and greenstuff." Lorie said, "They like clean, fresh water." Eric said, "They play, but they can't jump." Tyronne said, "They feel soft." Wallace said, "They can't climb." Robert said, "Dogs can kill them." Gregory said, "Guinea pigs eat bread crumbs."

The following three versions of "The Bees" were dictated on October 5. In this classroom of 28 children, 21 dictated and contributed to one or another account. A total of 71 different words are used in the three dictations; of that number, 15 appear in all three accounts.

The Bee Story

Karen said, "The father bee does not sting." Stephanie said, "The queen bee lays all the eggs." Carol said, "The father bee does not have a stinger." Melody said, "The workers gather nectar." Gary said, "The worker bees make honey." Margaret said, "The worker bees have stingers." Mark said, "The workers take care of the mother." Daniel said, "The workers make wax."

Bees

Gregory said, "The bees make wax." John said, "The worker bees make wax." John said, "The worker bees make the honey." Sandra said, "The father bees do not sting." Lorie said, "The bees make bee-bread out of yellow dust from the flowers." Tyronne said, "They have pockets on the side of their body." Valerie said, "We have three kinds of bees."

The Bees

Eric said, "The mother bee lays eggs." Wallace said, "They make bread out of yellow dust." Cleo

said, "The baby bees eat the bread." Roberta
said, "The father bee have big eyes." Eric said,
"Tanya is not here." Wayne said, "Rose is not
here today." Robert said, "I like honey."

Not only do the dictations represent a sizable and varied vocabulary but in addition they show a range and richness in syntactical structure. Sentences range from simple T units (subject, predicate, object) as in "The bees make wax." to "The bees make bee-bread out of yellow dust from the flowers." In only one instance was an awkward structure dictated, "The father bee have big eyes." In only two instances did they stray from the topic *bees* and talk about a current classroom situation, "Tanya is not here" and "Rose is not here today."

These accounts were obtained by Mrs. Foster, a marvelous first-grade teacher, a black teacher in an integrated class in Cambridge, Maryland. In this class the number of black and white children was almost the same. A few of the children had had some preschool experience. Note again, as stated earlier (p. 51), that it is virtually impossible to recognize a so-called black language.

•*Word Recognition.* The three dictations provide a veritable gold mine of instructional opportunities. Many words are available to be added to word banks (see p. 113). Word structures can be compared: bee, bees; sting, stinger; worker, workers. Books, encyclopedias, pamphlets, filmstrips about bees can be examined and words can be recognized. Auditory discrimination and visual-auditory discrimination activities can be devised based on the rich opportunities in the three selections.

By this time Mrs. Foster had moved along in her phonic skill training program to beginning consonant substitution (see pp. 76–79). With these selections she used words as follows:

not	*make*	*wax*	*like*
pot	rake	tax	bike
dot	take	Max	Mike
cot	lake		hike
lot	bake		dike
rot	cake		

First she placed the word *not* on the chalkboard, the children identified it, and then she placed the word *pot* directly below it and had the children identify it, and so on (see p. 77). Then she gave the children other appropriate known words from their dictations and had them try their hand at creating words by substituting different consonants.

Children love this activity because they see so readily that they can read many more words than they had realized and they learn that *they can create words*. This is an essential step toward word encoding (spelling), toward seeing phoneme-grapheme relationships (phonological encoding), and particularly toward creative writing. In each instance when a word is created it is also written. It is a thrill to hear children exclaim about the number of words they created out of one word.

For some members of the class, Mrs. Foster could also use a number of words such as *story*, *sting*, *free*, *ply*, *bread* and *Cleo* to reinforce their work with consonant blends or to introduce one not introduced previously.

Since making changes using blends is more challenging, it is good to provide a set of key words from which to select blends.

Key Words	*story*	*sting*	*free*	*fly*
stop	glory	bring	tree	sty
cloud		cling	glee	dry
bring		fling		
drink				
flap				
glad				

Key Words
trip
pray
green
blue

Changes can be made by changing to single-consonant beginnings.

story	sting	free	fly
tory	ring	bee	my
dory	bing	see	by

When children create a word that is not in word lists of common words or is a nonsense word and they can speak it, then they have attained a high order of phonic competence. For instance, they may create words as follows:

story	sting	free
pory	dring	kee
bory	cing	stee
kory	fing	dree

Again, however, be sure the children do not just make lists of words without having an opportunity to *speak* the words by reading them to each other or the teacher.

By now the reader's curiosity about why dictations about bees were produced and the amount of knowledge about bees displayed should be aroused. The following account is an example of how a teacher can take advantage of a situation and develop it into a learning experience providing much opportunity for extending children's concepts, interests, vocabulary, and language usage.

A girl had brought to school a portion of an old beehive that she had found and had placed it on the "pretty table" in the room. Mrs. Foster kept a table in the room on which a child could put something pretty (a flower or flowers, a shell, a pretty stone, a picture, and the like) or something interesting, such as the portion of the beehive. The hive provided an excellent opportunity to study about bees. Books and pamphlets were obtained from the school library, encyclopedias were consulted, a filmstrip was viewed. In brief, for a number of days bees were the center of interest. There was much discussion, pupil question asking, and pupil illustrating.

The children in this room, as in others like it, had no idea that they were reading "reading." They had learned from the very beginning that one reads about persons, places, animals, events, things, and the like. They had no idea that the preprimer or primer represented "reading." For these children reading anything, a dictated account or words in a book, on a filmstrip, or on television, was reading.

INDIVIDUAL DICTATION

Usually by early October a class is ready to do individual dictations. This results from the steady and careful weaning from whole-class dictations to group dictations to individual dictations. In the whole-class and group situations children learn gradually to perform on their own. But what is vastly more important is that each child has more to contribute and wants to contribute more than they have been doing. This eagerness to produce is a discriminating measure of "readiness" or, better than that, *progress*.

To obtain individual dictations requires adjustments in facilities as well as in pupil cooperation. A practical arrangement is to set up a dictating center. This can consist of a table and two chairs of the same height, one for the pupil dictator and one for the teacher recorder. Use of a small screen is desirable. The screen provides semiprivacy for the center. The teacher can see about the room by looking over the screen but the pupil is totally screened.

The list of "Things to Do" continues to serve an essential function. Pupils are not without activities to accomplish nor abandoned to idleness and distraction. They are on the "learning" road. While one child is dictating behind the screen, the others are engaged in activities chosen from the "things-to-do" list.

A plan of operation becomes essential. Obviously not all pupils can dictate at one time or even, in many instances, on the same day. Groups seem essential. The class can be organized either in (1) ability groups, or

(2) randomly organized groups. Each plan has advantages, but in many ways the former has the most. At times special interest groups will be formed. By now the teacher knows quite specifically about the children's different paces of learning. Usually a class of 25 or 30 pupils can readily be divided into three or four groups. A group should not number more than 10 children. Sometimes the least advanced group consists of only three or four children and usually they are not able as yet to dictate individual accounts. This small group continues with group-dictated accounts.

Usually two days are required to obtain individual dictations from an entire class. All children continue to examine the same stimulus, thereby enabling the less verbal children to benefit from the interaction with the more able ones. Then a group assembles in the area of the dictating center and one at a time comes behind the screen to the dictation table to dictate. While a group is waiting, the children think about what they are going to say, or they prepare illustrations, or reread previous accounts, or reexamine the stimulus.

Again a teacher used a box turtle as a stimulus, this time for the first individually obtained dictations. The following dictation is illustrative:

The Walking Fort
I called the turtle "The Walking Fort" because
that is what he is. He carries his fort on his back.
When he walks along, if he sees some trouble,
he pulls in his neck and his feet. Then he is safe
in his fort. I told my dad about the walking fort
and he said the turtle was like an army tank. But I
like "The Walking Fort" better.

David

Note how the freedom to dictate a personal response stimulated David. The quality of his ideas about "The Walking Fort," the order of the ideas, and the complexity of the sentences provides a very specific and rich accounting of David's creative ability with ideas and language and the nature of his experiences.

After each dictation was completed the teacher read it back to the pupil immediately to see if everything was in order. Then the two read it together. All this took but a few minutes. Now the pupil returned to his desk to make further use of the dictation. He could (1) underline known words, (2) check words against his word bank, (3) prepare or complete an illustration, (4) find words in the dictation in other sources, (5) work with his word bank, or (6) turn to the "what-to-do" list and select an activity.

When all members of the group finished dictating, the class engaged in other activities. This first group dictated sometime during the morning. In the afternoon a second group assembled and dictated. The following story by Edna is illustrative:

Race
I could run a race with the turtle. He has four feet
but he can't go fast. I have only two feet but I
could win the race.

Edna had just started illustrating her dictation when the others in her
group finished dictating. Then the group reassembled with the teacher
and took turns reading their stories to each other. One at a time they
stood by the teacher and read the story aloud to the group. This allowed
the teacher to follow the oral reading and to note which words the children had underlined and knew so she could be ready to supply the
unknown words as necessary. This helped the oral reading performance
and helped the listener hear and understand the story. Edna needed help
with *could* and *only*. Rereading the story aloud led her to recognize the
word *can't*. Somehow the demands of oral reading, language rhythm, and
the flow of ideas often aid recall this way.

At another time that day the teacher assembled the group of four
children who had not progressed to individual dictation. They dictated
the following account. Note that they no longer entered "Bob said" or
"Mae said." They had advanced to where they could identify their own
portions without the use of a name.

Bob's Turtle
My dad saw the turtle when he fished. The turtle
is little. The turtle can pull his head in. He has
spots on his back.
Bob
Mae
Gale
Jimmy

After the story was dictated, the teacher read it back to the group, pointing very briefly to each word as she proceeded. Then each pupil took a
turn standing by the easel and participating in a duet (teacher and pupil)
oral reading of the dictation. Bob was up first. He knew his own name and
said "turtle" when he read the title. When he came to the word *turtle* in
the first sentence, he did not recognize it again. This time, instead of
telling him the word, the teacher pointed to the word in the title. He
recognized it and made a discriminate decision—the two words were the
same. The teacher's resourcefulness helped Bob make a discovery. Bob
knew the word *fished* when they got to it and he recognized *turtle* the
next two times it occurred in the story.

The other pupils were paced through the story by the teacher. Then
the four returned to their seats to draw pictures to accompany their
dictation. Bob drew a picture of his father fishing, Jimmy drew one to
show the spots on the turtle's back, Mae drew a turtle on a rock, and Gale
drew a turtle walking. They knew that by the next day the teacher would
have reproduced a copy of the story for each.

Teachers sometimes voice concern about the time it takes to obtain individual stories. Such concern is not unfounded, but the best thing to do is to try the procedure and thereby discover that it can be carried through readily. Time does not become a factor. It did not in this case. Teachers working with comparable groups have been timed.

A group was assembled and the interest area was briefly discussed with the pupils. Thinking was stimulated and ideas were shared. Then, one at a time, the pupils sat down with the teacher and dictated. The stories averaged three sentences in length, with a few going to five sentences. In this demonstration, done late in September, the pupils had already had some experience dictating stories and expressing their own ideas.

After individually dictating a story, the children, one by one, returned to their seats with their stories and reread them silently. As they read, they underlined with a single black line each word they felt they knew. Guesses were not to be underlined—only words the pupils felt sure about.

When each child had dictated a story and the last one had had a few minutes to reread and mark his story, they all reassembled, and, one by one, they read aloud with the teacher as Dick's group had. The teacher clipped each child's story on the easel and pointed to each word, allowing for enough hesitation to encourage the child to say the word if he knew it or thought he did. Again, as with the previous group, the language pattern and context of the story often helped the pupil recall words that he did not recognize on his own.

The time for this series of events was 33 minutes. Dictating and writing took 23 minutes, oral rereading and sharing took 10 minutes. Even so, the whole procedure was unhurried.

Some typical stories are as follows:

Mr. Turtle
Mr. Turtle walks on four feet. He is very slow.

Spotty
The turtle has spots like my cat. I called him Spotty. That's my cat's name.

The Funny House
The turtle walks around in his house. His house has a hard roof. It's a funny house.

Slow Poke
The turtle is very slow. Sometimes he goes out on a street. Some get run over.

The words underlined are the ones that the pupils felt they knew when they reread their stories silently at their seats. Underlining this way is a positive approach to word learning, because the emphasis is on what is known. Also, it calls for a facing up to the facts: One either knows or does not know, or one guesses. Underlining therefore requires a certain amount of intellectual honesty. The need to "prove knowledge" occurs at the time of the oral reading. The teacher pauses a bit longer on each underlined word. If the word is unrecognized, the teacher supplies the word and the underlining is marked: +—/—/—/—/—/

When another group of eight was assembled all gathered around the turtle to watch, to touch, to talk and share ideas. Then, one by one, they sat with the teacher and dictated their accounts. The nature and quantity of each dictation varied, but they were similar one to another. Marni dictated the following:

The Lonesome Turtle
I believe the turtle is lonesome. He walks around
so slow and looks so sad. Sometimes he looks
out at us and then he pulls his head in again. I
believe he is lonesome.

Marni's reaction to the turtle reflects her personal dispositions (1) and motives. Her response to the turtle suggests strong regard for the welfare of others. The one little turtle in the big box being watched by so many people, poking his head out and pulling it in again, apparently aroused the sentiments expressed. Marni's general disposition found many stimuli that were functionally equivalent and that guided her to a form of behavior that was being labeled as, "That's Marni for you." This was not only Marni's way of reacting to animals, people, and events in her environment, but her way of coping with them.

It seems opportune here to repeat Ben Johnson's counsel in his statement, "Speak, that I may see thee" (12). Dictations give pupils opportunities to speak and to show themselves. Similarly, they give teachers an opportunity to learn what a pupil's distinctive characteristics are, because dispositions are in continuous flow. As Gordon Allport has stated, "Interests, ambitions, phobias, general attitudes, inclinations, hobbies, values, tastes, predilections—all are personal dispositions (some only secondary) and are at the same time motives" (1, p. 373). Thus Rick, dictating the following story, revealed his personal dispositions.

The Explorer
This turtle is an explorer. He goes around
exploring. He came out of the water to explore.
He explores our box.

Obviously the circumstances described represent an achieving, participating, gratifying learning environment. The instructional settings are productive. They are not an "Operation Wastebasket: A School for Failures" (17). Like the "School for Flunkies" this book is not a work of fiction. The children in these classrooms lived in a world of success. And there could be many more successes in all schools.

In this section three ways of obtaining pupil-dictated experience accounts have been described: whole class, group, and individual. The first few days and weeks of school are opportune moments for obtaining whole-class dictations, and any number of teaching-learning effects can be accomplished by starting early.

Children interacting as members of a class have the opportunity to get acquainted with each other linguistically, socially, culturally, emotionally, physically, and intellectually. Each stimulus permits the children to move about, to listen and talk to one another, to show or acquire regard for the rights of others. The whole-class accounts become a possession of each pupil, even though only five or six may have contributed literally. Their language unfolds what is cognitively and linguistically latent in all, because it is brought into operation functionally and dynamically by firsthand experience.

Much the same can be said for smaller groups, although there are a number of important differences. Each time a different group is formed, whether spontaneously or by the teacher, different kinds of social-personal arrangements occur. Understandings, habits, and practices relating to social choice and individual values are evident. The reconciling of conflicting individual and group desires becomes a powerful source for promoting adjustment and emotional reinforcement. In our mobile society such opportunities should help children adjust to changing social organization as related to learning and communication.

In both the whole-class and the group situations, individuals may be stimulated to do their own thinking and reacting, but as a member of a group they are susceptible and responsive to the language habits of others. The child is one among many and subject to the polarization that occurs along different lines at different times. But learning to adapt to change, particularly that resulting from the free exchange of ideas, is part of the flexibility of shifting group membership.

Individual dictations yield the best return to an individual and are best for achieving the reading skills aimed at by the teacher. The shift from whole-class and group dictations to individual dictation should be made as soon as possible. Many of the benefits associated with group circumstances will continue if procedures such as those just described are followed. The sharing of experiences and the oral interchange of ideas is particularly valuable.

Furthermore, the opportunity for each child to express his own ideas in his own way is most productive. He has the teacher's attention; his words are recorded; he is the author. At a later time, he can share his account of an experience with his classmates and he can share their accounts. The likelihood that he will recognize and remember words in his recorded acounts is greatly increased, because the words are of his choosing and represent his oral language-experience commitment.

STIMULUS INTEREST AREAS

Many people are familiar with the "acres of diamonds" story told so often by Russell Conwell, founder of Temple University in Philadelphia. He told about the man who searched around the world for an acre of diamonds and was unsuccessful. He returned home and started cultivating his garden and there he found his acre of diamonds. This is a most fitting introduction to the question of interest stimuli or what the children shall dictate about. Every classroom, school building, and playground represents an acre of diamonds of ideas. If to this is added the experiences children bring with them to school, it becomes readily apparent that acres of "interest" diamonds are available—personal, home, neighborhood and community, school, historical and cultural specialties, current and seasonal events, books and papers, TV and theater, and so on.

Personal

This is the world of "I," "me," "my," and "mine." What I am and what is mine have been impressed on me by each of my years of experience. As I have grown I have walked, talked, laughed, cried, eaten, slept, played, worked, given, received, loved, hated. Now that I am six, I know who I am and what is mine. What I know may not be what you know or how you see me, but it is my summation. I am developing my style of life. I may not be a well-rounded person, but already many rough edges have been rounded. I have my likes and dislikes, my fears and anxieties, my feelings of adequacy, my attitudes and biases, and a will to live and be loved. The effects of my experiences have shaped my affections, my expectations, my needs. If you want I will tell you about them. (Some children may require special reassuring that "you want," but that is all that is needed.) Already I have secret thoughts. I may reveal some and conceal others. But if you see me as a person—my hair and the way I wear it, my eyes, my nose, my smile, my walk, my talk, my friends—then I am more apt to be free and alert and willing to share my most precious possession—my self. The following stories dictated by children from either Seaford or Rehoboth, Delaware, are illustrative.

All About Me

I like to ride my bicycle. There is a hole at home and I like to play in it. I make mud cakes. I play with my dollbaby, and sometimes she cries, and these are real tears. She blows bubbles in her bubble pipe. I play in my house, too, with my books.

Debbie

Me

Me and my brother ride into Seaford to play at the Seaford school and my Dad drives my little brother in and he plays on the swings. Me and my brother, we go over there on the trapeze to play. And on the monkey bars. One night we went over to the football field. And tomorrow we are going up home.

Michael

I Come and I See

I come to school on a school bus. I see plenty of birds. I see all color leaves on the trees. I see green grass. I see people at the big school.

David

Myself

I have brown hair. I can read some books. I am in the first grade. I like to unfold my picture. It is called a snapshot. I like to build with my Tinker Toys. I like to watch television. I like to watch Superman. I am six.

Jimmy

Me

You don't know who my girlfriend is. Guess, Penny B. or Beverly. It is Beverly. She is pretty. She goes on my bus. My brother's name is Tony and so is Jeff's. My best boy friend is Jay Clark and I got some more. My hobby is sports cars. Tony collects sports car models.

Keith

Me

I cried all the time when I was a baby. I didn't want to go to bed.

Conrad

No matter what the stimulus, pupils have only their own experiences, first hand or indirect, to call on when they are invited to respond. It is easier for them to respond when they are asked to react to a direct experience. When they are asked to project, though, what they say is the product of a process that takes place in the pupils' minds. To a degree, each dictation has some of the revealing qualities that Henry Murray sought when he used a series of pictures to elicit from a subject data about himself (13). He suggested that a person's perceptual reactions yield information about the ways he looks at his world. He labeled the method the Thematic Apperception Test (TAT): Thematic refers to the themes dictated and apperception describes the perceptual-interpretive use made of a stimulus.

In a way, each dictated story is a TAT. Each is revealing, and the alert teacher can become increasingly more sensitive to the psychodynamics displayed. It is said that a TAT can yield information about seven aspects of adjustment: (1) thought organization, (2) emotional organization, (3) needs, (4) the subject's view of the world, (5) interpersonal relationships, (6) the subject's conception of and attitude toward himself, and (7) the dynamics of development and illness (9, p. 211).

This reference to the TAT and its use as a clinical test is not to suggest to teachers that they become amateur clinical interpreters. The stories and accounts children dictate are not TAT protocols. On the other hand, to a sensitive teacher the stories reflect the moods and traces of recent experiences, the psychodynamic features of a pupil's intellectual and emotional functioning. They can be revealing and helpful. Each dictation opportunity may provide a catharsis that may be helpful to a pupil and revealing to a perceptive teacher.

Home

Be it ever so humble, there is no place like home. Stories about home and the family are easy to obtain. It is a place dear to each one, and each in his way is ready to talk about some aspect of home. Home consists of mother, father, sister, brother, grandparents, uncles, aunts, cousins, pets, toys, bedrooms, bathrooms, living rooms, family rooms, kitchens, playrooms, yards, sidewalks, elevators, garages. All of these for some children, only a few for others. In almost every instance, be it ever so humble, pupils feel warmly about their homes. As earlier, the following stories were dictated by children from either Seaford or Rehoboth, Delaware, and are examples of the variety of topics children choose when dictating about home.

My Mother
My mother is nice. She does nice things. She is pretty. She loves me.
Steven

My Father
My father works in Oklahoma. My father loves me and I love him too. He buys me a lot of toys. He is nice.
Steven

My Father
My father is in the army. When he is not in the army, he teaches school. He sure is brave.
Jack

My House
My house is made out of bricks. My house is on Old Meadow Road. I like the living room because I have set up trains. My house has a basement and an attic. My house has three holes in the chimney.
Jimmy

My Pet Turtle
I have a turtle. It crawls around in the aquarium. I feed my turtle. Mopsy is my turtle.
Conrad

Baby
I have a baby sister. She plays with me. My baby sister gets me up for school in the morning.
Steven

My Family
I got a little sister, Donna Mae Davis. That's all except me, Debbie Davis. My mother's name is Evelyn and my father's name is Arthur.
Debbie

Nothing
I have a cat named Nothing. He comes at the window and we let him in. We named him Nothing because he is Nothing. He has fleas and he gives me them. We had him since he was a kitten. Nothing is three years old. He is a big Tom cat.
Laurie

My House
My house is big. My house is gray. Sometimes we sit on the steps at my house. Me and my mother sit on the steps. From far, far away it looks little. I don't have any stair steps. I do not live alone in my house. I live with my aunt. Her baby's name is Wade. I have a kitchen, a living room, a bathroom, and two bedrooms. One bedroom is yellow and one is pink. The kitchen is gray. My bathroom is pink. I sleep in my bedroom.
DeeDee

My Baby Brother
My little baby brother has a broken collar bone. When Tommy was little he used to cry a lot.
Scott

My Mother
My mother cooks breakfast for me. Then she takes me to school. She brings me in a car.
John

My Daddy
My Daddy sits at the fire place with me and drinks coffee with me. He cooks outside sometimes.
Scott

My Pets
I have a stray cat. I have a dog. Her name is Corky. My dog has a house and a pen is around it. I am going to build a house for my cat. I like to let my dog out, but he jumps up and I can't let him out.

Jimmy

My House
We like our house. I play with my dog, and we go in the house when it is time for supper.

Michele

John the Slug
I have a slug snail. And I like to look at it. He was in the yard.

Ricky

My Brother Pushed Me
When I go down the hill my brother walks. I ride in my wagon. My wagon is red. My brother pushes me full speed and I fall off. I didn't cry because I had my football suit on.

Conrad

The preceding stories were dictated by white and black children. Of the home stories, the *My House* story was dictated by a six-year-old black girl. Note the warmth and good feeling, the sensitivity to color in the various rooms, the quality of the language, and the orderliness of the ideas. All that most children need is an opportunity to talk and the receptivity of a teacher who understands and encourages.

James Hymes, writing about discipline in general made a statement that seems appropriate here (10, p. 49):

> Some youngsters have never really known a friend. They have been hit and hurt. Their parents even urge you to hit them if they are bad. Adults have never shown a warm side to these boys and girls. You will see the effect of this treatment at the very first. But don't forget: Their human nature is on your side. The fact that they have never truly known a kind person, a decent person, someone who could laugh and joke and talk with them, makes them all the more hungry for what you have to offer.

All the stories recorded in these pages were dictated during the first two months of school by six-year-old first graders, most of whom were attending school for the first time. A few had had kindergarten experience. Children will talk if encouraged to do so. They will enjoy doing so and look forward eagerly to each opportunity.

Neighborhood and Community

Everyone lives somewhere. Everyone has neighbors and a neighborhood. The city child knows his block and can tell you when he is near his neighborhood. Suburbanite and village children can do the same. The child in the country knows his home area and can tell you about it.

Each interest and stimulus provokes its own feelings and responses, its own vocabulary. Each has its own horizon. Note how this is reflected in the following stories:

The Acme
When my mother carried me to the Acme Market, I saw some toys and a tommy gun.

Frankie

Crickets
I like to find crickets. One is five and one is six.

Ronald

My Street
I live on the street that there was a river on, and when summer comes I am going to go out and pick up some sea shells that were in the river. My mother does not know there was a river. She thinks I found the Atlantic Ocean. I live on the same street that Laurie lives on.

Wayne

Where I live
I live in Nanticoke Acres. I like Nanticoke Acres because I have friends there. My house is brown. In the summer my father paints the house. I help my father paint the house. Pat Hill lives by me. Pat's house is red. The Bice's live by us. Their house is gray. They have a little swimming pool in their yard. Our road is made of stones.

Scott

The Centennial
Seaford is one hundred years old this week. We had lots of practices and yesterday our mothers came to see us out in the court. We had a program to celebrate the centennial. Keith and Raymond wore centennial hats. Some of the girls wore long dresses. We danced in the program. We had to have partners.

Mary

Firemen
I like firemen. They put out fires. They wear strong hats, and they wear these hats so that nothing can hurt their heads.

Sam

We Go Hunting
I like a BB gun that shoots BB's. That is my favorite thing. I like to shoot birds. I kill 'em with my BB gun. I go hunting with my daddy. My daddy has got a real rifle.

Conrad

I Help Daddy
I rake up the yard and Daddy helps me and so does my brother. We burn them up, and Daddy likes it. When we come home from school we have to rake the other side.

Jack

Things I Did Over the Weekend
I went to church on Sunday. I went out to lunch on Sunday. I went to the English Grill. We had a big meal.

Jimmy

Stop and Go
One day Dad was driving our car. He was driving in Maryland. He saw the red light and he stopped. Then it turned green. He started slow and then he went faster. The cops were after him. They caught him and gave him a ticket. He was going too fast.

John

Trip to the Firehouse
I went to the firehouse. And I went on the firetruck. I saw the boots and the coats and the hats.

Jane

Neighborhood and community resources are so numerous that ideas could supply an entire year's dictating program, ranging from the home to the zoo, the park, the theater, the courthouse, the mayor's office, churches, and the YMCA. Some do not require field trips. Although some visits would provide good experiences, valuable time should not be wasted by making trips too frequently.

Current and Seasonal Events

As all teachers know, the school year has a number of fixed special events: Halloween, Thanksgiving, Christmas, Lincoln's Birthday, Valentine's Day, Washington's Birthday, Easter. Some schools have even more. For the teacher using the language-experience approach, these events are a boon. The interest stimulated by them can be used to advantage for communication.

In addition, current happenings are a constant, novel, and variable source of stories: trips to the moon, inauguration of a president, a bridge collapse, a hurricane, a snowstorm, a centennial, a fire, an accident, and so on. They command attention and turn up in discussions in school corridors and cloakrooms. The alert teacher brings the discussions into the classroom and takes full advantage of the intense motivation they provide.

The Easter Bunny
The Easter bunny's ears are long. He is gray.
The Easter bunny has a little round tail. He gives all of us Easter eggs for Easter.

Pearl

Spring
In the spring we see flowers. There are pussy willows. We see daffodils. They are yellow. We have spring showers. Last night we had a thunderstorm. I saw some lightning in my window. We have seen a robin. This is a sign of spring.

Arlene

Valentine's Day
On Valentine's Day we went riding. We went to see where my boyfriend lives. We had fun.

Mary

The Pumpkin
Mrs. Johnson brought a pumpkin to school. The pumpkin is little. We put it on a shelf. We will make eyes in it and a mouth. Nathaniel said to put a tongue in his mouth then we will have a jack-o-lantern.

Frankie

Santa Claus
Me and my brother went to see Santa Claus last night. Santa Claus gave me a candy cane. I told him what I wanted for Christmas.

Ronald

The Inauguration

We watched TV. We saw Mr. Johnson. He was
made President. He put up his right hand and put
one hand on the Bible. A man prayed. A woman
sang. The people stood up and we did too when
the band played.

Beverly

Dental Health Week

I brush my teeth at school. I brush them every
day. So does Jimmy. He waits for me. We saw a
filmstrip about Tommy Tooth. Billy lost a tooth.
He put it under his pillow. The next morning he
found a quarter under his pillow.

Martin

The Pilgrims

The pilgrims came over on the Mayflower. The
pilgrims found out that there were Indians on this
land. I heard about the pilgrms and the Indians
had a Thanksgiving dinner.

Bob

Going to the Circus

We went to see the Hawks on Friday. We ate
supper early. On Saturday at 10:30 we went to
see Ringling Brothers and Barnum and Bailey
Circus. We saw a man jump rope on a highwire.
We saw some clowns and a mother clown with a
baby clown.

Scott

Abraham Lincoln

Abraham Lincoln has a memorial in Washington,
D.C. His statue is in the memorial. He was our
sixteenth President. His birthday was February
twelfth. He was born in a log cabin. When he was
President, he got shot. Lincoln was in the theater
watching a play and somebody came and shot
him.

William

The Coal-Mining Country

Mother and father and me went up to the
coal-mining country. We went to see my uncle
and aunt. I got some coal and I got some slate. I
seen the big diggers. Some of the things they put
on the diggers are big enough to drive your car
in. They have big trucks to haul the coal in. They
go in the coal mines.

David

Holiday Inn

We had a turkey at the Holiday Inn. We ate him.
My mother had a drink. I had a drink of a little

soda. My mother had another drink. We had little
swords with our drinks.

Lucy

Rocket
We watched the rocket go off. Part of the rocket
came off. We watched it go off. When it comes
down it goes under the water.

Jane

School and Curriculum

In 1963, when the directors of 27 studies concerned with different approaches to first-grade reading instruction met in Minneapolis, one of the variables they wished to control was reading-instruction time. No decision could be reached at that summer meeting. When they met again, in December, it was thought urgent that reading-instruction time be defined. Still no agreement could be reached (16, p. 564). A principal reason for this was that the language-experience people insisted that reading is a process and that a teacher can use any content as a source of reading material. In other words, all phases of the curriculum can provide material for reading instruction and require the use of reading skills.

Advocates of basic reader programs, phonic programs, linguistic programs and the like, limit reading instruction to a fixed time in the school day. In addition, their instructional materials consist primarily of the contrived plots and exercises provided in their basal reader collections, no two of which use the same stories or even the same themes. The vocabularies differ and the words are taught in different sequences with different controls for word introduction. Word attack skills are taught in varying order. Yet the instructors all agreed on a specified time limit to the otherwise "nonagreement" reading instruction—approximately 90 minutes.

The language-experience people, and to some degree the ITA (initial teaching alphabet) advocates, agreed that all parts of the curriculum provide materials and motivate interests that can be used for reading instruction. A look back at the wide variety of stories dictated by children provides much evidence to support this contention. In addition to the topics being widely varied, the vocabulary, syntax, grammar, and semantics clearly far exceed what is found in any basic reader first-grade reading program. If this has not already been noticed, it can be seen in the following pupil dictations.

Hatching Chickens
Today Jody had an incubator at school. It had
eggs in it. The incubator had a light bulb in it to
keep the eggs warm. One egg has hatched. The

chicken was wet. The heat will dry its feathers
and keep it warm.

Pam

The Guinea Pigs
Today Mrs. Ennis brought in two guinea pigs.
She let us pet them. We had fun. One was black
and white. The other one was all white. They eat
corrots, celery, and apples. They live in a cage.

Jean

A Magnifying Glass
A magnifying glass makes things look big
when you hold it over them. My daddy has a
magnifying blass to look at pennies when he
wants to put them in his book. There is a
magnifying glass at school that has a black
handle. I look at pennies with my magnifying
glass, too.

David

What Animals Do in Winter
The Snowshoe rabbit turns white in the winter.
This protects him in the winter from other
animals. When he is white, he can hide in the
snow. Some animals get very fat. Then they
hibernate or go to sleep for the winter. The
woodchuck and the badger sleep in a tunnel that
they dig with their front paws. The bears sleep in
a hollow log or a cave. When it comes spring,
they wake up and come out. The chipmunks and
the squirrels gather up nuts for winter and store
them in their nest.

David

Our Flag
We have a flag in front of the school. We have
one in our room too. The day before yesterday,
Mrs. VanTine took our flag down. When I brought
my flag, she put my flag up. The flag has fifty
stars. It has six red stripes and seven white
stripes. All the stripes together are thirteen.

Bill

The Intercom
I saw the intercom. Mrs. Pepper showed us how
it works. She called our room. Larry and Linda
and Nancy talked through the intercom.

Mitch

Election Day
Me and my brother rode down on his bike and my
bike. My father voted for Johnson. He voted
through the machine.

Pete

Science Fair

I saw a skeleton. I saw a egg in the water. If you put a lot of salt it will float up. I saw a turtle. I saw a big shell. Then we saw a alligator. We saw our chicks. And in the box there were two popped out and there were more to hatch. After we went back to the room, we saw a puppet show.

Karen

Seeds

When the seeds grow bigger, we are going to take the flowers home. We put seeds in the cups. We put some dirt in it and some stones in it. When the flowers come up, they will have roots on them.

Betty

Magnet

We played with the magnet. Everything that was metal it would pick up. It picked up a bar. It was metal. It picked up the bobby pins. It picked up screws.

Mary

My Project

The project I brought in for the Science Fair was the disappearing gas. I used some vinegar. I soaked steel wool in the vinegar for a few minutes. I stuck it in a bottle and added a little water to it and put a balloon in the top of the bottle. It will blow up inside the bottle

Conrad

Julie's Frog

Julie brought her frog in today. Mrs. McWilliams got a box to put the frog in. Kenny and Julie went out to get grass to put in the box. When they got the grass, the frog got out. Kenny caught the frog. The frog is big. The frog is green and it has black on it. It is pretty. I like the frog.

Carla

Animals

I like a cow because cows give you milk. A baby cow drinks milk from the big cow. We went on a trip to the farm. I saw some cows. They were black and white. The little cow was brown. They say "Moo."

Sara

Bicycle Safety

Sergeant Wells told us how to ride a bike. He showed us a movie. He showed us how to slow down or stop, and to turn right and left. The girl

crashed into a car. She had to go to the hospital.
After she was fixed, she obeyed the rules.

Steve

These children are not confined to a Procrustean preprimer or primer. They are not asked to tell again and again some silly plot about Dick Scott and Jane Foresman. Their reading-talking-thinking-sharing world is bound by all knowledge. From the very beginning of their reading days, they are reading about things they themselves have observed or heard or felt or smelled. Their attitudes toward reading are being shaped by experience and knowledge and not by forced plots with substandard language.

Stories, Dreams, and Wishes

The best school and community with its many firsthand opportunities cannot provide all the resources that children are able to use to stimulate and express their ideas. Children are creative and love to improvise. When encouraged, they create with eagerness and zest that clearly suggest pleasure. Talking about dreams and wishes requires self-revelation. Inviting the children to share these thoughts suggests that someone else wants to know about them and will be interested enough to read about them or listen to them. Telling about "my wishes" may cause many pupils to stop and think about themselves in a way they have not done before, and it may lead to better self-understanding. Books like *Is This You?* by Ruth Krauss[2] may help a child see himself in a different way and enjoy the ridiculous as good fun.

Creating stories is a wonderful way to stretch life. Stories begin as all invention and make-believe does, with an idea, frequently a once-upon-a time idea. How the idea interacts with things, people, and processes depends on each child's experience and ability to spin a yarn and, of course, on the degree to which the teacher invites and encourages story writing. It also reflects the amount of reading to the children that the teacher does. The following stories obtained from first-grade-level children are illustrative.

What I Want to Be
I wish I could be a cat so I could have babies. My cat has babies already. I would keep my babies warm. I would get a lot of weeds and make a nest. I would give them milk. I would climb trees and get birds and bring them to my babies. I would not let them die.

Caroline

[2]Ruth Krass, *Is This You?* (New York: William R. Scott, 1955).

When I grow Up
I want to be a road builder. I like trucks. I want to
drive a road scraper. It is hard.

Eddie

A One Time Magic Garden
We read a story and it had a magic garden. I
liked this story and I wish I had a magic garden. I
would plant some basketballs and some trucks. I
would plant a car that I could ride in with a motor.
Children could come along one time because no
one can come two times.

John

What I want to Be
I want to be a Soap Box Derby boy. Right now
my father and I are thinking about making a car.
We don't have to make a motor because the
starting place is on a hill. I want to have a motor
because I want to run the car on a street. If I keep
the car, I can race and I might win in the Soap
Box Derby.

Harold

My Favorite Dream
One day I had a dream about some monsters.
Near my house I saw a ten-foot monster and I
ran into my house. The monster was following
my foot tracks and I locked the screen door and
put a chair in back of the door.

Bill

The Pirates
The pirates were fighting some other men
because they wanted the treasure. The other
pirates shot back at them. When the last war was
over, one of the captains was killed. The other
pirates broke through the gates of the treasury
and got the treasure. The treasure was from a
treasure ship that sank down into the water a
long time ago. Now some of the pirates were rich
and some were poor.

Jack

My Pocket
I have a pocket on my dress. I carry tissues in my
pocket. My pocket has a big red apple on it. I
have two pockets on my dress. Sometimes I
carry my mother's mail in my pocket. Sometimes
I carry my toys in my pocket. The pocket I have
on my skirt has a tree on it.

Carla

The Man Who Didn't Want to Fight
One day a man said, "I don't want to fight but other people do." Then he said, "What shall I do? I know what I will do. I will build a house with a door that locks from the inside and no one can open it with a key. I will have no windows at all. I will have a hole for an air conditioner and a hole for two fans." So the little old man built the house. It was very cool. He built his house in the woods. The little old man lived happily ever after because he did not get in any more fights.

Pete

The Little Red Hen
The Little Red Hen found some wheat. She planted it. After the wheat grew, she took it to the mill. Then she made some bread. She asked Mrs. Duck if she wanted to help her make the bread. She asked Mr. Turkey if he wanted to help her. They both said, "Not I." When she got ready to eat it, she asked if they wanted to eat it. "Yes," they said. But Little Red Hen said, "You did not help me make it. My children and I will eat it."

Pam

Record Books.
Each child in first grade can keep a record book in which to place all the dictating he does for the year. A standard 8½-x-10-inch notebook will serve the purpose well. If the stories are typed, the typed copy can be taped or pasted into the book. If the dictation is recorded in manuscript by the teacher, it can be done directly in the notebook. Each story is dated, providing the pupil with a chronological record of his dictation. Throughout the year, a pupil will reread any or all entries. (As one boy said in February when he reread a story he had dictated in September, "That's the way I talked when I was little.") Drawings for each story can be made on the pages facing the pasted-in dictation, a drawing on the left and a story on the right. Notebooks can be exchanged and classmates can read each other's stories. The notebook serves many purposes and is especially valuable as a learning-to-read aid.

The titles of the entries in one boy's book show the variety of interests and themes that children derive:

How I Come to School	The Halloween Story
The Funny Man	The Trip to the Coal-Mining
Jane Jumps	Country
Helping at Home	Dandelions
My Weekend Story	Dick, My Brother

The Fireman's Big Truck
Help
Something Funny
The Lost Money
What I Want to Be
The Pilgrims
Santa Claus
When I Was Sick
What Animals Do in Winter
Teeny's Two Puppies
My Birthday
The Hands-Down Game
Going to the Reading Conference
The Late Snow
The Boy and Girl Who Ran Away
The Mousetrap Game

Our Family Garden
The Man Who Didn't Want to Fight
The Man Who Wanted a Family
Thanksgiving
Guess What This Is
The Book I Like Best
The Holiday I Had Off
The Puppet Show
Three Little Horses
Lincoln and Washington
A Magnifying Glass
What I Am
Two Guinea Pigs
The Easter Egg Hunt
A Funny Thing Happened

Note that some of the titles listed here are the same as those used earlier in this book. On occasion children select a common title for all to use and frequently reflect joint ventures, such as field trips.

This list represents only David's record of dictated stories. In addition, he had a long list of creative writings that he started in November and continued throughout the school year. Furthermore, not all his dictated accounts were placed in this notebook. Some were gathered in a science book, others in a health book.

In summary, the abundance of stimuli with which to motivate dictation should be strikingly apparent. Ideas and props are as extensive and numerous as experience and knowledge, not only of the immediate geographical area—home, community, and school—but also of the curriculum. Any teacher can tap this tremendous reservoir, and in so doing, get the children to examine more carefully the world about them, to see new horizons, to view the past and the future, and to act upon it all intellectually.

A look at the vocabulary displayed in the stories in the preceding pages shows how wide-ranging it is. Nomenclature in them is used correctly, concepts are refined and attained, and intellectual growth is stimulated and accomplished. Above all, attitudes toward knowledge and communication are fostered, as is the spirit of inquiry. Knowledge comes first. Reading and books are viewed as one means of obtaining ideas. Reading is learned as it is taught, not as an end in itself, but as a means of obtaining information or entertainment.

Individual Language and Experience Levels

Without a doubt, the chief use of language is to communicate meaning. Sounds have no intrinsic meaning of their own:

> A stream of speech consists of a succession not only of units of sound, but also of units which convey meaning to the speakers of the language. How do we know they contain meaning, and how can we test for meaning? The only way we can test with absolute assurance is by collecting large quantities of specimens of continuous speech from a speaker of a given language. (8, p. 13)

The illustrations of children's dictation provided in this chapter indicate the stream of language children use to convey meanings. Morphemes (words), unlike phonemes (sound units), have meaning and catalogue the vast universe of experience. The stories here show the range of experience of children, the influence of instruction, and the use of language to tell others about experiences and ideas.

Furthermore, by and large, the children communicated their ideas effectively. They learned to make themselves understood within the framework of the linguistic patterns of their society. If they lack adroitness in using the right expressions, this is a matter conditioned largely by opportunity to speak, by considerations of prestige within their social-cultural-linguistic environment, which now includes the classroom and the school, and by the taste, temper, and maturity of each pupil. To say that these children speak in nonstandard fashion is nonsense. Certainly they speak differently from the way they did when they were four years old; they change continuously and at varying rates in different groups. And such change will continue as fostered by the new opportunities provided by the school—if it is not stifled by a premature demand for "correctness." Finally, there is much confusion about correctness. Linguistically, what the children normally say is "correct." If one considers the forms that are admired and accepted by certain groups, though, their language may not be considered correct. The conventions of society are inescapable and represent a form of correctness that is a good thing. But at this stage of a child's life, attention must be focused on communication itself, so that the "why" and "when" of communication become soundly inculcated. Then language refinement, or how to conform to the best language patterns, becomes significant. Until then, children must manage to say practically everything they ever have a need to by learning to handle with ease the language that is their own.

If the language is a public language in which short, simple sentences abound, few subordinate clauses are used, sequence is limited, adjectives and adverbs are rigid and few in number, and reasons and conclusions are confounded, then the rate of change will be slow and attempts to bring about change will meet with resistance. If the language in the peer group in school involves this kind of communication only, then change to a more formal language will be slow:

> To ask the pupil to use language differently, to qualify verbally his individual experience, to expand his vocabulary, to increase the length of his verbal planning function, to generalize, to be sensitive to the implications of number, to order a verbally presented arithmetic problem, these requests when made to a *public* language user are very different from when they are made to a *formal* language user. For the latter it is a situation of linguistic development whilst for the former it is one of linguistic change [2, p. 99].

The task of reading instruction appears to be to preserve for the children the force and dignity that their language possesses while making available to them the possibilities inherent in a linguistic form oriented toward higher conceptualization. Their cognitive and affective states must be channeled in such a way that disequilibrium does not result. Small classes, individual attention, frequent opportunity to think, speak, listen, opportunities to use language not only to label and enumerate but also to categorize objects, events, and people, along with many opportunities to internalize the role of the speaker as well as the listener are all required.

This is what the LEA approach provides so abundantly. There are numerous opportunities for children to see, react, think, speak, be listened to, read, share, acquire increasingly more acceptable forms of language. The stories reproduced here reflect this clearly. Notice again the quality of the sentences; the range and size of the vocabulary; the use of sequence, prepositional phrases, and personal pronouns; the use of divergent and convergent thinking; the use of logical qualifiers; and the processing of relevant data to reach acceptable conclusions.

CLASSROOM SEATING

It is apparent that in classrooms reflecting the kind of instruction described the settings were "cleared for action." The hub of each action setting was and should be the classroom library (see Chapter 6), and being the hub, it should be centrally located. The first thing to catch attention in a room or pod of this caliber should be the library. A child entering the room for the first time should react at once to this setting: a table or two, book shelves about 3 feet high, chairs, one or two rocking chairs, and so on.

Then around the library center pupil desks are arranged in clusters of two, three, and four. Usually a three- or four-seat cluster is preferred. In each cluster the teacher can place a very able and achieving child, two who are also achieving but not at the same rate or level, and one child whose rate of learning is slower and level is lower and who could benefit from much help and assurance. In clusters of this type a marvelous *esprit de corps* develops. The children work together and help each other. The slow one is accepted, aided, and prized.

Action Centers

Around the room in appropriate places action centers can be established. These are rally points for a variety of purposes: a phonic booth, a science center, a word center, a listening post, a film viewing point, a reflecting site, a pretty table, a creative arts center, and so on. Care must be taken not to clutter but to keep the learning environment open and attractive. Activities should be changed periodically in keeping with the children's needs and varying circumstances. Pupils are free to move about *purposefully and thoughtfully*, at all times showing not only individual resourcefulness but regard for the rights of others. Care should be taken that a balance is maintained between close-ended activities and open-ended ones that encourage creativity and an extension of knowledge.

•*Word Recognition.* The many dictations provide innumerable opportunities for word recognition skill training. The number and variety of sight words becomes a rich and ready source.

The teacher can pause for a moment at a seating cluster and say "find a word in your word bank that begins like *d*own, or like *s*and, or *tr*ee, *sh*ow, *fl*y *th*e, and so on. These frequent brief stopovers are welcomed by the children and help keep them on an auditory-visual alert. Or she can ask them to find a word that ends like sing*ing*, or quick*ly*, or run*s*, or big*ger*, or sup*per*, and the like. Such actions give credence and endorsement to the value of repeated contacts. The word bank serves many useful purposes (see Chapter 4).

PHONIC BOOTH.

A phonic booth should be set up early in the school year. A phonic booth or phonic corner requires some privacy for both the participants and the class. One teacher set up a wooden box obtained in a nearby store (screens can be used, too). The box was about 1½ x 4 feet on the base and 4 feet high. One end and one side were removed. Two chairs were placed in the box on the base with a small table between them in the middle. The space was big enough for children to get in and out with ease and small enought to be cozy and offer some privacy. The box was decorated with a false window on the outside; on the inside, where the children sat, the walls were covered with words having a letter or letters underlined, such as b̲oy, t̲r̲ee, c̲hair, and t̲h̲ree, scattered all over the wall in different positions and different colors. This booth proved to be a boon to the phonic training program, especially for the slower children. Phonic "teachers" were designated for the booth and were available if someone wanted help, and all did. The pupils chosen as "teachers" were the ones best at these skills. Pupils could approach a "teacher" with their word banks and suggest they use the booth for phonic help. Of course, the "teachers" also sought out pupils. The booth was popular throughout the year and most helpful.

CONCLUSION

The purpose of this chapter is to describe how teachers can use the dictated experience accounts of children to initiate and maintain instruction in how to read. Most teachers are uncertain about how to get started at the beginning of the school year. To help them understand the *how*, *when*, and *what* of getting started, procedures were described in detail. Of special significance is the fact that if on the first or second day of school instruction is initiated as described, all the children can go home feeling that they have read. Favorable attitudes toward reading are fostered from the very beginning.

The use of a whole class as a base for obtaining dictation serves a useful purpose and is a means of getting started. By far the best procedure, however, is to obtain individual dictation. Transition from whole-class stories to individual dictation can be made effectively through groups that reflect some arrangement by ability or that are randomly organized. Children can see how an interest or stimulus is dealt with in the whole class or in one story, when three or four groups arrive at three or four similar but different stories about the same theme and individual dictations result in perhaps thirty versions. Teachers find that they can direct and obtain individual stories with greater ease if they operate out of group situations. As any teacher who tries the approach soon discovers, individual stories are most productive and have the best utility for instruction.

What to talk about or how to get children to talk has been described and illustrated with numerous children's stories. The major question is not what to use as a stimulus but how and what to select from among the innumerable possibilities. All living provides a ready source, with the curriculum and its many concepts as a structural fountainhead.

Certainly the language levels of children will vary from some command of a public language to good control of a formal language. Use of the children's language and acceptance of their level is the important guideline. Great care must be taken not to stifle their language by demanding "correctness." At this point in their language development the purpose of language as communication is paramount. Of course, this is true throughout life, and at a later time the formalities of language will have to be taught, but not at this early stage.

Bibliography

1. Allport, Gordon W., *Pattern and Growth in Personality.* New York: Holt, Rinehart and Winston, 1961.
2. Bernstein, Basin, "Social Structure, Language and Learning." In John P. DeCecco (ed.), *The Psychology of Language, Thought, and Instruction.* New York: Holt, Rinehart and Winston, 1967.
3. Bullock, Sir Alan, *A Language for Life, Report of the Committee of Inquiry Appointed by the Secretary of State for Education and Science* (England). London: Her Majesty's Stationery Office, 1975.
4. Cordts, Anna D. *The Word Method of Teaching Phonics.* Boston: Ginn, 1929.
5. Dewey, John, *Democracy and Education.* New York: Macmillan, 1916.
6. Goodenough, Florence L., and Dale B. Harris, *Goodenough-Harris Drawing Test.* New York: Harcourt Brace Jovanovich, 1963.
7. Goodlad, John I., *Facing the Future.* New York: McGraw-Hill, 1976.
8. Hamp, Eric P., "Language in a Few Words: With Notes on a Rereading, 1966." In John P. Dececco (ed.), *The Psychology of Language, Thought, and Instruction.* New York: Holt, Rinehart and Winston, 1967.
9. Holt, Robert R., "The Thematic Apperception Test." In Harold H. Anderson and Gladys L. Anderson (eds.), *An Introduction to Projective Techniques.* Englewood Cliffs, N.J.: Prentice-Hall, 1951.
10. Hymes, James L., Jr., *Behavior and Misbehavior.* Englewood Cliffs, N.J.: Prentice-Hall, 1955.
11. Jespersen, Otto, *Language: Its Nature, Development, and Origins.* New York: Macmillan, 1949.
12. Jonson, Ben, "Oratio Imago Animi," *Timber: Or Discoveries Made Upon Men and Matter.* In D. H. Herford and P. Simpson (eds.), *Ben Jonson.* Oxford: Oxford University Press, 1925-1952.
13. Murray, Henry, *Thematic Apperception Test.* Cambridge, Mass.: Harvard University Press, 1943.
14. Piaget, Jean, *The Origins of Intelligence in Children.* New York: International Universities Press, 1952.
15. Stauffer, Russell G., "Reading as Experience in Inquiry," *Educational Leadership,* 24 (February, 1967), 407-412.
16. Stauffer, Russell G., "The Verdict: Speculative Controversy," *The Reading Teacher,* 19 (May, 1966), 563-564.
17. Summers, Andrews, *Me The Flunkie.* New York: Fawcett, 1970.
18. Thomas, Charles K., *An Introduction to the Phonetics of American English.* New York: Ronald Press, 1947.
19. Waples, Douglas, B. Berelson, and F. R. Bradshaw, *What Reading Does to People.* Chicago: University of Chicago Press, 1940.

Chapter 4
Building a Word Bank

HOW TO DEVELOP A SIGHT VOCABULARY

When on the third day of school the teacher gave each child a copy of "The Box Turtle" dictation or the "Snowball" dictation reproduced exactly as it appeared on the large newsprint, this opened up a multitude of opportunities. Each child had produced an illustration of the turtle or the rabbit on which the teacher had written the title. This provided a one-to-one association of two symbol systems—language and iconic. The two reinforced each other and by so doing facilitated retention and recall. Now the illustration could be attached to the dictated account and thereby aid recognition of other words.

On this, the "first," occasion, as described on page 87, the teacher moved about the room and helped children underline any word they could recognize. Some children understand almost immediately what is meant by underlining and perhaps, more important, what is mean by underlining words that are known or can be read, or that, in brief, have become sight words. Two or more may underline each word, some may underline five or six, and some may underline only one or two. But usually all can and do underline.

It is not wise to hurry this phase and introduce underlining a day early. The recontact and reinforcement after the first 24-hour forgetting period (or remembering period) and then again after the second 24-hour forgetting period help establish a word or words as sight vocabulary.

The number of words each child underlines varies directly with each child's ability. This kind of pacing geared to each individual provides success for each and avoids making demands that are too exacting or too restricting. Bright children may underline all the words only to discover the next day that some words are not remembered. Then on occasion a line may be erased. If the word is identified through the power of context and closure, an essential word attack skill, the word can be underlined a second time. All this helps develop scholarly honesty (a mark of a true scholar is to be intellectually honest) and the determination to try again.

Those less able are also likely to underline a word or two or three because a new dictation has an impelling immediacy. These children lack ability at this stage to use word attack skills discriminatingly and to bridge a closure gap that exceeds more than a word. Usually it is wise not to have these pupils underline on the same day they dictate. If they can underline a word after a 24-hour forgetting period, the delayed recall proves to be a good safeguard. Then, too, these children probably should underline all known words twice and on different days as has been found profitable in some situations. Use of a different color (preferably red) to distinguish the second day underscoring is helpful.

Window-card usage is a superb way to determine ease and accuracy of recall. Recall and recognition are facilitated when context can be used freely. The power of comprehension or semantics or meaning is almost omnipotent. However, when a word window is cut into a 3 x 5-inch card, and the window is opened up on a word, the rest of the card occludes the other words and ideas and almost totally cuts off context. This means of isolating a word can be used readily. If the children can recognize a word isolated by a window card, it is very likely that they now have stored the word in their memory banks.

Pupils may come to the dictation area, sit by the teacher, and identify words they know. Or the teacher may move about the room and stop with different children.

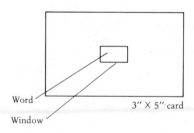

Word

Window

3" X 5" card

Children who recognize words readily in a whole-class story give an early indication of aptitude, particularly if they recognize words that they did not dictate. To do this is equivalent to recognizing words in a book. The words were not produced by the learner. Some children recognize only words they dictated and perhaps a few key words such as *Snow White*, *turtle*, and the like.

Recognition and retention are facilitated for a child if he produces words and ideas orally. Hence the opportunity to dictate becomes important. In a whole-class story, opportunity to dictate is limited to a few pupils. When group stories are obtained, the number of pupils who contribute to a story is increased. If the class is divided into three groups, as many as 18 pupils in a class of 30 may have an opportunity to dictate.

The best procedure is to obtain *individually dictated* stories. This can be done with greater ease than a novice teacher might believe possible. The account in Chapters 2 and 3 told how readily individual stories can be obtained.

A stimulus for the day might be a big red apple, as in one classroom. First, all the children talked about the apple and speculated about how it tasted. Pupil experiences with apples were related. Next, the teacher selected eight children to meet with, who took turns dictating about the red apple. Steve dictated the following story. Note that his account goes beyond the immediate experience of examining the apple. Pupils begin to add elaborations extracted from personal related experiences and on occasion add ideas that are largely imaginative. Thus by easy stages they begin to "tell a story" as they move beyond a literal accounting of the firsthand experience.

A Red Apple
Look! There's an apple on a tree. I am going to
climb the tree and eat it.
                                                    Steve

Steve underlined nine different words out of a total of 18 different words and 21 running words. Three of the words he recognized occurred twice and he underlined them each time. He also recognized his name. He knew these words on a second day, as is shown by the double lines.

In another class the teacher used crickets as a stimulus, and Ronald dictated the following:

Crickets
I like to find crickets. One cricket is five and one
is six.
                                                    Ronald

He underlined the word *I* and the word *cricket* and did so each time it occurred. Even though two uses of the word were plural and one was singular, he recognized each correctly. He also read his name.

Lisa dictated the following story and underlined the words as shown:

Coming to school

I come to school on a bus. My bus driver's name
is Mrs. Hastings. My bus number is twenty-three.
There are big children and little children on the
bus.

Lisa

Lisa used 23 different words and recognized each one. She did this with such ease that she was asked to underline the words only once. Accurate recognition was confirmed by using a window card placed over different words in the story in random order.

Recognition of words isolated by a window card may be facilitated if the words are exposed one at a time by following the word order in the story or by occasionally skipping a word. Some children recognize words better this way, because they sense the idea sequence and the word order of the story they dictated. A sign of growth in recognition skill occurs when such a child can recognize words checked in random order, for example, by shifting the window about, showing a word in the last sentence, then one in the first sentence, then one in the middle, and so on. Random-order recognition can be aided if at first only the substantives, or nouns, are exposed, then the action verbs, then the adjectives, and so on.

The use of a window card is a very important part of word attack skill learning. Each child can be given a window card to use at various times throughout a school day to test himself. Children love to do this and do it almost constantly for a while. If they do not recognize a word instantly, they sometimes amusingly take cautious peeks under the card in search of global ideas.

At this stage children love to test each other. This provides many action-centered opportunities for children to pair up in different ways and play window-card games. Some planned arranging can be done by the teacher, too, by deliberately placing a very good reader with one who needs help.

Psychologically speaking, window recognition, with the described procedural steps, is an exercise in cue reduction. The number of cues for recognition of a word is gradually reduced through (1) use of total story context, (2) teacher pointing a finger to different words, (3) window-card isolation of words in story sequence, (4) window-card isolation of words in random order. The number of cues provided by the original stimulus is reduced each time, until only a fleeting glance at a randomly isolated word may be sufficient for instant recognition.

For the stories just given, the children drew an illustration to accompany their dictation. Steve drew a big red apple hanging on a small branch of a tree. Ronald drew two stick-figure crickets, a big one and a small one. Lisa's picture was of a large yellow bus with a number 23 on the side.

Given an opportunity, children often display the pragmatic approach of associate-test-remember to word learning. Their pictures usually represent key concepts of the story context. The illustrations help them recall the story or words in a story; a picture can provide a semantic or meaning cue to word recognition as much as story or language context. Both pictures and language as forms of association are more logical, meaningful aids to recall than rote memory or studying words in isolation. Both forms have great potency when the child is the creator of the story dictation and illustration.

WORD BANKS

The reading market maintains its steady climb upward as it reflects the interaction of word-learning skill and reading attitude and interest. It shows a sudden point-three rise, though, as a result of response to the word bank idea. Investment in personalized word banks is wise and sound. It provides short- and long-term funds in what can become an upward-year bullish market. Optimism prevails, and the tightening demands for accurate recognition and reinvestment through functional use cannot dislodge the security confidence.

The bank stability removes peak-and-valley forgetting periods that are the frustrating liability of attempts at rote memorization of fixed word lists. Rote memorization has been categorized by repeated experience as an exercise in futility. The word bank, by contrast, with its dynamic, utilitarian pragmatism, results in the accummulation of a sound and functional vocabulary, invested with meaning and logical associations that facilitate retention and recall.

Every individually dictated story represents a personalized record of word usage. In the eyes of the pupil, the words in his story are "my words in writing." Possession is sometimes spoken of as nine-tenths of the law; similarly, in word learning it represents nine-tenths of retention.

Every time a pupil marks a word in his dictation as a known word, he is underlining a "my spoken word, my printed word" idea. In a way, he is awarding himself his own gold star. Each underlined word represents an achievement he himself recognizes. He recognizes the word and he draws the line. Should he forget the word, as he may do, the dictation context as well as the picture may provide the meaningful clues needed for recognition.

The underlined words that are recognized 2 and 3 days after dictation provide the deposits and reserves of the word bank. Deposits are made by a pupil through the teacher. Every underlined and recognized word *is printed by the teacher* on a small card (⅜-x-1½-inch). The words may be typed in primer-size type or handwritten. In either case, lower- and upper-case letters are used as the circumstances of good language usage require. Proper names, for instance, begin with capital letters. Typed words provide clear, well-shaped, and uniform letters. This is why pupil writing of word bank words is not sought at this time. If script is used, the same conditions should be observed. This makes for ease of recognition and for transfer of recognition to other contexts.

A word bank may be a small metal box of the kind made available commercially for filing 3-x-5-inch cards. Or it may be any similar box—a cut-down shoe box, a box for Christmas-tree ornaments, a candy box, and the like. It should have a lid or the accidents that frequently occur with young folks may result in a lot of spillage.

In the beginning the small word cards are placed in the word bank in random order—that is, not in alphabetical order. This dropping of words into the bank randomly is purposeful, however. All the *known* words are kept in the bank and can be withdrawn and redeposited readily. For instance, the teacher may tell the class to find a word in their word banks that begins like *b*aker. This starts a search through the bank to locate a fitting word. Required, too, may be a series of visual discrimination and auditory discrimination decisions. A child may need to check 10 different words and reject each (*t*urtle, *a*pple, *cl*imb, *t*ree, *f*eet, *c*at, *sl*ow, *l*ittle, *G*ale, *r*ace, *L*isa, *S*teve) before locating *b*ox. Such decision-making activities are enormously useful and superior to a dozen fabricated "skill book" pages. Different children fare differently. Some may find a fitting word with the first word examined and others may need to check a large number. Regardless, when all have located a word, the different fitting words may be compared. The task can be made more demanding by asking that they find as many words as they can that begin like *b*aker. Thus one child may produce: *b*ox, *B*ill, *b*ook, *br*ing. Even though *br*ing does not fit exactly because of the *r*-influenced *b*, it does fit in part, and at this stage should be recognized but set aside.

Word Bank Activities

A list of activities involving the word bank is as follows:

    I. Auditory-visual discrimination of beginning sounds
       A. Single consonants (*b*ox, *t*urtle)
       B. Single vowels (*a*nd, *i*t)
       C. Blends (*tr*ee, *bl*ue)
       D. Digraphs (*sh*e, *th*e)
   II. Auditory-visual discrimination of ending sounds
       A. Single consonants (loo*k*, ru*n*)
       B. Blends (sta*nd*, ju*mp*)
       C. Digraphs (pea*ch*, lig*ht*)
  III. Finding family words
       A. C*at*, b*at*, f*at*
       B. m*ake*, c*ake*, sh*ake*

IV. Completion or closure activities
   A. Using sentences like the following, children find a word or words that fit.
   Mary saw a _____ in the tree. (boy, bird, turtle, etc.)
   Bill likes to _____. (climb, walk, run, hide, etc.)
V. Conceptual classifying or categorizing
   A. Find names of things
      (hammer, cup, box)
   B. Find names of things you can do
      (run, jump, sit)
   C. Find names of people
      (Bill, Mary, Carla)
   D. Find only girls' names, or boys' names
   E. Find names of places
      (barn, pond, farm)
   F. Find words we can use at Christmas
      (tree, Santa Claus, snow)
   G. Find names of colors
VI. Finding two-letter words, three-letter words, and so on
   A. in, it, so
   B. toy, cat, man
   C. tree, trip, stop
   D. movie, drink, grass
VII. Finding words with structural changes
   A. run, runs, running
   B. show, showed
   C. drink, drinks, drinking
VIII. Finding compound words or two-in-one words
   A. woodchuck, somebody, Mayflower, firetruck.
IX. Alphabetizing: take ten words out of the word box and put them in alphabetical order.
X. Finding words that begin with capital letters
   A. Bill, Mother, Wilmington, Cambridge, La Plata

The list of things to do that serve instructional purposes and are not busy work is almost endless. Such a list should be posted so that children may from time to time freely select activities of their own.

Alphabetizing

Once the number of words in a word bank exceeds 30 or 40, the search for a single word may become cumbersome and demanding. Pupils become irked with the inefficiency of the system and are receptive to a better way to file words. This is the time to introduce alphabetizing.

When alphabetical filing is introduced, the best plan seems to be to place each letter on a small envelope, except that *X*, *Y*, and *Z* are placed on one envelope. The capitals and lower-case letters are written on the outside of the envelopes: *Aa, Bb, Cc, Dd,* and so on. Envelope size depends to some degree on the bank size; envelopes for thank-you notes or party invitations will usually do. Children deal with the alphabetizing in a very mature way. Invariably they are impressed by the efficiency of the system and its functional orderliness. They quickly learn to file each word card in the correct envelope according to the first letter of the word.

Now, much practical knowledge is acquired in a short time. Alphabetical order is appreciated in a way unmistakably different from rote repetition of the alphabet. The order of the letters serves a function; parroting the alphabet serves only to impress proud parents and naive teachers. Children begin to note the relationship between letter placement: *B* is toward the front, *S* is near the back, *M* is in the middle, and so on. When all the known words are filed, they see that some envelopes contain more words than others and that some are empty. When Pam started her alphabetical word bank, she had 44 words to file. Sixteen of the letter envelopes received words and 11 did not. In the *T* envelope she filed seven different words, with five in the *H* envelope. Pam said she liked her *B*-envelope words best—*bus, big, bicycle.* She started her alphabetical file in the latter part of September.

After the children have started alphabetical word banks, they can be introduced to a dictionary; any abridged dictonary designed for use in elementary school will do. Now the children can compare their word bank words and letter order with that of the dictionary. They notice that the *B* words in the dictionary are in the front of the book and that the *S* words are near the back, and so on, just as they are in their bank. Children are very responsive to being asked to locate in the dictionary words from their files. Some do this easily; others need help. Introduced this way, children do not develop fears about using dictionaries. Their attitude is favorable from the start, and the dictionary's utility value is impressively fostered.

All the children love to find a word bank word in the dictionary. Some actually learn to use the guide words at the top of each dictionary page. Some may have difficulty finding one word. On the other hand, some of the very able may find almost all their words. For instance, Pam found 40 of her 44 words and spent days doing so.

It has been said for years that knowledge of the alphabet is a fairly trustworthy predictor of reading success. But what is not usually added is that knowledge of the alphabet is equally as good a predictor of success in arithmetic and science (2). Ability to recite the 26 letters of the alphabet is evidence of a degree of mental maturity that enables a child to remember and repeat 26 (or even more) discrete unrelated items. Similar mental capacity would be revealed by committing to memory 26 children's names, or bird names, or tree names. It can be concluded that a child does not need to know the 26 letter names before learning how to read or do arithmetic. The alphabet letter names and their order can be learned in a natural functional way as described rather than by meaningless rote repetition.

WORDS, WORDS, WORDS

Up to now, we have been concerned with only a small aspect of word banks. A word bank can provide the security of a sound investment. The account can be drawn on at any time without depleting the principal.

Each dictated experience story becomes a treasure, even if it is dictated by the whole class or a group. Each individually dictated experience is even more treasured. The notebook with its chronological entries becomes a bank, too, a story bank much like the word bank. Both are cherished possessions.

How do these six-year-old bankers spend their day? Their banks are open Monday through Friday, usually from around 8:45 A.M. until around 2:45 P.M. Occasionally they are open through the lunch hour. The word bankers are neither miserly nor avaricious but frugal, prudent, and benevolent. All day long, they deal with words in one way or another, their own words and the words of peers. An atmosphere of industriousness prevails. "Busy work" is not needed. The teacher need not spend after-school hours preparing elaborate materials that are not as valuable to the children as those resulting from their own efforts.

What do the six-year-old word bankers do all day with their treasure? A search that yields tremendous pleasure is to locate word bank words in other places. One of the most thrilling places is a book in the classroom library, or any library for that matter. One day in September, Jane found 35 of her 50 bank words in one book. Jane's excitement and satisfaction spread to others in the room and similar searches were soon initiated. Sheila had only 10 words in her bank but she found 5 of them in one book.

The children learn that books are exciting and that it is thrilling to find known words there. But it is equally exciting to find words in newspapers. A newspaper has considerable status—Daddy reads it; so do Mother, Sister, Brother— everyone. A big advantage of newspaper words is that they can be cut out and kept in a special file. Sheila, for instance,

TRUCK   girl   house   fair

Winter   on   the   Billy.   a

Fire

found all her word bank words in newspapers and magazines. She was almost as proud of her cut-out words pasted on an 8½-x-11-inch sheet of paper as she was of her word bank.

Pam not only found most of her words in newspapers and magazines but she prepared special lists. She had six different sizes and shapes for the word *bus;* one was all capital letters of about 36-point type, another all lower case letters of about 8-point type; one had a capital *B;* one was in typewriter type, another in boldface, and one in italics:

bus   bus   Bus   **BUS**

bus   *bus*

Sheila and Pam and all the others assembled their own word pictures—the picture-dictionary idea, in a sense. Pam cut a picture of a bus out of an old magazine. Sheila cut out a picture of a fire truck and put the words *fire truck* on the back of the picture. Pam did not bother doing this; labeling was already too elementary for her. Sheila, on the other hand, used her words and pictures as a recognition test. First, she read the words. If she did not know a word, she would turn the picture over and look at it. Some interesting developments occurred; one boy, for example, said he "knew" some of his words so quickly because he knew by the size of the paper what picture was on the other side. Obviously, not all words could be pictured—*the, then,* and the like. The children soon discovered this and set up special lists of "no-picture words," "helper words," and the like.

Children were astounded to find that they could sometimes read every word on a page. Now the stilted and barren preprimers took on some value. Children were pleased when they could read every word in them. Of course, they wanted to read to others to display their prowess, so they worked with partners or met in small groups and listened to each other read aloud.

This kind of action-packed cutting, pasting, reading, and sharing requires freedom to move about. Children are quick to recognize and respect the need for orderliness and quiet. They move about in the room and share with each other as respectful good citizens. Naturally, because they are six-year-olds, this kind of conduct does not always occur. Teacher firmness and authority still prevail but only when pupil freedom exceeds the limits of social responsibleness.

Creative Word Usage

The words in a word bank can be arranged and rearranged on a word card holder. Anyone can construct a word card holder by stapling a piece of felt or the equivalent to a cardboard about 8 x 11 inches in size. The surface of the felt holds the word cards where they are placed. A good idea is to prepare a word card holder for each member in the class and even a few more. Keep them stored on a shelf readily accessible for use at any time. Cover the cardboard with varied colors of felt: black, red, green, blue, and so on.

By this time all the children will have thrilled to the sight of seeing their words and ideas appearing in print. They see their names in print, highlighting their contribution. Thus the thrill of authorship has been theirs and has spurred them on to greater effort.

Now, with the word card holders, they can, on their own, experience the pride of an originator of a different kind, through the creative use of the words in their word banks. A good beginning is to show pupils how to use words to arrange questions. The word card holder with a question can be shown to a teacher busy with another pupil and the answers can be a simple nodding of the head.

May I have the scissors?   May I have a pencil?   May I read to you?

This functional use of words promotes other creative uses. A child may discover that he does not have the word *have* in his word bank. Now he can use the closure approach to obtain it. He can set up on his word card holder: May I _____ the scissors? and show it to the teacher. He tells her what word he needs and she puts the word *have* on a word card have . This is an excellent way to add words to a word bank. Words requested in this way are seldom forgotten because they so clearly serve a communication purpose.

When pupils begin to form questions on their word card holders, a teacher must be prepared to cope with a barrage of requests. This soon eases up as the novelty wears off and as a vocabulary of key words builds up.

Going from questions to simple sentences and even to stories is an easy next step. Here are some samples obtained in a first-grade room early in the fall. Note that some of the structures are awkward. This results usually when a pupil does not have just the word wished and substitutes another word.

Gail: I go to school on the bus.
Sandra: I like to look at trees.
Steven: We like to eat hot dogs.
Dawn: **Fall**
          Mother sits on the swing.
          Houses are pretty.
          We like leaves.
          I saw some little acorns.

Bobby: We go to the shore.
         My family goes places.
         We go to Washington.

Carol: My mother is sick.
Nancy: Nancy and he go to my house.

The amount of thought and effort required to assemble sentences like these word by word may be far greater than seems apparent on the surface. First, each pupil had to think about what he wanted to say, controlled in part by the words in his word bank. Creativity was bounded and restrained accordingly.

Within the limits of the word bank, once the what-to-say had been decided on, it had to be remembered until the idea was completed and the necessary words had been assembled. Nancy, for instance, probably had no difficulty locating her name. Locating and identifying the other words may have required her to handle each word in her word bank. This kind of decision making requires top-flight, functional word recognition skill. It is a far cry from the flash-card rote drilling that is used in some other approaches.

Once a word bank is alphabetized it continues to provide means for developing and refining word attack skills. For instance, for Nancy to locate her seven words she had to recognize six different beginning sounds. Of this number perhaps the most challenging was *and*. The *n* sound in *and* is so dominant that it almost obscures the *a* phonetically. It is likely that in her phonetic-phonic (speech sound–letters representing sound) analysis she also had a visual image of the word. Regardless, she met the challenge and found the word *and* filed under *Aa*. Thus the total act of idea assembling on the word card holder established and reinforced essential phoneme-grapheme relationships.

This kind of idea structuring not only developed word recognition skills of the highest order but also began the "writing [makes] an exact man" technical expertness that Francis Bacon referred to (1). An attitude of correctness (correct thought, "I must say what I want to say") and persistence ("I'll stick with it until I've said what I want to say") was fostered. But above all, the attitude "What I want to say is functional only if someone else can read what I compose and understand what I say" was learned. So this structuring took place under the tremendously potent influence of a communication act—someone who writes does so for someone who reads. The author who knows his audience and writes for it is more apt to communicate effectively than one who does not.

In addition, syntactic power acquired through oral language usage was applied, reinforced, and developed in the composing act. In Nancy's sentence in the preceding samples list Nancy decided to write about "herself" (subject: *Nancy*) and "he" (subject: *he*). Then through the logic of discursive order, she had to dicide "what" about "Nancy" and "he" (predicate: *go*). Now she had established the subject and the subject's action, so she arranged the words in syntactical order. She also declared the "where" aspect of "go"—*to my house.*

Dawn's creative act reflects a more complex use of language and communication. She chose the topic "Fall" and wrote ideas related to it. This imposed an order of ideas about fall as well as a syntax order for each sentence.

It is far more important at this stage that children create and produce than that their attempts be "purified." Interest in written communication must be maintained as high as possible, so that the children will become absorbed in the thrill of this kind of communication.

Editorial work is initiated by the children. When they reread what they have composed they frequently change the structure because, as one boy said, "It doesn't sound right." Then when asked why he didn't use a more fitting word, he replied, "Because I didn't have it in my word bank." He had composed on a word card holder the statement, "We *see* the firemen yesterday." When he read it orally he said, "We *saw* the firemen yesterday." This editing shows the boy was sensitive to past and present tense.

How much time each pupil requires is not important. Nancy may have worked on her sentence off and on throughout the day; Dawn may have done her constructing in an hour's time. The word bank was constantly available, and since no deadline was declared each pupil could pace his own work throughout the day. At different times during the day, the teacher declared brief sharing periods. Children who had completed their compositions could share their material orally. This encouraged children to create throughout the day, day after day.

The children were free to move about in the room and read the compositions of others. They loved to do this. They enjoyed helping each other. At times, two worked together to compose a sentence using only the words in the word bank of one of the two. Pupils occasionally pooled their word bank resources, but the separation task later was so tedious that they tended to avoid this.

WORD RECOGNITION SKILL

The word bank provides one of the most valuable sources available for the development of word recognition skills. As has already been shown, the word bank supplies sight words that can be used to develop visual-auditory discrimination skills.

The word card holder is a valuable adjunct. In fact, as one teacher described it at a team teacher gathering, "The word card holder can become a freshly prepared skill activity page that serves immediate purposes."

Auditory discrimination is taught on the first day (see Chapter 3). As soon as a sight vocabulary has been acquired, auditory-visual discrimination skills can be learned.

The words in the word bank provide an excellent source of sight words. For instance, by mid-September, Pam recognized 25 words at sight. Two—*bus* and *big*—started with the letter *b*. In this beginning position the sound represented by the single consonant *b* can be heard readily. The teacher could do (and did) a number of things. Pam was asked to find a word in her bank that began with the same sound as the word *baker* for example. This word was spoken by the teacher, thus providing the auditory clue. Then Pam located the word *big* to provide the visual clue. The teacher then asked Pam to find a word that began with the same sound as *mother* (auditory). Pam found *my* (visual).

Now with both words on her word card holder, arranged one above the other ($_\text{my}^\text{big}$), another auditory-visual activity could be done. This time, the teacher gave Pam an auditory stimulus and asked her to decide which one of the two words had the same beginning sound as the one the teacher spoke. The teacher now said in rapid order "money," "boat," "bell," "may," "mix," "boy," and so on, expecting Pam to point each time either to *big* or to *my*. At this point the teacher paused to make certain that Pam knew the names of the two beginning letters. She had already determined that Pam knew the sound that each represented when it appeared as a beginning single consonant in a sound unit or word. Knowing the sound represented has the most useful value phonically.

Pam was not the only child in the room who knew the words *bus* and *my*. All had dictated individual stories "Coming to School," and all had used *bus* and many had used *my*. So group instruction could be done, too. Not only were the words ($_\text{my}^\text{big}$) placed on the word card holder, but also the words:

$$\left(\begin{array}{c}\text{turtle}\\\text{box}\end{array}\right)\quad\left(\begin{array}{c}\text{Bill}\\\text{Pam}\end{array}\right)\quad\left(\begin{array}{c}\text{furry}\\\text{cage}\end{array}\right)\quad\left(\begin{array}{c}\text{leaves}\\\text{red}\end{array}\right)$$

This listing of words provided an opportunity to distinguish eight different beginning sounds: *b* as in *big* and *Bill*, *m* as in *my*, *t* as in *turtle*, *p* as in *Pam*, and so on, and do so by keeping the letters in a *sound context* or syllable or, in each of these instances, a word. Later, distinction can be made between the sound *b* represents in *big*, *b* in *blue*, and *b* in *brown*. In each situation the sound context, or syllable, is of vital importance. In addition, the teacher could use a variety of spoken words as cue words. Useful were words like: *boy, baker, beautiful, biological*. Some words have only one or two syllables and others have three or more. This requires careful listening. Words that are not known (*biological*) are helpful because the children must focus almost entirely on sound and that is exactly what is wanted. This is an auditory (phonic, sound) and visual (sight, structure) discrimination skill training activity.

This kind of auditory (stimulus word spoken by the teacher) and visual (response word read by pupil) training can be initiated very early in a LEA reading program. In this instance the teacher introduced it in mid-September. The activity has much functional value. It helps children:

1. focus attention on beginning sounds
2. notice how beginning sounds are alike and different
3. identify the letters that represent a beginning sound
4. avoid confusing letter names with the sounds they represent
5. learn to recognize sounds and letter names in context rather than isolation
6. make and act on decisions about letters and sounds
7. facilitate the filing of words in their word banks

Pupil-teachers can soon be determined, once this kind of auditory-visual training has been initiated. Pam soon caught on to the skill and to the "teacher" role. Now she could look into another pupil's word bank, identify two words beginning with a single consonant (*bus, little*) and then provide orally a cue word (*barn* or *look*). Two or three or more pupils could meet around a table or on a rug in the magic rug corner and engage in this auditory-visual activity. The children loved doing this and did it frequently throughout a day. Again, the children were active, and what they were doing had functional value and it required teacher action on the scene and not after school. All the teacher needed to do was use the word wealth the children had acquired. As a result, the teacher was now free to direct and supervise small-group and individual word attack skill training.

Pupil participation became different, too. Pupils operated from the known (the words in their banks) to the unknown (words yet unlearned). Their chances for success increased because of this, as did their motivation. Most important, though, the pupils could serve as teacher and help refine the skills of their classmates. To do this pupils must know the *why* and *how* of the skills they teach. And, as every teacher knows, the best way to learn a skill is to teach it to others.

Word beginnings and word endings can be grasped and recognition can be refined by auditory-visual training. By the fourth week in September, Pam, a typical girl, and David, a typical boy, knew 44 and 50 words, respectively. By using their banks, they undertook various activities that went well beyond learning single-consonant beginning sounds:

*b*us	*d*river	*m*y
*l*ittle	*tr*ick	*p*ony
*t*wenty	*bl*ack	*r*ide
com*ing*	bla*ck*	pu*t*
driv*ing*	fa*st*	a*t*
		bi*g*

Children are quite responsive to this kind of word attack skill training because they work at their own levels. They know the printed words and how to set up similar activities. *Why* they are doing the training is no longer a skill-book busy-work mystery. Following directions is no longer the source of concern it tends to be in skill-book activities, because the children know not only how to follow directions but also how to give directions. Everyone works together throughout the day—partners, teams, groups, the whole class. Partners and teams are not fixed but vary from day to day and from activity to activity. The *esprit de corps* that results from work together toward a goal (learning to read) is tremendous.

If, on occasion, the pupils forget a word in their word banks, they are confronted with a unique relearning opportunity. They are not daunted, because they know what to do about it. They know that the best thing to do is to locate the word in the story in which it was first used and first underlined. The use of logical or context clues to recognition and recall is highly effective. It is not at all uncommon to find children double-checking their accuracy by referring to the original story. A practice found helpful with slow learners is to number the stories and then number, on the back of the word cards, the words learned in each story:

Front	*Back*
little	2
bus	1

In other words, the word *little* is underlined in the second story, *bus* in the first story, and so on. As has already been stated, the numbering of words is a crutch to learning or, better yet, a small intermediary step for the slow learners, but is unnecessary for the rapid learners.

CONCLUSION

The word bank file is a personalized record of words a pupil has learned to read or recognize at sight. The source of the words is a pupil's functional use of oral language to tell about an experience or relate an imaginary tale. The pupils identify the words they recognize. If they can reidentify them on at least two successive days, this provides good evidence that they will retain and recall the written word over a long period. Recognition is facilitated by identifying the word in written contexts such as books, newspapers, and magazines. The greatest aid to recognition is having the pupils use the words to construct sentences, ask questions, or develop a story. They do this by using small word cards and assembling the words syntactically on a word-card holder or spread out over the top of their desks. Filing words in alphabetical order in a word bank contributes to orderliness, to dictionary use, and to word recognition skill training.

Composing stories is a practical use of word bank wealth. In addition, the use of the words for word attack skill training is of great value. Auditory, or sound, discrimination (the basis of phonics) activities starts with the first day of school. Auditory-visual discrimination activities, or sound and sight activities, start with the first words in the word bank. This leads to a functional distinction between letter names and the sounds letters represent. It also prepares pupils for consonant substitution activities, the development of word families, and the use of phonetic respellings in a dictionary.

Bibliography

1. Bacon, Francis, "Of Studies," *Essays or Counsels, Civil and Moral.* In J. Spedding, R. L. Ellis, and D. D. Heath (eds.), *Works.* New York: Garrett Press, 1974.
2. Stauffer, Russell G. (compiler and editor), *Action Research in LEA Instructional Procedures.* Newark: University of Delaware, 1976.

Chapter 5
Creative Writing

It is difficult to write about the assets of a comprehensive approach to reading instruction and not be overly enthusiastic. Yet each facet yields so bountifully that exuberance about it seems natural. Creative writing, along with all other facets, prompts this kind of spirited reaction.

Creative writing both is and is not a good label for what really happens. Each pupil can invent, fashion, and fabricate and thereby derive the joy and elation that redounds to a creator. Pride of authorship and the self-esteem it evokes manifests itself in increased self-respect and in increased interest in the nature and quality of the writing. Creative use of language in oral communication is apparent among children almost from the time they begin to talk. So, gratifyingly, by the time children are of school age they have had much experience in using language creatively (see Chapter 1).

Now, though, they can produce their ideas in writing, share them with others in this medium, and store them for rereading at some other time. Over and over again, pupils can turn to their writings and realize each time that they are the authors as well as the producers. Not only is the written account and the creative use of language their language, but also the handwriting is theirs. Thus when written productions are exchanged and pupils discover that their writing is legible and that the content is interesting and holds attention, they have attained the pinnacle of authorship.

In the beginning what pupils write about is as important as what pupils talked about when dictation was started. Almost the same conditions hold. Pupils are most productive when they write about something they have just *experienced or experimented* with. This implementation for the creation of ideas results in a re-creation of ideas. For the unschooled, creative writing usually means "creating an imaginative plot or story" and a search for a John Updike or a Joyce Carol Oates. At this beginning phase of creating by writing such a search is out of place. What is wanted is writing in which the preoccupation is not with the creating of novel ideas or word painting but with the producing or recounting of ideas.

In brief, creative writing may be defined as a composition that reflects a child's own choice of words, ideas, grammar, punctuation, and encoding or spelling. The content may be nonfiction or fiction, documentary or imaginative, expository or narrative. The stimulus or the subject to write about may have been selected by the teacher, the class, or the pupil.

"Creative writing" requires certain other skills. Obviously, a child must be able to print, to form and produce letters, to group letters into words. The writing must be legible. Children must know the letters of the alphabet, must have an understanding about letter order in words, and above all must have some knowledge of phoneme-grapheme or letter-sound relationships so that they can encode phonologically. Because this is so, it is timely to elaborate on each.

Handwriting

Almost all educators agree that fundamental to the acquisition of skill in handwriting is the fostering of a favorable attitude toward handwriting. To achieve this, the very first steps in handwriting should be accomplished in a circumstance in which the children have a genuine purpose for writing. An ideal way to start, one abounding with personal pride and ego involvement, is to have first graders write their own names.

After children have made a drawing to accompany the first class story dictated, the teacher can show each of them how to add his or her name to the picture. It is now common practice in many schools for the pupils to have a copy of their names (usually printed or in manuscript writing) on their desk tops. They can then copy their names to the best of their ability, and thus be started on the road to writing by producing a word—a whole word that is filled with meaning.

Some children have considerable manual dexterity and they produce letters legibly and easily. Others can produce some letters but have difficulty with certain others. For example, Bill produced a legible *ill* but needed help with the capital *B*. Accordingly he practiced producing the upper case *B*. Steve had a fine *t* and a good *v*, but needed to master the large *S* and the letter *e*. Making a lower case *e* requires careful study for most children. Jack produced quite a good capital *J*, an excellent *c*, and a somewhat awkward *k*. The *a* he produced needed much adjustment. The lower-case *a* like the lower-case *e* proves a challenge to many children.

However, and this is a most important *however*, handwriting instruction was differentiated and individualized from the very beginning. Perhaps even more important, the teacher could praise each child for some letter formations. She could say to Bill, "That's a fine *i* and two very good *l*'s"; to Steve, "That's a great *t* and a good *v*"; to Jack, "That's a good *J* and an excellent *c;*" to Mary, "That's a good *M* and a fine *y*." To Bill she said, "Let's practice making capital *B*'s." Then she produced a capital *B* for him so that he could study it and copy it. She used lined paper that facilitated the production of both upper and lower case letters. Then she asked Bill to produce four letters in a *vertical* arrangement first and in a *horizontal* arrangement next.

B B B B B
B
B
B
B

Bill was not to produce more. She wanted him to concentrate intensely on these eight productions and to do as good a job as possible. Furthermore, as any experienced teacher can sustain, when the number of productions exceeds four or five the results become careless and the effort does more harm than good. Also, it seems easier to copy one under the other, or vertically, than to copy one alongside the other, or horizontally. It must be remembered that the intent is to study letter formation. To Steve she said, "Let's practice the capital *S* and the lower case *e*."

S S S S S   *e e e e e*
S   *e*
S   *e*
S   *e*
S   *e*

Because each child is working on his own needs, the incentive and willingness to try and try again is much greater than is otherwise true. Practice on specific letter forms focuses attention on specific needs. Children are quick to recognize how functional this kind of traning can be.

They see the value of a letter model. Because practice is individualized and localized to specific needs, it becomes very useful in acquiring and fixing legible writing habits.

Handwriting training once begun, usually on the first or second day of school, is practiced every day and often twice a day. Children respond to this instruction enthusiastically. The length of each practice session varies slightly but seldom exceeds 15 minutes.

When the children have fairly good control of the letters in their names, they start producing a friend's name or a neighbor's name. In a seating cluster of four the following names occurred: *Steve, Karen, Mitch,* and *Ronald.* By the time the children could produce legible writings of each name they had studied 15 of the 26 letters in the alphabet and had produced four upper case letters, *S, K, M,* and *R,* and 12 lower case letters, *t, e, v, a, r, n, i, c, h, o, l, d.* Moving from copying names to copying short sentences or phrases followed readily. The teacher could have a class or a group try their hand at producing, "My Mother is nice" a line taken from a dictated story, and copying it two or three times.

Extensive *copying from the chalkboard should be avoided.* It is difficult to do, it promotes carelessness, and, depending on where a child sits, it may be awkward. A sentence like "My Mother is nice" can be reproduced so that each child has a private copy. In brief, handwriting practice is done daily, focuses on individual abilities and needs, and avoids tedious copying.

Some school districts have developed their own manuscript alphabet and provide copies for each teacher and most times for each pupil. This being the era of easy reproducing of materials, many schools now provide each child with his own desk copy of the alphabet. In school districts that do not have their own form, almost any of the commercial forms can be used as a guide. For instance, the manuscript guide provided by the American English Book series[1] combines the best recent modifications of older, efficient styles of writing.

Of course, the teacher should plan instruction periods so that the children will have ample opportunity to acquire competence. They want to write legibly and with ease and speed; they are at the same time interested in producing neat and attractive papers.

Letters and Letter Order

Chapters 3 and 4 stressed the functional learning of sounds that letters can represent in a sound context or syllable and the names that identify the representing letters. The key idea is *functional learning.* By now, the

[1]Russell G. Stauffer et al., *American English Book,* Vols. I–III, (New York: Holt, Rinehart and Winston, 1960).

reader may have become keenly aware that functional learning best describes the LEA approach to learning. The words *work, operate,* and *function* all mean "to act in the way that is natural or intended," but *work* suggests success or effectiveness, *operate* stresses efficient activity, and *function* always implies activity that accomplishes the goal. To know letter names must be to know the purpose that letters serve or how they function in communication to represent sounds, and not just to be able to recite the alphabet by rote.

In speech the speaker produces sounds. When children come to school for the first time they possess sizable speaking vocabularies and tremendous phonological facility. They hear words spoken and can produce the sounds with astounding ease. It remains for the school to make them articulate about the use of specific letters to represent specific sounds and the blending of sounds into words. This is why learning auditory discrimination or the discrimination of sounds takes precedence in the initial stages of learning how letters represent sounds.

Transition from knowing letter sounds to knowing the letter names that represent the sounds in writing is readily accomplished, because once sounds have been learned, the letter names serve a practical purpose. Furthermore, letter names can be repeated orally as they appear in alphabetical order. Parroting the alphabet is an old-time way of showing off early erudition. Reciting any other list of 26 names would do. To know the sounds the letters represent, and their names, requires education that goes well beyond the alphabet parroting stage.

The order of letters within a word is what distinguishes one word from another. When beginning readers go beyond sight recognition of whole words, they become increasingly attentive to letter configuration and letter order as a means of recognition. Each act of auditory and auditory-visual discrimination requires a more precise distinguishing of letter features within words. As the reading vocabulary of children increases, they are required to note small differences of detail in order to distinguish one word from another, sometimes the distinction is as minute as wom*a*n and wom*e*n.

By the time children reach the stage where they begin to try their hand at creative writing, they have acquired a sensitivity to letter order in words. Each time they see a dictated story being written, they also see letters being formed and placed in a certain order. This is true from the very beginning when the teacher records the first dictated class story. The children see each letter being made and see the letters arranged in different order in each word. They see, too, the small white space between words.

When children select words from their word banks to organize sentences on their word card holders (see p. 119), attention is directed to some degree to letter order. When a word is needed to complete an idea, the pupil carefully observes the letter arrangement as the teacher writes the word. The same keen observation is made of the words reproduced by the teacher for a pupil's word bank. If a writing error or a typing error is made, the pupil sees how the teacher corrects the error so that the letter order or spelling will be correct. By the time pupils begin to write creatively, they have had considerable experience with letters and letter order in words. The first writing-spelling attempts are made with greater ease than might be thought.

Most important in all this is the *phonic training* the children have been receiving in consonant and vowel substitution. The more skilled they are at substituting letters and building new words in word families, the more apt they are to produce (or substitute) the right letter or the accepted letter order (spelling) when they are writing words. As a matter of fact, the spelling or producing of letters to represent a word is just about the best evidence a teacher can obtain of the effectiveness of her word attack teaching. Each error may be indicative of the need for additional very specific phonic teaching. That is to say, the phonological spelling attempts of individual pupils provide the best evidence of how successful the phonic program has been for the class.

GETTING STARTED

The discussion on creative word usage in Chapter 4 stated that children are very responsive to constructing ideas and building stories from the words in their own word banks. They spend hours of scholarly time in creative construction, and it seems that each success results in increased effort.

Daily construction soon has children wanting to use words that are not in their word banks. At first, they turn to the teacher for all needed words, and the semantic efficacy of this spelling and writing of new words results in superior retention. These are the words the children remember best, it seems, because they have filled recognized needs.

The need to turn to the teacher for a gap-filling word proves to be too long a wait for some, once they have gained confidence in creating sentences. As a result, they try to write a missing word themselves and thus make their first attempts at creating or producing a word through phonological encoding. The thrill of being a producer stimulates them to even further efforts. Of course, the alert teacher begins to urge pupils to try producing the words they need. Phonological independence can be activated by asking the children how they think a word begins and then asking them to write the word as they think it should be written. For instance, one child, Amy, needed the word "bright" to complete the sentence "Today is a bright day." She approached the teacher, Mr. Miller, for help and he recognized this request as another opportunity to advance the process of personal discovery, or learning by doing. Accordingly, he asked, "How do you think *bright* begins?" Amy hesitated; then he added, "It begins line *bring.*" With this clue she brightened and said, "*br.*" Mr. Miller pursued the advantage and asked, "What letter, a vowel, do you think comes next." She replied at once with *i.* "Good," said the teacher, confirming the choice of a vowel and praising her too. "Now try and finish the word." The child returned to her seat and wrote *brite.* Her phonological encoding gave evidence of a grasp of the consonant blend *br* phoneme-grapheme, a grasp of the long vowel *i,* and recognition that there was a *t* ending sound. The child learned or reconfirmed the knowledge that each word had a certain letter order, that letters represented sounds, and that they can be organized and assembled into a word. Her phonological action produced a letter order arrangement every bit as proper as the encoding adopted by society, *brite* and *bright.* Her producing *ite* told the teacher to provide discrimination training with words like *right, night,* and so on. For this child encoding a word had been an absorbing interest and a means of attaining a much desired goal.

This kind of teacher pacing provides opportunities for phonic growth and discovery, for developing a favorable attitude toward practicality of phoneme-grapheme relationships, and for stimulating curiosity about words. One discovery leads to another. As a result the *interest of pursuit* leads the children of their own accord to more and more encoding and the fascinating allure of writing words. The more words they encode phonologically, the wiser they become.

Usually producing these gap-filling words is the first attempt at encoding and producing in writing. Progress from supplying one word to encoding all the words follows rather naturally. And, as is universally true, once one or two children start writing or creating in writing, then others want to try too. Any alert teacher can determine the timing and thereby encourage others to create by producing ideas in writing. A word of caution, though. Be careful not to coerce children to try before they manifest this readiness.

Creative writing readiness is no mystery, it is not a wonderful discovery of pedagogy. It is simply a matter of systematic progress through personalized, differentiated, and structured instruction in phonics, in handwriting, and in creating ideas. Through pedagogical direction and organized use of (1) auditory discrimination, (2) visual-auditory discrimination, (3) consonant substitution, (4) vowel substitution, (5) the writing of upper and lower case letters, (6) the copying of words and short sentences, (7) the dictating of accounts, and (8) the use of the word bank words to create on a word card holder; do all this and *creative writing* is the natural outcome. Furthermore, the moment children engage in creating by writing, they further individualize themselves and become increasingly the distinctive beings that they are. These children live in school, and this is a change as significant as the one Copernicus introduced when the astronomical center shifted from the earth to the sun. In LEA instruction the child becomes the sun about which the actions, interactions, and transactions of education evolve and revolve.

Instructions to the children are simple and straight forward but require a teacher's integrity. Provide the children who are ready for creative writing with paper 12 x 18 inches in size. The top half of the paper should be unlined, providing space for drawing. The bottom half should have five lines with a ¾-inch space between and the two areas should be divided by a dotted line. Between each two of the five lines is another line dividing the ¾-inch space into two spaces each ⅛-inch wide. This kind of paper allows ample space for writing, the widest lines for capitals, the narrow ones for lower case letters. The space between the lines keeps a writing area open and uncluttered.

As was previously discussed, progress from oral dictation to writing is systematically developed in an integrated experience language-arts communication-oriented classroom. Many children in such an environment naturally begin to write their own accounts. Some children, however, do need closely supervised instruction in their first attempts at creative writing.

The teacher can assemble a group of not more than four or five children who seem ready for creative writing experiences but need close attention. Each child is given a piece of the prescribed paper. Then a topic and title are decided on. The teacher then directs the pupils to write the title on their own papers, encoding it with teacher assistance if needed, as was previously described. As with oral dictation, the teacher then focuses attention on the primary purpose of creative writing by asking the group or each child individually what they would like to say first about the topic, in this case, "Columbus." Ideas such as, "Columbus discovered America," or "Columbus had three ships," may be offered. Each child is then encouraged to put an idea, either his own or one of the group's, on his paper, encoding it word by word. It is important to note that the children or the child individually first decides on what he wants to say and then proceeds to write. It is sometimes necessary for the teacher to repeat the complete idea and then help each child individually. Sometimes, to get started, it is helpful to ask, "Do you wish to use one of the ideas" or "Do you have something of your own you wish to write?" When the child responds, the teacher can direct him to write the first word, show where to place it, and provide pacing help as needed. Then the teacher asks the child what the next word in his idea is and has him write it, being sure to leave a proper amount of space between words. It is important that from the very beginning, through praise and encouragement, the children learn that it is their *ideas,* vocabulary usage, and means of expressing these ideas that are of primary importance. Although the ability to encode

standard English spelling is a goal to be attained in later years, "correctness" is *not* now stressed or excessively rewarded by the teacher.

What to write about should never be an issue. A daily list of
suggested topics may be posted by the teacher, a daily list may be structured by the class, or children may just write about anything they wish.
The latter suggestion has a great deal of primacy. Writers are in many
ways alone. They coin their own ideas, select their own words, and are
brief or lengthy as they wish. This individualization carries over into what
to write about, too.

Quality handwriting is promoted largely because the children want
someone else to be able to read what they have written. Quality handwriting should be what is expected, but one must be cautious not to become
preoccupied with handwriting. The focus must be on the ideas a pupil
wants to record.

Even though phonics training continues on an intensive basis at a
time independent of creative writing time, children are likely to do much
phonological encoding. They are not phoneticians and most likely never
will be. However, they have acquired much phoneme-grapheme (letter-
sound) knowledge and this permits them to produce or encode words.
Gradually they learn an enormously important lesson about the English
language—*its encodings are highly irregular.* Thus they begin to realize
that the letter order used in dictionaries and in everyday writing has
become accepted even though it may not be the most appropriate or
efficient. Thus *bright* represents society's accepted letter order but is no
more "correct" than *brite*. Occasionally some word will stop a child tem-
porarily or even completely. When a temporary stop occurs the teacher is
provided with a teaching opportunity. The child can be paced phonologically, as described earlier. If a child is completely stymied, as with a word
like *yacht*, it is helpful to just supply the word. Above all, the children
must know that the teacher is available to help, not always immediately,
but soon.

While the children are writing, the teacher can move about the room
and offer aid as needed. Sometimes children are uncertain about what to
say next, and a question from the teacher such as "What will you say
next?" may help them bring out their ideas as they explain them orally.
Or a pupil may need just one word to complete an idea and the teacher
may say, "Is _____ what you want?" If it is the needed word, the
pupil will recognize it at once and acknowledge the help. Then, too, when
a pupil struggles too long with a spelling need, the teacher can help move
the child along. The teacher should be cautious, though, about creating
the attitude that a certain kind of adult perfection is being sought. What is
wanted is a perfection of pupil expression unhampered by adult standards. Improved performance will follow almost automatically.

The following writing resulted from a teacher's suggesting three top-

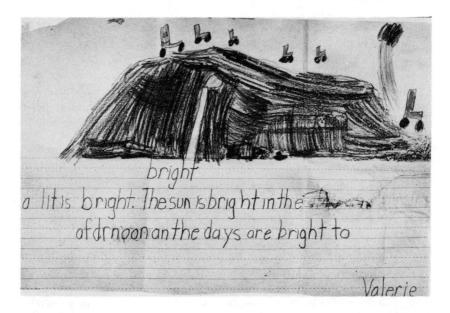

ics: *bright, different,* and *funny.* Valerie chose to write about *bright.* In Valerie's written production there are a number of astonishing plusses, and plusses should always be recognized first. She has a title, using one of the three suggestions, and it is of interest that she placed it appropriately. Of course, this was a word she could copy and this may, in part, account for the fact that she did not use an upper case *B.* Her first sentence starts on the left-hand side even though it does not begin with a capital *A.* The second sentence does start with a capital letter. *Light* is encoded phonologically as *lit* and apparently Valerie did not recognize the likely use of *ight,* as in *bright,* and transfer it to *light.* Remember, though, that most likely she copied the word *bright,* and if anything this is evidence of how little can be gained by copying. Copying is a rote performance focused only on copying. *Afternoon* was encoded phonologically as *afdrnoon* and reveals definite strengths—the *af* beginning and the *dr* for *ter,* the second syllable or sound unit. *Noon* has two *o*'s and this shows much recognition power. Invariably, children encode polysyllabic words sound unit by sound unit or syllable by syllable. This functional analysis of sounds and phoneme-grapheme representations displays a keen grasp of phonic-phonetic sound units. The word *and* as *an* may represent a speech pattern more than a faulty encoding. The use of *to* for *too* shows some strength in that she did not write *two.* Note, too, that Valerie inserted a period and did so at a fitting place. But perhaps of most significance are her ideas. First, she contrasts a light's brightness with the sun. Her next sentence is of compound-complex structure and is a gem of an expression.

Now take a look at Valerie's handwriting. Note that words are well spaced. Individual letters are well spaced and uniform in structure. Her execution of the letters *r, a,* and *e* is exceptionally well done. The letters with stems both up and down are consistently distinct.

All in all, why should I have made this labored analysis for the reader? The obvious fact is that there is really no mystery about it; no wonderful discovery of pedagogy. It is simply that we have children here who are intensely active and the task of instruction is to give their activities direction. Valerie and others were given the opportunity to realize an ambition, to gain discipline and perseverance, and to draw on their recently acquired know-how.

Valerie's drawing deserves examination, too. Notice the sky and the sun casting its rays on cars crossing the mountain. Across the mountain and in the darkness away from the sun, Valerie has a huge street light to illuminate the way for cars.

> Piaget sees cognitive growth as a slow process during which a child ... becomes more and more able to rely on thought as he builds mental structures of time, space, number, causality and logical classes.... Piaget calls this a de-centering process, because it involves becoming progressively less tied to the "here and now" [2, p. 58].

Valerie's drawing is a good example of this increasing range and flexibility of a child's mind. She was able to put herself in different places and showed awareness of the variety of relationships that can exist between people, objects, and events. She dealt not only with spatial relationships but also with scale.

On the whole, she showed an astonishing sensitivity to the concept of brightness in the world about her. She recorded her understanding in a detailed and varied drawing and in language. Both symbol systems help tell a great deal about the kind of person Valerie is.

Now examine Randy's account about the theme "Different." Note the encoding power. All 12 of the different words are produced according to their accepted letter order. The sentences are complete thought units and are properly punctuated. His handwriting skill is superb. The drawing is his *way of representing* differences and quite clearly constituted an experience for him.

The delight of a roomful of Valeries and Randys is immeasurable. Each child has a unique way of expressing ideas that can serve as personal identification almost as much as a signature or a fingerprint. In short, even this early in a writing career, a style of writing is evident. In instructional circumstances in which creativity in writing is fostered, an atmosphere of eagerness to write prevails. Writing becomes a pedagogical privilege and not a curriculum-prescribed task. The pride of authorship swells in each bosom. Each child produces his own version of a theme or topic or experience, and it is ever astounding how each pupil in a class produces an original interpretation.

Of course all this takes time: first, time to introduce a stimulus; then time to write and create and illustrate; and finally, time to share. Sharing time seems always to be the apex of achievement. Children are eager to share what they have done. Various ways of sharing can be planned—whole class, an entire pod, a group, a neighbor or buddy, and displays. Individual work can be put together into a book for the library table. Sharing may be done at set periods of time or during spare waiting moments in the school day.

PROMOTING CREATIVE WRITING

Once children have started to write, it becomes their preoccupation. They take great delight in writing and never seem able to do enough of it. (Some children arriving on an early bus spend their preschool time writing. Some want to write at recess and need to be told to run and play with the class.) Of course, the constant feedback provides instant gratification. Every letter, word, and sentence that is written is seen the moment it is done and can be shown to others.

Interestingly enough, drawings take a new look and new meaning. Somehow, because the children have produced the story, they become more attentive to the illustration. Drawings become more detailed and more supportive of what is said. Children seem to sense a close bond between the two mediums of expression and, therefore, use them jointly.

A paper, pencil, and crayon supply center should be set up to which the children can go any time during the school day. Paper is cheap. Pupils should not be allowed to waste it, but neither should they be restrained.

Paper of different sizes (15 x 12, 8 x 11, 3 x 7, and so on) should be provided, as well as newsprint 18 x 12, as already described. This encourages children to be selective and to think about writing as serving different purposes. The larger sizes of paper permit larger letters, a longer story, and a big picture. The smaller sizes of paper allow for accounts of various lengths and smaller writing. The children are responsive, too, to the demand to adapt letter writing to different paper size and line width. The smallest sheets may be used for notes to say thank you, extend an invitation, ask for help, keep a personal diary, take home, and so on. The larger sheet of paper also lends itself very well to being placed on an easel or corkboard or to being placed on the floor, where at times buddies can write a story together.

Even though children will write, write, write and find a multitude of things to write about, motivation must be planned. Selected stimuli direct the children to material within the curriculum—science activities and experiments, health activities, social studies, art, music, and crafts, and library and literature experiences. Numerous opportunities are available that can evoke marvelous pupil response. Children seem to be more candid when they write than when they talk; perhaps the aloneness of the writing act invites this. Stimuli selected by the teacher may include current events from newspapers, magazines, radio, and television. Children respond readily to writing articles for a class or school newspaper or a magazine. Here is a long list of topics most commonly written about.

animals	television	insects
pets	favorite food	parades
fish	picnics	school building
toys	swimming	school playground
Mother	public playground	school room
Father	neighbors	teacher
sisters	friends	desk
brothers	church	library
home	synagogue	school library
breakfast	uncles	librarian
dinner at home	aunts	picture books
barber	cousins	favorite books
beautician	grandparents	principal
dentist	best friend	principal's office
doctor	trips	snowman
illness	museum	snowballs
cars	post office	sledding
airplanes	dictionary	ice skating
airport	encyclopedia	roller skating
trains	favorite stories	birthdays

school secretary
school nurse
school custodian
art teacher
music teacher
physical
  education
  teacher
school cafeteria
school cook
lazy days
Sunday
Saturday
weekend
classroom art
  corner
classroom build-
  ing corner
Washington's
  birthday
Easter
Memorial Day
rivers
oceans
mountains
caves
ice cream stand
hamburger stand
drugstore
grocery store
shoe repair man
police
patrol cars
school patrol
lights
fairs

fairy tales
folk tales
games adults play
games children
  play
city buses
school bus
bus driver
leaves
trees
Labor Day
Father's job
Mother's job
family car
family camper
garden
flowers
lawn mowing
snow shoveling
Yom Kippur
Flag Day
Veterans Day
Election Day
first air flight
pilgrims
Thanksgiving
Indians
Columbus
John Smith
Martin Luther
  King
The President
winter
Christmas
Christmas trees
Christmas toys

Halloween
ghosts
auditorium
other teachers
other classes
rainy days
snowy days
hot days
cold days
Christmas gifts
Hanukkah
New Year's Day
Valentine Day
Lincoln's birthday
Canada
Mexico
other countries
Miss America
Miss Teen-Age
  America
comic papers
magazines
trouble
help
guessing
detectives
mystery
Dad's speeding
science
  experiments
vacation
summer
spring
night

As was noted in the section on the motivation of experience stories, field trips should be thought of as only one means of motivation. Field trips have the danger of overwhelming of young minds with more new ideas than they can easily assimilate. Trips should focus on one or two aspects of an experience, and before they are made pupils should review what they already know or think they know about what they will see. For a trip to a zoo, for example, a talk or a list of animals that may be seen should be prepared. Particulars known about animals can be listed; pupils can speculate about the height of a giraffe, for example, and the length of his neck and legs and so on. Contrasts can be drawn by speculating about whether or not a giraffe could stand up in a classroom or in a gymnasium or walk under a freeway or expressway overpass. Field trips, to be useful, should be dealt with wisely.

CONCEPT DEVELOPMENT

Of all the forms of development the acquisition of concepts seems, indeed, to be the most fascinating. Not enough can be said about how we acquire behaviors ranging from random activity to logical reasoning, or, to state it differently, how we proceed from concrete and factual criteria for decision making, to abstract and logical. Basically, concept formation consists of the perception of relationships among stimuli, as one author (17) put it, or between constituent-part processes, as others put it (5). Bruner et al. go on to say that the "working definition of a concept is the network of inferences that are or may be set into play by an act of categorizing" (5, p. 244). James Britton put it this way "as a child learns words in association with the objects of his environment he sorts those objects into categories: those categories are complexes, but since the naming will be for the most part in accord with social usage—the uses he has heard in others—these complexes will be pseudo concepts" (3, p. 211). But over the course of time the ability to think in concepts will be achieved and symbolically organized experiences will grow.

When a concept becomes a part of a system, as Vygotsky says, it can become subject to conscious and deliberate control. It can also become, as he puts it, a generalization and become a subordinate or superordinate concept.

Even though vocabulary and concepts are closely related, they are not identical. When a child has added a word to his spoken vocabulary (helicopter) and in turn to his word bank, it does not follow that he has acquired a systematized concept. Not only are there concrete-abstract differences but also superordinate and subordinate differences. Even so, words are the coin of the concept realm and help one gain admission. They represent a first step in the concept attainment process. Words are the principal medium of thought and the tactical instrument of instruction. Words are the principal medium for talk and for writing, and their varied use in different contexts helps extend and refine meanings.

Children love to play with words and the multiple meanings of words. Almost everyone has completed the sentence "Happiness is _____" for such ideas as "Happiness is an ice-cream cone," "Happiness is my baby brother," "Happiness is when the birds sing in the morning." Children can be invited to make this kind of response with many words and sentences.

Multiple meanings of words invite reaction, too: *run*—to go fast, run free, sail before a wind, race, melt as wax; *snap*—to close the jaws suddenly, grasp at bait, break a twig, talk back, snap fingers, crack a whip; *stand*—to be on your feet, take a position of firmness; a small place of business; *comb*—a device for adjusting the hair, the crest on a chicken or turkey; to search; *double*—twice as many, a double bed, a twin; to double over; *dress*—to put on clothes, put a room in order, arrange the hair, prepare a chicken for cooking; a lady's garment.

Opposites evoke varied responses: *hard-soft, big-little, ugly-pretty, high-low, sweet-sour, wet-dry.* Noun-verb usages invite other reactions: *foot*, as feet and to go on foot; *fill*, as material used to fill a hole and to fill something; *tie*, as a necktie and to bind. Words like *help, play, different, funny,* and *nose* invite ready response. All a teacher need do is write *help* on the board and invite children to write "help" stories.

"How I feel about _____" is always a good starter for a story. This encourages children to reveal their own opinions and feelings and can be rewarding as children discover how different pupils feel differently about milk, for instance, and why they feel as they do. Such topics as hate, love, honesty, safety patrol, war, and peace evoke interesting and sometimes startling responses.

Thus, in a refreshing, stimulating, and fruitful way, children's concepts, as a product of their thoughts, can be extended and refined by showing them how to notice the structure of concepts, both the perceptually obvious and the not too obvious, how to notice similarities and differences, relationships, novelties, levels, hierarchies, order, and so on. In addition, concepts in the content of daily living can be dealt with as concepts of space, time, number, people, humor, and so on.

The reading that children do from the very beginning, when they turn to the classroom library table to "see and read" illustrated story books or to locate words learned in the dictated stories, provides a vital source of concept development. When the children begin locating their word bank words in books, newspapers, magazines, and funnies, they are adding a new rich means of enlarging their concepts. Dictionaries, encyclopedias, and other similar sources provide maps, graphs, and illustrations that can extend and refine ideas. Most important, however, is the fact that the actual reading that children do provides a ready source of ideas for creative writing. Pupils start writing stories similar to those they read or have had read to them. They write their own fairy tales, myths, mysteries, plays, reports, descriptions, experiment accounts, and so on.

INITIAL CREATIVE WRITING EXAMPLES

The following examples are representative of what can be expected from a typical first-grade class when they start "creative writing." The topics they write about are of an immediate firsthand personal nature and illustrate how many different things children find to write about. Examine with care the writings reproduced photographically. They provide authentic productions for analysis. All the samples show the children's encoding ability or- their command of phoneme-grapheme relationships. Already they are astonishingly able phonologicians.

It must be remembered that each production reflects a great deal of persistent effort. Time was required as well as encouragement to write and encode. Teacher pacing on the encoding of some words helped establishe the how-to-do-it process *Copying must be scrupulously avoided.* Copying is nonproductive. Copying requires no thinking. Copying is contravening to sound phonic instruction. In brief, copying is a "no-no."

My brthr
His name is Eddie. He is three years old. He lics toplay wth crs and trucs.
John

The Fir
My hos got brnd don. My toys and my clos got brnd up to.
Alison

Philip has a Puampcinn. It is big.
Timmy

Stop and Go
Stop wen The lite is red. I Go wen the lite is green.
Katv

Wndr Wmn
I wish I wz Wndr Wmn. I will bet up the nzzis. I will jump of the mpir stat billding.
Denise

My New Baby Brohr
His nam is Michael Ray. He don't lik to lay down. He is alrges to milk.
Billy

I walk to school. Mommy gos nd kis my father.
Teresa

The first dictations that children do, especially the individual dictations, represent an almost endless source of instructional opportunities. This is even more true of the "creative writings." Because this is so, I shall elucidate some of them.

Handwriting

It is important, of course, that children acquire skill in readily producing legible handwriting. But if one needed to contrast this with the importance of acquiring skill in language usage, it would be of minor significance. Beth's work shows good production of 18 lowercase letters; some —such as her *a, o, m, n, s, t, f*—are excellent, others—such as her *r, c,* and *d* need further practice. The uppercase *I* and *B* are well done. So for Beth there is much opportunity for praise and for further instruction.

Betsey's writing is excellent. She produced 22 different lowercase letters and two uppercase letters. Many of her letters are very well structured and require only the refinement that writing and more writing can produce. Some of the letters can be singled out for immediate refinement through careful examination—the *m, r, e, u,* for instance. So she has her work cut out for her.

Betsev

I am a girl and I is six. I brought some book for the children to read. I live in a house

10-16

I just had a shoort har aot a wumincat it for me and I like it shoort the wumins name was ine. Beth

143

the nedl. We
got a nedl. it
had four nedls.
the dotrs name is
dotr Ralins. Katy 11-2-65

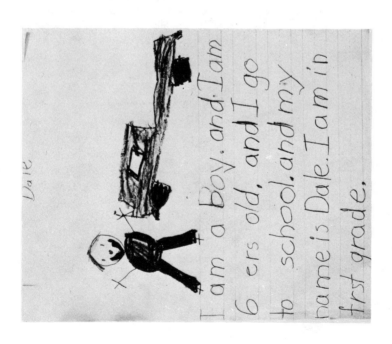

Dale

I am a Boy. and I am
6 ers old. and I go
to school. and my
name is Dale. I am in
frst grade.

Encoding

Examination of the encoding power of each of the children shows much strength. As described earlier, the children are urged to encode words as "best they can" using their phonological knowledge. Some respond to this immediately and eagerly. Some need to be paced through a word or two or three. And some need frequent pacing. Stress is placed on the production of ideas and not on producing accepted letter order.

An analysis of John's writing shows that he encoded according to American-English convention 10 different words: *my, his, is, Eddie, he, three, old, to, play, and.* One can only speculate about how he produced these words because one cannot tell whether he recalled by rote memorization of letter order (this is not likely), by visual imagery, or by phoneme-grapheming his way through. It is likely that he did the latter two (a combination of visual-auditory imagery) because the words are high-frequency words and he has heard and spoken them many times and seen them often in print, both in his dictated accounts, his word bank, and his wide reading experiences.

At this stage in reading instruction the best evidence a teacher can get of the effectiveness of her phonic analysis skill is the ability of children to encode phonologically. Encoding requires (1) knowledge of sounds a letter or combination of letters may represent in different sound contexts or syllables; (2) knowledge of letter names; (3) knowledge of letter shapes, both upper and lower case; and (4) ability to write legibly. This knowledge is acquired functionally, as described, and not by rote memorization. It is the *purpose* the letters serve—their shapes and their sounds—that facilitates their retention, recall, and use.

Even more significant is the ability of the children to use their knowledge of letters and the sounds they represent in new situations (words) and different combinations (blends, digraphs, diphthongs, prefixes, suffixes, silent letters). The positive transfer of letter-sound knowledge involves in each instance a *problem-solving* situation. Letter-sound or grapheme-phoneme knowledge must be highly generalized and transferred productively from word to word. Whenever the encodings are the same as society has declared them, even though there is much disagreement among phonetic-phonic specialists (7), the productions represent abstractions from the products of responding. In brief, such encoding is a measure of a child's ability to link sounds and letters used to represent sounds to *solve new encoding or spelling problems.* The test of successful learning is the *ability to use what is learned in a new situation.* Thus each encoding attempt provides evidence of transfer of phonic training knowledge with known words to the production of unknown words or successful problem solving.

A reexamination of John's production supports the preceding analysis of encoding problem solving and the transfer of knowledge. His encoding of *brother* as *brthr* shows a condition that occurs so frequently at this stage that it could almost be declared as characteristic—he did not use vowels. One can only speculate about why this occurs over and over again. Apparently at this stage of progress consonants play a key phonic role even though vowel variances have also been taught. More important, perhaps, is the fact that John produced the *br* blend and the *th* digraph influenced by the *r* sound. These productions by John represent quite keen phoneme-grapheme analysis and show that functional phonic teaching has been done. It also shows that more refinement is necessary in order to produce *brother*. Needed is more sound discrimination with syllable or sound units ending in *th*, with medial vowels, and with syllables or sound units ending in *er*. This to be followed by visual-auditory discrimination.

His encoding of *name* as *nam* shows that John did recognize and produce a medial vowel sound. Needed is more opportunity to note how many words are influenced phonetically by an *e* ending and how short vowels serve.

Supplying *yers* for *years* also shows much power. He produced the letter representing the beginning sound *y* and the ending sounds *rs*. He realized the need for a medial vowel and chose *e* probably from some grasp of *er* endings but not enough to have been effective in *brother*. It is more likely that a visual image of the word influenced his production. Needed, of course, is more experience with medial vowel digraphs.

The word *likes* produced as *lics* shows John well on the way to establishing that the letter *c* can represent the sound of *k* as in *can* and the sound of *s* as in *city*. The words *with* produced as *wth* and *cars* as *crs* again show much encoding power and specific needs. In *trucs* for *trucks*, as has already been said, John shows a need for further discrimination of sounds represented by *c*. Again he produced the fitting vowel. Thus John's production has provided specific diagnostic evidence so that additional good teaching could follow. In other words, provided here is superb evidence to support the instruction-learning truth that "*all good teaching is diagnostic.*"

Other highly significant factors evidenced by these creative writings are that (1) reading has been taught as a facet of language and not isolated from its primary purpose—to communicate; (2) phoneme-grapheme skill acquisition has been accomplished in functional auditory and auditory-visual discrimination circumstances; (3) because instructional items were chosen from the productions of the children and then the selected children grouped for instruction, they learned to set up expectations and make phoneme-grapheme encoding predictions; (4) the human eye and ear have discriminating power and this capability can be channeled into worthwhile purposes; (5) in childhood we take on the classification of experience embodied in our mother tongue; (6) different levels of generalization makes possible the higher forms of thought processing, including what may be called "reasoning"; (7) this basic training in discrimination, recognition, and decision making provides an essential foundation for the higher thought processes; (8) the children's world of representation is becoming a trustworthy storehouse of data that involves elementary value judgments and has predictive value to the degree that it is retrievable; (9) their looking, listening, and producing has permitted the children to perceive selectively, to focus, because they engage in writing with expectations; (10) what is organized through various means of language-type representation helps each child construct a phoneme-grapheme world that is functional and can be refined in the light of further experiences and instruction.

At this point the reader should be able to make a comparable analysis of Alison's production and that of Denise. If this is done before going on, then what follows can become an affirmation of the insights acquired. Alison encoded according to accepted letter order (spelling) 7 of a total of 12 different words, or a 58 percent achievement. It must be remembered that this positive percentage is achieved without any formal spelling instruction. Another interesting condition is evident in Alison's encoding effort that is very characteristic of almost all children at this stage. Once she had solved the encoding problem for *burned* by producing *brnd* she produced it that same way a second time. For the time being she had solved the problem "reason-ably" well and was satisfied. However, as is also an incredible corollary, a day or a week later, if faced with the need to encode this same word (burned) again, most likely she would have produced *burned* and not *brnd*. Why is this so? For a number of reasons; Alison may see the word *burned* encoded as *burned* elsewhere and compare her effort of *brnd;* another child reading her account may ask for help with *brnd* or may provide help. Thus *editorial* effort enters into the writing effort almost from the very beginning and does so on a "discovery learning" basis. Encoding of *fire* as *fir* shows a need for help involving final *e*, but shows great strength in the production of the beginning *f*, the medial vowel *i*, and the *r*. The word *house* as *hos* also shows power in initial consonant production, with some recognition of vowel diphthong because she used an *o*, and with the *s* ending. Encoding *down* and *don* shows good production power and the need for further focusing on vowel circumstances. The word *clos* for *clothes* shows initial consonant power extending to the blend *cl*, medial vowels, and some recognition of endings.

Denise produced seven words with society's accepted letter order out of a total of 15 different words for almost a 50 percent success average. Again, as others have shown, early encodings are often done without vowels—*wndr, wmn, wsh, wz*. Once produced, *wndr, wmn* stay the same. The production of *nzzis* for *Nazi* is quite an achievement as is *mpir* for *empire*. The words *state* as *stat* and *building* as *billding* shows growing control of phoneme-grapheme codifications and recognition of the suffix *ing* ending.

As a result of many creative writing opportunities (almost daily), *repetition* becomes productive. Written communication momentum provides the motivation. The numerous encoding requirements furnish both the practice and the contiguity that round out the functional use of basic learning laws. Behavior patterns are being established and refined and result in permanent change. Rereading provides immediate feedback and priceless self-rewarding. When others read a pupil's materials human ego plays an important role as aspiring social needs are satisfied. These consequences affect character, confirm habits, and produce tangible results. Thus the dynamic force of creating speaks concretely of motive and act, will and deed, and the disposition to write establishes a tendency to want to act or write again and again.

Each creative writing opportunity provides conditions of reinforcement: immediacy, frequency, acceptability, peer or social approval as well as teacher approval. The encoding opportunities are numerous, yet each child can set his own pace. The innumerable opportunities to produce phoneme-grapheme associations circumvent the necessity at this stage to learn by rote discrete spelling responses for each discrete spelling confrontation. *Generalization*, not rote memory, becomes the key factor in the acquisition of spelling ability.

Some people, usually outsiders, question teaching children to apply phonic knowledge to encoding in writing. It seems strange indeed that anyone should question such practical actions. There appears to be a conflict that Piaget labels as dialectical: "according to whether one emphasizes the creative role of adult social life, which leads to a corresponding on the transmission of knowledge by the teacher, or whether one concentrates on the no less constructive role of action . . . upon the activities of the student himself" (12, p. 67).

The basic purpose of this writing is to have children realize that they can communicate with one another in writing, much as they do in talking. Thus writing provides means whereby, as Piaget puts it, the two most central truths of the psychology of cognitive functions develops. Intellectual operations or cognitive processes proceed from (1) *effective action* and include (2) a *social dimension*.

Children invariably respond propitiously to writing, much as they do when they learn to talk. If, though, their early talking attempts were stopped to correct each error of pronunciation, syntax, or semantics, children would become utterly confused. Similarly, if early writing attempts were "corrected" for purism in spelling, in syntax, grammar, and semantics most children would never write. Teaching must be geared to practical, constructive, functional actions so that the efficacy of written communication may be grasped.

Children *develop a spelling conscience* in a natural way. When writings are exchanged and pupils discover that some of their encoding cannot be decoded they begin to realize that the medium (writing) is intended to convey a message (social communication). This is one of the ways pupils learn to be increasingly more attentive to society's accepted letter order encoding. In addition, when they see words in print and note that their encodings differ, they also realize the society's letter orders are different and frequently not phonetically consistent or regular. This beginning of a *spelling conscience* is a teacher's delight and a scholar's boon. Pupils want to encode words so that they can be read, and that is precisely why society develops and accepts certain letter orders for words (7). Attempts at *editing* begin early and spellings are changed or omitted words are inserted.

Syntax, Grammar, and Punctuation

A common critique of many children's first writings is that they use *and* over and over again to connect ideas and sentences. It is true that on occasion children in the LEA program do use these sentence constructions but only to a limited degree. Reexamination of the creative writings reproduced in this chapter show only three instances when a sentence was started with *and*.

The syntax or pattern of word formation in the various sentences shown is exceedingly good. First attempts at creative writing usually abound with *T*-unit type sentences (9)—subject, predicate, and object. This, of course, is acceptable. Even so, there is much early evidence of going beyond the T-unit structure by adding qualifying or elaborating expressions or having a compound subject or object. "My toys and my clos got brnd up to," "He liks to play with crs and trucs." "I brought some book for the children to read." Note the sensitivity to subject-predicate relationships and tense agreement of nouns and verbs. Adjective qualifiers are used and reflect pupil judgments about the nature and degree of things. Capital letters are used and in many instances appropriately. Because children attack encoding largely by sound units or syllables, on occasion they capitalize each syllable—barBeKu.

Periods are used and in most instances correctly so. Children know when they have finished an idea. One child, when asked how he knew when to use a period, replied in an annoyed way, "When I've said something." When children talk they know how to modulate their voices at the end of a declarative sentence or a question or a command. They soon display a similar response to written expressions. The reader is urged to remember that at this point this discussion has focused only on first attempts at creative writing and that no formal teaching of syntax, grammar, or punctuation has been done. On the other hand, the dictations the children have done have provided a superb foundation for the writing of ideas. In the dictations, as one can readily see by reexamination of the samples, the sentences used are invariably complete and show good use of vocabulary and syntax.

Sequence of Ideas

Because the writings reproduced here are recountings of personal experiences rather than attempts at producing an "imaginative story," sequence of ideas seems to result from the natural order of events. Recounting an experience starts with what happened first, then second, and so on: (1) my house burned down, (2) my toys and clothes burned too. As stated earlier, when dictated experience accounts were discussed, participating in a firsthand experience promotes orderly restating of events. Since no plot development is required and no punch line has to be held in mind, the order of ideas is sequenced almost naturally by circumstances.

Illustrations or Representations

Drawing reveals not only artistic ability but also self. The medium provides a means of expression, a way of projecting concepts by form symbolism rather than by words. Notice the use of detail, color, and plot setting in the illustrations reproduced. Notice, too, the manner in which space is used.

Writings Through the Year

The writing entitled *Fall Levs* by Iris was produced on November 1. By this date she had produced a number of writings in a steady flow. Her pencil seemed to flit across the paper. Her encoding proceeded at a steady pace because she had caught the "hang of things." Seldom did she make long pauses to ponder a phoneme-grapheme possibility, nor did she ask for help. Her word bank contained well over 100 words, arranged alphabetically. She was achieving excellently in the discrimination, recognition, and recall of words. The number of words she knew at sight far exceeded the number usually found in the preprimers of any basic reader series.

Pupils are *not* allowed to copy words from their word banks when doing creative writing. However, they are allowed to add words to the bank taken from their creative writing. In this instance Iris added to her bank: *fall, leaves, orange, turn,* and *ground.* However, a word to be added to a word bank has to be produced with the accepted letter order.

Three of the words (*fall, orange, ground*) could be added by Iris; but *leaves* and *turn* required teacher help. It might be thought that seeing (leaves) the standard encoding for *levs* might distress a child, but this does not occur. Children love the encoding challenge and frequently exclaim, as Iris did, about *levs*, "I was close."

fall levs   11-1
fall levs are fun to plae in. Sumare brown. and
sumare orange. and sum levs trn color. in fall
levs fall to the ground.

Iris

The following typical accounts were also written in November. Most were accompanied by a drawing.

Rake LeVs   11-9
I Rake up my Nxt dr nabrs. I get the
LeVes and Put the LeVesin the
Basket.

Tom

I playt with my friend. We playt on
Sunday. We like to play. Ann likes to
play with me. We playt with a cat.

Monica

My Ded Cat   11-9
Ones I Hade a Cat. He was white and
yellow. One night my father come
Fame my grandfathers house. Wenn
my Father Come home Fame my
grandfathers house he said Ruste is
Ded.

David

We went to the book Far. then we got
som books. Ther wer som big and
Little ones. I bot som last night. Then I
took thm home. Then I Read my book.
We will go to the far agen.

Jody

The following accounts show the progress of Darrell over a period of months. His first creative writing attempt was made on November 1 and tells about his watching TV. A "translation" of it follows in parentheses.

I wds the wid wsdn   11-1
wst on T Thn I wds OK Kobr
(I watch the wild western first on TV.
Then I watched O.K. Cracker)

Big Red   12-3
Big Red was a dog. Big Red won first pris. And
he plled a boy in a pind. I like Big Red. And he
was on a Movie.

Are School Room   12-10
We wrok in are school Room. We Read. We
have a tree in are Room and we decorate it. It
has Santa Claus and Candy Cans and staking on
ar Christmas tree and it has Pretty balls and it
has Prasits.

I got a foot ball and a   1-6
walkie-talkie for Christmas. And an record
player.

Me   2-10
I am tall. I do good work. I have blue eyes. I have
brown hair. I can count to 100 hundred. And I am
seven year old. And I am a boy. I am in the first
grade. The End.

Where I Like to Go   3-7
I Like to go to West Cheder a lot becus it is one
hundred mils away frum here. I go thaer becus it
has a big hill.

The Three Bears   4-18
The Three bears live in the woods. Thare was
father bear and mother bear and baby bear.
Thare house was mad out of wood. And thare
was a girl named Golde lox. She went to the
three bears house when the bears wer away
from the house because they wer wateing for
thare pareg to ceool. The End.

Darrell's writings are typical of a first grader. His first attempts reflect some sensitivity to letters and the sounds they represent as well as to letter order in words, word order in ideas, and idea order in an account. The encoding is mostly phonological. The titles vary considerably and show a wide range of interests. The quality of his sentences and his idea-order presentation shows constant improvement. His encoding according to standard orthography is increasingly more accurate. Whenever he meets a word or an idea that he cannot spell, he encodes it phonologically and goes on with his story writing. Note how he spelled *Goldilocks* (*Golde lox*) and *porrideg to cool* (*pareg to ceool*).

Darrell's handwriting showed marked improvement through December, too. After that, his skill was such that all his writings were equally good. By April, he was using space more economically by making smaller letters and spacing words more compactly. Darrell's own style of handwriting was being acquired and refined.

The writings presented here are only a sample of all the writing Darrell did during the year. Once children start creative writing, they seem to do it almost constantly. They want to write at home, at lunch time, at recess, during milk break. Interestingly enough, most parents cooperate when the children write at home by not spelling for them or putting words in their mouths. Most of the home-written stories are just like the ones done in school.

The following represent the range of interests and skills of typical first-grade creative writing from the end of October through the middle of March. The writing by Dawn is from November 3, Robby's from November 15, Louise's from December 7.

I like a trl to swim funny. Trl a funny Shell is a Trls house. A Trl is fun.

(trl = turtle)

Dawn

The praed
yesterday i was in a Praed. And i was in Amdlis niaber A. 54. And my papap was draving the Amblis.

Robby

(Amblis = ambulance; niaber = number)

Cismsy
I Horp It sts to snow. Cismsy is olms hre. We get sim toys. I like santo cls and I am shr he likes me to. My gil fan was sak.

Louise

In the classroom in which Louise was a pupil, her story about Christmas was typical. With a theme such as Christmas, one might think that a great deal of uniformity of writing and encoding might occur, but this was not true even with so dramatic a stimulus. On this particular day, December 7, 11 different encodings were used by the children in a class of 31: *Cismsy, clsmis, Crsms, Crsmss, Cesmus, Csim, Maerry Cismsy, Crhrimise, Cismisy, Marry Casmiss,* and *Christmas.*

Children write their own ideas and do their own encoding when urged to do so. Timmy, the boy who had spelled Christmas correctly, explained that he had been using the word at home and that was why he knew how to write it. On December 22, Katy also spelled it correctly. The five stories following hers were all written in January.

O Tannenbaum
We sing O Tannenbaum. It is a German song. A man named Luther cut down a Christmas tree and took it home and shoed his wif and children how the stars shined on it. O Tannenbaum is a folk song. The Germans were the first pepl to have a Christmas tree.

Katy

We were exspeermiting. We put a pensl on the water and it floted. We trieed some roocks and all the roocks sank.

Erik

Bright Snow-White Snow
I like snow it is fun. I like to make snowman. It is fun too. You can make a snow fort. It is fun too. And I like to go down a hill.

Karen

After School

After school I go home on bus thirteen. And when I get home I get dresst. And when I get dresst I go out and play. And I play in the farist. And I play in my fort. And today after school I am going to play with my dog. And after I play with my dog. I am going to play with my babby. And after I play with my babby. I am going to go to my freiend's house And when I get back from my freiend's house. I am going to play with my toys. And then I will eat my super And then I will woshst tv. Brian Smith

March 22

Clowds

I like clowds. Clowds give us rian sometimes. When rian comes down we have gray clowds. Clowds help us. We shuld be glad that God maked clowds.

Robin March 14

Our Volkswagon

We are going to get a Volkswagon. It will be blue outside and the inside will be white. Our Grandaddy is going to give us it. The Volkswagon is up in Washington. I am going to ride back with Mommy. I like to ride in the Volkswagon. My daddy can go to the plant esyer.

Mar 9 1967

When We Went to The Art Museum

My Daddy and my Mommy and me went to the
art museum. One man drew a lot of pictures. I
bote five little baskets when we went to the art
museum. It was fun at the art museum. We go to
stors sometimes. The mans name was Andrew
Wyeth. My sisters and brother stay at my
Mom-moms.

Anne

Second Billy Goat Gruff

Second Billy Goat Gruff is a goat. He is a little bit
tall. He has a small beard. Second Billy goat gruff
has small black horns. He has a brown fur. He
has brown huffs. He has a little brown tail. His
family is Big Billy goat gruff and Little Billy goat
gruff. I like it because Second Billy goat gruff got
over the bridge and because they got all the
green grass they wanted.

David

Hansel and Gretel

Hansel and Gretel and thair father were very
happy untill thair father had to marry a woman.
And she was called a Stepmother. She did't like
children. So that night the Stepmother and thair
father were taking. And Hansel and Gretel were
a sleep. Thair Stepmother and father made a
loud noise and woke them up.

Karen

This is a pretty boat. It is all different colours. It
can carry lots of people. It Travelseverywhere. It
takes many people to all different coutrys.

Brigitte

These two were produced in February and March:

George Washington

George Washington Father was name Frank. He
was our first Presudent. He choped down the
chery tree and George telled the trth to his father.
His Father put the hatchit up in the closit. He
fought the British.

David

My Mommy

My Mommy is pretty. She has blue eyes and
brown hair. Her name is Arinda. She is thirty-one
years old. She is nice. She spanks me
sometimes because I need it but when she is in a
good moond she doesnt spank me. She is
supertishesh because when she drops a comb
she steps on it before she picks it up. She is silly.
Yesturday she went out side in the snow with me.

She looks like my aunt. She is the most
wounderfulest mother I've ever had.

Jean

The following stories were obtained from children attending an independent school. Note that they are similar to what has already been shown. The range of interests is varied and fitting. Marked changes occur across the year, as is to be expected.

Once I went on a helucopter. I got to go up in
the air. I saw the impiyer stat bilding. The
impiyer stat bilding is vaire, vaire big. The
helucopter is neyt insiyde. I like to ride in a
helucopter. My hole famley went up on the
impiyer stat bilding. We looked down. It was
vaire, vaire far down and then we went back to
the houtele.

Bobby

12-17

Christmas day is a loving Day. Its a present for
God. Its a present for people. Christmas is like
tricker treating. And avry body liks that and I do
to. Its nice to have Christmas.

Billy

Billy's Christmas story goes on and on in this vein for four more pages and in doing so is representative of what some children do. Some not only write frequently, but also go on and on. An advantage of this kind of freedom and encouragement to produce is the opportunity for children to show preferences, inclinations, and aptitudes.

Velentine day   2-9

Velentine day is for loveing and giving to othr
people. You are shoing good manrs There are 1
days of Velentine. Velentine is on February 14.
and people like it and so do i to.

Tricia

Tricia continues like this for three more pages, commenting about "why Valentine's Day" and about things people do. Some people give gifts, some make cards, some put up a valentine box, and some have parties.

Once children start writing, they do so whenever opportunity permits. However, special times should be devoted to such writing so that teacher guidance can be provided effectively. Writing done at times other than those specifically planned is a special bonus.

One teacher introduced an idea that proved productive throughout the year. She made a 5-x-7-inch form with the heading "Write it. Don't say it," from which she could run off several blanks at a time. The children responded overwhelmingly. They could take a form from a stack in a box and write. They wrote memos to each other, to the teacher, to their parents, and to anyone else. Some used the memo forms to write reminder notes to themselves.

If pupils wish to have their stories typed, they must dictate their written accounts aloud to the typist (the teacher or a teacher's aide or a high-school student). Typed accounts are useful for a number of reasons. Since the typist is not copying from an original, she is not bound to reproduce the spellings of the child, so she can spell all words according to the standard orthography. When a child reads his material aloud, he frequently discovers syntax and grammar errors. Sometimes preoccupation with writing results in errors that usually do not occur in talking. A child may discover that he failed to insert a verb or a conjunction or a preposition. He can repair this now when he reads to the typist. In addition, children thrill to the opportunity of reading their authored products aloud. This procedure provides an opportunity for pupil editing.

When the typed copy has been completed, the pupil can read both his original and the typed version. It is astonishing how often the correct spellings are recognized. At first, children seem to take little account of differences in spelling, but, after a number of opportunities like this, they begin to compare the two versions and their spelling consciences develop.

At no time are the children asked to recopy their stories in order to correct their spelling. Some of the more sensitive children occasionally do so on their own. The teacher must be careful then that she does not create the impression that she wants all children to recopy and correct. What she wants is all children to write.

Even before the children start recopying entire stories, most do some correcting. Erasures are common; words are erased to produce them more accurately phonologically and orthographically. This is also part of the development of spelling conscience.

Punctuation and capitalization are corrected by the typist, and children respond to the adjusted versions. Failure to place periods is frequently an inadvertent result of the desire to get ideas down on paper. In their haste, children, just as adults, skip some of the communication essentials.

A primer-size typewriter allows children to type their own writings rather than write them by hand. Children love the typing privilege. It should be dealt with as a privilege, because this promotes respect for and responsible use of the typewriter. They learn readily how to insert paper and line it up. If some pupils experience difficulty doing this, an able pupil assigned as typewriter aide can provide the needed help.

A reexamination of the stories reproduced in the preceding pages reveals how language skills in written communication improve with usage. Notice how sentence length changes: The number of words per sentence becomes greater as the year progresses, as does the number of qualifying ideas incorporated into a sentence. The number of different words increases sharply. Early in the year, children tend to reuse ideas, seemingly because of the security this represents. The use of adjectives and adverbs increases, clearly reflecting a sensitivity to how nouns and subjects, verbs, and other adjectives and adverbs can be qualified. This more discriminate response results in a more acute examining of experiences.

Notice, too, how early encodings show considerable sensitivity to consonants but not to vowels. Consonant sounds are less variable. Consonants sounds are substituted for each other: *k* for *c* in *cut*, *s* for *c* in *city*, and so on. Vowels, on the other hand, are quite variable. One vowel can and does represent several different sounds. This is why dictionaries provide a vowel key, usually on every set of facing pages. Vowels are slippery, and people need help with them. Dictionaries seldom provide more than one consonant key, however. Children reflect these circumstances in their early writing attempts. They not only omit vowels but they substitute vowels phonologically: *cot* for *cut*, *frst* for *first*, *dotr* for *doctor*, *sum* for *some*, *nxt* for *next*, *far* for *fair*, *agen* for *again*, *plled* for *pulled*, *watering* for *waiting*, *trl* for *turtle*, *sts* for *starts*, *shr* for *sure*, *shoed* for *showed*, *pensl* for *pencil*, *bote* for *bought*, *trth* for truth.

This ability is phonologically noteworthy and represents tremendous sensitivity to the world of sounds and letters. The ability is an asset rather than a liability. Spelling power—that is, the recognition of how unorthodox conventional spellings differ—begins to show. Spellings "correct" by convention are increasingly used.

Similarly consonants are dropped or their order is reversed, and both silent consonants and vowels are dropped: *choped* for *chopped*, *chery* for *cherry*, *stors* for *stores*, *floted* for *flated*, *shoed* for *showed*, *pepl* for *people*, *becus* for *because*, *wrok* for *work*, *pris* for *prize*.

Again one might rightly ask how this kind of spelling production reflects spelling achievement as measured by standardized spelling tests based on conventional spellings. Reports of carefully documented studies indicate most convincingly that spelling achievement acquired this way is astoundingly high (14).

OTHER IDEAS ABOUT CREATIVE ACHIEVEMENT

A first-grade boy, rereading in May some of the pieces he had written in November, looked up and said, with an amused expression on his face, "That's the way I wrote when I was little." This boy was most likely prompted to turn to his earlier writings in order to enjoy again some of his own creations and bask in the glory of authorship. But his increased maturity and facility caused him to face up, through self-discovery, to his earlier shortcomings. Thus the modesty and capability of a scholar, who knows the power of change and growth, were being acquired early. He was also awakened to a sense of the delight and excitement of learning about communication and the intellectual power to be derived from precise communication. It is this kinship with self-knowledge and creative power that "makes him seem worthy to himself and stimulates him to further effort" (6, p. 2).

All children want to write. This is what Alvina Burrows and her colleagues wrote about so convincingly in 1939 (6); conditions have not changed in the 30 years since they made their four-year experiment. The creative use of language enables children to record what they think or feel is important and to communicate their experiences and imaginings. The language-experience approach to initial reading instruction bears witness to this burgeoning use of language.

Though theoretical positions may vary, psychologists have concurred for many years that certain variables affect learning rate. Some are personal—age, sex, intelligence, creativity, curiosity, motivation, intent, and so on. Some relate to the material to be learned—meaningful or nonmeaningful, verbal or motor, serial items or paried associates, similar or dissimilar items. Others are concerned with situation or the general arrangements for practice of skills and abilities (13).

In contrast to the general agreement about effects on learning, there is little agreement about sequence and organization of practice. Short distributed practice sessions appear to be most effective for whole learning, rote verbal learning, and simple motor skills, but when a task is complex, no general rule applies. On the other hand, it is known that active participation and understanding of the nature of the skills to be accomplished facilitate learning. Another principle of learning economy, accepted without much question, is that knowledge of results facilitates learning. Social psychologists have alerted us to the effects of group factors and social pressure on thinking and learning and to the potency of personal and social satisfaction. In gradual development of symbolic and cognitive behavior we see not only that maturation influences development but also that children seem to have a built-in knowledge of relationships (4, 11).

The word *creativity* has become a magic term recently (8). Creative thinking is distinguished by the fact that there is something novel about it and that it may or may not be tangibly expressed. Novel thinking, in which ideas are used in a new form or new connections, means transfer learning:

> From all this there comes, like a welcome breath of fresh air, a belief that children and others can be motivated by needs other than those of hunger, thirst, pain, and sex, that they can learn to know and to value the sweet taste of intellectual achievement [8, p. 10].

Creative and divergent thinking are thought of as almost synonymous, as thinking that may proceed by a variety of paths to diverse ends. Abilities required are ideational, associational, and expressional fluency; spontaneous and adaptive flexibility; originality; and elaboration.

Thelma Thurstone, in reacting to J. P. Guilford's ideas, says that she, too, has experienced "better results than we had hoped for" in her attempts to teach children to transfer from a specific ability to generalized thinking. She also found enthusiasm—children enjoy creating: "Perhaps if we did not do so much to keep children from being creative, they might like school better" (16, p. 39), she concludes.

Walter Loban, in his study (10) of the semantics and structure of language used by the same children from kindergarten through the sixth grade, related, to a solid base line, such diverse and significant aspects of language as the following. His list may serve as a guide to examination of the samples of children's writing in this chapter (10, p. 81).

1. flexibility of sentence pattern and of elements within the sentence pattern
2. proportion of organization and rambling
3. variations from conventional usage, grammar, and syntax
4. degree of coherence through subordination
5. diversity and range of vocabulary
6. extent to which generalizations occur
7. freedom from language tangles or false starts (mazes)
8. amount of language and length of units of communication
9. number of separate concepts presented
10. amount of concreteness and abstractness
11. use of affective verbs and other emotional language
12. use of figurative language (metaphor, simile, irony, hyperbole, personification)

The list, though not all-inclusive, presents elements certain to enter into any study of language proficiency. Furthermore, they apply equally to oral and written language.

Significant conclusions of Loban's study are that formal instruction in grammar seems to be an ineffective method of improving expression; pupils need many opportunities to deal with their own ideas in situations in which they want to communicate successfully with others; attempts to achieve flexibility within patterns other than basic sentence patterns should be the measure of proficiency; instruction in elementary school should have more to do with oral language.

Ruth Strickland studied children in primary grades for the relationship between their use of language and the development of silent and oral reading skill. She concluded (15) that at an early age children learn with reasonable thoroughness the basic structures of their language, that the oral language of the children she studied was far more advanced than the language of certain basic readers she examined, and that children in the highest category of reading age, oral reading interpretation, and listening comprehension also made more use of the common structural patterns in extended and elaborated form than did children who ranked low on these variables.

Reexamination of the samples in this chapter readily reveals their advanced language and how it differs from that commonly found in pre-primers and primers. The LEA approach did much for oral language readiness and for extending and refining perceptual experiences as children had opportunities to see, hear, touch, manipulate, write, draw, and talk about it all. Active contact with things and ideas may be why these children learned to read much as they learned to talk. Perhaps this is why educators have urged repeatedly that children should be guided to see and understand that reading is no more than talk written down. (1, 8).

CONCLUSION

This chapter on creative writing describes in detail what creative writing is, how to get first graders started at it, and what achievement to expect throughout the year. Other related topics—handwriting, spelling, phonics, motivation, concept development, and creative thinking—are also discussed.

Children use language uniquely and functionally long before they start school. They acquire this creative-talking facility by talking with others and among themselves as they play! Talk's purpose is to communicate. Skill in creative writing is best acquired in much the same way. The purpose of writing is also to communicate: Just as with speech, children will write to and for each other and themselves.

Creative writing is defined as a child's writing for some personal or social purpose in his own language. Each pupil selects his own words, ideas, and order and writes with his own handwriting and spelling. First steps occur when children use words in their word banks to express ideas. When a word not in a word bank is needed to complete an idea, pupils try their hand at writing and spelling without being overwhelmed because they have already acquired confidence in their vocabularies. Handwriting has to be taught functionally; it must serve a purpose from the very beginning. Phonic instruction pays off as children spell words phonologically. A spelling conscience is developed early as children discover on rereading that sometimes their letters and order of letters does not convey an intended word to others or to themselves. They also notice that sometimes a letter order they have used has produced a word that can be read but does not agree with conventional letter order.

Numerous ways of motivating creative writing are described and illustrated in this chapter. Many writing samples were supplied and appraised. Growth in written syntax, grammar, and semantics power was discussed. Writing, being more exacting than talk, yields greater returns when children increase their reading vocabularies, and so their language usage in general grows more rapidly. Children love to write and share, to be authors as well as readers. Some are more creative than others, in oral and written language as well as in expression in the arts. But all children love to create.

Bibliography

1. Boney, C. DeWitt, "Teaching Children to Read as They Learned to Talk," *Elementary English Review*, 16 (April, 1939), 139–141.
2. Brearley, Molly, and E. Hitchfield, *A Guide to Reading Piaget*. New York: Schocken Books, 1966.
3. Britton, James, *Language and Learning*. Briddlesex, England, Penguin Books, 1970.
4. Bruner, Jerome, "The Course of Cognitive Growth," *American Psychologist*, 19 (January, 1964), 1–15.
5. Bruner, Jerome S., Jacquelline J. Goodnow, and George A. Austin, *A Story of Thinking*. New York: Wiley, 1956.
6. Burrows, Alvina T., Doris C. Jackson, and Dorothy O. Saunders, *They All Want to Write*, 3rd ed. New York: Holt, Rinehart and Winston, 1964.
7. Deighton, Lee C., *A Comparative Study of Spellings in Four Major Collegiate Dictionaries*. Pleasantville, N.Y.: Hardcastle Press, 1972.
8. Guilford, J. P., "Intellectual Factors in Productive Thinking." In Mary J. Aschner and Charles E. Bish (eds.), *Productive Thinking in Education*. Washington, D.C.: National Education Association, 1965.
9. Hunt, Kellog W., *Grammatical Structures Written at Three Grade Levels*. NCTE Research Report No. 3. Champaign, Ill.: National Council of Teachers of English, 1965.
10. Loban, Walter D., *The Language of Elementary School Children*. Champaign, Ill.: National Council of Teachers of English, 1963.
11. Piaget, Jean, *The Origins of Intelligence in Children*. New York: International Universities Press, 1952.
12. Piaget, Jean, *Science and Education and the Psychology of the Child*. New York: Penguin Books, 1977.
13. Smith Karl U., and Margaret T. Smith, *Cybernetic Principles of Learning and Educational Design*. New York: Holt, Rinehart and Winston, 1966.
14. Stauffer, Russell G. (compiler and editor), *Action Research in LEA Instructional Procedures*. Newark: University of Delaware, 1976.
15. Strickland, Ruth B., "The Contribution of Structural Linguistics to the Teaching of Reading, Writing, and Grammar in the Elementary School." Bulletin of the School of Education, 40 (January, 1964). Bloomington: University of Indiana.

16. Thurstone, Thelma G., "Commentaries." In Mary Jane Aschner and Charles E. Bish (eds.), *Productive Thinking in Education.* Washington, D.C.: National Education Association, 1965.
17. Underwood, Benton J., "An Orientation for Research on Thinking," *Psychological Review,* 59 (April, 1952), 209-220.
18. Vygotsky, L. S., *Thought and Language.* New York: Wiley, 1962.

Chapter 6
The Library

The functional and psychological aspect of the LEA approach as defined and detailed in the preceding chapters is of such magnitude and potency that it is difficult to describe it phase by phase. The pedagogy is based on language usage for communication and abounds with teaching-learning procedures that are practical, timely, and utilitarian. Psychologically, the approach is one of action and accords true significance to intent and purpose.

We have already seen the degree to which language is linked with reality and with tangible usages that can be subjected by children to real action. Their language is supported by perception, experience, faith, and all the fundamental emotions linked to their activities. The single firm intention to communicate is an astounding regulator of interest, energy, and values. In addition, a strong feeling of mutual respect arises from cooperation among children in their school and social life.

All pedagogical and psychological aspects of the LEA approach operate from the very beginning in a functionally interrelated way. Increased reading power does somewhat evidence stages of progress. Individual physiological, intellectual, social, and cultural differences make stages of progress discernible. But, by and large, the functional use of language involves *all* aspects of communication at each stage.

A library is an integral part of the LEA approach. It was referred to in the account of the second day of dictated stories (Chapter 3). Once children learn to talk, they rattle on and on in monologues with themselves, monologues and dialogues with peers, and questions and answers with adults. Similarly, once children learn to read, they want to read to themselves and with and to peers and adults. To satisfy the zest for reading requires, in brief, a library.

SOME REFLECTIONS ON SCHOOL LIBRARIES

In a democratic society, education must serve all youth for personal-social-cultural purposes. As long as every adult as a member of an electorate possesses the power of the ballot, the civic demand that schools possess the resources of teaching and learning must go unquestioned. Printed and audiovisual materials are the basic tools of effective teaching and learning, including the "development of the discipline of critical thinking, the teaching of reading" (3, p. 3). Clearly, educational objectives can be fully achieved only when the nation's schools have a full complement of library resources, personnel, and services.

Libraries as creative centers can render two unique services. They can help develop reading interests and tastes and help lift the dead weight of poverty and ignorance. They are indispensable in meeting the demands of the information explosion (9). In the schools of tomorrow, pupils may spend more than half their time in school libraries and laboratories. Learning and teaching will then depend on the full utilization of the cognitive processes of questioning, problem solving, reflecting, inventing, and communicating. The intellectual and moral values gained will increase cultivated enjoyments, scholarly achievements, democratic commitments, and mutual respect.

The provision of a school library or a trained librarian does not ensure a measurable difference in an educational program. Other variables that must be present in the most effective program of library services are the teacher (of prime importance), the librarian (qualifications), and the principal (attitudes and cooperation) (7).

It is wise to conclude, therefore, that a school library is the resource center for teaching and learning and the command of the reading-thinking process is the foundation skill needed to use this resource. This means that skill in reading and library usage must be put at the top of educational objectives and that teaching and learning must be geared to it from the very beginning. This is precisely what is done in the language-experience approach.

Early in the 1960s Francis Keppel, as U.S. Commissioner of Education, reviewing statistics on libraries, said (9, p. 375), "This is a national disgrace. I call upon all of you, who know that a school without a library is a crippled school, to dramatize this shame of America—to carry your concern beyond your own councils to the American people." The statistics Keppel referred to indicated that the number of central libraries in elementary schools was about 44 percent; the number of full-time librarians employed in schools with centralized libraries was only about 51 percent; about 25 percent of elementary teachers were served by school libraries with librarians; and the number of books per pupil in elementary school with centralized libraries was 5.8.

No one can disagree with Keppel's evaluation of our school's libraries as "a national disgrace." Marked improvement has occurred in the years that have followed, but we still have a long way to go. Even more disgraceful is the way some school libraries, even some with full-time librarians, are being used. As long as librarians are viewed merely as custodians of books and libraries are visited only occasionally to find something to read in spare time, library services and, more particularly, the teaching of reading, are reflected on disgracefully.

Lack of a central library, or availability of a small and limited central library, and the availability of only a part-time librarian or no librarian at all will undoubtedly reduce the effectiveness of all reading approaches. It is claimed that their effectiveness is reduced proportionally as library facilities are lacking. A language-experience program, however, even crippled by library shortcomings, will yield better results than other programs similarly handicapped (14).

The Knapp Project planned a five-year three-phase establishment of centers across the country with major emphasis on elementary-school libraries. This is as it should be, because library attitudes, habits, and skills are best acquired from the very beginning of formal instruction (2, p. 5). Project director Peggy Sullivan in a report entitled "A Librarian's Dream Come True" (17) tells about the expert library help made available through the project, but she is emphatic in stating that this alone did not bring success. Cooperation of all school personnel, particularly teachers, was essential. At one cooperating college, students majoring in elementary education were asked which of several kinds of assistance they would most like to have in their first-year teaching jobs. Overwhelmingly their first choice was a centralized library with a qualified librarian.

Hazel Adams, as reading consultant in the Plainview–Old Bethpage school district, which collaborated with the Knapp School Libraries Project, reported in "The Changing Role of the Elementary School Library" that she saw many positive changes (1, p. 566):

> In one child's mind the library is no longer merely a place where he goes once a week to change a book (or, even worse, get a book for a book report he

must write). It is still a place where a child may on any day take out and return books, but it is also a center for information, a place for leisure time activities, for story hours, for discussion of books and a place to listen to music or view filmstrips.

The circumstances she described at the Central Park Road School in Plainview, New York, can be accomplished anywhere. All that is required is reasonable support and direction.

CLASSROOM LIBRARIES

Arranging a Library

Every teacher does some arranging in the classroom to facilitate the program and to make the room inviting. Most schools nowadays provide six-year-olds with more space than other classes. Desks are adjusted to their size and are mobile. Chalkboard and corkboard space are plentiful at the writing and eye level of the children. One corner of the room is usually an art area with easels and such for painting, drawing, molding, shaping, cutting, and pasting. Another corner usually houses the classroom library, with built-in and mobile bookshelves at a practical height for six-year-olds. There is usually a table or two, one for exhibiting books, magazines, and papers and one for reading and writing. Both have chairs. Also available are a small rocking chair, a large two-seater rocking chair, a stool, and a two- or three-step library ladder. Present, too, is a listening post with as many as six sets of earphones, a record player, a tape recorder, an overhead projector, a slide projector, and other audiovisual aids. Not all classroom library quarters are as well equipped as this, of course, but the more they are like this the better. It is readily apparent, too, that this corner is not easily confined but extends into the room. Some library corners are equipped with a rug and, in one first grade visited, people entering the library corner had to remove their shoes. This was a regulation of the pupils and was carefully enforced by them. It was not uncommon for children to lie on the rug to read or listen, and so they thought the rug should be kept very clean. Also "it looked better clean," as one youngster stated.

Even more fitting, influential, and tempting is the classroom library placed in the center of a room or open-space area. The outfitting of a centrally located area can be much like that described for the corner library: book shelves, two or three shelves high; a table or two with chairs; a book exhibit table; a rocking chair or two, one a single-seater and the other a large two-seater; a stool or two; a stand-up reading place; a rug. Located centrally, it becomes the hub of the classroom, just as the library should be the hub of the curriculum and the school.

It is impressive, indeed, to walk into a room or an open-space area and see the classroom library located in the middle of the room. It immediately creates the notion that books are important and that reading is important. A favorable first impression tends to have a lasting effect.

Classroom library centers reflect the personality and ingenuity of the teacher. The trick is to arrange the center so that children will be drawn to it like bees to flowers. If the place is too formal and is overdecorated, children will be concerned about messing it up, and this obviously defeats the purpose. On the other hand, if the arrangement is uninviting or too much like the rest of the room, that also defeats the purpose.

Children are quite responsive to a touch of something pretty. A small bouquet of fresh flowers, for example, adds charm and color. Children invariably respond to flowers in a pleased and proud way; they sense the respect the teacher has for them and what the flowers represent. Pupil-teacher regard becomes mutual. Artificial flowers will do when fresh-cut flowers are not available.

Caro Lane, supervisor of special education in Louisiana early in the 1950s, told the story of a little girl on her way to school carrying a single flower that she had picked on the wayside. When Miss Lane asked the girl about the flower, she replied that she was taking it to school to put on "the pretty table." Further inquiry by Miss Lane revealed that this teacher in her one-room school had brought a small marble-top table to school, calling it their "pretty table." If a pupil brought something pretty to school, it could be placed on the "pretty table." Such a table can also be an exhibit place for a good book.

Since the purpose of reading instruction is to get children to read, the place where they go to read should be as inviting as possible. Children who read only when in a "reading class" are not being taught a love for reading. The best index of the success of reading instruction is the amount of reading done and the eagerness with which children approach it.

Books for the Library

The classroom library should be readied before school starts in the fall. Children entering the classroom, perhaps for the first time, will see the library as part of the total room environment. Because of its inviting appearance, pupils may pause there, survey the area, and perhaps examine a book or two or a newspaper or magazine. Accordingly, the materials there when school opens are as important as the atmosphere.

There should be an array of colorful picture books with perhaps black and white illustrations, too. Some may have nothing but pictures, but many more should combine pictures and story: The children come to school to learn to read and they want to see words. Story books should also be available, with a lot of print but only a few pictures, books that look like books that Father, Mother, and Older Sister or Brother might read. Of course, the readability level will vary, but this is a boon rather than a liability. Many attractive books are now available that meet these conditions.

In addition, there may be a limited number of copies of basic reader materials, for instance, any preprimer or primer. Even though 30 copies of a preprimer might be available, *never* more than 2 copies should be in the classroom library. If preprimers and primers in four and five different series are exhibited, just two copies of each along with a few first readers may soon require a considerable amount of space. Using space this way is as unwise as putting out 30 books of one kind. Pupils, quick to note that the books consume a lot of space, sense that perhaps they have special significance, but this is just the opposite of the desired effect. No one in this day and age of vigorous attention to all aspects of linguistics will want to overexpose children to substandard language usage; yet that is precisely what will occur unless the precautions here noted are observed. Almost every set of basic readers includes at least two preprimers, sometimes three. If two of each from three sets are displayed, 18 books will be taking up valuable space. With primers and a few first readers added, the space consumed becomes inordinate.

Magazines are available in considerable number. The current month's copy, along with one or two from last year, should be displayed. Comic magazines are attention-getting material. Newspapers, some structured for school use at different levels of readability, should be exhibited. Adult community newspapers and adult magazines should be made available. Many children see these in their homes, on newsstands, or at the town library, and they should be led to feel that they are a part of their world, too. They like to "see and read" these much as adults do; children love to imitate and play adult roles.

The listening post should have a variety of recorded or taped stories, with some recorded just as they appear in some of the books. This way a child can either listen to the oral reading only or listen and follow along in the book. Nursery rhymes can be taped for listening, and stories with a musical background or records with only music can be supplied. Listening to music is as comforting and relaxing for children as it is for adults.

Some books on the display tables may lie flat; others may stand partially open to attract attention. The number of books, other than the preprimers and primers, should be about two per child; in a room of 30 children, the number should be about 60.

Using the Library

As already stated, the classroom library should be so arranged that a child entering the room for the first time on the first day of school is attracted by its appearance and curious about its offerings. *First* impressions are important impressions and, frequently, lasting ones; hence it should be readily apparent to each child that, in this room, this teacher is putting *first* things first.

High on the list of attitude determiners is the teacher's interest in books. Almost anyone can arrange an attractive area to display books, but the way a teacher handles a book, turns its pages, uses a book mark, speaks and feels about books are all tell-tale signs of appreciation of books. Not only does the teacher talk warmly and with enthusiasm about the books for the children but she also talks about what *she* is reading. Children just know she genuinely likes books: "Love for reading is not taught; it is created; not required, but inspired; not demanded, but exemplified; not exacted, but quickened; not solicited, but activated" (16, p. 4). On the first day of school, a tour of the room is in order, with the children following the teacher to listen, see, and touch. At the library, how books are really our best friend should be explained.

A dictated experience story, most likely not obtained until the second day, provides an excellent lead to reading: Recall the teacher's success (in Chapter 3) with a copy of *Snow White* that had been placed on the library table, along with other books using the words *snow* or *white* and some preprimers in which some of the children's names appeared. The class gathered in the classroom library even though they spilled out. The children loved the coziness much as some adults love the coziness of an easy chair.

Next the teacher picked up the copy of *Snow White* and had different children point to the words and read them. Then she opened the book and invited children to find the words on different pages. On one page they counted seven appearances of "Snow White." She selected other books containing the words *snow* and *white*. One girl found *snow* in *snowman* and identified it for the class. One boy found *snow* in *snowy*. He exclaimed that he had found *snow* but that it had, as he put it, "a funny tail on the end."

Once the children caught the idea, the teacher gave copies of different books to several children and designated them as leaders and then directed other children to gather with a leader and find words they could read. To Bill, for instance, she gave a copy of *Snow White* and had three other children join him at some other spot in the room. In a short time, there were eight groups scattered about the room buzzing like bees over the honey they were finding. The teacher moved from group to group to enjoy and endorse their findings and to be sure that all had a chance to "read." Pupils like Bill and Nancy found any number of words they recognized on sight. A few recognized only *snow* or *white* or both and their names.

After the children had located words for about 15 minutes, the teacher interrupted and had a short sharing session. Different pupils read aloud words they knew. One rule was imposed even though the pupil's enthusiasm made it difficult to enforce. Whenever a pupil read aloud, the others had to close their books and listen. It was easy to show the children how to keep a page place by placing a finger in the book.

On another day the teacher showed the children how they could find words they knew in magazines and newspapers. Visiting the library corner was now a reading pleasure. Children were busy locating words they could read as well as enjoying flipping through an entire book, magazine, or newspaper.

The teacher did not make an issue over the fact that some of the words were all capital letters, others all lower case letters, and some both. No point was made about the different print sizes and shapes. One day, when Nancy pointed out that her name was printed three different ways, the teacher listed all three (for everyone to see): all capitals, a capital N with lower case, and italic.

Even though much has been said about how to enlarge a word bank (see Chapter 4) and how to promote transfer of recognition to different print sizes and shapes and to different print media (see Chapter 3), little has been said about word cut-outs. In the library corner, or perhaps the art area, there should be a stack of old magazines such as *Good Housekeeping, Women's Day, Instructor, National Geographic,* and *Smithsonian* to which the children can turn not only to locate words but also to cut them out and keep a file of known words. One way that the children find rewarding is to have them paste the cut-out known words onto construction paper cut into such shapes as orange pumpkins around the Halloween season, Christmas trees, and snowmen.

In brief, the classroom library is the keystone of the reading, learning, communication arch. It will be the Mecca to which all pupils will turn if it is treated that way. It can be used in a variety of ways and will help to form the habit of using the library early in the pupils school life.

THE SCHOOL LIBRARY

The best way to illustrate the change that has occurred in libraries during the 1970s is to compare new elementary school buildings with those erected early in the 1960s and before. In the earlier buildings, the school cafeteria was somewhere in the center—a large, roomy, inviting place from which all morning the most enticing odors emanated. Any child in almost any part of the building could tell how the lunch was faring by the way his gastronomic juices were responding.

In the schools of the late 1960s, however, architects placed the library in the center of the school, so that now all classrooms have ready access to it. On occasion, the cafeteria in the rear of the building can be identified by faint odors. Food for the body is still essential, but because a school's chief objective is learning, food for the mind is given priority.

Reading is a matter of "feeding the mind" (5). In this regard Charles Dodgson, better known as Lewis Carroll, once delivered a lecture entitled "Feeding the Mind," in which he made an analogy between feeding the body with food and feeding the mind with ideas. Carroll says,

> I wonder if there is a thing in nature as a fat mind? I really think I have met with one or two: minds which could not keep up with the slowest trot in conversation; could not jump over a logical fence to save their lives; also got stuck fast in a narrow argument; and in short, were fit for nothing but to waddle helplessly through the world [5, p. 22].

As Kathleen Blake points out, Carroll advocates eating, because the good about eating is that when something is chewed interest is not in the health aspect of feeding the body but in the pleasure. Feeding the mind, much as with feeding the body, is done for the pleasure of it, for mastery in games of the mind.

Freud points out that play is the assertion of mastery for its own sake. In *Beyond the Pleasure Principle*, he said, "It is clear that in their play children... make themselves master of the situation" (6, p. 16). Similarly, Piaget, in *Play, Dreams and Imitation in Childhood* (12), speaks of three types of play: sensorimotor practice play, symbolic play, and games-with-rules play. In each, play is a form of mastery. Both men view play and feeding the mind as pleasurable acts of mastery. In a purer sense, reading as a game and for challenge of mastery is a form of mental digestion that results in a tidy and logically organized assimilation.

Carroll also points out that we feed our bodies because nature has internalized its demands to be fed. The same, however, is not true of the mind. If the mind is starved and neglected, human beings can continue to exist as animals, but scarcely as human beings. Thus it is a person's attitude toward and curiosity about knowledge (much of it gained by reading) that makes the difference. Bacon said curiosity is the seed of knowledge (4). Thus human beings are to be identified not solely as *homo sapiens* but as *homo ludens*, or "man the player." When human beings play games, especially intellectual ones, they are in the true sense thinking beings and mastery is the mainspring of their action.

The irony of this all is that most people are dissatisfied with their bodies. They diet, ingest vitamins and Geritol, jog and exercise, and invest millions in cosmetics and plastic surgery. Yet few are dissatisfied with their minds. People daily are fed a glutinous mass of intellectual junk (10), cheap periodicals, unnutritious television sugar plums, political pablum. While in school they are fed seedy malnutritious Sesame Streets, entertaining but unsound electric trains, ineffectual and abridged reading series, isolated and paralytic skill books. The numerous so-called reading methods are largely witless grovelings that dazzle and confuse. How wretched is the heart of humanity when in the method-mania of our times dares propose that a new alphabet of forty-four letters is a "method of instruction," or that such tripe as "Can Dan Fan Nan" has linguistic credibility. So for many their minds rot away, their thoughts are selfish and narrow, their decisions are näive and inept, their deeds are mindless and addleheaded.

Minds, to thrive and master, to remain fit and shapely, must be fed a balance of "roughage and smoothage, of vitamins and proteins, as well as carbohydrates and fats" (8). It was Bacon who said, "Read . . . but to weigh and consider. Some books are to be tasted, others to be swallowed, and some few to be chewed and digested" (4, p. 19). If the mind is to remain agile and adept, some ideas need to be carefully selected and thoroughly devoured. "If it is true that, 'you are what you eat,' it is equally true that you become what you think. Feeding the mind may be our most neglected area of public health, in its broadest social aspect" (8).

Democracy and ignorance do not go together. Citizens must not only be able to read but also to weigh and judge what they read. They must read widely, selectively, and frequently. In turn, their decisions about the value of what they read must be based on their examined experiences and verifiable knowledge. To do this the mind rather than memory must be trained. People must learn to raise their own questions, to seek answers dilligently and boldly, to analyze and act. The only fear scholars should have is the fear that they must face the consequences of their own decisions.

The school library should have a status similar to that of the classroom library. It should be the most readily seen, the most strikingly furnished, the best equipped, and the most invitingly designed part of the building complex. Where it is, a new attitude about the library prevails: Children use it, are proud of it, and treat it with the regard that our best friend merits.

Mary Gaver draws a sharp distinction between a classroom library and a school library as the centralized collection. She describes a library as an organized central collection of books and other materials, broad in variety and content, appropriately housed for ready use by children and teachers and under the direction of a full-time librarian (7). The best statement about school libraries is that of the American Association of School Librarians (3, p. 3):

> In the education of all youth, from the slowest learner in kindergarten to the most intelligent senior in high school, an abundance of printed and audiovisual materials is essential. These resources are the basic tools needed for the purpose of effective teaching and learning. . . . This fact holds true for the multitrack curriculum, ability groupings in subject areas, the expanded and intensified science program, the toughening of the intellectual content

in all courses, advanced placement and accelerated programs, the development of the disciplines of critical thinking, the teaching of reading, the provision of a challenging education for superior students, the meeting of needs of all students no matter what their abilities may be, ungraded elementary school classes, and similar practices and proposals.

Add to this the following lines from the same publication and the picture is complete (3, p. 11):

> The school library, in addition to doing its vital work of individual reading guidance and development of the school curriculum, should serve the school as a center for instructional materials. Instructional materials include books—the literature of children, young people, and adults—other printed materials, films, recordings, and newer media developed to aid learning.

Skill in library usage must be near the top of the list of scholarly reading skills. Learning and teaching will then fully utilize the cognitive processes of questioning, solving, inventing, and communicating. Students must learn how to select, analyze, evaluate, and organize information from all sources of communication.

From Thomas Petyt's *ABC* (1538), an abbreviated Latin primer, to Domenius' *Orbis Pictus* (1658) with its pictures and names to *New England Primer* (1727) with its rhymes and riddles and fables to the McGuffey readers (1840) with their graded selections of fiction and nonfiction and their pictures, illustrations, and instructions to the libraries of the 1960s is a record of over 400 years of gradual emergence of the role of materials in learning. It cannot be said that books have not been available for children. By 1710, books for children were in such abundance that "guides" were needed to identify the best ones, an evident change from Caxton's first printing of *Reynard the Fox* (1481) and *The Fables of Aesop* (1484) to Francis Seager's *The Schools of Vertue* (1557) and John Bunyan's *Pilgrim's Progress* (1678). The need for guides is obvious from then on merely by the multitude of such stories as Daniel Defoe's *Robinson Crusoe* (1719), Jonathan Swift's *Gulliver's Travels* (1726), Hans Christian Andersen's *Fairy Tales* (1846), Edward Lear's *Book of Nonsense* (1846), Lewis Carroll's *Alice in Wonderland* (1865), Louisa May Alcott's *Little Women* (1868), Mark Twain's *Tom Sawyer* (1876), Robert Louis Stevenson's *Kidnapped* (1886), Kenneth Grahame's *The Wind in the Willows* (1908), Eric Knight's *Lassie Come Home* (1940), E. B. White's *Charlotte's Web* (1952), and Sheila Burnford's *The Incredible Journey* (1961).

Nonfiction for children has sometimes been overlooked by historians of children's books. In early times the scriptures were taught through catechisms and books of advice and exhortation: Simon Patrick's *A Book for Beginners* (1662), for example, and John Quick's *The Young Men's Claim* (1691) (13, p. 49). From James Boswell's *Life of Samuel Johnson* (1791) to Carl Sandburg's *Abe Lincoln Grows Up* (1928), biographies and autobiographies have been popular with children, lured by human drama. Informational and hobby books have always been in special demand, too.

Graded readers can never substitute for the wealth of materials in a library. The 7 books in the McGuffey series were no more a substitute than are the 15 books of some modern series. Most authors and publishers of graded readers would be quick to deny that they intend to substitute for a library, but they cannot deny that the voluminous teaching practices recommended in their manuals, if followed even with little vigor, do not allow time for instruction in materials other than the readers.

A wide range of materials has been available for centuries and could have been abundantly supplied in the classrooms. Why have they not? Why, when in the twentieth century books are being published at astonishing rates (28,762 titles in 1967 alone) is reading instruction limited at the grade level to the use of basic readers? As long as reading is dealt with as a subject rather than a process, this stultifying practice is apt to persist. As long as reading instruction is paced largely by teacher questions about literal facts only, the material used for instruction is apt to be limited to graded readers because, once the teachers know the stories, they can use the same questions year after year. As long as reading comprehension is measured by a child's ability to parrot story facts, reading instruction is apt to be limited to graded readers. As long as reading instruction is viewed as primarily a sounding of words, reading for meaning will continue to be of secondary importance. As long as normative rather than individual standards measure achievement, reading instruction will remain primitive.

Librarians as well as teachers must aid the reading-learning-living process in such a way that pupils learn to take initiative. They must know when and why to seek the help of a librarian, just as they learn when and why to seek the teacher's help. One librarian, commenting on work habits nurtured by the language-experience approach, said, "These children know what they want and why, and their behavior as scholars is astounding, even among the first graders." Availability of materials, important in the preparation of scholars at all levels, is not enough. Children must be taught how to set reading goals and find personal and social answers in the facts they seek.

The American Library Association's *Standards for School Library Programs* declares general principles that should govern teacher-library relationships (3, pp. 65–67):

1. The teacher makes the library meaningful and useful to his students through his knowledge of the library's program and resources. . . .
2. The teacher motivates his students to make extensive use of library resources for classroom work and for purposes not connected with class assignments.

3. The teacher participates in the formulation of school library policies by serving on or communicating with the faculty library committee.

4. The teacher utilizes every opportunity to help the library in his school reach standards of excellence.

5. The teacher participates in the selection of materials for the school library and in the evaluation of the library's collection in his specialized field. . . .

6. The librarian provides teachers with many services related to materials that are helpful to them in connection with their teaching program. . . .

7. Using research skills successfully, satisfying curiosities through fact-finding, developing an interest in and liking for independent reading, and finding enjoyment in books, recordings, and other materials are important elements in the education of children and young people. . . .

8. The teacher brings his class groups to the library, sends small groups or individuals from the classroom to the library or its conference rooms to read, to learn library skills, or to do reference or research work, and makes collections of materials from the school library available in his classroom. . . .

9. The teacher keeps the school librarian informed about curricular changes and gives advance information about class assignments, so that resources are available in the library. . . .

10. The teacher becomes familiar with other libraries in the community. . . .

The librarian, on the other hand, renders the following services (3, p. 66):

1. builds systematically the collections of the school library so that materials are readily available for the curricular needs of students . . .

2. provides a variety of professional materials for teachers

3. acquires appropriate materials recommended for the library by teachers, as promptly as possible

4. assists teachers in the development of effective techniques for using the resources of the library and teaching library skills

5. keeps teachers informed about new materials that have been added to the library

6. helps teachers in the preparation of bibliographies and reading lists

7. locates information and performs other reference and searching services for teachers

8. serves as a resource consultant on curriculum and other school committees involving library materials . . .

9. provides informal in-service training for teachers about library resources, sources of information for printed and audiovisual materials, the evaluation of materials, and related topics

When the school library truly becomes the hub of a reading program in general and the LEA approach in particular, not only will the number of books and magazines read increase, but also the range and variety of reading interests will increase. Librarians in schools that are successfully using the LEA approach have kept accounts of such changes and report that an astonishingly large number of fiction and nonfiction books covering a wide range of interests is being selected, whereas prior to the introduction of this approach, especially inquiry reading (see Chapters 8 and 9), the number of books read and frequency of library usage was lower and the selections were limited largely to fiction.

For instance, Mrs. Lyons, librarian, reports that circulation at Wilmington Friends Lower School library increased from 9699 books in 1973–1974 to 11,703 in 1976–1977. These figures do not include circulation in the various classroom libraries or books sent to kindergarten and grade 1. Books in the sciences were in greatest demand, followed by sports, biographies, arts and crafts, geography and history, and finally fiction. There are a total of about 95 children in grades 2, 3, and 4, and they average a monthly circulation of about 200 science books.

In addition, a time period of about one-half hour can be set up on a daily basis as the reading hour. During this time everyone in the room reads, including the teacher or any other adults in the room at that time. The latter read materials at their level, but they must read. This is most important (11). Each morning the time for the reading hour may be changed: Monday, 9:30–10:00; Tuesday, 10:30–11:00; Wednesday, 11:00–11:30; Thursday, 1:00–1:30; Friday, 1:30–2:00. Children learn to check the reading hour time and anticipate reading. This looking forward to the reading hour is a most desirable attitude to cultivate. In some schools the entire school has a designated reading hour scheduled and everybody reads, including the principal, the school secretary, the custodian—everybody. It is a rare pleasure indeed to walk a school's corridors and see from room to room that everyone is reading.

Time should be set aside for at least a weekly sharing session. The sharing sessions can become an integral part of the whole reading-learning act, but it must not be allowed to become either perfunctory or muddled. The spirit of sharing must be maintained at a high level even if at times no sharing is done for two or three weeks or a little is done daily. Maintaining high spirit is of utmost importance.

For the individual student the library and librarian should supply a continuity of service that provides for cumulative growth in library skills and reading, listening, and viewing abilities and tastes from kindergarten to high school. The library should be a laboratory where students learn to research and study alone and in groups under teacher and librarian guidance. Guidance should be implicit, varied, and effective in every contact the student has with the librarian. Thus the library should become closely identified with a student's recreational reading as well as his academic pursuits. The library is the most important aspect of a reading-to-learn program. How and why the library serves this purpose must be stated emphatically and clearly. [An even more detailed account of the role of the library can be found in Chapter 8 of "Libraries and Reading Instruction" in *Directing Reading Maturity as a Cognitive Process* (15).]

Acting on Things

Sometime during the second week in school—the first week if it can be arranged—each first-grade class should visit the school library. Many of the children may already know where the library is, have seen how busy a place it is, and have peeked in and watched. The library, as the marketplace of the school, has the potential to capture interest both directly and subliminally. Pupils sense its active yet disciplined and dignified participation in the mental universe of dynamic inquiry and reason. The decisive criterion of a library of worth is its critical and empirical yet humanistic activity.

The librarian should be prepared to receive the first graders and the children should be prepared, too. The librarian knows six-year-olds, how they act, how to hold their attention, arouse their curiosity, stimulate their interest, and make them comfortable and welcome. The pupils' expectancies, if the visit has been anticipated, should not be overstimulated but eager and excited. If the classroom library is a yardstick, then its simulation can foster only the warmest attitudes.

Before going to the library, questions like "What do you think the library will be like?" "Why do you think the school has a library?" "Why do you think the library is so busy a place?" should be discussed. Reaction will vary according to the pupils' background and experience and should be expected, accepted, and used to advantage.

Many a carefully planned visit has been lost in the welter of too many things to see. Just like traveling on the same road a number of times, repeated visits make for familiarity and comfort. The first time, a general view of the library will do, with a brief reference to the check-out desk and a see-and-feel visit to the books for young readers (children must feel a book or two) and then a story session. Every librarian is a storyteller; he or she loves children, books, and stories, in that order. If each class is permitted to take back to their room five or six books especially selected for this occasion, the magic circle will have been closed. One or two of the children, allowed to carry the books, will expand with pride at the privilege. Then watch with what eagerness the books will be looked at, read, and thrilled to back in the classroom.

Thereafter, in weekly visits, the various aspects of the library can be examined so that the children will become acquainted with its resources. *Variety* and *library* become almost synonymous. The children come not only to select books to take out but to listen at story hours, poetry sessions, and panel discussions, for research, and for many other activities.

On a special visit, early in October, each child may select a book to bring to the classroom library. "Any book I like?" Asked one little girl. "Yes, any book you like," replied the teacher, "but one that you think the others might like, too." This added suggestion is not too binding or restricting and creates a number of positive conditions: First was "I like" and second was what "others might like." This may lead to more careful reflection over a book's interest and difficulty. On the same visit, some of the books in the classroom are returned to the library; others in the school may want to see them, too.

Of growing importance in the past decade has been the steady increase in the number and size of community libraries. Not only federal and state aid but also citizen committees have been ardent and active supporters of public libraries. Community libraries invariably have a sizable unit devoted entirely to children, with library hours scheduled to accommodate them. Children love to visit community libraries as a source of special pride. They can go there evenings, weekends, and summers. Visits require a certain degree of maturity and children rise to the challenge.

Interlibrary loans make additional sources available. One young fellow was truly astounded when he learned that the material he sought would be sent to his community library from a nearby city library. Age six is a marvelous age at which to learn that such resources are available.

Many families have libraries of their own, and giving books at Christmas and birthdays is common practice among many people. Book clubs for children and their subscribers are increasing, too. Children who have libraries in their homes love to share their books with classmates.

Why Read?

Children read for enjoyment or to satisfy personal curiosity, but also to share. There are people, of course, who read just to escape or to fill a friendless void, but they are the exception. The majority of people are social and want to share, and it is this spirit that is to be cultivated as desirable in a classroom.

Children share ideas as they dictate whole-class stories and group stories. When they dictate individual stories, they share their versions with a group or the class. The spirit of sharing permeates the classroom. Even before the select-a-book October visit to the library, the children have shared reactions to books in the classroom library: Why I liked this book, this story, this page, this picture, this sentence, this idea, this word provide the impetus for sharing. Varied sessions provide change of pace, fill voids, stem from spontaneous eagerness to share immediately or border on outburst. Other sharing times can be carefully planned as a specific part of the school day.

A child may have very specific personal reasons for choosing a book to bring to class from the school library and will want to tell others about it. At least, he must be given the opportunity to do so. A good procedure is to provide a small lectern as a physical base for the book and a psychological base for the child. He may feel more secure behind the "wall" that a lectern provides. Some children are very verbal and secure, overconfident, in fact, whereas others are just the opposite. The teacher should help in all instances. The shy children, still pretty much in private worlds, may do no more than stand up and show their selections, but they are up, and that is important.

Ideas gained through books are an excellent source for dictated stories. Or the books may provide ideas for sentences assembled on word-card holders and adding words to the word banks. Sharing a book may take many forms. (Chapter 4 indicates more.)

Independent Library Visits

All first-grade children have school library time for book exchanges, stories, exhibits, and the like. When they reach a certain level of progress in reading and word recognition, though, and qualify for group directed-reading-thinking activities, they have earned a special privilege. Library visits can be made individually for as long as half an hour at a time, but usually only once a week, to read at leisure.

The reading performance required for this privilege is ability to read orally and silently and to comprehend material at the basic reader primer level. This does not mean that a pupil has been led through a particular basic reader series but that because of his skills and experience at reading the pupil can pick up almost any primer or its equivalent and read it. Many children reach this level of performance early in December, others not until January or February, and some still later.

Once children have the skills needed to go to the library alone then, of course, they require additional instruction on library use. Usually, five or six pupils in a room have advanced equally so the librarian is not taxed with special instruction. Location skills and use of the card catalogue are taught. Children should learn how to enter a library quietly and go about their business. Purposes for going to the library are examined, just as are purposes for reading in a directed reading-thinking activity.

Independent library users are granted another special privilege about once a month. Because they are reading widely and have more opportunity to deal with books that they think others in their class might enjoy, they may on certain occasions select two books to take to their classroom. The books are issued in the children's names, demanding certain responsibilities. Each child is given an opportunity to tell the class why he selected the books, and he must check on their whereabouts to return them at the end of the loan period.

CONCLUSION

This chapter describes how a classroom library, school, community, and home libraries are an integral part of the language-experience approach. Once children have learned to read, they want to read, and this requires materials.

The provision of the best of library facilities does not ensure measurable differences in reading programs. Other variables are the experience and attitudes of the teacher, the librarian, and the principal.

Considerable progress has been made toward changing the condition of school libraries since the early 1960s. Nevertheless, we still have a long way to go, not only in making libraries available but also in utilizing them properly. Full-time librarians are needed. Projects like the Knapp School Project are helping us see more clearly how and why better libraries are needed.

A classroom library is a major contributor to the success of the language-experience approach. Such a library can be the center of a room, physically and pedagogically. Teachers can be as creative as possible in their arranging and use of a classroom library and will find that their ingenuity will pay huge dividends. Their own interest in books and reading will be mirrored by the children. Enthusiasm need never be quarantined.

The library is rapidly replacing the cafeteria as the physical hub of the school. Food for the mind is as important as food for the body. Much leadership has been provided by the American Library Association, especially through its *Standards for School Library Programs*.

Books for children have long been available. By 1710 they were so abundant that guides to the best ones were needed. Today many guides, catalogues, and bibliographies group books by subject, by category, by title. A library can be abundantly supplied with books.

Class and group visits to a library are described. In addition, much emphasis is given to independent visits of children to the school and community libraries. Reference is made also to the value of home libraries.

Bibliography

1. Adams, Hazel, "The Changing Role of the Elementary School Library," *The Reading Teacher, 19* (April, 1965), 563–566.
2. American Association of School Librarians, *A Proposal to the Knapp Foundation to Demonstrate the Educational Value of a Full Program of School Library Services*. Chicago, Ill.: American Library Association, 1962.
3. American Association of School Librarians, *Standards for School Library Programs*. Chicago, Ill.: American Library Association, 1960.
4. Bacon, Francis, *Essays*. New York: Scribner, 1928.

5. Blake, Kathleen, *Play, Games and Sport: The Literary Works of Lewis Carroll.* Ithaca, N.Y.: Cornell University Press, 1974.
6. Freud, Sigmund, "Beyond the Pleasure Principle," *The Standard Edition of the Complete Psychological Works of Sigmund Freud,* trans. under general editorship of James Strachey, in collaboration with Anna Freud, assisted by Alex Straches and Alan Tyson, 24 vols. London: Hogarth Press, 1957.
7. Graver, Mary V., *Effectiveness of Centralized Library Service in Elementary Schools,* 2nd ed. New Brunswick, N.J.: Rutgers University Press, 1963.
8. Harris, S., "Feeding the Mind," *Durham Morning Herald,* Durham, N.C., November 5, 1974.
9. Keppel, Francis, "The Unlimited Future of Libraries," *School and Society,* 92 (December, 12, 1964), 374–376.
10. Newman, Ernest, *Strictly Speaking.* Indianapolis: Bobbs-Merrill, 1974.
11. Petre, Richard, "Reading Breaks Make It in Maryland," *Journal of Reading,* 15 (December, 1971), 344–348.
12. Piaget, Jean, *Play, Dreams and Imitation in Childhood,* trans. G. Gattegno and F. M. Hodgson. New York: Norton, 1962.
13. Sloane, William, *Children's Books in England and America in the Seventeenth Century.* New York: (Columbia University Press) (King's Crown Press), 1955.
14. Stauffer, Russell G. (compiler and author), *Action Research in L.E.A. Instructional Procedures.* Newark, Del.: University of Delaware, 1976.
15. Stauffer, Russell, G., "Libraries and Reading Instruction," *Directing Reading Maturity as a Cognitive Process.* New York: Harper & Row, 1969.
16. Stauffer, Russell G., "The Role of the Teacher," in *Reading for Meaning,* Proceedings of the 34th Annual Education Conference, Vol. 3. Newark, Del.: University of Delaware, 1952.
17. Sullivan, Peggy, *A Librarian's Dream Come True.* Chicago, Ill.: Knapp School Libraries Project, 1964.

Chapter 7
Directed Reading-Thinking Activities

In the previous chapter, brief reference was made to that time in the progress of beginning readers when they have advanced enough to be introduced to directed reading-thinking activities (DRTAs) in groups. A distinction of group directed reading-thinking activities is that pupils move toward efficient reading practices by learning to think clearly and consistently in the medium of a group, refining a systematic approach to reading, so that they can use it while *on their own*.

Growth toward reading maturity must have an early start and an aim. John Dewey referred to democracy as the best form of social cooperation; similarly, group directed reading-thinking activities provide the best form of pedagogical and intellectual cooperation. In the actions of a group, sound intellectual and emotional dispositions are acquired and ease of reading increases. The intellectual habit of reading for meaning not only must be developed early but must be adjusted to varied use and to continued growth. By reading for meaning the reader may avoid premature crystallization of ideas by putting faith in aspirations, inquiry, and fastidiousness. Without these qualities, reading and thinking become a vagrant use of energy and incline one toward dogma and cant.

If this all sounds challenging, then it serves its purpose well. Teaching reading and thinking is a serious business. It must be dealt with as such if children are to learn how to participate in a mental universe in which they can find self-respect and social respect.

THE DIRECTED READING-THINKING ACTIVITY PLAN

A group directed reading-thinking activity has two distinguishing features: All members of a group read with about the same competence and all read the same material at the same time. The primary objective is to develop skill in reading critically. A critical reading performance requires that readers become skilled at determining purposes for reading. Readers either declare their own purposes or adopt the purposes of others; but if they adopt others' purposes, they make certain they know how and why they are doing so. Critical readers also speculate about the nature and complexity of the answers they seek. This they do by using their experience and knowledge to the fullest. Critical readers, then, read to test their purposes and assumptions. As a result, they may (1) find the answer(s) they are seeking literally and completely stated, (2) find only partial answers or implied answers and face the need either to restate their purposes in light of the new information or to suspend judgment until more reading has been done, (3) need to declare completely new purposes.

To be a critical reader requires a command of three intellectual skills. The first of these skills is known as the art of inquiry, or of asking relevant questions. Allied with this is the ability to conjecture, estimate, hypothesize. Scholars do not raise questions in an intellectual vacuum; rather, by virtue of the knowledge and experience available to them at the time, they conjecture about answers. If they accept the questions that someone else raises, it is of even greater significance that they speculate about answers. By doing so they become personally committed and cognitively involved. The second skill required is that of processing information. Scholars do this in a prescribed (not random) order, as dictated by their reading goals. In many ways the human mind acts like a computer. If it is properly programmed (inquiry-regulated, goal-set), data are processed appropriately (as evidence is weighed selectively). The third skill is that of validating answers. This scholars do either by testing their judgment against that of a peer group or a group of authorities or by actually trying the answers to see if they are correct. Thus, in brief, critical readers first inquire; then they process ideas selectively; and finally they get feedback by testing answers.

This problem-solving approach to reading may be used with both fiction and nonfiction. The purpose in either circumstance will vary according to the reader's ability to perform critically, creatively, and maturely. Reading efficiency will vary according to the purposes declared and the nature and difficulty of the material.

Proof that answers have been found either in part or completely may be presented to the group by means of oral reading or by written reporting. Both means of providing proof should be used.

The group size considered most acceptable for good teaching ranges from 8 to 10 members. Groups so limited in size permit each member to compare and contrast his thinking with that of others. In the dynamics of interacting minds, each can observe how others use evidence, make assumptions or educated guesses, adapt rate, provide proof, and perform creatively.

A plan of action may be outlined as follows:

I. Identifying purposes for reading
   A. individual pupil purposes determined by
      1. pupil experience, intelligence and language facility
      2. pupil interests, needs, and goals
      3. group interests, needs, and goals
      4. influence of the teacher
      5. influence of the content
         a. nature and difficulty of the material
         b. title, subtitles, and the like
         c. pictures, maps, graphs, charts
         d. linguistic clues
   B. group purposes determined by
      1. experience, language facility, and intelligence of each member of the group
      2. interests, needs, and goals of each member of the group
      3. concensus of the group or subgroups
      4. influence of the teacher
      5. influence of the content
II. Adjusting the rate of reading to the purposes declared and to the nature and difficulty of the material. Adjustment is made to acquire efficiency by
   A. survey: overview a selection or text
   B. skim: read swiftly and lightly for single points
   C. scan: read carefully from point to point
   D. read critically or study: read, reread, and reflect so as to pass judgment
III. Achieving reading purposes by
   A. adapting rate to purposes and the nature and difficulty of the material (reading efficiency)
   B. recognizing comprehension needs and seeking help in
      1. clarification and attainment of purposes

      2. concept attainment

      3. evaluation of information in the light of purposes declared

    C. requesting immediate help in word recognition or concept attainment through the use of

      1. context, or meaning, clues

      2. structural, or sight, clues

      3. phonic, or sound, clues

      4. glossary, or meaning, sound, and sight clues

IV. developing comprehension

    A. reporting information answering individual or group purposes by

      1. oral rereading of passages that support or refute

      2. a statement of findings

      3. recording answers

      4. anticipating further consequences in light of findings

    B. pursuing original purpose(s) further or redefining purposes

    C. recognizing the need for other source material

    D. developing and refining concepts

V. Fundamental skill training activities of discussion, further reading, additional study or writing by

    A. increasing powers of observation or directed attention

    B. increasing powers of reflection by

      1. abstracting or reorganizing old ideas, conceiving new ideas, distinguishing between ideas, generalizing about ideas, and making inductions and analyses

      2. judging or formulating and assessing propositions

      3. reasoning or inferring, demonstrating and systematizing knowledge deductively

    C. mastering the skills of word recognition in picture and language context analysis, phonetic and structural analysis, and dictionary usage

    D. developing vocabulary and concepts by word meaning, semantic dimension, analogous words, contrasted words, word histories, new words

    E. developing adeptness in conceptualization and cognitive functioning by making and testing inferences; making particulars, classes, and categories; understanding, reversibility, mobile equilibrium, and conservation

    F. mastering the skills of oral reading or voice, enunciation, and expression; reading to prove a point or to present information; reading prose and poetry to entertain; and reading in chorus

DIRECTING THE BASIC DRTA STEPS

Purposes for reading or questions raised provide the directional and motivational forces that keep a reader on course. Purposes are also the key element in versatility, and versatile, efficient reading ability is the major goal of instruction.

The reading-thinking process must begin in the mind of readers. They must raise the questions and to them belongs the challenge and the responsibility of judgment. The teacher keeps the inquiry process active and changes the amount of data to be processed. Another view of DRTA instructional procedures might be outlined as follows:

I. Pupil actions (PRP)
   A. Predict (set purposes)
   B. Read (process ideas)
   C. Prove (test answers)
II. Teacher actions (WWP)
   A. What do you think? (active thought)
   B. Why do you think so? (agitate thought)
   C. Prove it! (require evidence)

To acquire refinement in the use of the reading-thinking process requires constant practice under the watchful eye of a competent teacher who is the coach, the agitator, the mentor, and the pedagog as well as the teacher. Four recent studies show quite clearly that what the teacher does makes an enormous difference. The first study, done by Edmund H. Henderson at the University of Delaware, examined individually formulated purposes for reading in relation to comprehension and purpose attainment. The results justified concluding that pupils differ in the success with which they attain purposes and that pupils who set better purposes are more likely to attain them and also more likely to be more successful in attaining purposes supplied by someone else (8). The second study, done by Richard M. Petre also at the University of Delaware, provided substantial evidence that when children were taught according to DRTA recommendations, an open-communication-system premises, the quantity, quality, and variety of pupil responses was significantly better than when they were taught differently. The DRTA procedure yielded superior results no matter whether pupils' instructional levels in reading were above, at, or below grade level (9).

Jane L. Davidson, at the University of Michigan, replicated in good part the Petre study and in addition analyzed the kinds of questions asked by teachers. She found that teachers who followed DRTA procedures asked more questions requiring interpreting and inferring than teachers who did not. As a result, students' responses were at levels of thinking higher than the literal level. She, too, found that the DRTA procedure was effective regardless of whether students read at, above, or below grade level (4).

As might readily be predicted, instructional level is an independent variable in the critical-reading process. It is what is done to promote critical reading, regardless of level, that makes the difference. In other words, children can be trained to be thinking readers at any level. A fourth study, done by C. van Eyk Grobler at the University of Delaware, set out to analyze the behavioral expression of aggression fostered by DRTA open-communication procedures compared with those fostered by closed-communication directed reading activity (DRA) procedures. As Grobler says,

> Bearing in mind that this study represents *ex post facto* research, the level of significance attained nevertheless justifies the following specific implications. The D-R-T-A approach tends to generate a greater degree of constructive behavior and less destructive behavior and appears to be particularly effective as a treatment for intellectually slower children [6, p. 111].

It is indeed encouraging to know that the intellectual potential of children can be nurtured not merely by imparting knowledge to them but by aiding them to master the cognitive-affective skills that will permit them to overcome such difficulties as may be encountered when reading and to do so with self-reliance.

It should be evident that the DRTA plan represents a procedure to be used when reading almost any material. Its arrangement provides an orderliness useful to problem solving, abstracting, and analyzing information, including propaganda analysis and similar activities in which reading serves as a means in the search for truth and beauty. The attitudes of expression and cultivation, of decision making in terms of consequences, of using one's knowledge and experience evaluatively, of attaining ends that are meaningful and vital, of accepting change and suspending judgment can be taught and acquired.

Literate people differ from those who are illiterate in what they do about learning. A student or a reader starts with a problem or purpose to be resolved, collects relevant facts, and judges their value in determining a means to an end. Both the literate person and the skilled reader perform like the inquiring researcher; they establish hypotheses and set out to prove or disprove.

If the teacher properly arranges the conditions of intellectual interaction, children can investigate the hidden processes of their own and other people's thinking and thus avoid being docile, unimaginative, and stereotyped in their own thinking. Furthermore, authority and dependency are oriented toward the textbook and the group rather than the teacher. M. L. Johnson Abercrombie says on free group discussion:

> Perhaps from the educational point of view the most important feature is the wide range of behavior which is useful; in different ways it is as useful to listen as to talk; to agree as to disagree; to critize as to approve. The topics covered are so varied that no one person can for long retain a dominant position as the most knowledgeable or the most clear-headed. Sooner or later even the cleverest finds himself in a web of confusion out of which he is helped maybe by the most inarticulate. Often indeed it is the academically weak student who can offer a direct common-sense way out of the maze in which they all are stuck. Any one student may be at one moment the teacher, at another the pupil, and the tact, patience, and skill which students severally or jointly may command when they undertake to teach another are worth seeing [1, p. 75].

Those skilled in teacher education will recognize at once that the pursuit of such purpose is primarily a matter of outlook and philosophy. The ends described can be accomplished in almost any kind of learning situation. Children acquire from repeated experience the attitude that they can think and can find out what they want to know. They acquire craftsmanship and artistry. Knowledge becomes as intriguing as a great adventure.

Three Basic Steps

The basic steps in effective development of a group directed reading-thinking activity can be used whenever a group of children is dealing with the same material at the same time under a teacher's guidance. The plan is useful regardless of the material. Basic readers can be used, but any textbook, magazine, or newspaper may be employed.

DEVELOPING PURPOSES FOR READING

The key step in a directed reading-thinking activity is developing purposes for reading. They are the directional and motivating influences that get readers started, keep them on course, and carry them through to the end (12, pp. 12, 24–35). Versatile readers adjust their reading rate to their purposes and to the nature and difficulty of the material being read. By focusing on purposes from the very beginning of formal reading instruction, readers learn to appreciate their use and value. Young readers will not be too articulate about what they are doing, but with experience and maturity, they will begin to see how to be deliberate. Of all the reading skills, the one that authorities and teachers and readers bemoan as most lacking is versatility. It is the author's conviction that students can complete high school and college and accomplish this high skill if appropriate methodology is used from the very beginning of reading instruction.

Three ingredients essential to directed reading-thinking instruction are the teacher, the group, and the material. The teacher and the material determine to a large degree the nature of the skills acquired by the pupils.

Teachers must avoid being the instrument of authoritarian indoctrination. Their teaching must be such that the group is never intimidated by the tyranny of a right *teacher* answer—one that the group dares not to question.

If teachers are to direct a reading activity so that the pupils' thinking is both required and honored, they will, in a very important sense, be emotionally removed from the give and take of the reading-thinking process. The role of the teacher is that of an *agitator,* as one second-grade girl described it, an intellectual agitator. In this capacity the teacher asks and asks again: "What do you think?" "Why do you think so?" "Read the line that proves it." These directives are sufficiently specific to stir the minds of all schoolchildren. When the pupils state what they think, express their opinions, and listen to the ideas voiced by others in the group, they will read to see who in the group is right or wrong or partially right or partially wrong and why.

In these circumstances the pupils will not be reading to find an answer asked by the teacher. They will not fear being wrong and provoking the displeasure of the teacher. Neither will they be preoccupied with currying the teacher's favor. If they fail to find an answer, the blame for the failure will not be projected onto the teacher, because it was not the teacher's question. This is how the teacher is emotionally freed from asserting the tyranny of right answers.

In turn, all members of the group are involved in the act of "feedforward," or creating hypotheses, conjectures, and purposes and using them to guide their reading and to test their significance. It is in the context of the group that the adequacy of reading and meaning is tested. It is the group that demands that individual predictions, to be acknowledged, must be warranted by available evidence. The group sits as auditor, authorized to examine the evidence, verify the questions and answers, and accept the results.

Selections, on the other hand, must be well written and reflect conflicts, issues, incidents, eventualities. These maintain and propel a reader's interest and carry him on to the end. The ever-present human interest factor provides the motivation that facilitates a grasp of the social relationship of the story heroes as readers follow their problems. This is what permits readers to grasp a story and reduce human behavior to its elements. In short, because a story makes sense, it keeps the motto "on with the story" uppermost in the mind of each reader. Events that lead from the beginning to the end of a plot unfold in gripping sequence and hold the reader's attention, which is not released until the climax has been reached.

Pictures vital to telling a story must be built into the presentation of a plot. They must be planned to help carry a plot forward; to aid the reader by strengthening, reinforcing, and developing visual images; to establish and develop concepts; and to heighten drama and interest. At no time must the pictures reveal what is intended to be told by the story. In other words, pictures as well as words provide the medium for telling a story. If it is allowed that a good picture is worth a thousand words, then it must be agreed that picture and story should not repeat the same thousand words.

DEVELOPING HABITS OF REASONING

Let us now consider the second aspect of a directed reading-thinking activity: reasoning while reading. Interestingly enough, the word *reason* is derived from the word *ratio,* which means "a balance." What is it that readers balance while reading? They balance their experience and knowledge and the yardsticks provided by society that they have learned to use against those of the authors. To the degree that readers have examined carefully the experiences and knowledge they use, they can be critical readers. In other words, critical reading can be initiated at the first-reader level.

While reading a story entitled "The Paper Umbrellas," pupil predictions indicated the degree to which children can use evidence to reason about story outcomes. After examining the pictures on the first two pages, the children thought that the boy would help the lady pick up some pictures. They also thought that a strong gust of wind might blow the pictures so far away that it would be difficult to locate them. On the next two pages of the story, they discovered that the boy had to move very fast to prevent one of the pictures from being blown down an open manhole. He did manage to save the picture. However, when he looked about he saw people approaching a bus holding newspapers over their heads. Now he was concerned about his own newspapers, and the source of the papers that the people were carrying.

The children put to work the information they had acquired. Some predicted that the newspapers being used as umbrellas had been taken from the boy's stand. Others thought that the people had carried the newspapers with them from their offices or places of work. Still other children felt that if the people had taken the newspapers, they had also paid for them. One lad thought that, because the boy was gathering the pictures, perhaps the old lady stood by his newspapers and took care of them.

DEVELOPING HABITS OF TESTING PREDICTIONS

In the preceding instance, children used evidence to reason and predict, leading to the third step in a DRTA: testing to find out whether predictions made or hypotheses declared are right or wrong. Testing is done by first reading diligently to determine the nature and quality of an answer and then reading the particular lines orally to prove to the group that predictions were either right or wrong. Under these conditions there is immediate feedback and the data processing is continuous, guided by the pupils' directives. Most strategic is the instant and constant testing that is done as readers either substantiate or deny their hypotheses and provide proof to the group.

These three steps—predicting, reading, proving—are the PRP of a directed reading thinking activity. The PRP process is repeated each time a pause is made in the reading to prove and predict. Stops can be made at different points, thereby requiring readers to put ideas to work. The demands are different at each stop. With little information available, as with the use of a title only, many conjectures are possible; in other words, *divergent thinking* can occur. If three-fourths of a story has been read, then predictions should be limited, because the story outcome is now in sight. In other words, *convergent thinking* is now occurring.

Organizing a Group

In directing a class through the different phases of the language-experience approach, an intimate knowledge of pupil progress is obtained. The dictated-experience phase, the creative use of word bank cards, the creative writing, the reading of library books, the location of known words in different contexts, the facility with word attack skills—all provide evidence of achievement and progress. Even so, it is desirable to identify specific criteria and weigh their significance.

An early sign of progress is a pupil's ability to recognize and remember words used in a whole-class or group dictated experience story. Some will do as Bill did in Chapter 3, when he recognized and remembered 35 of the 37 different words. Some will remember only a word or two. Most children will range between these two levels.

When the children have progressed to the dictation of individual stories, the number of words they recognize and the ease with which these words are recognized increases. This is especially true of average and above-average children, who may add as many as 8 to 10 new words per dictation. Slower learners may continue at their one-to-three-word-per-story pace, but they will remember the words.

As they acquire word attack skills, children show increasing ability to attack and recognize their own dictated words. This is a significant early sign, because it provides evidence of resourcefulness in the use of word attack skill, essential to participation in a group DRTA.

The number of known words that children identify in newspapers, magazines, and the like, is also a good yardstick. The ability to transfer recognition skill to different contexts and different print shapes shows flexibility.

By the time pupils' word banks total 150 words or more, their prowess will be well established. Some pupils may "memorize" this many words, but this seldom occurs. The words will have been learned functionally in a communication context and will be recognized and remembered because of their utility as well as their configuration.

By the time vocabulary is this large, creative writing will usually be well under way and the word bank may no longer contain a copy of each known word. The maintenance of a word bank may begin to be a liability. It takes time to add the words, and because some are seldom used again, the bank begins to lose its utility. This is the time to introduce a selective entry of words. Now only words of special significance are added— unusual words like *gigantic* and *Nanticoke*; special words like *settlers* and *cogwheel*; names like *Christopher Columbus* and *Pinocchio*; lovely words like *sparkling* and *glossy*. Thus the word bank becomes a concept bank.

One of the most significant indicators of progress is the amount of reading being done. It is not so much the number of books that is important as it is the evidence that a favorable attitude toward books has been fostered and that the children are reading. Not only will pupils be reading book after book but they will be reading to and with each other. Teaming up promotes smooth and expressive oral reading and facilitates the use of word attack skills.

In brief, then, pupils are ready for group instruction when their word bank words total about 150 or more, when they read orally with considerable ease, when they love to read and turn to books readily, and when they show facility in attacking a word they do not recognize immediately. A formal check can be made in each of these areas if a teacher feels insecure about his knowledge of a pupil, but the check should be made in such a way that it will not reflect on the pupil or stifle an interest in reading.

It must be remembered that a particular girl or boy may not perform equally in each of these aspects. Nevertheless, if she or he participates in group instruction, where all read and react to the same story at the same time, it will be done with eagerness and confidence.

A DIRECTED LISTENING-THINKING ACTIVITY

At this point in the DRTA discussion we must stop to examine the pedagogic utility of directed *listening*-thinking activities. The spontaneous development of the intelligence is characterized by the progressive establishment of systems of transformation or conversions; similarly, there are "operative" structures in the development of a succession of stages in directing reading (listening) thought processes (10). As already pointed out in earlier chapters, expectations begin to influence subsequent behavior very early in life; children project their own wishes, hopes and fears, and habitual ways of feeling and thinking about things or their personalities.

James Britton puts it this way,

> I look at the world in the light of what I have learned to expect from past experience of the world. That is to say, there is on the one hand my world representation—the accumulated record of my past experience—and there is on the other hand the process of representing to myself whatever of the world confronts me at any given moment. It is as though, in confrontation, my world representations were a body of expectations from which I select and match: the selecting and matching being in response to whatever cues the situation offers (but influenced also by my mood of the moment). What takes place in the confrontation may contradict or modify or confirm my expectations. My expectations are hypotheses which I submit to the test of encounter with the actual. The outcome affects not only my representation of the present moment, but, if necessary, my whole accumulated representation of the world. *Every encounter with the actual is an experimental committal of all I have learned from experience* [3, p. 15].

John Dewey says, "From this point of view, the principle of continuity of experience means that every experience both takes up something from those which have gone before and modifies in some way the quality of those which come after" (5, p. 27).

In the educative process, growing as developing is not enough. Education and/or teachers must specify in which direction growth takes place. Thus every DRLA and DRTA becomes a moving force whose value can be judged on the basis of what it moves toward or into. Adults must exercise the wisdom of their own wider experience. They must (1) see what attitudes and habitual tendencies are conducive to continued growth; (2) understand individuals and to a good degree what is going on in the minds of those who are learning; (3) recognize what surroundings lead to growth; (4) and, above all, know how to utilize surroundings, physically, psychologically and socially.

The most important attitude that can be formed through DLTA and DRTA activities is the desire to go on learning. The precious gift to learn from experience, to formulate hypotheses or make predictions, and to revise thinking in the light of experience is what education must develop if children are to grow.

Children love to be read to. Furthermore, they love to respond to a pause in the reading and tell what they think will follow and why. This in essence is a directed listening-predicting activity. People of all ages, as a matter of fact, enjoy pauses in the reading of a story to make an educated guess about what may follow. What is more, even preschoolers will begin to tell why they think as they do.

Take, for instance, a picture story book such as Bill Peet's *Whingding Dilly*,[1] read three pages and show the illustrations; almost instantly the class will be involved. The children will make such predictions as "He wants to be a horse"; "He wants to be a great horse"; "He is sad." Then read through p. 7 and show the marvelous illustrations and predictions will follow: "Scamp is running away"; "He will find another home"; "He will go to another country"; "He won't come back because Orvie laughed at him." This will continue through the story, episode after episode; children become attentive, participating listeners, making predictions and changing them in the light of new information. Thus the precious gift of cognitive action is developing: attending to facts, making decisions, altering decisions, and examining outcomes.

A DIRECTED READING-THINKING ACTIVITY ILLUSTRATION

The aims in a directed reading-thinking activity in a group situation are twofold. The first is to teach children the skill of extracting information of predictive value from a given context of either fiction or nonfiction. The information children extract depends on how it fits into their personal store of experiences and knowledge. At times, the ideas or assumptions called into use will interact with each other freely, at other times more rigidly. The likelihood of extracting information of good predictive value is increased if the ideas and assumptions relate flexibly to each other. This happens when a plot is well developed or when a selection is well written and within the children's comprehension. Thus various combinations can be examined and their usefulness tested as material is read.

To accomplish effective utilization of this skill in different content areas DRTA training must use both fiction and nonfiction. The transfer of this skill from fiction to nonfiction materials is not necessarily automatic. Pupils must see the relevance of the reading-thinking process in all areas. This way they can continuously relate what is learned in reading class to the job of being a student in all subject areas and to the practical reading tasks of everyday life.

The second aim is to provide, through the group, ways of behaving as a thinking reader that will be useful to pupils when they read on their own. In a group in which the pupils' thinking is uppermost, each pupil's fund of experience and knowledge, can become clearer. What a pupil "sees" in a story, title, or illustration depends on how he has perceived

[1]Boston: Houghton Mifflin, 1970.

and organized previous information, how things are alike in some respects and different in others.

If the information received earlier is too generalized, too close to being nonverbal, too dependent on haphazard concrete-perceptual experiences, pupils may become aware of these inadequacies in the group situation. Otherwise, left on their own or educated in nonthinking, parrotlike repetition, they may never learn to question the validity of their own ideas and concepts. When this happens, pupils use their loosely structured concepts inappropriately and fail to extract information of predictive value; hence they continue to perpetuate their blunders and shortcomings. Persistent and intelligent effort is required if the new constructs that pupils make are to be at a higher level than those previously made.

Pupil Awareness of Conceptual Resources

How can students become aware of their own conceptual resources and limitations in a group directed-reading situation? The role of the group can provide a milieu conducive to sound mental construction rather than compounding wrong concepts. The favorable conditions are these:

1. All in the group examine the same material.
2. Each pupil reacts in terms of his own private stock of experience and knowledge.
3. Pupils are motivated because they share ideas and the spirit is competitive.
4. The information extracted and the assumptions made are contrasted and likenesses and differences are noted.
5. The activity itself provides the means for the creative use of ideas.
6. Each pupil's personal integrity is at stake.
7. Each pupil's educated guesses must be defended, proved or disproved.
8. Available evidence must be presented to the group for acceptance or rejection. The group is the auditor, jury and judge.
9. Pupils learn to have the strength of their convictions and not to be dominated by loud verbalizers.
10. Pupils learn to respect the thinking of others, to study how they examine evidence and how they prove points.
11. Pupils learn to temper their emotions in the crucible of group interaction, to be enthusiastic without being obnoxious, to rejoice without being offensive, to accept mistakes without being stifled.

12. All this is done under the direction of a prepared teacher who knows the content, the important concepts to be attained, and how to promote thinking in others without putting words in their mouths. A teacher must know the *effect* being sought.

A DRTA Account

The outline of a directed reading-thinking activity has been presented and certain basic principles and assumptions underlying the development of an effective group DRTA have been declared. Practices in each of the five basic steps were briefly outlined. It was pointed out that, in essence, a DRTA has two parts—a process and a product. The first four steps— identifying purposes, guiding adjustment of rate to purposes and materials, observing the reading, and developing comprehension—comprise a process cycle. Each step of a DRTA sets the cycle in motion: check comprehension, reset purposes, adjust rate, read. In fact, it might be shown that each time a reader stops to reflect, even in the middle of a sentence, he sets a similar cycle in motion—he pauses to check his understanding, decides to proceed with the same or different purposes, quickly adjusts rate, and then reads on. The product of the DRTA is the extension and refining of fundamental skills. This is the time when, by direct attack, an attempt is made to increase powers of observation, reflection, and conceptualization.

Basic readers are adaptable to the fundamental purposes of a DRTA in a group situation. Controls of vocabulary, concepts, interests, illustrations, and story length can make this true. The rate of introduction of new words and new concepts is usually controlled and permits pupils to try newly learned word attack skills and comprehension skills without being frustrated. At the primary level in particular, stories are about events or ideas within the scope of most children's experience. Gradually the content reaches out beyond their experiences—socially, historically, numerically, geographically, esthetically, scientifically, and humorously— but at an adjusted pace, so as not to overwhelm children. The length of the selections should be such that the material can be read easily in the time limits imposed by the demands of the total curriculum.

"A One-Time Magic Garden" (13, pp. 101–106) is one of a series of first-reader stories prepared to develop reading-thinking skills by means of a well-contrived plot and well-paced vocabulary. The plot moves forward steadily from the first page, the plot introduction page, through a series of related episodes to the climax. The title is bound to the story and helps orient the reader toward the main idea of the plot. The answer to "A One-Time Magic Garden" is not provided until the very end. Curiosity about its meaning helps the reader speculate and stay on course.

A One-Time Magic Garden

"This must be magic," said Bill.
"Dad just put it in this morning.
Then it was little, but see it now."

"I can see it go," said Cooky.
"It is going up as fast as a bird.
I wish I could go up on it."

"You can," said one of the twins.
"I will show you how."

101

(Illustration) Along the entire left margin of the page is shown a huge cornstalk, and the children, as well as the dog, are climbing the stalk.

Ted jumped on and said
it was fun.
Next Bill and Red
jumped on, too.
Soon all but one of the twins were going up.
Ned just looked at the children.

He thought, "They are going up
faster and faster.
When will they stop?
How will they get down?"

Then the girls called to him.
At last he jumped on, and
away they all went,
up . . . up . . . up . . .
102

(Illustration) The group is standing in the presence of a friendly green giant. In the background are trees bearing toys instead of fruit.

"Good morning," said the man.
"My name is Uncle Green, and
this is my magic garden.
I just give things away.
Take all you want."

"All we want!" said Cooky
"I want so many things.
I will take balls, bats, and skates."

"I want new skates, too," said Ned.
Then away he ran to get them.
103

(Illustration) The green giant is presenting a coat made of corn husks to the youngest girl in the group.

Susan sat down to talk
with Uncle Green.
Soon she said, "It is cold up here.
Can you give me a coat?"

"I have just the coat for you,"
said Uncle Green.
"It is good at all times.
Put it on when you are cold and
when you are hot.
Put it on when it rains, but
do not get it on upside down."

Susan put on the funny-looking coat
and went for a walk.
104

(Illustration) The green giant is seated on a chair-shaped tree stump and is watching the children picking different toys from the trees in the garden.

All the children were happy.
They were laughing and playing
in the garden.
Uncle Green sat down alone to see the fun.

Then Ted said, "I do not see Ned.
Help me look for my twin brother."

"I do not see Susan," said Nancy.
"We must look for her, too."

"I can find them," said Uncle Green.
"No one can hide in my garden."
105

(Illustration) Two of the children are looking down a huge cornstalk through an opening in the clouds. The green giant and the other children are approaching the sky opening. Far below a village can be seen.

"Here we are," called Ned.
"Susan and I know how to get down."

Uncle Green laughed and said,
"You are looking down my magic hole.
You can go down there like a fireman."

Ted said, "We will go now,
but we will come up in the morning."

"No, no," said Uncle Green.
"This is a one-time magic garden.
No one can come up two times."
106

Meeting New Words in Context

The frequency with which words are met is vital for retention. As any experienced first-grade teacher can confirm, and any new teacher soon learns, one or two contacts with a word are not enough to effect retention, even among bright children. Teachers can also confirm that presenting words in isolation by rote drill to supply needed recontact with a word seldom does the trick. Flash cards misused are the shackle of the learner, the despair of the naïve teacher, and the frustration of the well-meaning parent.

Analysis of vocabulary usage shows that strictly from the view of the "mechanics" of reading, the repetition of old and new words within the preceding story is good. The psychology of learning has for years been clear about the efficacy of meaningful repetition of or recontact with what is to be learned. Each new word is used a minimum of four times in "A One-Time Magic Garden." J. B. Stroud puts it this way (14, p. 373):

> The two great experiences used to insure retention are thorough initial learning and subsequent practice or review. No matter how thorough the initial learning is, forgetting is to be expected in time unless subsequent practice is engaged in. Such practice may take several forms, as in rereading material previously studied, using the material in different contexts, engaging in symbolical practice by direct recall, class discussion.

Far more important, though, is the meaningful and appropriate introduction of words according to the natural communication demands of the context and concepts of language and pictures. Thus each page of the magic-garden story can provide the basis for many examples of the semantic-concept triangle (16). The picture provides *experience*, one of the two ingredients for meaning. The story provides the *language*, the other ingredient. This is the base of the semantic triangle and provides the foundation for meaning. When the two ingredients are joined in the mind of the reader, a *concept*, or idea, is fashioned. This is the apex of the triangle and represents the peak attainment of conceptualization.

Because the words in "A One-Time Magic Garden" are used in a conventional way, agreed on by our society, the children who read this story should meet each new word in the story context. *The words should not be presented prior to the reading and in isolation.* Because of the appropriate and timely use of the words and because the children will be intent on reading for meaning, the likelihood of their recognizing the words on their own is high. When the pupils are talking no one needs to stand by and prompt or tell them what words to speak. Similarly, when the children are reading, no one needs to stand by as they meet new

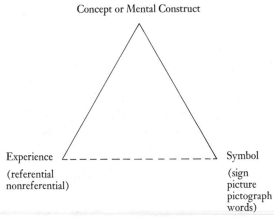

Semantic-Concept Triangle

words, because they are used appropriately in a meaningful setting. In this selection the words and their meanings are quite common. If the efficacy of context is not enough, the pupils have the opportunity of using, on their own, the phonic and structure clues they have been taught.

When a teacher writes new words on the chalkboard and tells the children what the words are, or helps them analyze the words before they meet them in context, the pupils do not have an opportunity to use the word attack skills they have been taught. The teacher, by so doing, short-circuits marvelous learning opportunities.

It is commonly thought that experience is the best teacher. But this is only half the story; the other half is, "particularly if it is secondhand." Life is filled with second-hand experiences, and much of what we learn is gained through them. One need not jump off a bridge to understand the danger of doing so nor touch a burning match nor fall on ice nor lose a dog to find out what these experiences mean. Reading is a rich, indispensable, and dynamic source of such experiences. Therefore, from the very beginning, children should be taught to read in such a way that they acquire the attitude that reading can give them new ideas and change old ones. It is most important that the teacher's attitude toward reading foster a sense of reading to learn, and acquire experience.

Data Processing, Feedback, and Testing

One way to program the reading of a selection is to permit the reader to process varying amounts of data, or evidence, and speculate about events to follow. In the case of "A One-Time Magic Garden," because of the nature of the title it is suggested that speculation be invited in response to the title only. The predicting (weighing of evidence), data processing (reading), testing (selecting relevant data), and evaluating (confirming or rejecting hypothesis) should occur in four steps:

1. prediction from title clues only
2. prediction from first-page clues
3. prediction from the first three pages of clues or evidence from half the story
4. prediction from five-sixths of the story, or the first five pages, with the reader using all the information except that on the last or climax page

If this segmented treatment were given to every six-page story, the purpose of a DRTA would soon be defeated. The procedure would soon become as stultifying as the DRA recommended practice in so many other instances: readiness (teacher tells, teacher asks questions), guided silent reading (teacher watches pupils read), comprehension check (pupils answer teacher's questions and tell back the story), oral reading (pupils read a page orally, taking turns and following in the book to detect pupil errors), readiness, and so on, as the cycle is repeated (11). It is important, therefore, that the teacher vary the amount of material (information) to be processed and do so from story to story.

In a DRTA procedure the purpose of dealing with various amounts of information is to teach children to be reading detectives. Throughout the instruction time pupils must discover for themselves the predictive value of clues in one-sixth, one-fourth, one-half, two-thirds, and five-sixths of a story. That this kind of thinking-reading performance can be initiated in the first grade is easy to prove.

The teacher initiated the purpose-setting session by asking them, "What do *you think* a story with a title like this may be about?" This question is usually sufficient to get things going. Occasionally, though, particularly in the earlier DRTA sessions, it may be helpful to rephrase the question and ask, "What do you think might happen in this story?"

Here are some of the predictions made by one group of 10 six-year-olds. "It may be a trick garden." "Maybe it grows only one time and then the people have no food." "This could be a make-believe garden with only fairies and princesses." "Maybe they have the biggest tomatoes. My dad did one year." Each of these conjectures reflects a use of ideas suggested by the title. Notice how each varies and reveals something about the child and his experiences and language.

Urging this teacher to tell the children that this is a story about a giant cornstalk and a giant's garden that grows toys would have been a betrayal of story secrets that would have yielded little. Children know about gardens and magic. They know what it means to grow things and how magic might help.

Four of the children made conjectures—a good number. At times all in a group may offer a different conjecture, and at other times only one conjecture may be heard. But the teacher must always be willing to accept the responses that emerge. If only one response is made, or even no response, the occasion demands restraint by the teacher. It is tempting to step in and offer ideas, and sometimes this is permissible, but it is preferable to try to discover what kinds of information are needed to arouse responses and why the title clues did not stimulate responses. If this kind of restraint is exercised and alertness to additional clues is maintained, the children will gain in thinking power and assurance. They are the ones who must experience and discover what to do with information. The teacher should not set up barricades against learning by giving ideas.

Before proceeding, the teacher asked the other six children in the group which of the four ideas they thought was the most likely. Three thought the trick-garden idea was good; one thought it would be about tomatoes; and two thought it would be about fairies and princesses. All had done some thinking, and each had made a decision. There had been no coercion.

STEP 1. TITLE CLUES

Have the pupils read the story title silently to judge the likely nature of the plot that follows. A title that has been chosen carefully not only to name a story but also to be useful in developing reading-thinking skills serves many purposes. It can be the equivalent of a *central theme* or main idea. In this case the title is highly suggestive of a possible outcome of the story: "A One-Time Magic Garden" has special meaning. A trained reader will keep this in mind throughout. All clues and all items of information are oriented around this idea. The title gives direction and focus, and in this respect provides a set of clues that embraces the entire plot.

The title permits and encourages *divergent* thinking. As J. P. Guilford has said, this means the producing of a diversity of ideas that are logically probable (7). The ideas are reasonable or credible within the limitations of the facts available. Divergent thinking prompts *creative* thinking, or ideational fluency. E. Paul Torrance says:

> The creative reader sensitizes himself to problems, gaps in knowledge, missing elements, something incorrect. This calls for the formation of new relationships and combinations, synthesizing relatively unrelated elements to discover new uses, and building onto what is known. In this research for solutions, there is the operation of ideational fluency (the production of a large number of possibilities [15, p. 60].

"How can we find out who is right?" asked the teacher. She received a quick reply: "Read!" They knew what it meant to read to find out. "Read to the bottom of page 101 and then close your books," said the teacher.

Children asked to be independent and to recognize a need and know what to do about it must be trained. Just prior to a first reading, pupils need to review briefly from time to time what to do if they come to a word they do not know. The steps are as follows:

1. Read to the end of the sentence (meaning).
2. Look for picture clues (meaning).
3. Break word into syllables (structure).
4. Sound it out (phonics).
5. Ask for teacher help.

At the intermediate level the fifth step becomes the consulting of a glossary or a dictionary.

In order to know that they do not know a particular word, the children will first have to see it. Visual discrimination is their first reaction, that is, perceiving likeness and differences of structure. Once they know that they do not know a word, then what action to take is of first importance. In reviewing the five steps for the children, context, or meaning, clues must always be listed first. The potency of meaning is so great and the idea of reading for meaning is so important that meaning must always take precedence. Also, once pupils have an idea of what a word might be, the skills of phonic and structural analysis become meaningfully or contextually functional.

As soon as the group knew how far they were to read, they took off. The first picture had helped to focus on the nature of the plot and its direction. All knew that children were involved and that a cornstalk was growing tall.

The teacher observed the silent reading and recognized it as a most important time in the learning-to-read training program. All reading teachers agree that the object of instruction is to develop self-reliant, independent, discriminating readers. All agree, too, that it is the teacher who sets the climate of DRTA by words, tone of voice, manner, and skill-training facility. If children are to be self-reliant in their use of comprehension and word attack skills, the teacher must direct instructional experienes that will foster such skills and attitudes.

A first step on the road to word recognition independence is to foster the attitude: "Try it yourself and then get help if you need it." One of the advantages of structured basic reader material is that by controlling the number of new words on a page, the ratio of new words to running words (or previously learned words), and the relationship of new words to picture content, readers are encouraged to try the unrecognized words on their own before seeking help. This is only half the process, however. If children are to try out their fund of word attack skills, they must be given the opportunity to do so. The best opportunity for children who are learning to read is to meet new words for the first time in a context. It follows from this that the teacher *must not* present the new words prior to the reading of a selection in a mistaken notion that this is preparing the children to read. When this is done it prepares them for a kind of mental servitude, denying them the freedom to determine their own word recognition needs and to apply the skills they have been taught.

Next in importance is the pupil's willingness to ask for help. Teachers sometimes say that children will not ask for help, and this is true when they have been deprived of the healthy give and take of discovery learning. Teachers who find that children do not ask for help should examine their own behavior in relation to the learning environment. When their behavior is open, accepting, scholarly, and understanding, pupils will know that they do not know and will ask for help when they need it. When a pupil asks for help with an unknown word, such a question as, "What do you think the word might be?" or "What have you already done to find out what the word could be?" are often all the assistance that is needed. If this is not sufficient, more direct guidance can then be given.

After the first page has been read and all books have been closed, the comprehension check can be started by a number of questions from the teacher, who may ask, "What do you think now?" or "What do you think will happen next?" or "Were you right?" Each question serves a particular purpose.

"What do you think now?" and "What do you think will happen next?" set similar lines of thought in motion. The latter question focuses more sharply on "what next" ideas. It invites anticipation and speculation about events to come and calls into play the use of ideas garnered thus far. To make educated guesses, pupils must screen and evaluate ideas and make decisions about events to come in light of events that have already occurred. The first question elicits almost the same responses but lets the pupils decide for themselves that "what next" ideas are called for. In other words, "What do you think now?" is somewhat less directive than "What do you think will happen next?"

"Were you right?" focuses on the reading purposes and an evaluation of right and wrong, or partially right and partially wrong. This is a good approach that meets with favorable response. The pupils know whether what they had predicted actually occurred. They know, too, that the test of their predictions will be to read the line(s) that prove or disprove or partially support. The question "Were you right?" focuses on proof. Pupils schooled in the processes of DRTA will not wait to be asked the question since they know that when all books are closed, comprehension will be checked and evaluated. The question also focuses on the human drama by focusing on the reader.

In this instance the teacher asked, "Well, were any of you right?" The boy who had spoken about tomatoes replied to this immediately by saying, "I wasn't right about the tomato but this may be a magic cornstalk!"

Now the teacher said, "Read the lines that gave you this idea." The boy opened his book and read eagerly: " 'This must be magic,' said Bill. 'Dad just put it in this morning. Then it was little, but see it now.' "

The oral *rereading* by the boy to prove a point was done with considerable smoothness and expression because he was preoccupied with making a point and not the saying of words. He did not read monotonously word by word or in a singsong, high-pitched voice. The reason is obvious: He was providing evidence in defense of a point, not evidence that he could say words.

The oral rereading was not motivated by purposes different from the purposes that motivated the original reading. Such notions apply only in situations where the pupils reread a story aloud after it has been read silently. Even then the purposes are usually fabricated by the teacher and neither motivate nor deceive the children, who soon realize that all that is wanted is a routinized pronouncing of the words. In DRTA, oral rereading is motivated by the same purposes that initiated the silent reading, although they are somewhat different now because information has been acquired. This is correct, for this is feedback time, the time to read to prove or disprove. This time contrasts with the feed-forward or predicting time in that it represents the omega of the feed-forward and feedback cycle.

When the lines were read orally, the other members of the group kept their books closed, which necessitated their listening discriminately to the lines being read. They had to decide whether the lines being read were correct and supported the point being defended. This kind of training in listening is very important because it requires attentiveness and discernment.

"I think I was right, too," said one of the girls. "I believe it is a trick garden. The story said it was going up as fast as a bird." Then she read aloud the lines that supported her view.

The pupils who found that their predictions were wrong were not distressed. After all, they too had thought well. They readjusted their thinking according to the new information. They knew from experience that circumstances like these require flexibility. As a result, they were developing emotional stability and cognitive maturity as well.

It is readily apparent that the children are being required to interpret and make inferences. According to B. Bloom's *Taxonomy*, making inferences and interpretations rates high in the cognitive domain (2). Especially noteworthy is the fact that the children are being required to infer and interpret in an empirical story context situation and not in an isolated skill book situation or in reponse to a simpleminded teacher question such as "How long do you think the plant has been growing?"

STEP 2. FIRST-PAGE CLUES

"What do you think will happen next?" asked the teacher.

"I think they will crawl up on the stalk," said one child, "and find some magic."

"I think this stalk isn't strong enough to hold them," said another child.

"I think they will grow a lot of magic corn and have the best popcorn in the country!" said a third.

"Read pages 102 and 103 and see what you think then," said the teacher.

The teacher might have probed for more conjectures, but sensed that all the children were sufficiently questioning in attitude to go on. A most important skill for teachers in such situations is to know when to have the pupils read on. No one can spell out all such circumstances, nor would one want to. Each situation varies and the teacher must be flexible. The motto should always be: On with the story.

This time the teacher did not realert the children about how to handle word recognition needs. They knew what to do. More important, they knew that they could ask for help and receive it without angering a dissatisfied teacher or being scoffed at by the group. The learning climate was good. To know that you know that you do not know may be the beginning of wisdom, but the next step is equally as important: to *know what to do about what you do not know.*

Throughout this silent reading session the teacher stayed alert not only to requests for help, but also to the pupil's reading performances. The teacher watched their reading posture, lip movement, finger pointing, and facial reactions to plot development, reading rate, and so on. Not all pupils finished and closed their books at the same time, so, taking advantage of these seconds by carrying on a private conversation with the few pupils who had finished early, the teacher asked, in a low whisper, "Did you find out what the magic garden is?" Children respond especially well to such personal encounters and welcome the attention. Furthermore, this serves as a double comprehension check. A pupil reluctant to speak up in the group may be drawn into active participation in this way.

After all the books had been closed, the comprehension check began immediately. The teacher merely said, "Well?" as an invitation to respond. In rapid order the children now read aloud lines to prove points about the garden and Uncle Green.

STEP 3. ONE-HALF OF STORY

Speculation about what might follow was so ripe that all the teacher needed to do was listen.

"I think the green giant will keep them in the garden," said one, "and they can't go home. That's why they call it one-time."

"I think they will get home again but they can't take the toys along," said another.

"Uncle Green looks very friendly. I think he will help them get home again with all kinds of toys," said a third child.

The pupils were, of course, responsible for reading both the pictures and the text as they went on to the next two pages. The most obvious sources of information in materials of this type are the pictures. At this stage of reading progress, pupils should be schooled to turn first to the pictures. Notice, too, how throughout this presentation the pictures helped to carry the plot forward. In this instance the pupils were primed to see how the children returned home. Neither picture provided such evidence. Both provided information but raised questions such as, "What is Uncle Green giving Susan?" "Why do Ned and Nancy look worried?" Answers can be found only in the text.

Notice, too, how the facing pages (104 and 105) help to carry the plot forward. The ideas presented were not what the children had expected, yet they are plausible and fit plot development. The content did not sound contrived. The surprise in the plot held the readers' attention and kept them involved in unraveling the story. This is as it should be. A good deal of careful planning, writing, and arranging is required to set up a series of stories that will be useful in the teaching of reading as a thinking process.

Again the teacher observed reading performance and made short but timely personal visits. These checkup sessions keep the readers focused on meaning. Attention had, of course, been given to recognizing words, but words are recognized so that the plot can be comprehended.

Once books were closed, the comprehension check session immediately got under way. "The children didn't go home," said one boy with a certain amount of concern. "Why do you think they didn't?" asked the teacher. "Maybe this is a trick garden and they are trapped," was the reply. "Yes," said a girl. "Uncle Green looks too happy. I believe he tricked them."

STEP 4. FIVE-SIXTHS OF STORY

"How many think the children are caught?" asked the teacher. Almost all hands went up. Two children felt sure they would get home again but did not know how. One boy thought the "one-time" idea meant that they could go home but never come back. "Read on and find out," said the teacher. This comprehension appraisal was brief, enthusiastic, and reader oriented. The children grasped the puzzling element and were eager to go on to resolve the puzzle.

All too often the last picture in a story designed for this level gives away the ending, leaving no need to read on. The last picture in this story did not give away the ending and was itself puzzling. The pupils had to read to find out and the teacher knew this.

Almost before the teacher could look around, the books were closed again. It was obvious by the "ohs" and "ahs" that the pupils had reached the end. All knew what "one-time magic garden" meant. During the discussion that followed, the teacher asked a girl to read the line that proved the "one-time" point.

Before dismissing the group, the teacher printed the so-called new words introduced in this story on the chalkboard. Then she asked different pupils to pronounce the words. Reading the words in isolation at this point was a good test because the words were first met and dealt with in context. If the children do not recognize a word in isolation, the teacher can ask them to turn to the story and reuse the context clues.

Chapter 2 in *Directing the Reading-Thinking Process* (11) enlarges on the discussion of DRTA plans and provides five different accounts such as this one on the "One-Time Magic Garden." The illustrations show different grade levels of materials and the use of nonfiction as well as fiction. The reader is urged to turn to this text for further study.

Analysis of Variants and Covariants

The diagram provided here is designed to help a teacher understand *how* and *why* varying the number of "stops-to-predict" or "pauses-to-reflect" or "think-outs" or "feed-forward" pauses is essential. To create different

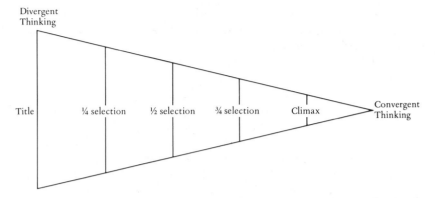

intellectual challenges and reading environments a teacher deliberately plans "think-outs." This is done to (1) vary the style of DRTA actions; (2) avoid the monotony and mindless routine of following the same plan for each DRTA; (3) note how well the children cope intellectually with varying amounts of data; (4) see how effectively the children move from divergent thinking demands (creative) to convergent, or closure, thinking.

In reality the DRTA instructional situation becomes basic training in processing information. During the "think-outs" or "feed-forward" pauses, the children are trained to mentally turn over and over a problem or a question or a conjecture so that all aspects or phases may be taken into account; they must weigh evidence, draw accurate inferences, balance claims and counterclaims, all in order to make judgments. This is clearly a matter of applying the mind. All this is done by varying the quantity, quality, and type of material being read.

Varying the amount of information a reader is to use to make judgments can be done in innumerable ways. In the diagram presented the division is by quarters. Stops can be made by thirds, halves, or page by page. The entire selection except for the last, or "who-done-it," page can be read before a prediction stop is made. Pauses can be made within a page. Depending on the nature of the material, paragraph pauses can sometimes provide needed training opportunities. It is the amount and quality of the information that makes the difference. Much weighty information can be offered in an axiom, a formula, a digest statement, a theorem, and the like.

Illustration stops can also be made. For instance, when reading well-illustrated fiction, the mind can be challenged by looking at the first and last picture, or only the last picture, or all the pictures. Similar action can be taken when maps or graphs are used.

A chart can be prepared listing ways in which pauses to predict can be made. This helps pupils to understand what is intended. In addition, pupils can select a plan of action and follow it. Each plan should be used frequently enough and should be discussed so as to be grasped.

It must not be assumed that pausing at each quarter or third of a selection places equal demands on a mind. Quality or conciseness of information usually cannot be judged by the space it takes. Nor may it be assumed that each pupil will weigh evidence for decision-making purposes in the same way.

It must not be assumed that in all DRTA teaching sessions the pupils are told exactly how far to read. Such a procedure could develop over-dependence on teacher directions. Therefore, on occasion, pupils are told to read until they find an answer. This places a different responsibility on the children and requires another kind of decision making.

CONCLUSION

This chapter is concerned with the fact that reading-thinking skills must be taught as early as possible in children's reading-to-learn and learning-to-read program. A major advantage of introducing children to directed reading instruction by means of the comprehensive LEA approach is that they learn the rudiments of reading in functional communication. They learn to read much as they learned to talk.

Learning to read differs from learning to talk, however, in that it is directed at acquiring skills that are to be used deliberately and purposefully to acquire knowledge. Accordingly, as soon as children have made certain advances in learning to read, they need to be taught how their new skills can be used, refined, and extended so that higher utility will result.

The outline for a directed reading-thinking activity, or a problem-solving approach to reading, presents five basic steps. The first four are very similar to the steps usually associated with reflective thinking. This is thinking and acting that enables readers to direct, act, know, and convert. It frees them from merely impulsive and unregulated reading, which may be largely imaginative, to reading that is concerned with critical and creative ends. The steps outlined show that reading is not a single unitary activity but a process that must be adapted to the purpose of the reader and the nature and difficulty of the material.

How children acquire critical and creative ability almost from the beginning of their school careers depends to a large degree on how the teacher directs reading instruction. The teacher must direct it so that pupils' thinking is required, honored, and refined. The teacher must oversee the PRP process and foster in each pupil the attitude of *predicting* or setting purposes (feed-forward), *reading* (reasoning), and *proving* or testing (feedback) the ideas read in the light of the purposes declared.

Pupils in an LEA program evidence certain readily recognized signs of achievement and readiness for group instruction. The best evidence, of course, is the amount of reading they do and enjoy. Other signs are the size of their reading vocabularies; the rate of growth of their vocabularies as well as their range and complexity; the quality of oral reading; the nature and quantity of creative writing; the ability to use sound, or phonic, knowledge and sight, word structure knowledge, and meaning or context knowledge in decoding a word; and their attitude toward reading.

The most essential teaching variable is the teacher. It is the teacher's attitude toward reading and thinking and instruction that makes the difference. There must be dedication to the proposition that reading is a mental process and that efficient reading-thinking skills must be taught.

Bibliography

1. Abercrombie, M. L. Johnson, *The Anatomy of Judgment*. New York: Basic Books, 1960.
2. Bloom, Benjamin, et al., *Taxonomy of Educational Objectives, Handbook I: Cognitive Domain*. New York: McKay, 1956.
3. Britton, James, *Language and Experience*. Baltimore: Penguin Books, 1970.
4. Davidson, Jane L., "The Quantity, Quality, and Variety of Teachers' Questions and Pupils' Responses During an Open-Communication Structured Group Directed Reading-Thinking Activity and a Closed-Communication Structured Group Directed Reading Activity." Ph.D. dissertation, University of Michigan, 1970.
5. Dewey, John, *Experience and Education*. New York: Macmillan, 1938.
6. Grobler, C. van Eyk, "Methodology in Reading Instruction as a Controlled Variable in the Constructive or Destructive Channeling of Aggression," Ph.D. dissertation, University of Delaware, 1971.
7. Guilford, J. P., "Frontiers in Thinking That Teachers Should Know About," *The Reading Teacher, 13* (February, 1960), 176–182.
8. Henderson, Edmund H., "A Study of Individually Formulated Purposes for Reading in Relation to Reading Achievement Comprehension and Purpose Attainment," Ph.D. dissertation, University of Delaware, 1963.
9. Petre, Richard M., "Quantity, Quality and Variety of Pupil Responses During an Open-Communication Structured Group Directed Reading-Thinking Activity and a Closed-Communication Structured Group Directed Reading Activity," Ph.D. dissertation, University of Delaware, 1970.
10. Piaget, Jean, *Science of Education and the Psychology of the Child*. Baltimore: Penguin Books, 1970.
11. Stauffer, Russell G., *Directing the Reading-Thinking Process*. New York: Harper & Row, 1975.
12. Stauffer, Russell G., *Teaching Reading as a Thinking Process*. New York: Harper & Row, 1969.
13. Stauffer, Russell G., et al., *Away We Go*. New York: Holt, Rinehart and Winston, 1960.
14. Stroud, J. B., "The Role of Practice in Learning," in *The Psychology of Learning*, Forty-first Yearbook of the National Society for the Study of Education, Part II. Chicago Ill.: University of Chicago Press, 1942.
15. Torrance, R. Paul, "Developing Creative Readers," in Russell G. Stauffer

(compiler), *Dimensions of Critical Reading,* Proceedings of the Annual Education and Reading Conferences, 1963–1964. Newark, Del.: University of Delaware, 1964.

16. Walpole, Hugh, *Semantics: The Nature of Words and Their Meanings.* New York: Norton, 1941.

Chapter 8
Inquiry Reading I

The first chapters of this book were devoted to how individual pupils learn to read by means of LEA procedures. Teachers were urged to start with whole-class-dictated stories, then move to group dictation, and on to individual dictation by early October. The account told about how pupils dictated their own ideas and used their own vocabularies and experiences to learn to read. The words they first learned were self-identified. The sentences that they assembled on their word-card holders from words in their word banks were of their own creation. The creative writing was their own and reflected their ideas and experiences as well as their hand-writing. The books they selected in the classroom library and in the school library were largely of their own choosing. The ideas they chose to share with their classmates were of their own choosing. In fact, each phase of the teaching-learning circumstance was predominantly individual.

It was equally apparent that each pupil and each activity were group and class based. Each child was a member of a class and of within-class groups that varied according to pupil purposes, interests, and needs. Stimuli to evoke interest and response were in most instances presented to the entire class. Reactions stimulated each child's individual sensory pathways but also required and inspired each to share ideas with the class. Oral language was used to share reactions and exchange ideas. Dictated stories, word bank idea creations, and creative stories were shared with the class. Books were read, enjoyed, and shared. Library visits were made by whole classes and by individuals.

In brief, communication of ideas constituted the principal crystallization of school life—intellectually and affectively, socially and individually. Interests, values, sympathies, and respect developed mutually. When the children worked by themselves, their conduct was marked by individual concentration, and when they were in a group, by effective collaboration. The children were learning to see other points of view and to coordinate them. They were acquiring new coordinations in the development of thought and feeling.

The account of directed group reading, in which each member reacted to the same material, described teaching-learning experiences quite different from the earlier ones. Now children were being introduced to the practices and procedures of a disciplined scholar. The practices were introduced as soon as the children's reading ability permitted, so that they could begin early to acquire sound habits and skills through repeated reinforcement. In a sense, the group DRTA provides the setting for pupils to learn to deal with the logic of thought. Jean Piaget puts it this way in one of his discussions about the progress of seven-year-olds (1, p. 41):

> With respect to intelligence, we are now dealing with the beginnings of the construction of logic itself. Logic constitutes the system of relationships which permit the coordination of points of view corresponding to different individuals, as well as those which correspond to the successive percepts or intuitions of the same individual. . . . The mental instruments which will facilitate logical and moral coordination are the operation in the field of intelligence and the will in the field of affectivity.

In a way, then, this chapter on inquiry reading is an invigorating and exhilarating remodeling of a *group* directed reading-thinking activity that for elucidation and comparison might be labeled an *individualized* directed reading-thinking activity. Inquiry reading procedures reflect and utilize practices and procedures, skills and attitudes of group DRTA actions. This chapter details further growth and development in the expanding educational lives of scholars coping with a curriculum that presents a variety of materials of varied difficulty.

Inquiry reading or individualized DRTA has a number of distinguishing features.

1. *Interest areas,* or the nature of the inquiries to be made, stem by and large from the children.
2. Inquiry areas are made more definitive and manageable by

categorizing and *subgrouping* specific points of interest within the scope of the children's understanding.

3. Inquiry is intensified by the raising of *questions*, thereby connecting it with pupil experiences and curiosities.

4. Motivation and inquiry impetus is strengthened and personalized by *pupil speculation*, thus taking into account the experiences, knowledge, and capacities of individuals or the powers and purposes of those taught.

5. *Materials are selected* that fit the needs (questions and speculations) of the pupils and that can be grasped (capabilities) by them. For the inquiry to be educative the materials must be adaptable to the individual; this is what regulates the quantity and difficulty of the material. Materials are selected from the range of multimedia possibilities.

6. *Obtaining answers*, adjusting inquiries, and internalizing information become the key factors in transactions that regulate the growth attained by the learner.

7. *Sharing information* includes the total social setup of the learning situation in which each pupil is engaged. Sharing requires thorough preparation and planning ahead, flexibility and firmness, with enough orderliness and clarity to hold attention.

8. *Audience interaction and evaluation* must manifest politeness and courtesy and avoid ritualistic forms. Judgments about the presentations must be fair and intrinsically worthwhile.

A principal pedagogical difference between the two teaching-learning procedures is the distinction between *group* instruction and *individualized* instruction. This is not to imply that there is no individualization of instruction during group DRTA time; there is, as has been shown again and again. Neither is it true that there is no group instruction during the individualized time; there is. The skills and abilities acquired in both instances are also interrelated, but the pedagogical emphases vary. On the one hand, in group DRTA's the formalized skills of a scholar are acquired and refined in the crucible of group interaction under immediate teacher direction. The conditions require immediate justification and defense of a position taken and judgments made. Through group interaction pupils acquire the humility of scholars as well as self-esteem and intensification of action. Here is where falsely directed self-will, pride, and sophistication are tempered so that pupils can become as realistic and rational as possible. Speculation or educated guesses or predictions make for free inquiry and for the empirical test of proof. The creative character of productive hypothesizing is decisively different from that of unproductive guesswork: Pupils engaged in hypothesizing want to prove their points; those not so engaged are fearful of doing so.

These cognitive skills are acquired and refined not in a day or a week or a year, but across the years and through the disciplines of accuracy and the hope of discovery. As children grow physically and intellectually and their interests and tastes expand and become refined, as they meet with the increasing demands of a spiraling curriculum, they must acquire the cognitive reading skills of a scholar. They must acquire minds that are disciplined and dignified, competent and productive, vigilant and independent.

A scholar learns to be self-reliant, enduring, open-minded, stable, humane, organized, confident yet humble. The skills and abilities acquired in group DRTA's are to be applied and extended by the children when they are on their own. Each must grasp the Socratic challenge to be and to know oneself, and for this, on the other hand, the individualized DRTA sesssions provide excellent training. The children learn to pursue their own interests, to refine interests into tastes, and to test their knowledge against the dimensions of a class that is essentially honest and critical.

Group DRTA's and individualized DRTA's provide sharply contrasting conditions, as the following account shows:

1. In group DRTA's pupils are grouped by the teacher, and the group members have about the same reading ability.

    In individualized DRTA's children are grouped according to their interests.

2. In group DRTA's group size is limited to 8 to 10 pupils.

    In individualized DRTA's no limit is placed on group size. Pupils may pursue an interest alone, in a group, or as a class.

3. In group DRTA's all pupils read the same selection at the same time. Basic readers can be used as well as other materials.

    In individualized DRTA's children seldom if ever read the same material at the same time. The library as a multimedia center becomes the principal source of material and a wide variety is available to be used. In addition, specialists can be consulted.

4. In group DRTA's teacher direction is constant. The teacher stays with the group until the DRTA is completed.

    In individualized DRTA's the teacher is a general director and collaborator and keeps the different enterprises going through the eight instructional facets and across the weeks.

5. In group DRTA's the time required for one DRTA is about 30 minutes.

    In individualized inquiry-type reading the time span may range from one to three to five weeks or more.

Nevertheless, the approaches have a number of pedagogical features in common:

1. Purposes for reading are declared by the pupils. The power to frame and to pursue purposes is bound to intellectual freedom and is the moving spring of action.
2. Answers to questions are validated.
3. Pupil actions and transactions do occur. Both are cooperative enterprises.
4. Pupil interactions are effected by the situation in which they share. The primary source of social control resides in the very nature of the DRTA being done.
5. The teacher is responsible for knowing individual pupils and for a broad knowledge of subject matter.
6. In each the procedure must be flexible enough to quicken the free play of individual experiences and cognitive powers and yet firm enough to keep the activity on course.
7. In each the intellectual freedom fosters the power to frame questions, to judge wisely, to evaluate desires by consequences, to select and order ideas, to pursue chosen ends into operation.
8. In each the ideal aim is progressive development of the power of the intellect and of self-control.

ALTERNATING INSTRUCTION

Plans to alternate between group DRTA's and inquiry reading individualized DRTA's are determined by a number of conditions: the reading abilities, maturity, interests, and tastes of the children. At the first-grade level the bright children will have a large enough reading vocabulary and sufficient word attack skills to begin group-type DRTA's by December. Usually the best source of material at this stage is found in a well-structured basic reader series. The readers should be examined with great care to be certain that the "stories" have (1) plots that are well developed and are not naïvely patronizing; (2) illustrations that help carry the plot forward but do not "tell" the story; (3) vocabulary controls for "new word" introduction; (4) language structure that reflects the language usage of our culture and is not distorted by warped syntactical arrangements; and (5) length that can be read in a 20-to-30-minute period. Group DRTA's should then be done on a basis of two or three per week for a period of three consecutive weeks. Instructional time must always be allowed for phase V, or the extending and refining of concepts. At the end of a three-week group DRTA session instruction turns again to dictation, to creative writing, to handwriting, to vocabulary development, to extensive wide reading, and the like. Of course, some of these activities are never ending, such as creative writing, handwriting, vocabulary development, extensive reading. This is the measure of variation suitable to activities in first grade. The six-year-olds seem not to have either the maturity or reader competence to engage in inquiry reading as described. Usually, too, the so-called average pupils are ready for group DRTA's by January and the less able by February or March. Invariably in a class of 28 randomly grouped children two or three pupils are not advanced enough even by April to engage in group DRTA's. They do, however, engage regularly in group DLTA's and enjoy doing so. They are quite responsive, also, to doing directed picture-thinking activities. Pictures structured in a series of episodes much like a series of comic strip cartoons can be shown one at a time to elicit "what next" predictions and "why-do-you-think-so?" thinking.

What to do in second grade and beyond is dealt with in Chapters 9 and 12. At this point it is sufficient to say that at the second-grade level both group and individualized DRTA's are introduced and alternated on a one- two- and three-week cycle. By fourth grade and beyond attention focuses ever more acutely on individualized DRTA's or on inquiry reading. Now time patterns alternate in such a way that approximately two-thirds of the instructional time is devoted to inquiry reading and about one-third to group DRTA's.

INSTRUCTIONAL PROCEDURES—FIRST GRADE

When the group DRTA activities end and the pupils return to a more intensified listening-speaking-writing phase, they do so with a new zest and an interesting degree of levity. The children sense the difference in structure and freedom between the two techniques and relish the variance. Their perspective toward and regard for the intensive integration of the facets of language is augmented.

Interests

Pupils are much more apt to pause and reflect over what to do and what to read when a group DRTA session ends. In three weeks they have become accustomed to the group DRTA routine and its provocative orderliness; such reaction is desirable and comforting. The thing to do when the change is made is to take advantage of their momentary pause.

This is a good time to introduce means for taking more personal initiative in selecting creative writing topics, in selecting reading materials, in sharing ideas, and in listening activities. The children can plan for this amplification of self-selection freedom, by examining their own likes or interests or tastes. A sharing session in which the children speak about what they might like to read can be held. Some pupil is sure to respond almost immediately by naming a book he wants to read and, thus, set others thinking and responding. Or if the question is qualified to what they might like to read about, attention is focused on interests or topics. It is almost like the distinction between interest as a value and interests as the values to which ever more complex goals to action are assigned (1, p. 35). Interest involves a value judgment, and interests suggest the forming of values.

The "interests" mentioned by the children might be listed on the board so that they can be examined. If this procedure is too formalized, some children may turn away because they find it difficult to make such self-analysis and to project likes and dislikes in so formal a way. One must therefore proceed with caution and keep within the projection range of the children. A small list is best for a start. Self-examination and decision making about actions are not easy without the stimulus of books and the library.

Interestingly enough, there will be more reading of nonfiction during the rest of the school year. This shift seems to be prompted by a number of conditions. The stimuli that promote creative writing and dictated materials are so varied that they arouse wide curiosity. As has already been indicated in earlier chapters, the topics range all the way from safety pins to battleships to orbiting spacecraft. In addition, the rest of the school curriculum proves a fruitful source of ideas. Science and health activities yield a large return. Social studies and current events are also promoters of inquisitiveness. Of course, the omnipresent television is a ready source of ideas, as are newspapers, magazines, and the radio.

Word Recognition

Now that specific steps have been given describing what readers should do when they encounter a word they do not recognize instantly in the group DRTA situation, the same rules are reviewed for self-selection reading purposes. Obviously, pupils may encounter more words they do not recognize while reading a book they have selected than when reading the stories in a basic reader that the teacher has selected. They may also experience a greater desire to unlock more unknown words. Most likely they will be making more attempts at word recognition than before the group DRTA sessions. Accordingly, it is wise to review the steps and post a chart listing them.

First, the reader always reads to the end of the sentence or even the paragraph in which the unrecognized word appears. He does this because getting the idea proves to be effective. It is a fitting use of both interpolation or extrapolation of ideas. It keeps attention focused on comprehension and that is what reading is all about. In addition, he may study the picture for meaning clues.

Second, he tries to analyze the word by breaking it into sound units or syllables and noting common endings and beginnings. This breaking down into sound units facilitates recognition of phoneme-grapheme representations.

Third, he tries to sound the word and pronounce it. Chances are good that if he blends the sounds correctly, he will recognize the word because it is already in his speaking-meaning vocabulary.

Fourth, he turns to the teacher for help. The mark of a scholar is to realize that when he has tried all the skills at his command and failed, he must turn to someone more skilled. The important decision is the full recognition that he does not know and needs help.

Throughout the self-selection reading period, word attack skills are taught as they are throughout the group DRTA period. The members of a group can be called together from time to time to discuss words they attacked successfully and to tell how they did it. This kind of sharing of knowledge about words and about word attack skills is particularly beneficial.

Some of the words so identified may be added to the selective word bank. In addition, some of the words may show up in creative writing. If this happens it is evidence of the highest order that the children are functionally using the words they have learned.

Sharing

Prior to this time, sharing was done in a number of practical and partially spontaneous ways. A pupil might have found a page in a book that she wanted to read to the class. If when she approached the teacher it seemed not too disruptive to ask the class to listen, the teacher invited them to do so. Then it might be discovered that three or four others had something to share: a new word learned, a way they unlocked a word, a picture, a funny sentence, a creative story.

Sharing time may be scheduled daily. Pupils may request some of the sharing time by listing their names on the daily scheduling board. Of course, the teacher stays alert to all the pupils and makes certain that all who want to participate do. Sharing time may also be used to fill waiting minutes; so many of these seem to occur in the life of first graders. They await the milk break, the television program, their turn to go to the auditorium, recess, lunch, and so on. Waiting and sharing can become almost synonymous and make waiting a pleasant experience.

Sharing time is best scheduled for longer terms, though, either once a week (good at first) or twice in three weeks. Some of the most important reasons pedagogically for fixed times are as follows:

1. If pupils want to share something with the class and wants the class to give its undivided attention, they should *plan* what they want to share. This is not to imply that some planning was not done for the first kinds of

sharing but to say that now deliberate effort is made to plan. The teacher and pupils talk about how to plan different presentations: oral reading, new words, a monologue, a team skit, a puppet show, and so on.

2. When pupils have planned what they want to share, they must give thought to *different ways* of sharing that are unique and will hold the attention of the class. A pupil may want to share something about George Washington, for instance, and make a tricornered hat to wear, or about April showers and wear a raincoat and hat, or about skiing and show ski shoes, or about words and prepare an illustration or a mural for a set of sequences in a story. Some of the sharing may be written, but most of it will be oral.

3. Some pupils are quite original about how to share, but others are not and become concerned. So it is helpful to prepare a *ways-to-share poster.* Each sharing idea can be written on a 3-×-5-inch card. The cards can then be arranged by putting them on a card holder, by pinning them on the corkboard, by keeping an orderly pile in a box, or by keeping them together with a rubber band. This permits pupils to reexamine ideas and select one that they think will serve best. Some will need help in decision making, so the teacher is always available and observant.

4. After pupils have planned what and how they will share, they need to *rehearse* the presentation. This is a key aspect of sharing. To be effective and to ask others to be attentive, one must be prepared. There is not much difference between staging a play and staging a sharing session. Accordingly, pupils have to learn how to rehearse, privately, without disturbing the class. Pupils are unbelievably ingenious at both quietness and secretiveness.

5. Thought must be given to *personnel.* A pupil must decide if he is going to do the sharing alone or if he needs help. Thus monologues, dialogues, teams, and casts are planned and scheduled. Partners vary from session to session and purpose to purpose and much interaction results.

6. Some thought must also be given to the *time* needed for a presentation. This may prove challenging to some, but, if the idea is not carried too far, all can give at least an approximation: a very short time, a little time, pretty much time, and the like.

Records

Now that the approach to reading instruction resembles that of individualized self-selection, some form of record keeping is in order. The best procedure is to have the pupils keep accounts. This is all a part of the self-regulatory aspect of being a scholar—to know one's interests, to convert interests to tastes, to pursue one's interests, to share one's interests, and to keep an account.

This, then, is the time to introduce book-record cards. Cards 3 × 5 or 5 × 8 inches provide just the right amount of space. Most pupils prefer the 3-×-5-inch index card, but some do better with larger ones. Index cards are excellent for the purpose; they are lined and durable. They are readily filed, too, in various types of container. Commercial file boxes are made especially for different sizes of index cards; shoe boxes and the like also serve adequately.

Records must be simple enough that the children can keep them and, at the same time, must be effective enough to serve the purpose of a record. One procedure practical enough to meet all purposes is as follows:

1. For every book a child reads, a card is prepared.
2. On the first line or two of the card the book title is copied.
3. A line is skipped and then the author's name is copied.
4. Another line is skipped and a double entry is made on the next line: (a) First the number of pages in the book is listed, (b) then the number of pages read is listed. A card might read: "36, 36," or "36, all," or "36, 10." The first two entries show that the entire book was read. The third shows that 10 of the 36 pages were read.
5. A typical card might be as follows:

| *Lucy and Red* |
| Micha Trimor |
| 44   44 |

By the time record keeping is introduced, each pupil will have done a considerable amount of creative writing and will have enough handwriting skill to keep records. Even so, checks by the teacher always help the children maintain readable and accurate accounts.

When record keeping is first introduced, it tends to set off a wave of entries. Quantity seems to have high priority. Let the competition run its course. It will not last. This is especially true when the children with many cards discover that the teacher seems just as enthusiastic about Jim's 10 cards as Myra's 30.

Notice that the children are *not* asked to add a *comment* about the book. Comments, at this stage particularly, tend to become stereotyped and redundant. Let it be known, though, that if they wish to say something about a book they may. Discretion must then be exercised so that children do not get the notion that the teacher really wants a comment. If this happens, it is better either to drop the idea entirely or to require all to say something. Usually, though, when comments are voluntary, this evokes more and better responses than otherwise.

Above all, make it clear that a pupil does not need to read an entire book. Just as adults do, some pupils discover that a certain book is not interesting and they put it down after reading some of it. Or, because of the nature of their interest, they do not want or need to read the entire book to obtain what they wish. This kind of scholarly discipline promotes selective reading. A child may read an article in an encyclopedia, for example, and wish to make a record card.

The teacher should examine the book entries periodically. This is a good time to discuss books with children. A recent or an old entry may be discussed. If properly handled, children are pleased to share with the teacher and to have their cards examined.

When children have read the same books and kept similar entries, a stimulating procedure is to have a round-table discussion.

Direction

By this time the reader may be curious as to why this chapter has been labeled individualized directed reading-thinking activities. It is true that the activities engaged in during the fall of the year and in the first phases of the program were directed by the teacher. Now, though, the contrast between group and individualized reading-thinking activities sharpens and clarifies the dimensions of each. In addition, more of the activities are now being directed toward developing pupils who can deliberately bring to bear specific scholarly actions on a self-selected reading goal.

True adaptation to their peers comes about gradually as the budding scholars learn to present their ideas and make them understood. They learn to subordinate themselves to the ideas they are presenting and to their audience. They learn to cooperate with others in the presentation of ideas and to show increasing appreciation for the points of view of others. They begin to seek justification or proof, not only in group DRTA situations but in all situations. They appreciate the need for regulated and conclusive discussion. They learn to think before acting, to plan, to anticipate responses and questions, to be ready—in other words, they are learning to be deliberate and to reflect; Piaget refers to reflection as "internalized social discussion" (4, p. 40). The pupil begins to see the value of actively pursuing a goal consistently and in a disciplined way. They avoid being offensive, ridiculing or scoffing or being overly critical. They show appreciation for the flow of ideas and the amenities that accompany the interchange of ideas.

Above all, they learn to examine their own interests and tastes and gain increasing appreciation for the depth and seriousness of the questions they raise. Somehow they begin to sense that values reside not so much in the answers we give as in the questions we raise. Thereby, they uncover the elemental motivation to learning and to thinking—the *power of intellectual commitment*.

All this requires careful direction by the teacher in setting a course toward the true goal of education, to prepare thinking, reflecting, responsible scholars. We cannot wait until children are in high school to set progress toward these objectives in motion, but we must do so from the very beginning of formal instruction. In a reading instruction world harassed by materialistic publishers and prejudiced, corrupt, and dogmatic extremists, we cannot afford for one minute to withdraw to a corner of mental timidity and emotional cowardice and extend the nonreading void in which so many children are caught. We must strive militantly to provide reading-thinking direction as defined here, and we must do so in the name of scholarship.

A LANGUAGE ACTIONS FOUNDATION

For the rest of the school year the reading program is in all respects a language arts program, a communications program. Reading serves a purpose. It is a means to pleasure in relaxation or entertainment as well as a means to pleasure through the learning of new ideas. Reading can be silent or, on occasion, oral. Oral reading is meant to prove a point in both the group and the individualized DRTA sessions. In the latter, oral reading is also for sharing a story or an idea. Entire books or parts of books are read. Encyclopedias are used, as are dictionaries and other similar sources. Newspapers and magazines are read. Books are read in science, health, history, music.

Much listening is done, too. Pupils listen to the dictated stories of their peers. Sometimes they hear 8 or 10 very different versions of the same episode, and they begin to sense that each person views things just a bit differently from his neighbor. Pupils listen to creative writing accounts. They attend sharing sessions, and, almost every day, they hear the teacher read aloud. This is a delightful time of the day, and they never tire of it. Fiction and nonfiction as well as poetry are read, and the teacher's reading of poetry is really beautiful. So they are learning much by reading and by listening. Many new ideas are being taken in and many old ones are enriched.

Much opportunity to talk has been provided from the very beginning. Not only did the children dictate stories to the teacher and have a chance to say things their way, but they also had a chance to read their dictated stories to others. They read their creative-writing stories, too. In the sharing sessions, they helped stage different kinds of presentations and had many opportunities to talk. They appeared in front of their classmates on many occasions and in many ways—sometimes screened from them, as in puppet shows, sometimes wearing masks or costumes, sometimes behind a lectern or a table or a stand, sometimes next to a map or a chart or a picture, sometimes in a semidarkened room showing slides or overhead-projector transparencies, sometimes in a play or a skit. These opportunities help develop poise, confidence, and ease and they make the presenting person sensitive to the audience.

Almost since the first copying of names, the children have been writing. They occasionally added a word to their word banks, being very careful to form each letter correctly. They wrote many, many creative stories and accounts. They kept their own reading records. Writing served in many ways, and they learned that if they wanted someone else to read their writing, they had to write letters and words clearly.

This is an action program based on the active use of language. As one first-grade girl said, "We are on the go all the time." They are always doing something—reading, writing, listening, speaking, planning, going to the library, making visits in and around the school and the community. This is truly a first grade on the go.

CONCLUSION

Much individualized instruction occurred prior to the initiation of group directed reading-thinking activities, but now a new slant is given to such instruction, because the training in the group situation helps the young scholar-readers to be more self-reliant and resourceful as reader-thinkers. They see more clearly how to set purposes for reading, how to attack words, how to search for meaning, and how to be versatile reading detectives.

Individualized instruction helps readers learn about themselves, their interests, their tastes, their ambitions, their perseverance, their judgment. They learn how to select material that both answers purposes and is readable. They see the classroom, school, and community libraries as true resource centers.

How to examine one's interests and select from among them one or two to be ardently pursued becomes a crucial matter and requires direction by the teacher. Equally important, though, is how to share interests and knowledge with one's peers. If classmates are to listen and be attentive, presentations must be made in such a way as to hold their attention. This means that, to share, one must plan and rehearse so that the sharing is done with the ease of a professional stage presentation. To do this, the pupils and the teacher may help in planning, rehearsing, and staging. Props may be required. Time needed should be determined, so that a class schedule can be prepared. All this requires a considerable amount of resourcefulness and dedication.

Accomplishing all these features makes the language-experience program an all-embracing language arts program. Required for success are ability to declare interests, to locate materials, to use materials, to plan ways of sharing, and to share. In other words, children read, write, talk, listen, and think, in functional communication.

Bibliography

1. Piaget, Jean, *Six Psychological Studies,* edited by David Elkind. New York: Random House, 1967.

Chapter 9
Inquiry Reading II

The objective conditions described involving the experiences and language of children at the first-grade level have set a definitive course for enriched growth through further instruction. One condition that should stand out clearly when instruction and learning are conceived as described is that the materials must fall within the life experience of the children. This, however, is only a first step. Next is the progressive development across the curriculum and across the years of the reading process so far acquired into a fuller and richer and more organized form. The experiences and the capacities that have been developed and utilized should provide the foundation for all further learning. The skills so far acquired make possible vast new educative growth.

At a staff meeting of all primary-level teachers late one September, a second-grade teacher said, "I have never had so many children who could read so many words and who know what to do when they encounter a 'new' word." It was evident that she was enthusiastic and was giving whatever happened in first grade her tacit endorsement. Even so, her first measure of achievement was "words known" and her second measure was "attacking an unknown word." This is typical of persons oriented toward traditional memoriter procedures. How much more fitting it would have been had she commented about the pupils' attitude toward reading, their wide interests, the nature of their comprehension, their resourcefulness, their cooperative actions, and above all their enthusiasm.

The achievement of children measured at the end of their first year, at the beginning of second grade, and on a carefully controlled replication study (15) showed strong performances in LEA programs. The tests used in these studies measured only certain limited aspects of reading achievement and little if any in the other facet, language (4, 15, 16). Even though the test of creative writing showed excellent achievement, it was an adapted test and needed more validity and reliability to be sound. Not measured were the children's regard for reading, their resourcefulness as readers, their range of interests and tastes, their versatility with oral and written language, their library usage skills, their ability to interact and to cooperate, their sharing abilities, their listening abilities, their self-directive learning behavior, or above all, their abilities to set goals and pursue them.

First-Year Accounting

Because the LEA approach is founded on activity and respect for work done, the skills acquired are functional and readily tabulated. This is so because the aim of instruction is understanding and communication.

Dictations provide a chronological record of performance. Each child has a booklet in which dictations are kept in order from September through May. Each dictation is dated and thereby helps identify specific achievement and progress. Achievement shows quantitative and qualitative changes in amount dictated, such as number of sentences, length and complexity of sentences, number of running words, number of different words, sequence of ideas, use of nomenclature fitting a topic of interest, range of interests, number of words underlined as known words, and nature and quality of the illustrations. The dictated accounts also show objective evidence of regulated instruction and the choice of interests and conditions that interacted with the existing capacities and needs of those taught to create worthwhile experiences. The accounts show too what consideration was given to the powers and purposes of those taught. Most of the dictations are accounts of firsthand experiences structured by the teacher, some accounts are based on remembered experiences of earlier days, and some few accounts are creative, imaginative stories that reveal still other potentials.

These specific measures of achievement provide recognizable accounting for the children too. Any child can look back at any time and react. One child in March looked back at a September dictation and said, "That's how I talked when I was little." In addition, children can compare accounts with each other.

Parents can be shown graphic and comprehensible evidence of achievement. The specifics so far declared are a far cry from the inexplicable and enigmatic letter grades usually found on report cards.

School records can be filled with a digest accounting of specifics. Such documentation is useful not only for immediate purposes but also for subsequent years. As a result, instruction can be more readily geared to achievement and growth potential.

Word bank evidence is bountiful and meaningful for instructional accounting but even more so for learner reassurance and optimism. A weekly total of bank words and new additions can be readily maintained and dated. When the words are alphabetized, the number of words filed under each letter can be maintained. The accounting serves different purposes: children can see that some letters begin many words (b, d, m, r, s) and that some begin only a few words (e, h, j, k, v); that some represent varied sounds (*c*at, *c*ity, *c*hild, *t*op, *t*he, *t*ree,); and that *x*, *y*, and *z* words are somewhat unique. Skill in locating a word in an alphabetized word bank is twofold. First, the ease with which a child turns to the middle of the bank for a word like *m*other, or the front of the bank for *b*aker, or the back of the bank for *s*ummer reveals a grasp of alphabetical relationships. Second, locating such words as *car* under *c*, not *k*, and *phone* under *p*, not *f*, demonstrates a functional knowledge of letter-sound, phoneme-grapheme variability. Words can be categorized as *thing* words, *animal* words, *people* words, *place* words, *space* words, and so on. Again a wealth of documented information is available for precision accounting.

Creative writing and encoding folders are a rich source of documentation. Each entry is dated and provides a chronological record for evaluation and comparison. Handwriting evidence is bountiful, such as ability to form upper and lower case letters and ability to space letters and words. Punctuation usage is readily appraised: periods, commas, question marks, exclamation marks, quotes. The range and nature of the topics written about provide evidence to the scope of the child's interests. Of special importance because of its twofold nature is the encoding. First, it reveals the number of words so well established that they can be produced when needed in the accepted letter order (spelling power). Second, the encoding shows a grasp of phoneme-grapheme relationships and the ability to produce them. Third, the phonological encodings reveal adaptability and versatility in encoding effort and the need to teach, reteach, and establish more functionally those productions not grasped: *lite* for *light*, *treting* for *treating*, *frst* for *first*, *dotr* for *doctor*, and so on. Perhaps the most important information is the frequency and nature of the writings, because these reflect not only children's interests but also their attitude toward writing and their confidence in their phonic (phoneme-grapheme) ability, handwriting, and ability to create. It also reveals the *nature* of the pupils writing, how they construe the world about them, the kinds of action verbs they use, the value judgments (adjectives and adverbs) they make, their poetic tendencies, their scale of values, how they shift from egocentric diary form writing (intrapersonal) to sociocentric (interpersonal) communication.

Library usage provides still another accounting. Weekly visits to the school library show pupils' responses to the opportunity; their reaction to books, magazines, and so on; the items they select to take with them. The classroom library provides similar evidence, but because of its ready access provides even more. The record of books read in part or entirely and the comments about the reading are excellent sources. Sharing books, book illustrations, and words provides still more accountings. If the major outcome of reading instruction is the acquisition of a desire to read, then in many ways the library provides the best single measure of instructional success. The most important attitude that can be formed is that of the desire to go on reading.

The DRTA instructional sessions provide yet another means of assessing achievement. Because this is a structured group circumstance flexible enough to provide free play of individual capabilities and firm enough to give direction, certain key educational values can be identified. Cognitively the participants are learning to make their reading actions purposefully directed, to extrapolate information of predictive value, to deal with an array of options or expectations, to make well-formed judgments, to prove points by providing evidence. Socially, a child learns to cope with the reactions and challenges of others, to commune with others, to stand his ground, and to observe conventions and courtesies.

These numerous accountings, if anything, prove conclusively that in reality "all good teaching is diagnostic." The range and variety of data available cannot be matched in any diagnostic center or any paper-and-pencil test. It is the cumulative effect of firsthand functional situations that represents the principal difference.

All in all the pupils have engaged in many activities that have challenged them, aroused their confidence, and showed them how to be resourceful and persistent. They have enjoyed reading about many things and sharing with others. They have felt that they were respected by their classmates as well as their teacher. From the start, their language and ideas were accepted. Gradually, they changed some of their language as well as ideas, because they realized they could achieve things better that way. In brief, they have emerged as young scholars intent on discovering and mastering knowledge in a steady, self-regulated, teacher-directed, affectively tempered way.

INQUIRY READING: NEXT STAGES

The previous chapter described in detail the circumstances surrounding the introduction of *group* directed reading-thinking activities and the alternating of instruction with *individualized* directed reading-thinking activities. At the second- and third-grade levels and then at the fourth-grade level and beyond a variation of the alternating plan serves best to take into account the continuous development of the mind and character of the children.

The summer between first and second grade usually results in a fair amount of forgetting, as school records show and teachers confirm. This is especially true for the low achievers. In some school districts where memoriter methods of reading instruction prevail it is the rule to start *all* second graders in reading in a primer-level basic reader. Even though such practices are devoid of motivation and interest (the pupils know the stories), the actions are justified on the grounds of "review." If they use other basals the vocabulary is new and makes too many demands.

However, evidence in various research studies (15) shows that children nurtured on the eclectic approach not only maintained their skills and abilities but improved them. Their attitudes toward reading and creative writing were such that they practiced during the summer and consequently showed improvement. Of course, not all improved, but so many did to such a degree that overall they contributed to a resounding success story.

The opening of second grade in the fall should not expose the children to an extended period of review. The motivation should be refreshingly stimulating. Some skills, such as how to deal with words not recognized at sight and word attack skills, may be reviewed. Also reviewed are skills of determining interests, selecting materials, and sharing. All this is done while reading, though, and not as isolated drills on warmed-over material.

Getting started in second grade is an exciting adventure, with the first month of school being devoted to an all-out language arts effort. In the studies cited in *Action Research in L.E.A. Instructional Procedures** it followed naturally from the life experiences of the children that they talked and dictated about the summer. They listened too, and read and reread about such summertime doings as trips, swimming pool adventures, seashore days, storms, picnics, playground games, skate boarding, boating, and the like.

Creative writing may be reactivated along about mid-September. Word attack training should be engaged in for the purpose of just reading and especially for encoding. Reviews are made of auditory discrimination,

*See Appendix B.

visual-auditory discrimination, consonant substitution and vowel substitution, and the vowel key.

Library usage should be reintroduced. Again classroom libraries are in the center of the room or pod and are stocked with an array of books and magazines and papers. Among the papers should be daily papers and copies of *My Weekly Reader* ranging from so-called first-grade level to sixth-grade level. At no time should any second grade be limited to only second-grade level Weekly Readers. To do so is to deny individual differences and violate the basic tenets of a multivaried LEA approach. School central libraries are also visited. Books varying from science to social science, from poetry to fiction were presented. Not only did the books encompass different interests but they were also of different readability levels.

Increasingly on the national scene, public libraries are being made available throughout an entire year, but especially during the summer. Book mobiles also make more visits at this time, and school libraries are being kept open throughout summer months.

Throughout September, experiences of the summer provide a fertile source, a starting point, a means by which learning and instruction function in relation to a purpose-increased command of the reading-thinking process. By the end of the month both the teacher and the pupils will have discovered many things. Pupils will have either started reading or continued reading at a pace they can maintain. Pupils find this month of self-appraisal worthwhile; they can get their feet on the ground without spurious and unseemly pressure. As a result, they approach reading-writing-listening-speaking activities confidently, cooperatively, and industriously.

The teacher is doubly alert. She notes levels of performance and makes inventories of needs. The month becomes an inventory-accounting month in a very true sense. For instance, she notes pupil word attack skill abilities and requests for help with words; she then gears instruction accordingly. She notes the kinds of books selected for reading, the nature of pupil's interests, and the efficiency of the book-card record keeping. She talks with children individually and hears them read aloud. She studies their creative writings. In brief, September is a marvelous time to get acquainted personally and educationally and to set a course.

Group directed reading-thinking activities are begun in October. The children are grouped at levels each member can attain without frustration. Groups have no more than 8 or 10 children. Usually three or four groups are formed and usually basal reader materials are used for instructional purposes. Some children can handle third-reader-level material or higher with ease, some read at the second-reader level, and some use first readers. Always at least one pupil needs to continue intensive effort using only pupil dictations. On no occasion, though, are all the children at a primer level as described earlier.

The group DRTA's follow the patterns described in detail in Chapter 3. The increased maturity allows for refining predictive abilities, formulating hypotheses or questions, dealing with facts and options, making decisions about the quality and accuracy of answers, and so on. What to do when a word is met that is not recognized instantly is carefully reviewed. In brief, a reading process is being taught, a way of attacking information obtained through the printed word and related illustrations.

Inquiry-type reading is activated approximately in November. When this occurs basic readers are totally removed for a period of three to four weeks and instruction is devoted to inquiring into pupil ideas and interests. The interest to be pursued may be introduced by the teacher or by pupils. The teacher takes full advantage of life-experience circumstances. Because this is the Halloween season, related topics may be used. Masks—their origin, use, production, and nature—make an interesting topic for a week or so. Samples of masks may be examined, and pupils may ask questions (e.g., "Who made the first masks?" "Why did witch doctors wear masks?" "When did we start using Halloween masks?") Speculation about likely answers reflects pupil capacities and experiences. By refined standards this speculation may appear meager and even haphazard. But this is to be expected at this introductory stage. Groundwork is being laid and maturity and repeated opportunity are needed to develop polish. This of course is true of all activities, even those largely physical. Pupil speculations may be as follows: "Long ago people made masks"; "The first mask was an animal head"; "Witch doctors scare away colds"; "Indians wear masks to dance"; and so on. Books about masks are made available in the classroom library. Pictures are examined and encyclopedias are consulted. The children read about, view, and discuss masks, and they share ideas about them. Usually take several forms: writing creatively, reading to the class, making illustrations for viewing, and making masks. Invariably such a topic evokes a widening horizon and related issues are examined. Early people and their culture are talked about, read about, and written about. Medicine men and witch doctors prove interesting topics. Halloween masks, pumpkin faces, and the like, prove of interest. Materials used for masks are studied.

An interest area such as masks may occupy a class for two or maybe three weeks. Sometimes in a three-week period a different interest is pursued each week. Most times one interest area occupies a class for at least two weeks.

The intent of inquiry reading is to impress the pupils with the nature and breadth of knowledge, and with the library as a principal source of knowledge. In addition, they must learn that a basic reading program does not constitute all reading, but that one reads in varied sources not only about certain basal reader characters but about persons, places, things, and events. No topic should ever be considered in isolation. Every interest has a setting, (place) a social context (persons), a time of discovery and development (history), a future, and above all a connectedness, by class or species or category.

Alternating from group DRTA's to individualized DRTA's or inquiry reading can be done by such a plan for the rest of the year. Roughly, *the alternating should occur every three weeks.* Proceeding this way avoids the repetitious pitfall of basal reader stories. Multimedia centers are constantly featured as sources of reading material. Nonfiction materials or materials from other parts of the curriculum help expand curiosities and experiences. Problem solving is featured. Creative writing is utilized functionally. Dictation continues but in a more knowledge-seeking manner. Word attack skills are used and refined. Vocabularies are extended. Concepts are attained.

By the time a second session of inquiry reading is initiated the children will have learned a great deal about themselves, the school, and knowledge in general. As a result each succeeding opportunity takes on a more refined structure. Each planning session results in a more careful self-examination of likes and dislikes, interests and tastes, and motivations. At the same time pupils respond to their classmates. Above all, they begin to realize that one does not just read but that one *reads about something.* This in turn helps focus attention both inwardly on self and outwardly on the world, particularly the immediate life-experience world.

Gradually, too, reading and collecting ideas occur with an eye to *sharing.* No longer are the children reading just for themselves. Because they are going to share some and perhaps all they have learned, reading becomes more selective. This is true even among the less able. Sharing promotes rereading, a get-your-facts-straight attitude, and reflection.

How to share becomes crucial. By spring of the year new ways of sharing are sought. At this time numerous ways can be listed and some published listings prove helpful, such as the one by Amy E. Jensen (12) or the one by Jeanette Veatch (20).

Pursuing the alternate plan as described in second grade helps children realize that reading skills are acquired in a variety of reading situations and serve a variety of purposes and that comprehension skills are of greater value than word attack skills. At no time do they get the notion that reading involves only reading day after day and week after week in a "basal reading series." Certainly they never get the notion that reading means just to read aloud. It seems that at last the oral reading tradition can be broken. Children need not fear "reading aloud," for they are beginning to realize that reading can be done to search for answers and for individual enjoyment.

Teachers are beginning to realize that a good reading program provides a broad-based foundation for the development of reading power in all areas of knowledge. Perhaps of most importance is teacher realization that the contrived fiction of basal readers, their gratuitous and warped use of myths and folktales, their impropitious use of poetry represent a meager and uninspiring diet. No longer will teachers feel that so-called library reading is supplementary to basal reading. This indeed was one of the most baleful attitudes foisted on reading instruction. No longer will a second or a third set of basal readers be used as supplementary readers. No series of basal readers can ever serve as a substitute for the range and depth of a library. No longer will teachers have the mistaken notion that they must listen to every child read orally two or three times a week and make meticulous notes. Quite to the contrary, the teachers' meticulous notekeeping will follow the comprehensive discriminating registry described in the accountability portions of this chapter.

INQUIRY READING: ITS EXTENSION AND REFINEMENT

Probably one of the most näive notions that has prevailed is the idea that certain reading skills can be introduced only at the third and fourth grades and beyond. This is not true. The basic skills of comprehension are the same at all levels because they are basically thinking skills. What does change is the increasing maturity of the children, the nature of their inquiry or their purposes for reading, and the scope and depth of their interests and tastes. Paralleling this is the change in the nature (science, literature, mathematics) and readability or complexity of the materials. As a matter of fact, examination of one of the numerous "flow charts" accompanying basal readers shows that the comprehension skills defined at the early primary level are the same at each succeeding level. The difference lies in the increasing maturity and skill acquisition of the children. Accordingly, the extension and refinement period continues throughout school, indeed throughout life. Always the continuity of experience says that the extension is based on that which has already been learned. So in the progress toward refinement and efficiency, purposes become increasingly more probing, interests become wider, tastes are deepened, attitudes are acquired and fashioned. In short, reading becomes a principal source of personal pleasure and a means of obtaining limitless knowledge.

When reading instruction is based on the sound premises as described it involves:

1. Group-type directed reading-thinking activities at all levels, even, as M. L. Johnson Abercrombie described, at the medical

school level (1). Her account of the processes of perception and reasoning are invaluable.

2. Individualized-type directed reading-thinking activities or inquiry reading to develop self-regulatory readers able to cope with material at the breadth and depth of knowledge of the curriculum.
3. Integrating reading into the language arts and at all times viewing it as *one* of the communication arts.
4. Acquiring a reading habit so that reading will always be a source of pleasure and a means of developing intellectually and emotionally.

Although there are statements in the Bullock report that should be questioned, there are many that should be applauded. One such statement merits repeating here.

> Associated with the notion of the specialized teaching in reading, both in the U.S.A. and here, is the commercially produced programme, sometimes called the "reading workshop" or "reading laboratory." Again on the face of it such programmes appear to offer a ready-made route to the development of reading skills. However, the fact that a pupil can become adept at completing the reading tasks in this rather narrow context does not mean that this ability will automatically transfer, and that he will be able to apply it at will in his other reading. Moreover, we have seen little evidence to support the view that there is any long term value in "booster" courses using these programmes [5, p. 117].

Three sentences further on is an added judgment that warrants being reproduced in bold face as it is here.

> **However, any real gain in reading development must come through the generation of a strong motivation, and this means reading to satisfy a purpose. This is more likely to arise from the wide-ranging opportunities of the curriculum than from the arbitrary stimulus of "laboratory materials"** [5, p. 117].

In many ways it would be better perhaps to discard the word *curriculum* and speak of it always as the "progressive organization of knowledge." As John Dewey says, for an experience to be educative it must "tend both to knowledge of more facts and entertaining of more ideas and to a better, a more orderly, arrangement of them" (8, p. 102). It is then, too, that (1) inquiry reading is directed by some leading purpose or idea that results in action; (2) the purposes are tested by the consequences they produce when they are acted on; (3) accounting is a matter of reflective reviewing and summarizing. This is so because reflection "is the heart of intellectual organization and of the disciplined mind" (8, 110). In this respect *reflection* means to review what has been done on a gross basis so as to extract the net meanings and thereby supply capital investment for dealing with new inquiries.

Interest Areas

The inquiring minds of eight- and nine-year-olds now well into the oper-
ationaly phase of intellectual development show an astounding degree of
curiosity, and seminal ideas, and a range of exploratory skills seeking
purposeful direction. Because this is so an instructor needs only to set the
power to the demands of the content in the different areas. As a result,
instruction in how to read in the content areas does not wait until some
mythical moment in the secondary schools. Texts on reading in the content areas are aimed at this level and this is a ridiculous oversight, but
perhaps even more ridiculous is the notion that there is a "reading content" that is not in the "content areas." One does not read reading. Always
one reads about something even when the something is poorly contrived
fiction.

At the beginning of a four- to six-week inquiry reading session a
number of days are devoted to declaring, selecting, and talking about
interests. First, a range of topics is declared: space, weather, oil, sports,
oceans, mammals, famous Americans, ham string muscles, diesel motors,
Amtrak, supersonic flights, and so on. In this classroom each topic was
listed as shown and enlarged on briefly by the pupil who proposed the
idea. To this the instructor added two: mountains and Queen Elizabeth II.

Categorizing

The following day the class selected three of the topics for exploration:
oceans, space, Queen Elizabeth II. To make the topics more definitive
and to further utilize the experience and knowledge the students already
have, *ideas* relative to each topic were declared. Each of the three topics
reminded the children of a variety of related items.

Oceans	Space	Queen Elizabeth II
fish	astronauts	Queen Elizabeth I
currents	flights	Queen Mother
pollution	space shuttle	Prince Charles
oil	satellites	coronation
fishing	explorations	25th anniversary
transportation	stars	duties
exploration	planets	castles
crabbing	sound barrier	knights
sea battles	control centers	Robin Hood
oil spills	launching pads	coat of arms
shipwrecks	equipment	dictators
hurricanes	food	crowning
sharks	pollution	Queen's guard

(continued)

Oceans	Space	Queen Elizabeth II
icebergs	winds	changing of guards
whales	maps	crown jewels
lobsters	weather	
swimming	Milky Way	
shipyards	comets	
boating	moon landings	
Atlantic Ocean		
Pacific Ocean		

Again each idea proposed was discussed briefly by the pupil who made the suggestion. The list provided an index to the acquisitiveness of the children and their alertness, and their brief discussions showed the earnestness and depth of their curiosity. Thus instruction was deliberately proceeding in such a way that the experience and the capacities of the students provided the starting point for further learning.

How to make the range of proposals less wieldy was resolved in part by subgrouping or categorizing. The *ocean* listings were grouped under topics as shown and was done by the children. They must see how items go together.

OCEAN

Sea Life	Conditions	Shipping
fish	currents	transportation
sharks	pollution	shipyards
whales	oil spills	clipper ships
lobsters	hurricanes	
	icebergs	
	oil	

Different Oceans	Things to Do
Atlantic Ocean	fishing
Pacific Ocean	crabbing
	swimming
	boating

By this time all the children will have contributed in some fashion. A few might dominate the topic discussions if the instructor allowed. The eagerness of some is an early indication of the degree of curiosity; the reticence of others can be offset by wise handling and by giving them an opportunity to participate. This preliminary declaring of interests and "sharing of ignorance" not only arouses curiosity and motivates but leads to an insight into what is known and what is not known. In brief, this forum has provided an accountability opportunity for the children. The accountability is unto themselves, and this too is a mark of a true scholar.

Raising Questions

The listing of topics and the categorizing has opened up naturally into a "what we know" and "what we do not know" phase. It is the latter that prompts the questions. Thus the sessions up to this point have focused instructionally and equally on two things: First, problems grow out of the life-experiences of the learner and are within the range of curiosities and capacities of the students; second, what is done is of such a nature that it results in arousing in the pupils an active desire to seek information and produce new ideas. Thus the questions to be raised, the problems to be solved, stem from the pupils and are not imposed from without.

Different approaches are feasible. Sometimes questions are raised by all class members. Other times pupils select an area of interest and then assemble in small groups to raise questions. Both approaches have advantages and are workable. If the latter approach is used, further organization is needed. A group chairperson is needed to head the question-raising session and a secretary is needed to record the questions, all under teacher guidance.

Obviously the nature and quality of the questions will reflect the experience, capacities, and keenness of the children as well as the nature and quality of instruction received. If, as Socrates said, "A question well asked is half the answer," then training in the art of question asking is a must. Repeated opportunities to ask questions and examination of their quality help refine the art of question asking from the *what, when, who, where* level to the *why* and *how* level.

The questions raised are recorded much as they are asked. This is especially so for eight- and nine-year-olds. By the time children approach the latter phases of the operational stage they are ready to clarify a question, usually by making it more pointed. The questions are reproduced and each member of a group is supplied with a set. When group members embark on the answer-seeking course a good procedure is to place each question on a separate 3-×-5-inch, 5-×-7-inch card or even a regular-sized sheet of paper. This provides space for recording answers or making notes and sets up a ready filing system.

Illustrative questions or purposes:

Whales
1. How much do whales weigh?
2. How fast can whales swim?
3. Why do we catch whales?
4. How do whales have babies?

5. Why do whales blow water out of their heads?
6. How can we save the whales?

Ocean Currents
1. What makes an ocean current?
2. Where are the ocean currents?
3. How many ocean currents are there?
4. Are ocean currents like river currents?

Oil
1. How far down must they go to get oil?
2. How do they test for oil?
3. How do oil rigs stand up in storms?
4. Do all oceans have oil?
5. What happens if an oil line breaks?
6. Is the oil from ocean drilling as good as the oil from land drilling?
7. How are tankers loaded that are bobbing in the ocean?

Astronauts
1. What are astronauts' suits made of?
2. What do astronauts eat?
3. How do they sleep?
4. How do they go to the toilet?
5. How do they wash?
6. What must they study to be an astronaut?
7. How big is a "cabin-in-the-sky"?
8. Why do they take pictures of the stars?
9. Why can they see stars better than we can?

Prince Charles
1. How old is Prince Charles?
2. Did he go to school?
3. Does he live in a castle?
4. What does he do?
5. Must he help the queen rule?
6. Can he marry anybody?
7. Does he have an armored car?

Questions are indeed marvelous motivators and binders. The asker always remembers his or her question. John Dewey attributes to Plato the idea that a slave is a person who executes the purposes of another. Because the pupils are learning to ask their own questions, they are learning to be free intellectually. In turn the freedom to question is accompanied by a responsibility that directs activities in the learning process. In a sense, raising questions is an exercise in scholarly self-control and implementation.

As Dewey said, "A purpose is an end-view" (8, p. 78). In other words, questions involve some understanding of likely consequences and their significance. In brief, raising questions or purposes can develop into command of a complex intellectual skill. It involves reflection over what is already known, noting what similarities there are between other related experiences, and the making of judgments or decisions. Questions supply the foundation for a plan or a method of action.

Speculation

Raising questions does in a sense cause a condition of disturbance that produces both a puzzle and a challenge. The puzzle aspect may be quite far-reaching as the inquiries go beyond just *information*-seeking questions to *explanations*. But the challenge of putting the puzzle together proves particularly stimulating. The anomalies and deviations provoke an expectancy and in the atmosphere of a group of eager, live-minded children evoke a spirit and attitude akin to that of scientific inquiry. In all cases the act of questioning is paralleled with anticipations or expectations. When this is not so, the result is impulsive rather than purposive action.

Again, as Dewey has pointed out, it is foresight of consequences that transforms impulse into purpose. In so doing, immediate, impulsive responses are offset by reflection and judgment. In brief, overt action is postponed and anticipation and expectation give direction and impetus to what might otherwise be blind.

The essential point, then, is for the teacher to instruct in such a way that purposive question-raising occasions are carefully planned, directed, and utilized. This is done by requiring pupils to exercise their intelligence, to draw on their experiences and knowledge, and to speculate openly about likely answers. The pupils' questions stem from some knowledge and reflect their experience and horizons. Thus the invitation to speculate, to anticipate, causes them to make comparisons, to consider the relation of their fund of experience, their observations, information, and judgments. Mere foresight is not enough. The scholar must learn how to weigh and judge a likely end-view, to objectify so that a more genuine purposive plan may be formed. As L. Susan Stebbing said, questions can readily become rhetorical in form and then become a "stylistic trick" (19). "To pursue an aim without considering what its realization would involve is stupid. . . ." Similarly, to pursue an aim without first examining relevant connections between what you think you know and what you want to find out would be equally stupid. No matter what the pupils' level of ignorance or level of knowledge in regard to a question, they must learn to take advantage, so to speak, of their "stupidity."

First attempts at speculation, especially by eight-year-olds, are apt to be limited. ("I have no idea" may very well be the answer.) But once again it is the teacher's business to help promote and shape the learning process by encouragement. (The teacher might say, "What do you think it might be?" or "Take a guess" or "Try anyway.") Repeated opportunity and thoughtful urging will cause all children to respond as they begin to realize that they "do know something." Often it is helpful to stimulate speculation by aiding them to relate the question to previous experiences and concepts. At times their speculations may be close to the truth and on other occasions far from the truth. Either extreme proves helpful.

The question "How much do whales weigh?" produced a range of speculation among eight-year-olds from 50 lb., to 400 lb., and to 1 ton. However, a 10-year-old addressing himself to the same question said, "There are different kinds of whales and they all have different weights. In addition, I must know if it's a baby whale or a grown whale." "How fast does a whale swim?" produced from eight-year-olds such speculations as "30 miles an hour," "a mile a minute," "about as fast as a horse can run." Again, 10-year-olds wanted a more precisely worded question.

Even though writers are not all in agreement about the nature and variety of conceptual conflict, all seem in agreement that epistemic curiosity results in motivation and aroused potential when knowledge is sought for practical or social ends (3, pp. 274–285). Berlyne defines epistemic curiosity as "the brand of arousal that motivates the quest for knowledge and is relieved when knowledge is procured" (3, p. 274). In addition, he says that declared expectations are usually accompanied by high arousal. When the uncertainty represents the best estimate that can be made, it tends to produce a general alertness or vigilance. F. C. Bartlett speaks of *gaps of information* and how thinking by *interpolation* or *extrapolation*, fills in these gaps (2). This is what gives behavior guided by knowledge "its special characteristics: its rationality, its flexibility, its stamp of voluntary and conscious control" (3, p. 264).

Selecting Materials

The multimedia center (library) and the librarian become involved in the quest for knowledge early in the inquiry instructional scheme. Some books or periodicals related to the interest areas declared may be identified by the librarian and placed in the classroom library as soon as interest areas are declared. Caution must be exercised, though, so that the items made available do not overpower the children but serve to arouse or intensify curiosity. The primary purpose of such librarian-teacher-identified materials is to enliven the discussion and stimulate subsequent question asking and speculation.

Once pupil speculation has occurred the search for answers begins. If at all possible, visits to the school central library or a community library should be made. Visits to both places are highly desirable, especially to the community library. Such a visit has a prestige factor that produces scholarly status.

Pupils go to the libraries armed with their questions. They know what they are looking for and this keeps the search on course.

Of course, pupils must learn about library usage: the books, encyclopedias, newspapers, magazines, films, film strips, slides, consumer reports, records, collections, and consultants available. Every community has available people knowledgeable in different specialties: the mayor, state and federal representatives, lawyers, doctors, engineers, craftsmen, electricians, carpenters, artists, farmers, actors, architects, and so on. Consultants can render invaluable service. They not only are a ready source of information or explanation but also serve to inspire. Interviewing can be done in the school, by phone, or by visits to the consultant. Each method has its values and should be used at one time or another. Interlibrary loans are possible and materials may be obtained from a state library or even the Library of Congress. The Federal Bureau of Records has an enormous supply of pamphlets on an endless variety of topics. Visits to museums, zoos, parks, art galleries, and the like, to see and to talk with the museum directors provide another ready source for many.

How to select and how to reject materials represents skills that are not learned with one opportunity. This is one more reason why the proposed alternating plan from group directed-reading-thinking activities to individualized (inquiry reading) directed-reading-thinking activities is essential. As already pointed out, at the third- and fourth-grade level, four inquiry reading sessions (as described here) may be accomplished across a school year. At fifth grade and beyond, this number may reduce to three sessions. This is so because the nature of the inquiry and the sharing becomes increasingly more thorough as knowledge seeking moves from the informative to the explanatory level. Similarly, across the years the children learn by repeated opportunity to be resourceful in their search and increasingly more persistent. Specific skills acquired are listed on pp. 253-258.

It is apparent that instruction is required and that the instruction must be geared to the level of the learners and their ability to assimilate. Library usage instruction should be coordinated by the teacher through the librarian. Joined instructional effort year after year will help the aspiring and maturing young discoverers to realize with increasing insight the meaning of the fairy tale ending:

Snip, snap, snout,
This tale's told out.

Obtaining Answers

Once materials have been located, time will be spent not only in reading but also in listening, seeing, talking, writing, and organizing. There is a great likelihood that at no time during the ensuing days will all the pupils be reading at the same time. If this were to occur then all sources of information other than the printed word would be ignored. This is not the way of inquiry and research.

On occasion, however, an inquiry reading period may result in a reading session. A class may select, for instance, to pursue famous authors of children's literature and their writings. As a result, the class may be busy reading books by the authors selected or reading biographies and autobiographies.

The teacher's role at this "obtaining answers" stage is vital. Even though the powers and purposes of the children have been utilized so far the task of locating answers and organizing them is the crux of the instruction and the learning. If the pupils are to achieve, it is clear that the materials must be within their grasp. Accordingly, the teacher moves about, giving help or encouragement as needed. She may go from team to team or even from child to child and inquire about progress: "How are you faring?" "Can I help you?" "Do you have all the materials you would like?" "Can I help you with words or ideas you don't understand?" Care must be taken that children don't flounder and lose desire to proceed. The important thing is that the children know the teacher is present and is eager to help. When the children realize that the attention and help are offered sincerely, they will not only seek help but will patiently wait their turn.

This is *not* the time to "test" children by saying, "Tell me what you have read or learned so far" or "Tell me what these words mean." The teacher's role is that of stimulating and facilitating inquiry, by helping, guiding, directing, and reassuring. When this is done appropriately the children do not acquire the notion that they are "reading for the teacher." They are reading to satisfy their own interests and purposes. The pupils want to get out of this situation all that they can, and to do this they must view the teacher, the librarian, the consultant, as aides to turn to, a constant resource and a steadying guide.

The art of taking notes or making notes is difficult to master and requires many opportunities under instructional guidance. This is why each inquiry reading session provides invaluable teaching-learning times and does so across a school year and *across school years*. The opportunity for skill acquisition and skill refinement is provided and needs only to be capitalized on wisely.

The art of searching for ideas needs to be learned in such a way that success and encouragement offset frustration and despair. Pupils must learn how to thumb through material and obtain an overview, and they must know how to use an index, a table of contents, chapter introductions, and chapter summaries. They must learn how to skip about and occasionally study-read a paragraph or two, how to note an idea or mark a passage, how to check new concepts. Perhaps most important, particularly at grades 5 and beyond, is to learn how to obtain an overview reference and then to decide whether to skim-read, scan-read, study-read, or reject the material entirely (18, 19). Versatility skills in reading are in essence versatility skills in studying.

Search of materials and note taking must never be allowed to reach the low level of copying verbatim from any source, especially from an encyclopedia. This is why "how to search" needs to be taught, as has been so aptly described by Dorothy Grant Hennings and Barbara M. Grant (11) and by Alvina Burrows (6). Alvina Burrows says, "In the realm of thought and factual knowledge, control of exact data contributes to the status of the nine year old in his group. Exactness of information ranks high" (6, p. 81).

Especially needed is time to reflect, to think about the ideas, to see how they fit together. Probably the greatest influencing factor at this stage of the inquiry process is to decide on how the information being acquired is to be shared.

Sharing Information

The numerous advantages of working in and through a class or even two or three classes become readily apparent when decisions are made about how the information being collected is to be assembled for presentation. This decision making, perhaps more than any other factor, helps overcome the "copying" practice. In addition, it helps develop an understanding for organizing ideas, selecting ideas, dramatizing ideas, and above all doing it in such a way that audience attention is held. Now attention focuses on the audience and the demands for clarity, brevity, style, engagingness, and acceptability.

Needed are different ways of sharing. Excellent ways are available (12, 20, 11). Each different way needs to be studied to determine its singular advantages and disadvantages, its maximum effectiveness, its ease of use, and its particular magnetism. Accordingly, it is wise to list only five or six ways of sharing for any one inquiry reading session. By so doing the children will not be overwhelmed, but will have opportunity to compare techniques, and will over a period of time, get to see how different techniques serve differently.

For instance, in the classroom in which the previously listed topics were declared and categorized, eight ways of sharing were listed:

1. a mural
2. a television-type interview
3. a diorama
4. a puppet show
5. a quiz game
6. a series of posters
7. demonstrations
8. short talks

Each of the eight methods was then studied briefly to show its advantages and disadvantages and to compare one with another. For instance, a mural required long sheets of paper that could be readily manipulated, decisions on what should be depicted, how items should be shown, and whether items should be shown chronologically, by best use, or in some other way. If a television interview approach was to be used, an interviewer and interviewees were needed. Should this be a talk show only or should illustrative materials be used? A diorama required judgments about what to produce, how to use space depth, how to make the diorama large enough to be seen, how to explain the diorama, and so on.

In the meantime, especially with third- and fourth-grade children, short sharing periods might be scheduled two or three times a week. To do so maintains interest and evokes a questioning attitude. A new or unusual word, a book, an illustration, a story character, and oral reading of a short passage are some good short-term ways of sharing.

Invariably the method of sharing influences what information is gathered and how intensely it is studied. This is why it is wise to determine the different ways of sharing while information is still being sought and assembled. Usually the pause to select a way of sharing causes children to double-check information and to be sure of its authenticity. For instance, if a mural is decided on, the children must decide what episodes to depict, how to illustrate each, and who will do what.

Now, too, comes a *preparation for sharing* time. These are marvelous moments: selecting, arranging, rearranging, rehearsing. Overall, these activities represent a spirited integration of effort and creativity.

Rehearsals are needed, and regardless of the method of sharing, rehearsals take on a refining role. Rehearsals are similar to play rehearsals. They are businesslike and determined. Flaws are taken out. Presentations are sharpened. Then when the presentation is quite polished it is *timed*. This serves a dual purpose: first, each presentation must be scheduled and it is necessary to know how much time to allocate; second, it helps sharpen the action.

Table 9-1   A SHARING SCHEDULE

PUPIL NAME	INTEREST AREAS	SHARING METHOD	TIME NEEDED	PROPS NEEDED
Bill, Ronald, Mark, Phil	whales	mural	20 min	pointer
Helen, Mary, Jean	planes	diorama	10 min	table, pointer

Next it is time to prepare a sharing schedule. This can be done as shown in Table 9-1.

The last few days of sharing time are devoted to the actual presentations. A workable plan is to schedule two or three days for intraroom sharing and one or two days for interroom sharing. As stated before, the integrity of children is astounding. When the rehearsals and presentations are under way, there is little if any attempt to take sneak previews. Of course, all the pupils are busy readying their own projects and have little time to waste.

Usually classroom furniture needs to be rearranged either to face a front stage or to create a theater in the round. If at all possible, a lectern should be available. There should be a short break after each presentation as one team prepares to leave the stage and another moves in. This provides a brief time for class interaction.

Another excellent means of sharing is to gather all third graders or all sixth graders in the school auditorium and then hear one presentation from each third- or sixth-grade class or a cross-age grouping. This provides the students with experience on a larger stage and of course with a larger audience.

A sharing session on dolls proved to be of interest to boys as well as to girls in one fourth grade. It was done somewhat as follows, over a period of three days:

1. One group told about doll hospitals. Almost every major city in the country now has one. These hospitals mend, restore, or renovate dolls. Even grown-ups call with treasured dolls to be restored.
2. Another group told about ancient dolls—Egyptian dolls, Roman dolls, puppets—and showed pictures.
3. One girl told about American Indian dolls and demonstrated how they were made.
4. Two boys and girls showed pictures from and told about famous doll stories: Emma Brock's *Drusilla;* Rachel Field's *Hitty;* Rumer Godden's *The Doll House;* Margery Bianco's *Little Wooden Doll.*

5. The mother of one of the boys had a sizable doll collection that she showed to the class. Then she told them about some of the famous doll collections in museums, like the collections at Yale University, the Smithsonian Institution, and the Kansas City Museum.

M. W. Sharpe, a supervising teacher for UCLA in the Los Angeles elementary school, prepared an excellent list of activities that she labeled as follow-up activities but that may as readily be labeled as sharing activities (14). Other excellent ideas for sharing are found in Amy Jensen's article (12).

All the activities listed supply ample evidence to support the premise that the sharing period provides an ideal means for children to use all their language art skills and to acquire and refine such skills. The sharing time should not be a contrived time. It can be one of the most natural, vital, and stimulating times developed within the confines of a school.

It should be apparent, too, that much of the sharing occurs outside the walls of a single classroom. Because the pupils have something to offer, the activities spill over in a natural way into the rest of the school and thereby provide a sound base for open school actions and interactions. Fourth-grade pupils may share with primary-level pupils or with sixth-grade pupils. At times they may share with pupils in a single classroom, at other times with all the pupils in a building in a school auditorium. As a matter of fact, sharing can spill over to parents and other interested adults.

Audience Interaction and Evaluation

Piaget begins a section in his book *Six Psychological Studies* with the title "The Progress and Socialization of Behavior" and the statement that, "In an activity-oriented school, where the children are at liberty to work either in groups or alone and to talk while working, one is struck by the difference between these children and classes of younger children" (13, p. 39). If this statement were changed to include classes that are not activity-oriented, then it would serve this book: The best way to describe this difference between classes is to refer to the reactions of visitors. Visitors are nearly always astounded by the individual concentration children exhibit when they work by themselves and the effective collaboration they show when they work in a group.

As Piaget says, "True discussions are now possible in that the children show comprehension with respect to the other's point of view and a search for justification or proof with respect to their own statements" (13, p. 39). "True discussions" occur with amazing frequency in the epistemic approach to reading instruction. The children substitute reflection and deliberation for impulsive behavior, and this is of utmost importance in the development of intelligence and emotion. A system of values, closely related to realities and results, one that is based on mutual respect and reciprocity, gradually emerges for each pupil. The children attribute equivalent personal values to each other, and this kind of respect produces honesty and tolerance between peers and friends. It shows regard for rules and regulations essential to study and intercommunication for efficient functioning in a classroom, a library, a school, or even a community. It leads to forms of conduct and moral feelings that emanate from within, and are less subject to external dictation. Individuals see the why and how of subordinating themselves to the laws of reciprocity.

Of all the benefits that derive from the use of the LEA approach and the broader epistemic approach, the progress and socialization of behavior is most significant. Children will perform as described if they are given the proper opportunity, encouragement, and pedagogical direction.

Audience response must be evolved in such a way that social control stems from pupil realization that they are in a situation in which they are cooperative or interacting parts. Order and respect reside in the shared work being done, enterprises in which all have an opportunity to contribute and, in turn, to which all have a responsibility. The teacher must be flexible enough to permit pupils to respond openly and yet just and fair enough to display good manners, politeness, and courtesy. At the same time, members of the audience must avoid a merely formal response.

Again the instructional advantage resides in repeated opportunities for inquiry reading across the school year. Pupils will acquire the attitudes and habits essential to social control in an atmosphere charged with the harnessed power of pupils learning to be thoughtful, fair, resourceful, and self-reliant individuals.

In classrooms where inquiry reading instruction is done, visitors are especially welcome at sharing time—not only children from other classrooms but also parents and school administrators or community authorities. Sometimes the presence of an instant eye camera from a local television station adds greatly to the instructional and learning momentum.

It is obvious sociocentric skills are slowly refined during the early school years. Piaget's research led him to believe that egocentrism was especially pronounced in the early school years, and as Flavell puts it,

> social interaction is the principal liberating factor, particularly social interaction with peers. In the course of his contacts (and especially, his conflicts and arguments) with other children, the child increasingly finds himself forced to re-examine his own percepts and concepts in the light of others, and by so doing, gradually rids himself of cognitive egocentrism [10, p. 279].

But, of course, audience response must be paralleled by the development of responsibility on the part of those making presentations.

They must present in such a way that they do not end up talking to themselves. Flavell states that to the extent that a presenter takes "an accurate measure of the other's listener role attributes, and then actively uses this knowledge to shape and adapt his message accordingly, to that extent ought the communication be an effective, non-egocentric one" (9, p. 8). Flavell further concludes that as a child develops he becomes increasingly aware of the need to pay attention to the characteristics of the audience (9, p. 212).

Edgar Dale expresses very well the hopes and prospects for education in his comprehensive *Building a Learning Environment.* He says that as we develop sharply improved instructional experiences we must remember that human beings are both tough-minded and tender-hearted, durable and compassionate. Human beings can learn the "arts, skills, and attitudes required to take charge of their own lives; in fact, they often do so with distinction" (7, p. 13). What is needed, however, is a "higher level of communication," a "revolutionary approach to improved media, methods, and materials of instruction" (7, p. 13). Then he asks, "Are we up to it?"

In the instructional practices described throughout this text, essentially three factors are dealt with that serve as mediators of self in a wholesome way: motivation, commitment, and sharing. Possibly the highest form of motivation stems from commitment, namely, *intellectual commitment.* It has been suggested repeatedly that pupils be urged to express themselves, to relate their experiences and knowledge to the event at hand, and to use it to predict, anticipate, plan, and evaluate. This honoring of pupils' analyses of events and judgments about them develops confidence, poise, and a desire to seek, to know, and to modify. Therefore all learning should involve the development and refinement of decision making and the need to weigh alternatives.

The best way to instruct in this way is to start at the "level of the learner," by involving each learner intellectually and by leading each on to new insights and understandings. High-level motivation stems from the pursuit of objectives that the student has helped declare, because they become his commitment.

The fulfillment that results not only from finding answers to one's own questions but also from sharing answers found with others provides reward and equilibrium. To prepare a presentation by rehearsing and cutting and fitting and then to earn the plaudits of peers goes a long way toward fostering self-esteem. In the process, pupils begin to realize time and again that plaudits are not the sole key to motivation. It is the inner solace that makes the difference.

In addition, each opportunity to participate through an open-minded, self-structured inquiry into knowledge permits pupils to experience varying degrees of success and failure. Often ends are not truly fully achieved, and this calls for a wide range of defenses, ranging from repressions to rationalizations to the realization that self-regard requires a consistency of esteem and a defense against anxiety. This is the consequence of living in the world of many options. One must learn the responsibility of making choices, and to do so in an educative environment is indeed healthy.

SKILLS ACQUIRED IN INQUIRY READING

The major point to be made about reading skills is not that a group DRTA program is best fitted for use in developing reading skills or that an individualized program of instruction will best do the job. Rather, it is the knowledge that each has a distinct and different contribution to make to developing the all-round skills of an efficient reader. This knowledge is more important than to declare here what reading skills are best accomplished in an individualized program. It is good to keep in mind that in the group DRTA approach all read the same teacher-selected material at the same time. In an individualized program all pupils may be reading different material that they selected on their own.

Reading skills that are most effectively taught in an individualized reading program based on the premise of self-selection are as follows:

•*Locating Materials.* Pupils need to learn where different materials are kept and how they can be obtained. This skill is many faceted. It requires technical knowledge of libraries (a classroom library, a school library, a community library, specialized libraries).

•*Selecting Materials.* Once materials have been located, there is the equally important job of wise selection. How does one survey a book, an encyclopedia, a book shelf to select what is wanted?

•*Using Materials.* In the use of materials a number of questions can be asked: When does a person read an entire book or a portion of a book? When does a person quote or paraphrase? When does a person withdraw a book for use outside a library? These are only some of the questions.

•*Searching Persistently.* Pupils learn to pursue an interest or a question until an answer is found.

•*Being Resourceful.* Pupils learn to know when they have what they need to satisfy their curiosity and when to look further.

•*Identifying Personal Interests.* Because of the wide variety of available books and materials, selection is required. An individual cannot read all that is available, even if he has the capacity and inclination to do so. As a result, readers are forced to examine their likes and dislikes.

Identifying Purposes for Reading. In an individualized situation, readers are on their own. They have to decide what they want to read and why. To a degree they can check their purposes for reading against those of others.

Reading Extensively. With the library as only one major source of material, reading will be limited only by the reader's purpose, capacity, and level of aspiration.

Reading Intensively. An individualized reading situation is most apt to allow a student to read and reflect and read again so as to understand as thoroughly as possible. To share ideas one must be accurate.

Assembling Information. Whether making a thorough or an extensive study, the reader must learn to assemble relevant material. This means reading selectively, accepting that which fits the requirements of the purpose and rejecting that which does not.

Organizing Information. When material has been wisely selected, readers are faced with another language arts task that may require considerable reflective reading if they are to develop a timely and appropriate organization of ideas.

Keeping Records. If pupils do no more than borrow a book, read it, and return it, they forget it. If they borrow many books, read them, make endless notes, and return the books, the quantity will obliterate the meaning of the material. Record keeping must be done selectively, efficiently, and concisely; and it must be done frequently if pupils are to understand the why and how of records.

Learning Word Attack Skills. If word attack skills are properly taught in a group DRTA program, individualized reading instruction will help only to reinforce the skills. If anything, the pupils learn to be even more self-reliant. Properly taught, pupils can test their skills in the wide world of many books and many words. This is what an individualized reading program should do.

The best test of word attack skill is the ability to cope with demands in materials not structured on a "controlled" vocabulary and syntax basis. One of the advantages of basal reader materials is the pacing of "new word" introduction. A "new word" is only a new word in the sense that when it is used in a basal series it is labeled as "new" on its first appearance. This, in turn, is supposed to mean that the "new word" is well embedded among "old," known words. Because this pacing occurs the semantics of the sentence and paragraph in which the word appears for the first time should facilitate recognition. Interpolation, closure, or semantics—in brief, meaning—should do the recognition trick. In addition, when phonic (sound) and structural (sight) analysis skills are used, their recognition should be accomplished. All this is possible though *only* because the controlled vocabulary comprises words of such high frequency that they are in almost any child's speaking-meaning vocabulary. This is what makes recognition likely. (See Chapter 10 on word recognition.)

However, when children turn to varied sources—books, magazines, newspapers, filmstrip captions—they may encounter readability controls but not a "controlled vocabulary" in the sense described for basal readers. Because this is so they may come upon unknown words or words not in their speaking-meaning vocabularies. Or they may meet three or four or more unknown words in a sentence or a paragraph, and as a result the semantics or meaning base is so limited as not to be helpful. In addition, they may need to deal with nomenclature for a particular topic and not be familiar with it: A story on the topic *whales* may include *marine, mammals, dolphins, porpoises, sperm, whaling, fins, gills, aquatic,* and so on. This is when pupils, or anyone for that matter, begin to realize that where there is no meaning known or where there is a lack of experience this is the greatest liability. Experience (which provides meaning) and language do develop together and thereby serve communication.

Pupils faced with unfamiliar nomenclature learn either (1) to be resourceful in the use of phonic and structural analysis skills and in dictionary usage or (2) to turn to the teacher or some knowledgeable person for help. The practical application of word attack skills is probably the most productive opportunity. Word attack skills are reviewed, honed, and used beginning with structural analysis and continuing on to phoneme-grapheme decoding. Although the children may speak a word like *marine* (məren) readily, they may require the dictionary to discover its meaning and even then may require the help of an adult. *Dolphin* (dol fin) may be readily spoken but again probably requires help with the meaning.

It should be readily evident that reading material such as this requires word recognition skill and on-the-scene instruction and also requires concept attainment know-how. Required, too, is pupil confidence, reassurance, persistence, and patience, as well as a capable teacher. This kind of practical learning situation can never be put into a skill book. This is why pupils trained only on skill book diets fail so miserably, particularly on standardized tests at the fourth-grade level and beyond. Skill books do not develop the key essential to skill acquisition—*the ability to transfer knowledge to new and practical situations.*

During the weeks devoted to inquiry reading invaluable opportunities occur for word recognition and concept development skill training. This is just one more reason why four to six weeks are required. Such intense training needs to be followed by period of a different type of training or there should be alternation between (inquiry reading) individualized DRTA's and group DRTA's.

•*Acquiring Concepts.* As in the case of word recognition skills, concept development should be taught, extended, and refined in an individualized program. This provides the essential framework without either overwhelming the pupil or permitting the development of carelessness and indifference.

•*Sharing Ideas.* All the skills involved in sharing ideas are best accomplished in a program of individualized instruction. Pupils learn why and how to share in circumstances in which they have something to share and a reason for sharing.

•*Listening.* A natural event in the sharing of ideas is learning to listen and to be attentive. New ideas, presented in different ways and by different people, provide the medium. Not only do pupils learn to listen selectively and under varied conditions, they also learn to study these conditions so that when their turn comes they may hold the attention of the audience.

•*Asking Questions.* Like note taking, questions might be considered subordinate to listening. However, the asking of questions begins at an earlier stage and is a more active, participating process. The quality of the question is determined by the listener's knowledge and experience as well as ability to listen. Pupils can learn to ask probing questions to clarify or extend knowledge or to expose prejudices and distortions. They can learn also to ask questions tactfully, to take their turn, to pursue a point. Obviously this is best done in the learning-sharing atmosphere created by a program of individualized instruction.

•*Reading to Learn.* The privilege to read and read and read can become an overwhelming responsibility. To be free to go to a book shelf or a library and select book after book again and again can be very demanding. "What to pick now? I've read all about horses" may result in a pause in which the child thinks: "Do I like to read? How much do I want to read? What are others reading? Why?" These are the kinds of self-searching questions that can confront a pupil privileged to read. This kind of soul-searching, can be of tremendous value and can result in wiser and more deliberate ways of selecting.

•*Reading to Learn.* Pupils who are permitted and encounraged to read wisely and given extended time to do so may sooner or later discover that their reading interests go far beyond reading for fun. Pupils learn to examine their likes and dislikes and the likes and dislikes of others and the permanency of these conditions, so they extend their reading horizons, vary their selections, and learn more.

•*Gaining Self-respect.* The privilege to pick and choose, and to do so according to one's likes and dislikes and at one's own pace, is an excellent way to learn not only to examine oneself but to respect one's own judgments.

•*Knowing When to Get Help.* At a time when all members of a class are busy on their own, the right to seek teacher help takes on the aura of a privilege. Pupils see more clearly with repeated experience when they need help, why, and how much. Being on your own also means knowing when you are no longer able to achieve on your own.

•*Setting Standards.* To be your own most severe taskmaster is something to be learned as early in one's education career as possible. "Build for quality not for quantity" may be the standard for many days. For others it may be: "Read for quantity; read, read, read." Setting standards and imposing them on one's own conduct is the crux of the learning circumstance.

Among the important incentives to setting high standards are honors, praise, and rivalry. One of the most significant factors operating is the effect of the immediate satisfaction of a job well done. The reward is not as remote as a grade at the end of a marking period; it therefore exerts much influence on standards set and maintained. Meritorious achievement, group sanction and esteem, and personal interest are the notable sources.

•*Reading Orally.* To read aloud to an audience something they have not heard before and to hold their attention is one of the high aims of oral reading. Pupils begin to realize this at an early point in an individualized DRTA program. Then they see the need for oral reading practice and for quality performance.

•*Speaking in Public.* To address a class and hold its attention requires the same kind of thoughful preparation. Pupils are made intimately aware of these needs as they deal with the recurring experience of individualized DRTA sessions. Pupils are readily caught up in the *esprit de corps* that becomes a part of a sharing session and produces an atmosphere conducive to easy and spontaneous speech.

·Appreciating the Moment of Silence. If one steps into almost any library, the busy silence that permeates the atmosphere is immediately manifest. There is the hush and tranquility of thinkers at work: quiet work, quiet thoughts, quiet animation. Overall the library silence is an unplanned silence. The librarian does not ring a bell for a moment of silence. Rather, it reflects an attitude of scholarly respect for the rights and privileges of others.

CONCLUSION

The eclectic program described thus far has the sanction of cognitive conventions and the precedent of the communication arts. The general conclusion that should be drawn is that command of the reading process and its adaptation to the various knowledge areas is effected by the whole situation in which students share and of which they are interacting parts. Thus command of the reading process takes on new dimensions and urgencies.

Those who participate in inquiry reading do not feel that they are dictated to by any one individual or that they are subject to the domination of some superior adult. This does not mean that there are no occasions when a teacher or librarian does not have to intervene. But the main line of control is based on the activities carried on and on maintenance of actions and interactions. In brief, the primary source of control physically and intellectually resides in the nature of the work being done.

Reading becomes a means of self-realization, self-regulation, and self-relaxation. Reading as one means for acquiring knowledge and/or pleasure is done not only for oneself but to share. As Bacon said, "Reading maketh a full man." Sharing is done by talking, demonstrating, illustrating, dramatizing, writing, and, of course, oral reading. The last is done to prove points, to share favorite passages, to dramatize, to enjoy a poem. In turn, listening skills are sharpened as pupils attend to the various presentations, each making different demands.

Inquiry reading provides numerous opportunities for cooperating and interacting. Oral interactions are done on a pupil-pupil and pupil-teacher basis. Pupils learn to plan, to think about their audiences and anticipate their responses. Stated differently, pupils are learning to be deliberate and to reflect. Piaget refers to reflection as "internalized social discussions" (13, p. 41). Thus pupils learn to show appreciation for the flow of ideas and the amenities that accompany the interchange of ideas.

In addition, pupils learn how their peers respond to different presentations and topics. They are gradually learning to obtain release from the "prison of their own perspective" (9). Pupils are acquiring know-how in the areas of role taking, role perception, role playing, role enactment, empathy, sympathy, and the like. Undoubtedly there are age-dependent skills involved but their extension and refinement are more likely to occur through the repeated opportunities of inquiry reading in any one year, but especially over the years.

Above all, children learn to examine their interests and tastes and gain increasing appreciation for curiosity, the nature and scope of knowledge, and language. They begin to sense that value resides not so much in the answers we give as in the questions we raise. Thereby they learn the elemental motivation to learn and to think—the power of intellectual commitment.

Thus it should be very clear that the activities engaged in are for the most part self-generated, reflect the pupil's natural and acquired curiosities, and are the modest fruits of their individual preoccupations. When they are grouped, as they are in many instances, the children do produce a significant achievement. *Above all*, it can be said, the children were chiefly led into these endeavors by their *own consuming curiosity* about the world around them. Armored with the exuberance of childhood and the desire for action and adventure, they rapidly grew in scholarly ability.

Bibliography

1. Abercrombie, M. L. Johnson, *The Anatomy of Judgment*. New York: Basic Books, 1960.
2. Bartlett, F. C., *Thinking*. London: Methuen, 1958.
3. Berlyne, D. E., *Conflict, Arousal and Curiosity*. New York: McGraw-Hill, 1960.
4. Bond, Guy L., and Robert Dykstra, "The Role of the Coordinating Center in the Cooperative Research Program," *The Reading Teacher, 19* (May, 1966), 565–568.
5. Bullock Sir Allen, *A Language for Life, Report of the Committee of Inquiry Appointed by the Secretary of State for Education and Science* (England). London: Her Majesty's Stationery Office, 1975.
6. Burrows, Alvina T., *Teaching Children in the Middle Grades*. Lexington, Mass: Heath, 1952.
7. Dale, Edgar, *Building a Learning Environment*. Bloomington, Ind.: Phi Delta Kappa, 1972.
8. Dewey, John, *Experience and Education*. New York: Macmillan, 1938.
9. Flavell, John H., *The Development of Role Taking and Communication Skills in Children*. New York: Wiley, 1968.
10. Flavell, John H., *The Developmental Psychology of Jean Piaget*. New York: Van Nostrand, 1963.
11. Hennings, Dorothy G., and Barbara Grant, *Content and Craft: Written Expression in the Elementary School*. Englewood Cliffs, N.J.: Prentice-Hall, 1973.
12. Jensen, Amy E., "Attracting Children to Books," *Elementary English, 33* (October, 1956), 332–339.

13. Piaget, Jean, *Six Psychological Studies*, trans. David Elkind. New York: Random House, 1967.
14. Sharpe, Malda W., "Individualized Reading: Follow-Up Activities," *Elementary English, 41* (January, 1959), 21-24.
15. Stauffer, Russell G. (compiler and editor), *Action Research in L.E.A. Instructional Procedures*. Newark, Del.: University of Delaware, 1976.
16. Stauffer, Russell G., "The Verdict: Speculative Controversy," *The Reading Teacher, 19* (May, 1966), 563-564.
17. Stauffer, Russell G., et al., *Communications Through Effective Reading.* Haddonfield, N.J.: Learn, Inc., 1972.
18. Stauffer, Russell G., et al., *Rapid Comprehension Through Effective Reading.* Haddonfield, N.J.: Learn, Inc., 1969.
19. Stebbing, L. Susan, *Thinking to Some Purpose.* London: Penguin Books, 1939.
20. Williams, Lois E., *Independent Learning in the Elementary Classroom.* Washington, D.C.: American Association of Elementary-Kindergarten-Nursery Education, 1969.

Chapter 10
Word Recognition

By now the reader must be fully aware that word recognition skill attainment has been discussed in almost every chapter. It is impossible to treat it differently in a book based on actual classroom instructional practices. Word attack skill instruction must be circumscribed only by the curriculum and age-dependent skill development and not confined to "ready-made routes" (skill books) that are limited and so general that they provide little evidence to support their value.

Accordingly, up to this point much has been written about context clues, auditory discrimination, visual discrimination, auditory-visual discrimination, consonant substitution, alphabetizing, vowel key variability, dictionary usage, and concept attainment. The reader is urged to reread the sections enumerated and to note again that in each instance skill development is taught in functional situations based on *pupil recognition of a need* and on *purposive actions* (see pp. 65–79).

The need for skill training should stem from actual reading situations in which *comprehension has been blocked* by an unknown or unrecognized word. This places the premium on recognizing a felt need and on meaning and puts word attack skill in perspective as an *auxiliary aid to comprehension*. Thus need for a word attack skill stems from a reading communication context in which communication is blocked. When this occurs the skills acquired are retained because the skill utilization resolved a felt need and not because some adult was to be impressed with a rote performance in an isolated context.

WORD RECOGNITION DEFINED

What does a child do, or what does any individual do for that matter, when he stops at a word he does not recognize at first sight? Obviously he *sees* the word first or, in other words, he uses *visual perception*. But seeing the word is not enough or the word would have been recognized. Next, he tries to *sound* the word with first visual clues and then sound clues. He analyzes the word to discover letter clues (graphemes) to the sounds that they may represent (phonemes) in this particular word context. Then he blends the sounds together so that, with the appropriate intonation, he can say the word. All this may not be sufficient, because *meaning* clues also determine phoneme sounds and intonation, so he may have to read on to find the meaning.

Word recognition, then, involves the ability to use context or meaning clues, phonetic or sound clues, and structure or sight clues. If this makes learning to read seem most difficult, how is it that year after year many children learn to read on their own? Their success implies three things. First, the skills of word recognition cannot be too complex or else these preschoolers would not be able to work out their own reliable systems. Second, there must be some pattern to the development of these skills or else the children would develop as many different systems as the well-meaning adult phoneticians have done. Third, there must be a latent power that facilitates recognition residing in meaning and communication or else the words would remain unknown.

Compare a reading performance in which immediate word recognition fails with one in which no difficulty is encountered. Recognition becomes the act of simultaneously seeing the word and identifying its meaning. Meaning directs the entire process.

Since meaning plays a dominant role in both situations—dealing with words that are not immediately recognized at sight and words that are—it is apparently the most functional key to word recognition. This is the position taken throughout this book, because it emphasizes *communication*, to which all other aids are subordinate. One deals with the phonetic elements not merely to say a word but to help in grasping its meaning. The same is true of the use of structural aids.

A PUZZLING CIRCUMSTANCE

Acquiring facility at word attack cannot be too complex for if it were, children would not acquire it on their own. Year after year, teachers take professional courses in reading instruction and always show much concern about word attack teaching. Year after year, tests to determine teacher knowledge of word attack skills show astounding ignorance. All this is true because the neophyte, unaware of the complex word attack skill programs of authors and publishers, proceeds functionally to the heart of the problem and acquires simple yet effective methods. Teachers, on the other hand, all of whom can read with considerable skill, do not use the word attack skills of the neophyte and find it difficult to memorize the complex programs being published.

The children are right. There are only a few procedures needed to read almost any word that is already in their speaking vocabularies. The skills they use and the order in which they learned them are most likely: auditory discrimination, auditory-visual discrimination, consonant substitution, vowel variability, structural variation, and dictionary usage.

It puzzles some people and escapes others why word attack is taught in grades 1, 2, and 3 and then is forgotten in grades 4, 5, 6, and beyond. The reason is simple. Children learning to read have a large functional speaking vocabulary. If a word they are trying to read is in their speaking-meaning vocabulary and they can decode the word so as to speak it, they then recognize its meaning or use. Thus speaking-meaning recognition functionally embraces reading recognition. This makes the following conclusion obvious. The best way to introduce children to skills that are functional is to use words they have selected from their own individual speaking-meaning vocabularies. This closes the circle described earlier (nonrecognition to recognition) in communication or in a situation where language is serving its purpose.

MEANING CLUES TO WORD RECOGNITION

Of all the means for decoding a word not recognized instantly at sight the most effective and advantageous is the use of meaning clues. This is especially true during preprimary and primary years for most children, and well beyond those years for some, because their oral language-semantic vocabulary so vastly exceeds their recognizable printed language. Thus the principle of closure facilitates the grasp of meaning and the insertion of a fitting word. For instance, in the sentence "I like a turtle," the child who had dictated the idea recognized the words *I*, *a*, and *turtle* instantly but hesitated over *like*. The child had been urged to produce the words he knew and hone in on the unrecognized word, *like*, semantically or by meaning. The principle of closure might have been tested purely if the setting were: "I _____ a turtle." However, this setting, like all such settings, was a transfused closure and was not pure in a psychological testing sense. It is transfused because the word *like* is in place syntatically and semantically rather than a blank space. It permeates the entity of the idea and literally diffuses meaning throughout. Not only do meaning clues or comprehension clues dominate, as they should, but they are aided by the evident phonic clues represented by the phoneme-grapheme representations or letter-sound representations in the word *like*. Thus phonic analysis can serve in its most functional capacity as an auxiliary aid to comprehension.

Every time children reread material they have dictated, the recognition of words is enormously facilitated because (1) they were the producer of the words, (2) they arranged the words syntactically, (3) the principle of closure transfuses meaning literally, and (4) phonic clues provide a timely and functional auxiliary aid. The superiority of a context situation such as this over meeting a word in isolation is unquestionable. Thus, from the very beginning the children are learning to read for meaning in empirical language settings.

Almost identical conditions are found when children use a word card holder and compose ideas by using printed words. If they need a word not in their word bank and the word is supplied by the teacher, fitting in the right word completes the closure. As already stated, children tend to remember very well words obtained in the rich, firsthand context of composing, for language is being used to communicate and reading skill is acquired functionally.

When children are asked to use language context clues to recognize a word, they are not being asked to guess. Quite to the contrary, they are being asked to use their intellectual powers to their fullest. They are being asked to comprehend so thoroughly that they can make logical cognitive deductions. Convergent-type thinking is being required as pupils focus all the information at hand on the missing word or concept.

Certainly the process of reading comprehension is arrested when an unrecognized word retards comprehension. Pupils facing up to the fact that they do not know are taking the first big step toward wisdom. The cost in time to stop, think, reflect, and act is infinitesimally small as compared with the penalty of ignorance.

Every reader, the highly skilled as well as the semiskilled one, uses context clues to meaning because, as C. M. McCullough put it, the "verbal woods are full of context aids to reading" (5, p. 225). Not all readers, however, are articulate about what they do. This is a function of a good instructional program.

What, then, are the context aids to reading that are available to readers as they make their way through the verbal woods? McCullough lists and defines context aids to reading as follows: the experience clue, the comparison or contrast clue, the synonym clue, the summary clue, the mood or situation clue, the definition clue, the familiar expression clue (5, pp. 226-227).

A. S. Artley (1) also lists context aids that a reader can use as clues to word meanings. Even though some of the aids he classified are similar to those listed by McCullough, they merit listing again. They are typographical aids, structural aids, substitute words, word elements, figures of speech, pictorial representations, inference, direct explanation, background experience, subjective clues.

Language used to communicate is a storehouse of meaning. This is true whether the language is oral or written. The printed page is a reading detective's paradise of clues. Every word, every word order; each idea, each idea order; every line, sentence, paragraph, and page; all punctuation; all mechanics—all aid the knowing reader searching for understanding.

The innumerable demands on oral language made by day-to-day living force all children to face up to the comsequences of what they hear. They catch tone, mood, intent, and word order because they influence what children wish or do. Children will learn to be equally as attentive to the meaning of printed words if their experiences with them demand meaning. Learning to use printed words to communicate requires direct and continuous teaching. Learning to use all the many context aids to written communication also requires direct and continuous teaching in a situation that demands understanding on the part of the student.

Reading or the recognition of words must not be thought of as a parroting situation. Printed words must be dealt with by each reader as they occur in a communication context. They must not be predigested for him. He must learn to take full advantage of every clue available in the search for meaning.

Over and over again pupils must be given an opportunity to search for meaning as they read—to unlock every word. The context clues described thus far must be taught repeatedly so that each pupil will in the course of his reading training become as accomplished in his use of these clues as he is in the use of oral communication clues.

If we add the clues defined by modern structural linguistics to the context clues as enumerated by McCullough and by Artley, we obtain a complete picture. Linguists approach language meaning through language signals. Although linguists are on occasion charged with neglect of meaning, C. C. Fries points out that he and others have constantly insisted that meaning cannot be ignored. He says:

All language, as we view it here, concerns itself with meanings. Or, perhaps, we should say rather that human beings are basically concerned with meanings and use language as their tool to grasp, to comprehend, and to share meanings. It is the linguist's business to turn the spotlight on the tool—language—itself in order to examine the physical material of which it is composed and to determine the ways this material has been selected and shaped to accomplish its function of mediating meaning [3, p. 97].

Language as the storehouse of man's experience and of the meanings that grow out of that experience provides man with a means which he can share his experience. Just as the semanticists point out that "the word is not the thing" (3, p. 99), so the linguists point out that *the language itself is not the meanings*. Language is a code of signals. The person wishing to communicate effectively learns the language signals by which meanings are sent and received. The signals can be dealt with discretely for purposes of analysis, but in operation they function as a continuous system. In fact, the systems of patterns are, through frequent and intensive usage, learned so thoroughly that they become a part of an undifferentiated background. The identification and recognition of the patterns in speech are almost instantaneous and automatic. people are not conscious of the code through which messages come and go, of learning to talk, or of having to learn to talk; unless something interferes, they are conscious only of the messages conveyed.

According to Fries (3, pp. 65, 105, 106), there are several important layers of signaling patterns: lexical, grammatical, and social-cultural signals.

Lexical signals are the morphemes of words that function in our language code. They consist of two contrasting patterns. First, the difference in lexical meaning is represented by the different words. For example:

Every *step* seemed harder to take.
Every *stop* seemed harder to take.

In speech the difference between *step* and *stop* is signaled solely by the difference in their vowel sounds. In print it is signaled by the vowel shape. *Step* and *stop* are similarly separated from *stoop, steep, strap, strip*. In writing as in speaking, or in reading as in listening, it is the particular message or meaning to be transmitted that determines the sequences to be used and how they are to function as signals. When the lexical signals *step—stop* and the meanings connected with the pattern ("Every (*stop, step*) seemed harder to take") are known so completely that identification and recognition of the language signals is instantaneous, then attention to the carrying physical patterns (speech or print) sinks below the threshold of attention. When the signals are not known completely, conscious effort must be given not only to the lexical signal or signals that are not instantaneously recognized but also to the meanings connected with the total pattern. Meaning is essential to accurate identification and recognition even at the structural-unit level of lexical signals or at the word level.

Second, there is a co-occurrence of other lexical sets that identify a particular meaning out of a variety of meanings that a lexical signal or word may represent. The lexical item *spread* represents different meanings. In each of the following sentences the co-occurrence of other lexical items, especially those underlined, help determine the particular meaning applicable in each sentence.

> "With canvas spread, she was following the Adventure." "Soon they were out where the full wind caught the spread sail." "He would not put on a full spread of canvas in a strong wind." "Tiger was her cat. Spread out on Patty's knees, Tiger was dreaming of. . . ."

Listeners and readers familiar with our language usually are not conscious of the use of lexical sets in recognizing a particular meaning out of many that a word may have. However, such responses are acquired in the learning of a language. The reader is apt to grasp instantaneously the meaning of *spread canvas, full spread,* and *spread out* without giving deliberate attention to the co-occurring lexical sets.

Although pupils may, when reading, deal successfully and effortlessly with lexical sets that have been learned in their speaking-listening communication world, teachers should not assume that all meaning shifts are grasped. Pupils need to be made articulate about such changes. One method is to require them to single out for discussion such varied meanings as are illustrated, for example, by *spread.* Other uses can then be dealt with such as *spread butter,* a *table spread,* a *bedspread, spread-eagled;* and attention can be given to co-occurring lexical sets.

Grammatical signals are the signals of meaning carried by grammatical structures, of which there are three patterns. One of the patterns is the contrastive arrangements on the form-class level, or words as the *parts of speech.* In these patterns of grammatical signals, it is not individual words that function as the structural units but classes of words. In the context of actual usage, the words become marked as belonging to one of four major form classes (3, p. 106). It is the markers that signal the form class or part of speech.

Skill and efficiency in the use of language context clues for word recognition purposes are of prime importance in the mature reader's competency because such skill and efficiency are essential to understanding. Reading without understanding is not reading. Mature readers must exert a determined effort to get as close to perfect comprehension as circumstances permit. Therefore, they use every available technique to unlock meaning; and for them, unlocking words means to unlock the meaning of words.

Attaining this skill and efficiency in the use of language context clues word recognition results from constant, diligent effort. Therefore, the directive "to read to the end of a sentence" is only a beginning. It is a beginning, however, and it does initiate the attitude and habit of seeking meaning.

Daily practice should be provided to develop skill and efficiency in the use of language context clues. Through such practice children will grasp the idea that getting the meaning is of first-order importance and that sounding out is only an aid to achieving that purpose. The teacher can use the examples presented as pattern guides in taking advantage of similar opportunities and making the learning of language context clues a daily practice.

Language context clues are important from the very beginning of the learning-to-read program. As the syntactic, grammatical, and semantic demands of language become more complex, the need for training in the use of language context becomes more urgent.

Picture Context Clues

It is impossible to write a book about the teaching of reading and put the entire discussion of word recognition into one chapter. A look at the index to this book will show that discussion of word recognition occurs at many points. Naturally, the ability to recognize words is an essential, ongoing part of reading.

When basic readers are carefully structured, deliberate effort is made to provide picture clues as well as language clues to word recognition. This kind of structuring should continue throughout a basic series, but it is especially important at the beginning-to-read level. In presenting a word like *family*, ample language clues can be provided, and the family can be shown in a picture. Thus the context for the word *family* can be like that of a picture dictionary. The pupil can be given the new word *family*, a language definition, and an illustration. In a well-structured basic reader series, these three elements are provided so often that the pupil has a picture dictionary literally built into the reader.

Just as words and illustrations are used in a basic reader or in a picture dictionary, they are also the hallmarks of any well-structured dictionary, even an unabridged dictionary. As a matter of fact, unabridged dictionaries would be more useful if they provided more illustrations.

Picture context clues can be most helpful to the beginning reader, to the maturing reader, and even to the most advanced reader. Illustrations specifically directed at providing ideas to support or elaborate on the meaning of a single word are worthy of careful study. Basic reader pictures and glossary illustrations can contribute greatly to the total word recognition process and to comprehension. Such pictures are not only worth a thousand words but can also supply the means by which the reader is able to clarify one word.

The desirable path to pursue, then, to acquire word recognition skill is to give first-order priority to the value of context clues, both language and picture clues. The plan described here is a realistic and far-reaching plan. Its important facets are immediately apparent from the early phases of the learning-to-read program. An overall design concerned with meaning and long-range efficiency within the framework of ordered excellence goes far beyond a program that seeks only phoneme or grapheme constancy.

VOWEL KEYS

All the activities described thus far prove useful almost simultaneously. It is regrettable that they cannot all be learned simultaneously. By teaching skill activities one after another there is implied a discreteness that does not exist in actual language use. In addition to the discreteness imposed by spaced and sequenced instruction is the fact that some children learn rapidly and some do not. This program does not harness any child. Children may acquire skill at their own rates of assimilation and accommodation. Because all are invited and encouraged to be active participants, they tend to make better progress than would otherwise be true.

By the time children have progressed to the vowel-key preparation stage, they will have had much experience with words, with letters and how they represent sounds, with word families, with blending sounds, and with attacking the words in their dictated stories that they do not recognize instantly at sight, or in the stories of their peers and library books. All this provides superb readiness for another step and another skill in the word attack armory.

In the recognition and use of consonants, the ability to make consonant substitutions is paramount. Word families can be enlarged by substituting consonants, but also some of the consonants substituted represent different sounds, as k in cat, s in city, and so on. Accordingly, the concepts of consonant substitution and consonant variability have long-term utility, as detailed in the section on dictionary usage. In a similar way, a major understanding about vowels is their variability. Each vowel represents several different sounds, and the same sound may be represented by different single vowels and vowel combinations. The concepts of consonant substitution and vowel variability are constantly reinforced because of their utility.

One procedure useful in helping children deal with vowel variability is to return to the word family game. One way is to make words by changing a word beginning and then by changing endings.

cat	let	black	fold
fat	met	track	cold
fan	men	trap	colt
man	pen	trash	comb

Or the children can make a free-wheeling substitution in much the same pattern

cat	bath	fable	like
can	math	table	mike
man	mask	take	mile
tan	task	shake	pile

Another way is to keep the medial vowel constant and change both ends

cat	net	tin	not
man	peck	sit	rod
lad	when	thick	log
blast	beg	him	frost

This causes children to focus on vowels as well as consonants. These kinds of exercises can be done as a group with either the teacher or one of the group making the changes and the children responding orally to the words. Equally as effective is to have the children either singly or in pairs make their own lists of meaningful words changing the single consonant, consonant blends, and/or consonant digraphs as directed (see pp. 78–79).

From this step, changing the medial vowels follows rather readily. First list the five vowels as a guide: a, e, i, o, u. Then the words can be made using common high-frequency words.

not	ten	hut	far	beg
net	tan	hit	for	big
nut	ton	hat	fer	bag
nit	tin	hot	fir	bog
nat	tun	het	fur	bug

From this to the construction of a vowel key is a ready transition. Start with a one-syllable word containing a long $\bar{a}$ sound such as $\bar{a}te$. The best plan is to use the key word used in a dictionary key. By so doing the alphabet-card key and the key in the dictionaries the children use will be in agreement. The practicality of the key is readily apparent, first in auditory discrimination: "Does the vowel heard in *day* have the same sound as the vowel heard in *ate*?" Then try such words as *make, big, late, can, cake, cane, sit.* Do this until the decisions can be made readily and, of course, correctly.

The teacher can start each pupil's vowel key by writing on a 3-×-5-inch card the five vowels and then a key word for long $\bar{a}$: $\bar{a}te$. Be sure to use the correct diacritical mark.

a   e   i   o   u
āte

Next add a word like *căt*, with the short *ă* sound. Again do auditory exercises first with words with short *ă* and then with words using another short vowel. Next put *āte* and *căt* together and do sound-discriminating exercises again. First, use words that have either a short *ă* or a long *ā*. Then use words that have different vowels so that the pupil must decide that the vowel heard represents neither a long *ā* or a short *ă*. Thus *vowel variability* is introduced.

Proceed in the same way with each of the five vowels. Each time, add the key word to the vowel key. Vowel variability is now brought into sharper focus, both visually and phonically. A key may appear as follows:

a	e	i	o	u
āte	mē	īce	nō	ūse
căt	gĕt	sit	nŏt	cŭt

This accomplished, add the *r*-influenced vowels one at a time. Words like *cär, hër, sïr, nör, fûr* serve as good key words. Be sure always to start with auditory discrimination training.

Not all children will build vowel keys at the same time. But once the construction of keys starts in a room, other pupils become interested and attentive and frequently exceed teacher expectations.

Vowel keys can also be used in poor teaching. Supervisors, principals, and visitors are impressed when they see vowel keys on desk tops of first graders. But the keys can be almost completely nonfunctional if they are foisted on the children. This when it happens is a terrible loss, because the attitudes of the children are influenced negatively. In addition, they fail to acquire an essential skill. Vowel keys should not become a decorative front.

When does a vowel key serve pupils? Before a key is built in any classroom, the teacher should be sure of being able to answer this question with conviction.

A vowel key helps children attack words in their experience stories. Because the words represent the words that the children speak and that already have sound value for them, the pupils' chances of unlocking, or sounding out, a word are increased if they can use vowels as well as consonants.

A key is useful in unlocking words that occur in sources other than a pupil's or classmates' dictation. They may be attacking a word in a library book, a newspaper, or an encyclopedia.

A key is most helpful in creative writing. As was shown in Chapter 5, pupils at first tend to omit vowels in words in which consonant sounds seem to predominate, as in *hf* for *half, dfr* for *different, crmms* for

Christmas. But as they continue with creative writing and increasingly develop phoneme-grapheme sensitivity, they look for help with vowels. At this point they turn to their vowel keys. However, a word of caution is in order, for use of a vowel key for writing can defeat both purposes easily. The children may begin to feel guilty about word spellings and curb their writing; in that case, the vowel key becomes a whip rather than a tool. It should be pointed out to them periodically how to use their vowel keys for help with a word. Better yet, when they ask for help with the spelling of a word, they can be shown how to use their vowel keys. The concept of vowel variability thus becomes firmly established.

STRUCTURAL VARIATIONS

When children talk, they correctly use such meaning changes as *run-runs-running, ball-balls, paint-painted-paints-painting, slow-slowly, rain-rainy-raining.* (A reexamination of the dictated stories in Chapter 2 shows this to be true.) They appreciate the functional uses of inflectional and derivative changes.

When they reread their dictated stories, they learn to read such words without confusion. They see how *run, runs, running,* are different, and they add a card to their word banks for each word change. Some teachers reinforce visual recognition by making direct comparisons of words in columns:

run	paint	rain
runs	painted	rainy
running	painting	raining

Taught this way, the children experience little trouble in dealing with such changes. As a matter of fact, they soon become proficient at changing words deliberately. Motivation for this runs high, because children can display a new skill and they can add words to their word banks. Knowing words like *snow, call, walk, pull, fish, watch,* and *go* leads to ready change to and recognition of *snowing, snowed, calling, called,* and so on.

Success with such changes influences creative writing. After the first flurry of writing, children begin to be attentive to word endings and spell words much as required. (Another look at Chapter 5 on creative writing will provide evidence of this.)

When creative writing is done daily and the stories become longer and longer, another very interesting sensitivity appears. The more children write, the more they face the demands of spelling and the more resourceful they become. Much of their spelling is phonological. When a polysyllabic word like *Halloween* is spelled, it may very well be done by phonological parts or syllables and be produced as *hal O en, needle* may be spelled *ned l, doctor* as *dot r, pumpkin* as *puanp cinn.* Another interesting variation occurs at this stage of progress, the capitalization of the first letter of each syllable. *Decorate* may be written *DeCorAte*, *West Chester* as *West ChesTer*, *Christmas* as *CisMas*, *Tannenbaum* as *Ten N Bam*, *Museum* as *Mu See Um*, and so on. This is more apt to occur when words appear in a title and so may reflect sensitivity to capital letters in titles.

Providing numerous opportunities to use and produce language is a natural way of dealing with variations. At such times, as the pupils begin to respond, more teaching opportunities become available and the teacher can capitalize on the alertness evidenced by systematic teaching of discrimination. For instance, some children delight in locating a polysylabic word in a dictionary and seeing that they have syllabized it correctly on their own.

DICTIONARY USAGE

In Chapter 3 early use of the dictionary was described in reference to word banks. As soon as pupils accumulate so many sight words that locating a word they want becomes cumbersome and time-consuming, the orderly arrangement of a word bank takes on significance. The moment an alphabetical system is introduced, the children recognize its merits. They delight in taking their 25 or more words and alphabetizing them.

Organizing the word bank yields a number of practical learning opportunities:

1. The children recognize the value and purpose of the orderly arrangement of letters alphabetically.
2. The letter order is now known functionally and not by rote.
3. Positions within the alphabet are learned through practical usage. It is soon learned, for instance, that the letter *b* is near the beginning, *m* near the middle, *w* near the end. Repeated filing of words establishes such spatial relationships functionally.
4. When a word is filed, its first letter becomes significant. Not only does it represent a sound and serve pronunciation purposes but it also serves either a filing or a location purpose.
5. The subtlety of some sounds and letters is brought into sharp focus. To file *(k) car*, *(s) city*, *(ch) chief*, *(f) phone*, *(skw) squeeze*, *(sh) shake*, *(gh) ghost*, *(j) giant*, *(wh) who*, and *(th) then* requires keen consonant discrimination. Also, filing words like *(a) apple*, *ate*, *are;* *(e) east*, *end*, *earn;* and so on, requires special attention to vowels and the variability of vowel sounds.
6. All the attention directed to beginning letters, letter order, and the sounds that letters represent calls attention to the order of letters within words. Thus sensitivity to spelling or the letter order within words is increased.

The day is almost at hand when the letters of alphabet charts no longer appear around the walls of the rooms of every first grade and other primary grades. Almost everyone who attended first grade before 1975 has seen a huge alphabet staring admonishingly across the room. The big capital letters followed by the sad and diminutive lower-case letters challenged each child. Not only were the letters large, much larger than anything ever produced by a child on paper, but also they were up so high and so far beyond eye level that they looked distorted.

At last, schools are providing each child with personal desk copies that are clear and readable. This alphabet helps in the early use of a file-box word bank, because letter location can be checked on it. From the desk alphabet and word bank filing to the dictionary is an easy transition. Each child should have a copy of a desk dictionary, such as *Webster's Elementary Dictionary* (10). The children must have a real dictionary, not a "Pixie" dictionary.

Now some learning sport can be indulged in. The children can be asked to locate any letter and its first entry. Some are sure to have trouble with this, so teams may be formed. But their delight when they are successful is well worth the effort. If the alphabet has index tabs along the side, the dictionary is especially helpful. (Tabbed dictionaries cost a bit more, but the pedagogical return far exceeds the cost.) All the children might locate the same word, one that all can read, of course. The teacher might write *snow* on the board and have each child or each team locate it in a dictionary.

Once begun, interest in the dictionary persists. Some children locate each word in their word banks and enter the dictionary page number on the back of the word card. Some select one word under each letter entry in their word banks and locate that in the dictionary.

As time goes by and progress is made in the various phases of the approach, the likelihood of pupils turning to the dictionary increases. The building and use of the consonant key and, particularly, the vowel key results in more frequent reference. If the card vowel key is the same as the dictionary's, the children should be alerted that this is the card's source. This is a good time to show the bright ones how phonetic respellings make use of consonant substitution, the vowel key, and the diacritcal marks. It is not at all uncommon for a number of bright first graders to use a dictionary for pronunciation by the phonetic respellings. Some children begin to use the dictionary to edit their own creative writing. Caution must be exercised. This is a commendable practice; however, children should not get the impression that dictionary usage and perfect spelling is the object of creative writing. Such an attitude could have dire consequences. The purpose of creative writing in the early stages is to express ideas in writing, not to teach spelling or dictionary usage or editing.

Introduction of dictionary usage is not delayed until third or fourth grade. As can be seen, elementary steps in dictionary usage can be introduced early in first grade and steadily augmented as circumstances and abilities warrant. Approaching the dictionary this way alerts children early in their school careers to one of the most functional tools in a scholar's life.

Not all the skills of dictionary usage are taught at this point, of course. An account of what can be done makes this quite clear. The refined skills of dictionary usage for learning etymologies, pronunciation, synonyms and antonyms, usage levels and dialect distribution, common English spellings, and consulting the many explanatory notes require special training and maturity. For some, this may be a lifetime process.

ROOTS IN ACTION

Printed language, like spoken language, is a form of symbolic condensation and is regulated by *interpersonal exchange* and *cooperation.* "Thanks to language," says Piaget, "the child has become capable of evoking absent situations and of liberating himself from the frontiers of space and time . . . also . . . objects and events . . . are experienced within a conceptual and rational framework which enriches the understanding of them" (3, p. 89). From the time sounds are associated with specific actions and the acquisition of language, children gradually enter an objective universe. They do so by a series of adaptations of linguistic fitting and alerting, or internalizing and externalizing, or assimilating and accommodating. In fact, it is to the degree that children are able to communicate with language that they learn to cope with their social world and its unfolding realities as well as with their inner lives.

Oral language facility is acquired by children either spontaneously or by elicitation in a world of increasing intercommunication with adults, siblings, and peers. Facility with printed language should be acquired in a similar way. Children can then adapt thought to others and to reality more effectively. This is why the language-experience approach to learning to read provides a functional transition from oral language to printed language for all children, almost regardless of their abilities and backgrounds.

The communication of ideas, either spontaneous or elicited, provides the teaching vehicle. Gradually, children discover the riches of the world of realities through their own interpretation, through that of their peers and teachers, and, through books. At first, their responses, oral and written, are rudimentary and closely linked to actions, but, as they continue to use written language of their own creation and by others, they discover the need for certain regulations. So they begin to make adjustments that reflect certain common obligations.

Methods for decoding a printed word not recognized at sight are first discovered and refined by decoding their own recorded language. Recall and recognition are thus facilitated by authorship and semantics. Children make ready and constant application when they read their own language and then that of their peers and finally that found in books and other printed sources. Thus, reading and word attack application are closely linked to interest and activity-related values.

Techniques for unlocking words are best acquired functionally. When a skill helps a reader along the printed pathway to comprehension, its utility is recognized and its use becomes efficient. Word attack skills are acquired because they are functional and facilitate comprehension. Thanks to printed language and the rich exchange among individuals that it affords, the refinement of word attack skills grows more functional. Rules are not memorized or taught in isolation as a means of readying a child to deal with printed language. The lack of consistency within the majority of so-called phonic rules is recognized functionally. As a result, variability does not produce the anxiety of failure.

Apparently phonics must be kept in perspective to recognize its contribution to reading and the learning-to-read process. The following generalizations about word attack skills and phonics are timely and relevant.

1. Children should *always* read for meaning.
2. Words to be dealt with should *always* appear in meaningful context.
3. Context or meaning clues to word recognition should *always* be tried first when attacking a word not recognized at sight.
4. Phonic generalizations are useful while learning to read. This is true particularly if the printed words being dealt with are already a functional part of the subject's speaking-meaning or oral language vocabulary.
5. Generalizations about structure are useful while learning to read. Knowledge of common inflectional changes and affixes helps readers deal with words that are already part of their speaking-meaning vocabularies.
6. Ability to substitute consonant sounds, to recognize variations of vowel sounds as marked diacritically, and to blend sounds together are essential to dictionary usage.
7. A dictionary helps word recognition for both pronunciation and meaning. For pronunciation, a dictionary provides phonetic respellings of consonant substitution, diacritical vowel marking, syllabification, and accent. The dictionary also provides a diacritical key for convenience and accuracy. Meaning clues are provided through definitions, illustrative usages, word histories, and pictures.

8. Rules are so great in number and so complex in detail that only the most skilled phonetician is apt to know them all and use them correctly. All readers depend on a dictionary for help. Therefore efficient use of the dictionary should be taught, starting with the first grade.

CONCEPT DEVELOPMENT

Even though a discussion of concept development appears in Chapter 5, further discussion is warranted, because the acquisition of concepts is a lifetime job and skill in concept attainment rates top priority in anyone's life but especially so in the life of a scholar.

Comprehension as a functional invariant of all reading instruction requires that, from the very beginning of instruction, the reading-to-learn phase take precedence over the learning-to-read phase. The semantic and syntactic aspects of the developmental process of learning to read are essentially one, precisely because of their similar directions, whereas in speech this is so because of their reverse direction. Children learning to read bring with them a rich supply of concepts, meanings, and words acquired in their world of oral communication and need only to learn to recognize printed symbols of speech. As this learning progresses, the instructional emphasis should rapidly shift from recognizing printed words to recognizing concept development. This shift occurs because reading in all phases of the curriculum and further school work becomes a principal source of knowledge or of cognitive structures. The everyday concepts and words the children bring to school and build on in early school life are hewn from concrete experience. Concepts of a historical, geographical, sociological, numerical, or scientific nature evolve from maturation of everyday concepts and a "mediated" approach that give them body and vitality (9).

The Nature of Concepts

Basically, concept formation consists of the perception of relationships— among stimuli, as one author put it (8), or between constituent-part process, as others put it (2). Bruner et al. go on to say, though, that the "working definition of a concept is the network of inferences that are or may be set into play by an act of categorizing" (2, p. 244). They have found it more meaningful, however, to regard a concept as:

a network of sign-significate inferences by which one goes beyond a set of observed criterial properties exhibited by an object or event to the class identity of the object or event in question, and thence to additional inferences about other unobserved properties of the object or event [2, p. 244].

To this definition they add clarity by means of an apple illustration. An object is seen; the object has criterial properties; a set of these criterial properties is observed as *red* (a shade of color), *shiny* (a degree of brightness or dullness of appearance), and *roundish* (shape). Undoubtedly, other properties or attributes are observed, although Bruner does not list them and apparently assumes that the three listed are sufficiently illustrative. Now the network of sign-significate leads the observer to conclude that the object observed is an apple. As an apple, the object has class identity. To make this inference the observer, as pointed out, undoubtedly noted other criterial properties of *apple*, because any number of other things also possess the properties *red, shiny, round* (ball, tomato, and so on). Also observed must have been fruit qualities, texture of surface, size, and so on.

On the basis of the inferences made thus far, particularly the class identity, other assumptions may now be made. Assumptions or inferences may be defined as a weighted average of previous experience and knowledge. The inferences are based on observed properties and result from extrapolations, that is, a going beyond the information already given. It could be assumed, for instance, that the apple is delicious and possesses, therefore, a certain relation of sugar to acid content, or that it is nonpoisonous and is uncontaminated by sprays. Or it might be assumed that if it is left unrefrigerated, the apple will rot after a certain period of time. It is apparent, then, that when these complex concepts are wisely made and appropriately used, we can reach new generalizations or concepts for which we have no direct evidence at the moment.

It seems obvious, as Vygotsky says, that when a concept is a part of a system, it can become subject to conscious and deliberate control. He defines consciousness as "awareness of the activity of the mind," and this self-reflective awareness of meaning always implies a degreee of generalization. Generalization, he says, in turn means the "formation of a superordinate concept" that includes as a particular case the given concept. Vygotsky says, "A superordinate concept implies the existence of a series of subordinate concepts, and it also presupposes a hierarchy of concepts of different levels of generality. Thus the given concept is placed within a system of relationships of generality" (9, p. 92). He illustrates this emergence of a system of analyzing the circumstance in which a child has learned the word *flower* and later learns the word *rose* and uses them interchangeably. When, however, *flower* becomes generalized and more widely applicable to include such subordinates as *petunia, tulip,* and *rose,* the relationship of the two changes in the child's mind. Thus, he says, a system is taking shape, and the child's knowledge of flowers as a superordinate concept and of rose, petunia, and tulip as subordinate concepts is becoming systematized.

Probably one of the clearest accounts of concept formation and attainment and the learning and teaching of concepts is the final report on *Strategies and Cognitive Processes in Concept Learning* (4). During the three years of the project, concepts in various disciplines were studied, and a definition of *concept* was formulated. An analogy between *concept* and the concept of *dog* was used.

> A dog is a domesticated, carnivorous mammal of the family Canidae; in other words the concept, *dog*, is comprised of the defining properties by which all instances of dogs are put into the same category and also by which dogs are discriminated from other animals. Similarly, *concept* is defined as a product of learning, or, more broadly, of mankind's experiences, having four characteristics—definability, structure, psychological meaningfulness, and utility [4, p. 1].

Treating concepts in terms of defining characteristics should assist teachers in identifying and differentiating concepts from other products of learning such as facts, principles, and problem-solving skills.

Types of Concepts

Even though much has already been said about concept attainment and development, Chapters 5 and 8 of Russell's *Children's Thinking* (7), in which he classifies concepts into types, will prove helpful not only from a teaching-learning point of view but also from a curriculum point of view. He classified concepts into seven types and added an eighth:

1. mathematical concepts
2. concepts of time
3. scientific concepts
4. concepts of self
5. social concepts
6. aesthetic concepts
7. concepts of humor
8. miscellaneous concepts

Mathematical concepts include those of numbers and their manipulation in the fundamental operations and application in problem solving, measurement or quantities of weights and measures (gram, pound, ton, inch, yard, acre), space relationships and relationships of objects in space (size, shape, position, cup, round, space module).

Concepts of time are in many ways more abstract than those of space because there are fewer specific clues available. Extension of time concepts from day and night to morning and evening, from yesterday, today, and tomorrow to long ago and eternity, from arranging events in chronological order to making and using time lines requires careful and frequent study as well as increasing maturity and a going from immediate specific experiences to the general and remote.

Scientific concepts include the concepts of mathematics and time and go beyond concrete measures to explanations of observed happenings. The many contacts possible with children's natural environment can help them immeasurably to classify and order, to note hierarchies, to overcome animism, to overcome egocentric responses, to grasp the nature of proof, to distinguish between fact and superstition, and to grasp laws.

Vocabulary development and concept attainment is an arduous task. Skilled teaching and an alert, attentive, curious scholar are required. The teaching-learning must be done in each phase of the curriculum and at each stage of development.

CONCLUSION

This chapter presents compactly the basic word attack skill program useful to the learning reader. It illustrates why acquisition of fundamental skills is neither complex nor difficult. Each year some children starting to school for the first time have already learned to read and have developed, much on their own, functional word attack skills.

As in all communication, word attack learning should always give first attention to the use of context or meaning clues to recognition. This means that skills are first developed by using words selected from a language and a morpheme sound unit.

Word attack skills serve readers by helping them reach into their speaking-meaning vocabularies and by helping them to use the dictionary. The former takes precedence in the early stages of reading instruction, because the children already possess large functional speaking-meaning vocabularies. As soon as the words met in print are not found in their speaking-meaning vocabularies, the children must turn to a dictionary.

Sound pedagogical training is accomplished by using the children's speaking-meaning vocabularies and then gradually going on to the vocabularies of others, as expressed in books, magazines, and newspapers. Sound psychological training comes by using practices of learning based on logical usage, meaningful repetition, meaningful transfer to new contexts, instant feedback, and frequent retention exercises.

Concept development is a must in any instructional situation, but especially so in inquiry reading in which basic skills for reading in the "content areas" are acquired. Words are the coins of the concept realm and represent a first step in the hierarchy of concept attainment. It behooves us to make concept development strategies sound, comprehensive, and orderly, since concepts are requisite to all learning and communication.

The teaching of word recognition must have its roots in the pupils' actions. From the time children first associate sound—words—with specific actions and begin to acquire language, they gradually enter an increasingly objective universe. Their knowledge must govern the purpose and action of functional word attack skill teaching. When it is, the utility of skills is recognized and their use becomes increasingly efficient.

Bibliography

1. Artley, A. Sterl, "Teaching Word Meaning Through Context," *Elementary English Review*, 20 (February, 1943), 68–74.
2. Bruner, Jerome S., Jacquelline J. Goodnow, and George A. Austin, *A Study of Thinking*. New York: Wiley, 1956.
3. Fries, Charles C., *Linguistics and Reading*. New York: Holt, Rinehart and Winston, 1963.
4. Klausmeier, Herbert J., and Chester W. Harris, *Strategies and Cognitive Processes in Concept Learning*. Final Report, Project No. 2850. Washington, D.C.: U.S. Department of Health, Education, and Welfare, Office of Education, Bureau of Research, March, 1968.
5. McCullough, Constance M., "Phonic Knowledge Demonstrated by Prospective Elementary School·Teachers," a paper presented at the American Educational Research Association Meeting, Chicago, February, 1963 (mimeographed).
6. Piaget, Jean, *Six Psychological Studies*, edited by David Elkind. New York: Random House, 1967.
7. Russell, David H., *Children's Thinking*. Boston: Ginn, 1956.
8. Underwood, Benton J., "An Orientation for Research on Thinking," *Psychological Review*, 59 (1952), 209–220.
9. Vygotsky, L. S., *Thought and Language*. New York: Wiley, 1962.
10. *Webster's Dictionary of Synonyms*. Springfield, Mass.: Merriam, 1942.

Chapter 11
Spelling Instruction

It is both amusing and agonizing to realize that spelling has for so many centuries been a demon to many. Comenius referred to it as "that most troublesome torture of wits" (7, p. 258). However, Huey points out that Comenius further says that spelling does not need to be troublesome. Huey also states that spelling instruction, too, does not need to be a problem to teachers or students.

Until the mid-nineteenth century spelling instruction was closely allied to reading instruction. The history of American reading instruction shows that the *New England Primer* had to compete with England's *Perfect School-Master*, a speller designed to teach "exact spelling," reading, and writing. In 1702 George Fox's *Instruction for Right Spelling* and "plain directions for reading and writing true English" came on the scene and was used widely for the next 75 years (9, pp. 25–30). However, as Nila B. Smith adds, "Perhaps the most successful of the Spellers of this period was Thomas Dilworth's *A New Guide to the English Tongue.* . . . The first American reprint was made by Benjamin Franklin in 1747" (9, p. 32). These spellers not only dominated the reading instruction scene but foreshadowed changes that gradually influenced instruction widely: the transition from religious to moralistic content; and the inclusion of such secular materials as stories, riddles, and dialogues. In these times and until the appearance of the McGuffey Readers in 1840 spellers "served in the same capacity as the basic reader does today" (9, p. 66). Then Smith cites a five-stanza poem showing that "spelling was still used as the foundation method for inducting children into the mysteries of reading.

Verse 3
So as you wish to be a dunce,
Pray go and fetch me them at once.
For as you will not learn to *spell*,
'Tis vain to think of *reading* well [9, p. 67].

Why was it all so dull? Because children had to spend endless hours naming letters in syllables and words before doing any reading. Throughout this time, learning the alphabet was the first step. With the appearance of Webster's speller in 1798 a new emphasis resulted, "that of teaching the sounds of letters as well as their names" (7, p. 69). Now *articulation* followed by *elocution* dominated reading and spelling instruction. Worcester's Primer, which appeared in 1828, apparently was the first to recognize the "word method" as well as the "alphabet method." Horace Mann in the 1830s was a staunch advocate of the word method and roundly ridiculed the A-B-C method. Huey, too, strongly advocated the word method, silent reading for meaning, functional phonics, vocabulary development, and the importance of awakening in children a real desire for reading.

Repeatedly throughout this book the point has been made that the uses of language both in and out of school entail a meshing of communication skills. The language arts, both those of expression (talking and writing) and those of impression (listening and reading) reflect clearly that the relation of meaning to language is the same regardless of the modality being used. Even so, the mechanical aspects of written and spoken language have been greatly overstressed, to the neglect of the vastly more important function of language in relation to the central thought processes. As Alvina Burrows et al. point out, "For purposes of analysis these skills can be separated from the context in which they function. Similarly, for practice leading to mastery, a degree of isolation can be effected in teaching and learning. Yet the skills do not exist as ends in themselves . . . one learns to spell in order to communicate, not to write lists of words or to win spelling matches" (2, p. 244).

So, although the history of spelling and reading instruction shows a remarkable meshing, this came about not so much as a means of communication but as a mechanical, rote skill acquisition in isolation. Rote learning has always been the pitfall of instruction, but this is doubly true for spelling. Furthermore, this rote learning approach was carried to such extremes that parroting letter names in word order was for centuries said to be the "royal road to reading." However, with the advent of public schools and the masses it was soon discovered that rote memorization had damnable pitfalls. There has been mounting criticism since the 1820s, but to no avail. Altogether this mechanistic approach has been most laborious and retarding.

Spelling to Communicate

There has been a great wind of change in the primary schools since most of the adults of today were primary school children and many of the old beliefs have been blown away. New and exciting things are happening; this is the only stage in the whole of education when the child is educated as a whole person, and his many interests can be encouraged [4, p. iii].

Thus writes Lady Plowden in her foreword to John Blackie's remarkably insightful and forward-looking book, *Inside the Primary School*. Blackie says that one by one the many hindrances "masquerading as aids" have been disappearing and that writing and learning to write are more pragmatic. The pragmatic dimension, said Ernest Horn "includes the relation of language to the purposes of the sayer and the sayee ... *it is purpose* that guides the construction of ideas and holds them together. Pragmatically considered, such terms as meaning, significance, and value, all imply the question, 'For whom?'" (6, p. 288). Thus from the beginning handwriting instruction requires a good model because what is written must be so legible that it can be read; then dictation along with teacher transcription furthers the "for whom" aspect as talk is written down; and then comes the stage when the child wants to write and does. "This process may be fast or slow according to the child's capacity, but it will be essentially the same in every case" (4, p. 71). At this stage it is clearly essential that the writings convey a genuine personal experience and have something to say that the children really want to say. At this stage, too, it is quite debatable whether or not vocabulary size or use of "substandard" language affects learning to write. As Celia S. Lavatelli says, "Not knowing five synonyms for 'beautiful' and saying 'He done it' are unlikely to impede school learning" (8, p. 55). Furthermore, in the modern school the writing that conveys a genuine personal experience uses a much wider range of interests and is about persons (social), places (geography), things (artifacts), events (affairs and phenomena), logistics (mathematics and science), music and arts, and even poetry.

This is the context in which children can and should be introduced to writing. It follows naturally from purposeful communication and the need to be understood—in brief, it is a pragmatic introduction. Children learn to talk so as to communicate with a parent, a peer, a sibling, an adult.

They should learn to write in order to communicate, in much the same way as they learned to talk.

Writing as handwriting was discussed in Chapter 5 (pp. 127–129). The model provided was both personal and legible as each pupil learned to produce the letters in his or her name. This initial learning was then extended to handwriting training using the names of peers; after this, training continued with the copying of sentences from personal dictation. Each child mastered letter formation in keeping with his or her own performances or demonstrated capability. In this kind of instruction, mastering letter formation is individualized and thereby circumvents mass rote indoctrination.

Encoding in creative writing was prefaced on a number of skill advances. Foremost was the phonological encoding of children clearly based on phonic instruction focused on phoneme-grapheme relationships. Evidence supports the conclusion that children so taught to write *do not fear* producing words or doing encoding. They thrill to the "written communication" process and love to write. It is truly as Burrows et al. (1) said in their superb book, "They All Want to Write," for they do.

It is at this stage of progress that left-to-right word attack skill is recognizable. Most of the phonologically encoded words are produced with the first letter(s) correct: *diffrt* (different), *kis* (kiss), *lite* (light), *tret* (treat), *frst* (first), *har* (hair), *cot* (cut), *nedl* (needle). Many of the encodings also show endings being correctly associated by letter sound and produced. This production of beginnings and endings reflects the basic psychology of learning law that the children are attentive to extremes. In turn, the achievements reflect consonant knowledge and, particularly, consonant substitution know-how. In addition, because the two extremes are produced there results a kind of natural focusing on the medial letters, usually vowels. This, as skill increases, leads to vowel production and vowel variability recognition.

When polysyllabic words are encoded phonologically the children do so intuitively by word sound units or syllables. Early in their creative writing careers they sense that encoding can be done more readily through syllables, because a syllable (sound unit) usually has a beginning, an ending, and a medial letter, except of course in open syllables. In fact, in many instances the children capitalize the beginning of each syllable: *decorate* encoded as *DecKorAte; western* as *Ws Drn; woman* as *WoMan; Goldilox* as *Gold De Lox; neighbor* as *Na Ber.*

At this stage of writing to communicate children do so many astonishing things that it is difficult to avoid overenthusiasm. The feats just described seem phenomenal but other feats are too. For example, reexamination of the creative writing samples discussed in Chapter 5 shows that many of the words (and not only phonetically regular words) produced are encoded according to accepted letter order, or, if you wish, are correctly spelled. This most likely reflects a number of phenomena. The words correctly spelled had not been studied as "spelling words" and their correct reproduction was not expected or rewarded. Their correct reproduction probably shows that because the children have been reading quite widely and have been working extensively with words (word bank activities, cutting out words, etc.), they can *read* the words readily and thereby a strong visual image has most likely been embedded in the central nervous system. Often when children encode a word like *leVes* they will say, "Something is missing," and seem to know that *leVes* does not look like *leaves*, or that *frst* does not really look like *first*. Students of spelling have contended for years that children are more likely to spell correctly words they can read and for which they have meaning than words they cannot read. Apparently words that can be read leave a strong visual-perceptual imprint.

In addition, the children do not lose sight of the syntactical order for word arrangement. In short, they do not forget what they want to say and how they want to say it while they work on the encoding of any one word. The message is the medium.

"It is commonly supposed that there is only one right way to spell every word in the language . . . but evidence from recently published dictionaries points the other way," says Lee C. Deighton, whose book *A Comparative Study of Spellings* (3) shows that four major collegiate dictionaries list variant spellings for more than 2000 words in the common language and show disagreement on spelling for about 1770 words. The following are illustrative: *aging* or *ageing; air-line* or *airline; armfuls* or *armsful; blond* or *blonde; bused* or *bussed; dripped* or *dript; gage* or *gauge; gobbledegook* or *gobbledygook;* and so on.

Two of the dictionaries Deighton used for his study carefully avoided the use of the word *preferred* and even frequency was not an explicit basis of choice. This indecision about which variant is "correct" reflects in good part how across the years the spelling variants for almost all of our words evolved slowly until an accepted letter order became established, and this is how so-called correct spelling developed and came to mean the production of the *accepted* letter order.

On the other hand, to write and encode so that others can read is the communication purpose of all writing. The only likely exception is a personal diary in which one does not write for others.

Thus the phonological encodings in early creative writings can in a broad sense be taken to reflect a phylogenetic development of encodings and the gradual acceptance of preferred spellings on frequency. The circumstances are different though from historical development because the young encoders of today are constantly encountering the accepted letter order encodings in their reading, so that although they may encode leaves as *leVes* and first as *frst* one time, the next time they see the words in print they see them encoded as *leaves* and *first*. This leads directly to another skill, that of *editing*. Children do learn to edit their own writing and that of their peers. They do it by listening to what has been written, by oral rereading, and by actual proofreading.

Instruction that focuses on writing for communication acknowledges early that "perfect" writing is utopian castle building. A writer strives to write with clarity and effectiveness and struggles for a lifetime. Children want to communicate and to do so clearly and effectively, and they learn across the years as they mature to gain increasing command over writing skills. At each stage of growth, however, writing is done to communicate, and it must be taught that way. Therefore it is of utmost importance that the early attempts at writing be dealt with wisely. Children must be made to feel secure, to want to try and try again, to edit and gradually to refine and polish. This allows for assessment, improvement, and even grading when all is being done in the interest of developing better communication skills. What is needed is to improve children's confidence in their own capabilities and especially their desire to communicate in writing.

SPELLING

As we said earlier, knowledge of letter names is indicative of possible success in learning to read, write, deal with numbers, and so on. Children who can repeat the alphabet show that they can handle 26 items mentally and do so in a fixed order. Far more significant is the ability to learn the *sounds that letters represent* singly or in combination. In speech letters represent sounds. Children who can talk bring with them to school a tremendous phonological wealth acquired in the wonderfully unique way in which children learn to hear words, to note their sound elements and stress, and to remember to produce them as heard. All that remains for a school to do is make the children facile in the use of specific letters to represent specific sounds and especially the blending of sounds into words. (This is a good time to review the sections on word recognition, particularly auditory discrimination, pp. 51–53.) Knowing the purpose of letters, the sounds they represent, and their names is far different from parroting the alphabet.

The material that follows is devoted to formal spelling instruction and describes a functional procedure to develop spelling power without violating either the philosophy or the principles of learning declared in this book. Spelling is done in all writing. In the primary-level phases, spelling goes through a gradual transition from phonological "perfection" to adult-imposed (frequently phono-illogical) "correctness." In the beginning, as we have seen, children put down phoneme-grapheme relationships as they hear and see them. Often their productions are phonologically accurate as measured by dictionary respellings. Children's instinctive phonological sense is astounding and must be taken advantage of. Gradually, children acquire a consciousness of letter order as they see that their spelling (encoding) differs from that in books, newspapers, and so on. Some children begin to ask for adult-type spelling because they experience difficulty in rereading what they have encoded, especially when they try to reread their accounts after a week or so.

Formal spelling instruction involving dictation from a selected word list prepared by vocabulary authorities can be initiated in the second grade for most children. The most efficient procedure is the *test-study, self-correction* method, which involves pupil decision making and learner responsibility and permits progress at an individual pace.

In mid-October of the second year, "formal" spelling can be introduced. All the previous functional spelling, reading experiences, and word recognition training will have provided sufficient readiness. It must be kept in mind that formal spelling has to be introduced in such a way that it *will not stifle creative writing.* Instruction must also be differentiated. To impose the same list of words on all children is disastrous, if not ridiculous. Accordingly, each pupil's instructional level has to be determined first. This is readily done and is interesting for the children.

First, a spelling list—such as those published in most language arts series or spelling series for use in the elementary grades—should be obtained. In the first and second grades, a random sample of 20 words is sufficient. At each level beyond that, random samples of 25 words should be used.

A random sample should be fair and unbiased and can be obtained as follows: If the total number of words in the first-grade list is 200 and the size of the random sample wanted is 20, simply divide the 200 by 20. Then select every tenth word on the list to compile an adequate and unbiased sample of 20 words. A similar procedure is followed at each grade level until a list for each grade level is obtained.

The next step is to test the class to determine ability or instructional levels. Each child should have a sheet of paper on which he can put 20 or 25 words in a column. The following instructions from the teachers must be understood by all the children: "I will pronounce or say a word and will speak it only *once.* As soon as you have heard the word, write it on your paper. If you are not sure of the spelling of a word, try it anyway. You may be right. If you don't know the word at all just draw a line." These instructions may be repeated and illustrated on the chalkboard until all understand. Be certain, though, that the testing situation is not made to seem a dire circumstance and that it does not create anxiety. What is wanted is that the children do the best they can and show what they really can do. It should be stressed that each word will be spoken *only once.* Allowance must be made for instances in which a child really does not hear a word (in which case it is repeated), but these repetitions are definitely exceptions. Because this is functional spelling and patterns must be set correctly from the start, the words are *not* put into sentences and no effort is made to distinguish homonyms by using sentences (see p. 290).

Children who spell 70 percent or more of the first-grade list of words correctly are tested again, using the second-grade-level list. On the first day of testing two lists will most likely be enough of a challenge. Testing should continue the next day and until all in the room spell less than 70 percent of a list correctly. The following distribution is illustrative of one that is likely to occur in a second-grade class of 30 children:

NUMBER OF CHILDREN	INSTRUCTIONAL LEVEL
3	0
5	1
10	2
8	3
4	4

This means that in this class there are five spelling groups, each at a different level. This is so even though three of the children were unable to achieve 70 percent on any list. These three may not be made isolates or removed from the class when spelling instruction occurs. Two adjustments can be made that will help the children be productive, help them save face, and help them maintain a positive attitude. For this group five words can be selected from their word banks and used as spelling words. Thus the number of words is restricted and the words used are chosen from among words that they can read and have dealt with on numerous occasions. Both adjustments have high merit.

Adjustment can also be made for the second group. Rather than administering the usual 20 words each week the number can be reduced to 10. There is nothing sacred about the use of 20 words; such an adjustment violates no standard and will more likely provide successful experiences for these children. The other three groups will be tested and will work with a 20-word list.

The *test-study* method proceeds as follows: On Monday, each group is administered a test of their prescribed words. The teacher has the five lists and speaks one word from each list in turn. The children in the first group spell the first word as soon as it is pronounced. The children in the second group spell the second word spoken; those in the third group, the third word; and so on.

Each word is spoken only once. The children are instructed that if a word like *one* or *won* (a homonym) is spoken, they must ask which *one* is meant. This gives the teacher an opportunity to reply, "How many do you know?" If the child knows both words, the teacher should indicate which word is meant. This may sound a bit complex, but children catch on to the procedure quickly. Whenever they are writing functionally on their own they must know whether to use *one* or *won*. No one will stand by and tell them. Therefore they must learn from the beginning to be self-reliant, resourceful, and alert to possible homonyms.

The teacher must pace the pronunciation of the words at an even tempo and allow enough time for each child to write. Classes and teachers tend to establish their own tempos. No child must be frustrated by the pacing.

Why is a word spoken only once? Spelling is largely a conditioned-response reaction. One seldom pauses while writing a paper or a letter to repeat a word once or twice; one just writes. When a word to be spelled is spoken, the pupils must be ready to spell it at once. Chances are good that they will be much more successful this way.

Why is a word not used in a sentence? This is not done for two reasons. First, and of utmost importance, the words dictated *are words each child can read.* This means the child not only has a quite distinct *visual image* for the word but also has a *meaning* or meanings for the word. Second, if children wait until a sentence containing the word has been read and the word is spoken again in isolation, many distractors have been put in the way. Such interpolated tasks can readily interfere with and block recall. Emphasis must be on the immediate, conditioned-response reaction.

While administering the tests, it is best for the teacher *not* to walk around the room. A fixed place should be established for all spelling occasions and each word should be spoken clearly and without distortion. As progress is made through the word lists, the pupils may be oriented occasionally by saying, "This is word number five," or, "Group 1, 'my'; Group 2, 'tree'; Group 3, 'flower'"; and so on. This helps all the pupils stay together and keep pace.

When the five lists have been dictated, the *self-correction* phase is introduced. Each child is given a typed copy of the words he or she was just asked to spell. (This means, of course, that there must be three lists available for the first group, five for the second, and so on.) Each child then checks his or her spellings against the list. In this way the children discover their own successes and their own errors. They learn to recognize and deal with their own needs. Because the children are tested at their own levels, they are not apt to miss more than three or four words; that is, they should spell 17 or more words out of 20 correctly without having first attempted to memorize the list. This degree of success is a result of their reading ability, phonic phoneme-grapheme (letter-sound) ability, and independent writing ability. It results, too, from the fact that the children are administered words at their own instructional levels.

If a word is misspelled, a check mark (√) is placed next to it. The number of misspelled words is then indicated at the top of the page; if none were misspelled, this is indicated with a zero. In the beginning, a quick check should be made by the teacher to see how accurately the children have checked. Once the technique is learned an occasional teacher *spot check* will suffice. Children are basically honest and have a tremendous amount of integrity. They will diligently check their papers when they realize that this pretest gives them the opportunity to find those words they do not know. This in turn allows them to concentrate their study efforts on those few words not spelled correctly. A small amount of supervision on the part of the teacher, not so much to uncover dishonesty as to discover *honest oversight*, is sufficient. If the teacher finds a word misspelled that has not been marked, the child is alerted but not told which word it is. All the teacher does is change the number at the top of the paper. Then the child must check all the words again to find the misspelling.

Each misspelled word is studied immediately. Traditional methods suffice here. First, the pupils study the correct letter order, repeating it over and over. Then they close their eyes and visualize the word while repeating the spelling. Again, they restudy the word while looking at it. Then they *cover both* the misspelled word and the correct spelling and write the word again, next to the misspelling. They check immediately to see if they are right and repeat the action as follows:

thes √   this   this

In the beginning all this takes a bit of time, but it is worth every second of it. In a month or so the children will have caught on so well that everything will proceed easily and efficiently.

Nothing more need be done in spelling on Monday. On Wednesday, the same procedure is followed. Everybody spells the same words again, even if they had perfect papers on Monday. The children who spell all the words correctly on both Monday and Wednesday are through for the week. The children who do not are tested again on Friday. If children miss the same word on Wednesday that they missed on Monday, they study it more intently on Thursday. Their failure to retain the correct letter order during the period of delayed recall from Monday to Wednesday showed that the word had not been learned well enough and needed more reinforcement.

The week's activity just described permits a number of psychological learning actions to occur. First, the test-study method takes advantage of each pupil's reading ability, visual-perceptual word recognition ability, sound-letter word attack training, creative-writing experience, and rote recognition of word letter order as evidenced by conditioned-response reproduction. Second, the self-correction method takes advantage of the individual discovery of success and failure, focusing on specific personal errors. Self-correction employs firsthand oral and visual clues, oral and visual imagery, repetition, and double checking. Further, because the children perform at their own instructional levels, the number of errors made is not so large as to be frustrating; usually no more than three words are misspelled. The second check on Wednesday provides a delayed-recall retention check to see how effective the previous learning has been. In addition, each of the pupil's skills is reactivated. Pupils who show twice that they do know the spellings are excused from further checks and so rewarded for their knowledge. For the others the third check on Friday again yields evidence of retention and accuracy of recall.

Additional delayed-recall checks should be made biweekly or monthly. On these occasions the words missed in the preceding two or three weeks are used again in the test-study procedure.

When spelling is taught this way, it becomes a pedagogical pleasure and a challenge to the learner rather than drudgery and frustration. Rates of progress vary according to a child's level of achievement. Bright children may be spelling a so-called fifth-grade list by the end of the year. The opportunity to proceed at a pace in keeping with their ability spurs all, but especially the bright students, and the achievement gap between them and the slow learners becomes increasingly larger.

Instruction can be varied by giving the able spellers 25 or even 30 words to spell each week. Or, if they continuously achieve perfect scores on Mondays and Wednesdays, they can be given a new list on Fridays. On the other hand, it has been found quite helpful to reduce the number of words per week for the slower learners. Administering only 10 or 15 words at a time helps them along. It is better to attain a perfect score on 10 words with regularity than to be overwhelmed by having to spell 20 words.

At the third- and fourth-grade levels and beyond, the spelling gap between the top performers and the others widens even more. Good teaching increases individual differences. It is not uncommon for fourth-grade classes to have some children spelling at ninth- and tenth-grade levels.

CONCLUSION

Individualization of instruction or differentiation of instruction are terms that receive endless lip service from educators but seldom if ever are implemented. Efforts to provide instruction that promotes pupil individuality are frustrated by the rigidity of grade standards, impractical attempts at homogeneity, and the foisting on teachers of publisher-designed undiversified materials. Consequently, teachers frequently are "fooling themselves and cheating their pupils". (5, p. 17)

What is wanted is for the children to achieve as rapidly and as smoothly as possible and to do so in harmony with their social and emotional well-being. Even though children cannot be grouped homogeneously on all traits, they can generally be so grouped on a single trait. Ability to spell is not really a "single trait," but it approaches such a classification more completely than many without producing weird distortions. The practices described in this chapter do permit arranging pupils relatively homogeneously by a single criterion. At the same time children are not locked into a level but can move forward at a rate in keeping with their ability while maintaining high standards of achievement.

In a randomly structured class children will differ widely in spelling ability just as they do in reading ability and so on. However, making an inventory of abilities as described is conducive to almost totally individual pacing. Each pupil can move forward at a rate appropriate to his or her unique ability. This is true even though in a typical class of 30 pupils five or more instructional levels invariably result.

In a class organized for differentiated spelling instruction children can grasp a perception of maturity and progress that will help them seek greater achievement. The spelling class experience may help them make the transition to similarly productive learning habits in other pedagogical activities. In addition, the teacher's recognition of the children's achievement and progress will unquestionably influence their morale and well-being. All of us seem to try harder as we attain recognition and approval. Self-esteem is based not only on the opinion of peers or the teacher, but on the clear personal recognition of achievement that results from the self-correction technique. This direct recognition and approval first by the individual, and then by the teacher, peers, and parents is far superior to tangible rewards of tokens or prizes.

Finally, because producing the accepted letter order of words (spelling) is being constantly reinforced and demanded in creative writing, transfer of spelling knowledge to actual usage occurs. Creative writing requires not only a legible product but also a product that accurately conveys the ideas being encoded. Learning how to produce such writing is, above all, the aspiration or goal-striving behavior that produces a realistic attitude toward success and continuous improvement in spelling.

Bibliography

1. Burrows, Alvina T., Doris C. Jackson, and Dorothy O. Saunders, *They All Want to Write*, 3rd ed. New York: Holt, Rinehart and Winston, 1964.
2. Burrows, Alvina T., Dianne L. Monson, and Russell G. Stauffer, *New Horizons in the Language Arts*. New York: Harper & Row, 1972.

3. Deighton, Lee C., *A Comparative Study of Spellings.* Pleasantville, N.Y.: Hardscrabble Press, Inc., 1972.
4. Department of Education and Science, *Children and Their Primary Schools, A Report of the Central Advisory Council for Education* (England), Vol. 1. London: Her Majesty's Stationery Office, 1967.
5. Goodlad, John I., and Robert H. Anderson, *The Nongraded Elementary School.* New York: Harcourt Brace Jovanovich, 1959.
6. Horn, Ernest, "Language and Meaning," in Nelson B. Henry (ed.), *The Psychology of Learning,* Forty-First Yearbook of the National Society for the Study of Education, Part II. Chicago: University of Chicago Press, 1942.
7. Huey, Edmund B., *The Psychology and Pedagogy of Reading.* New York: Macmillan, 1913.
8. Lavatelli, Celia Stendler, *Piaget's Theory Applied to an Early Childhood Curriculum.* Cambridge, Mass., American Science and Engineering, 1970.
9. Smith, Nila B., *American Reading Instruction.* New York: Silver Burdette, 1934.

Chapter 12
The Universality of LEA

It is timely to pause here and reexamine the basic meaning of the term the *Experience-Language Approach to instruction*. At this point in our discussion this term is too limited, not allowing for the comprehensive meaning and usage of functional communication. Since, though, a label is needed, we might speak of the *LEA approach to the communication arts*. Or perhaps it would be best to label the approach *the language arts approach to communication effectiveness*. Each of the labels seems to circumscribe the approach but from different points of view.

The conception of LEA detailed in this book embraces the total communication arts. This gives the experience-language a dynamic and embracing dimension. Whenever communication goes on, utilization is made of the basic sense of communication, which summed in one phase, is to be understood. This is the efficacy of the preschoolers learning rhythms whereby they generate and acquire a system of language. Whatever language they acquire during these formative years—oral language, sign language, or body language—is acquired *to satisfy their own purposes*. Thus oral language acquisition involves the facets of speaking (producing) and listening (receiving), and sign and body language, using visual perception (seeing and receiving) and physical encoding (producing). The acquisition of this extensive communication network provides a natural foundation for learning to read and write.

The bases for formal instruction in the four facets of language are thus clearly defined. *First,* and foremost in all language instruction, must be the condition that it be done in such a way that children learn the refinements while "satisfying their purposes." Language production that results from intention to communicate is functional in nature. *Second,* language provides the basic symbolization for thought and for thinking. Thus language is used not only to communicate but to reflect, to dream, to project, and instruction must emulate this. *Third,* language is used in all areas of the curriculum, not only in literature, and instruction in the use and refinement of the facets of language must cover this wide range. Thus total communication includes the full spectrum of communication modes, and pedagogical development and refinement must spring out of progressive differentiation across the spiraling curriculum. This is so because language is a code that represents the learned behavior of society and is readily influenced by both the culture in which it is used and the teachers in that culture.

The previous chapters have detailed pedagogical procedures that promote, develop, and refine the use of experience and language with special attention to written communication or reading and writing. This chapter will focus briefly on those years beyond third grade and on special uses of the approach.

THIRD YEAR AND BEYOND

Once the cycle of instruction has been activated as described thus far for kindergarten through third grade it needs but be extended and refined at each succeeding level. The two distinguishing features of directed reading instruction are the use of (1) group-type procedures and (2) the use of multiplex differentiated inquiry (individualized) reading procedures. Both provide a fundamental medium and have unique advantages. Both give rise to disciplines that, although not mutually exclusive, are clearly different. In brief, a well-rounded program of instruction to be sound must include both procedures.

If the use of these two all-embracing techniques is essential at the primary level with children whose intellectual capabilities are evolving under the power of representative intelligence and who are learning to cope with the separate and multiple perspectives of each other and the curriculum, then it is even more essential at this more advanced phase of intra-personal cognitive functioning. At this level it is also essential to their interpersonal or social universe. The period from 8 to 11 years marks the expansion beyond the constructions characteristic of the concrete operations period. Now children "can anticipate the outcome of a large number of instances taken together. Thus the notion of probability as a ratio of favorable cases to possible cases is gradually established" (7, p. 113). Indeed what is most striking about the use of group DRTA's and individualized DRTA's over this long period of formation of concrete operations is the functional unity that combines the cognitive reading actions into a whole. Now one can see the systematic unfolding of an integrated process that is not only cognitive but social and moral as well. What is remarkable is that during the earlier period the actions and interactions involved things and events based primarily in the present and of a sensorimotor type, but now transactions are based primarily on the coordination of cognitive and affective components. Thus children are gradually freeing themselves from the concrete here and now and are able to cope with a variety of possible transformations. Their interests now also include the past, the non-present and the future. New perspectives are opening up. The *cybernetics of self-regulation* extends to adjustments that are "both retroactive. [loop systems or feedbacks] and anticipatory [probability systems and feed forward] constituting a permanent system of compensations" (7, p. 157). Furthermore, Piaget and Inhelder go on to say that there is no behavior pattern, no matter how intellectual, that does not involve affective factors, the two are inseparable and irreducible. In short, reading has become primarily a matter of "feeding the mind" (1). For minds to thrive, they must be fed a balance of the sciences and social sciences, of the humanities, of mathematics and economics, of prose and poetry, of biology and zoology, and so on.

Because intellectual development proceeds in a sequence of states, pursuing instruction in directed reading-thinking activities year after year provides a regulating force that is determined simultaneously by maturation, by cognitive actions, and by the enrichment resulting from the ongoing internal reorganization of mental schemes. Gradually the art of *critically weighing evidence* in light of the inquiries being made and the content authenticity is consolidated as a tool of thinking. Generative learning occurs when instruction is sparked by the children's own inquiries, thereby helping teachers to meet children at their level of questioning and on a common intellectual plane. In brief, it is the processes of thinking, the logical methods of inquiry, and the stabilization of affective social and moral conditions that are being developed.

In addition, the quantity and quality of student inquiries increase when the questions teachers ask reflect the spontaneous questions of children (2, 6) and their level of cognitive maturity. An open communication system permits instruction to proceed on a cooperating intellectual plane. This is so because raising open-ended questions and asking for evidence is a kind of instruction that fosters self-regulatory intellectual action rather than contravenes. The teacher, although always in control, takes account of the whole learning context instead of falling into the pitfalls of teacher-raised fact questions and robot-type "behavioral" responses. The aim in reading as in scientific work is to extract information of predictive value. To observe accurately, to speculate wisely, and to draw reasonable conclusions involves intellectual skills that are not easy to learn and may take a lifetime to acquire. Every instructional opportunity at every stage of development and progress must be utilized.

Another important difference between the DRTA way of directing the reading process and didactic instructor questioning methods is the extent to which the emotions are aroused. Disagreements among students occur as similarities and differences in personal reactions are voiced. Clashes between opposing basic assumptions occur. What is important is that students learn to recognize the extent to which their emotions are involved, keep a clear head, and not let their reactions block learning. In brief, they must acquire the art of noble detachment.

Concepts must be isolated, analyzed, and internalized. Misapprehensions, subtleties, exaggerations, falsifications, ambiguities, vaguenesses, figures of speech, idioms, and the like, must be located, unraveled, and classified. The relationship between thought and word is more than a symbol-experience construct; it is a process that undergoes constant change. Syntactically infants may start with one- and two-word sentences and go on to increasingly more complex sentences. Semantically, however, they usually start from a whole, a meaningful complex, and gradually learn to divide and master the separate conceptual structures (11).

Comprehension and concept attainment are the functional invariants of all reading instruction. Language development as a part of maturation influences much of a person's progress from thought that is predominantly perceptual and intuitive to thought that is conceptual and logical. It is not enough for children to have had an experience, especially verbally; it must also affect their way of organizing experiences. Piaget starts from the central postulate that action (motor or cognitive) is adaptive and is the source from which mental operations emerge. A child's verbal accommodation to a reading-learning experience is helpful but will produce lasting effects only if, through further self-regulation, generalization to other tasks results.

Of course, reading can be done for simple entertainment or just to pass the time. Accordingly, reading can be either regulated or unregulated. But when reading to learn is the instructional goal, the reading process must be critical and productive.

Critical reading becomes a means of making judgments based on values and a choice of the relevant. To make decisions and deal with alternatives requires mental discipline. In essence, the dimensions of critical versatile reading are as follows: ability to actualize concepts and intentions; ability to sift through information and determine its relevance to one's predictions while at the same time actively following an author's intentions and fidelity; ability to deal with constraints and variants and invariants in terms of the purposes established; ability to maintain in dynamic equilibrium such personal components as convictions and inclinations; ability to accept the responsibility of exercising choice among different options on the basis of consequences; and ability to internalize the knowledge gained and apply it in new situations.

In the years from 8 to 11 intelligent actions and thought must be refined increasingly through the personal and group exploration of group DRTA procedures and individualized DRTA procedures. Questions must become more insightful and be derived from intellectual actions rather than being affective "off-the-top" moot points. Actions in turn must be organized and combined and become constructive with a view to learning the result of the coordinations through operative deduction. The search for answers must become increasingly thorough and definitive. The social interaction of students must reflect both interdependence and equality. Thus answers are sought and ideas are explored in different contexts, in different media, at different degrees of complexity, and from different perspectives. Undoubtedly the cognitive skills described are not acquired in a day or a week or a year but across the years and through discipline.

Communication Refinements

Each school year should start with inquiry reading-type instructional procedures. This approach fosters a reexamination of interests that have been augmented by summertime adventures and explorations, summertime leisure, summertime reading, and summertime reflection. It reintroduces the pupils to self-analysis and self-determination by encouraging them to select interests to pursue and materials for study and research. Each year, preparation for sharing tends to be more creative and extended. Sharing is done with the zest of an invigorating first opportunity.

This is a period of reassessment of self for pupils and of estimation of pupil abilities for the instructor. Dictation continues at each level and is activated during this time of familiarizing and adjusting. This means of communication warrants attention and refinement across the years. Dictation to a teacher or an aide is expanded by use of tape recorders and especially by dictating to a classmate or to older, more advanced students.

Creative writing is activated by writing about summer experiences and summertime dreams. Increasingly, and by degrees, a personal style is acquired. This is especially so where originality and style are encouraged and where writing instruction introduces refinements and variations in such discreet doses that creating is not stifled. Succeeding years will show a dual trend. More and more writing will be done in account form to recount or report some current event of social or political significance, to detail an experiment or its results in science. The fiction writing will vary in style, in plot development, in sensing of nuances. All of this is to be expected and is to be refined through encouragement, instruction, and masterful imponderables.

As the amount of writing increases and the nature of the writing varies and changes, pupils become increasingly occupied with putting down what they wish to say and less deterred by how they put it down. This is to be desired and reflects the course of most writers—put down what you wish to say and struggle with refinement later.

So after ideas have been recorded and read and reread, the need for adjustments becomes apparent or new ways to express ideas become evident. As a result the idea of a second copy is introduced and editorial work is done. Usually, desire to clarify an expression, to make semantic changes, to intensify, leads to adjustments in grammar, in punctuation, in spelling, and in vocabulary usage. This editorial effort leads to the third, or final, polished copy.

In general the plan can be expressed as:

Draft One: *Write*
Put down ideas.
Draft Two: *Refine*
Adjust ideas.
Polish expressions.
Tighten structure.
Check mechanics of punctuation and spelling.
Draft Three: *Polish*
Make final copy.

Of course, as the year spins on, instructional attention is given to writing refinements. What must be avoided is red pencil abuse. Writing can be refined without violating the spirit of writing. Each phase of instruction must be both tempered and pointed. Thus a concentrated effort is made to standardize all spellings. This is best done by focusing only on spelling for a week or more while doing editorial work. A good procedure is to alert a pupil to the need for spelling corrections by placing a check mark at the beginning of a line, indicating that in that line there is a word or words spelled incorrectly.

√ and when the clouts moved by

or

$\overset{2}{\text{√}}$ in the desel enjine there was a

In the fourth grade and beyond it is also timely to have periodic student evaluations and sharing. Appraisal can be done by a three-member team. They decide (1) what about the presentation was best liked, and (2) what changes might be made if the presentation were made again. Both reactions keep attention focused on the positive and deemphasize the negative. Comments must be constructive and give thought not only to the nature and effectiveness of the presentation but also to the self-regard of the participants.

The Progress and Socialization of Behavior

Piaget begins a section of his book *Six Psychological Studies* with the title "The Progress and Socialization of Behavior" and the statement, "In an activity-oriented school, where the children are at liberty to work either in groups or alone and to talk while working, one is struck by the difference between these children and classes of younger children" (7, p. 39). If the last phrase were changed to "and classes that are not activity-oriented," then the statement would well serve this book: The best way to describe this difference between classes is to refer to the reactions of visitors. Visitors are nearly always astounded by the individual concentration children exhibit when they work by themselves and the effective collaboration they show when they work in an interest-oriented group.

As Piaget says, "True discussions are now possible in that the children show comprehension with respect to the other's point of view and a search for justification or proof with respect to their own statements" (7, p. 39). "True discussions" occur with amazing frequency in the cognitive

approach to reading instruction. The children substitute reflection and deliberation for impulsive behavior, which is of utmost importance in the development of intelligence and emotion. A system of values, closely related to realities and results, one that is based on mutual respect and reciprocity, gradually emerges for each pupil. The children attribute equivalent personal values to each other, and this kind of respect produces honesty and tolerance between peers and friends. It shows regard for regulations essential to study and intercommunication for efficient functioning in a classroom, a library, a school, or even a community. It leads to forms of conduct and moral feelings that emanate from within and are less subject to external dictation of situational ethics. Individuals see the rationale for subordinating themselves to the laws of reciprocity.

Of all the benefits that derive from the use of the LEA approach and the broader cognitive approach, the progress and socialization of behavior are by far the most significant. Children will perform as described if they are given the proper opportunity, wholesome encouragement, and pedagogical direction.

SPECIAL USES OF LEA

Immature Six-Year-Olds

A major advantage of the language-experience approach to initial reading instruction in particular is the degree to which superior children are given numerous opportunities to produce at their expectancy levels. This is so because instruction does not require all children to proceed as one. At the same time similar advantage accrues to the slowly developing children. They, too, can use to the fullest their limited but functional intellectual wealth by engaging in language-experience-type activities at their own rate of assimilation and accommodation while at the same time receiving more intensive instruction in their specific needs, and they can be provided with the kinds of experiences they need to gain maturity cognitively, socially, and emotionally.

Early identification of maturity for response to beginning reading instruction can be quite accurate. Teacher judgment is perhaps as trustworthy as any and when coupled with some diagnosis (see 10) can be quite to the point. A basic plan for early screening is "predicated on a strong and enduring commitment to provide successful learning experiences for students before a pattern of failure in school is established. . . . The purpose of a system is to evaluate student behaviors over a long period of time within the classroom environment, and to offer to teachers immediate feedback from a team of specialists" (3, p. 4). Then what remains to be done, of course, is to differentiate instruction.

A plan developed at Seaford, Delaware, during a period of years when I was consultant there proved most effective. All pupils starting school at West Seaford Elementary School were assigned randomly to four different first-grade classrooms. At the end of the first three weeks of school, the four teachers and the district reading supervisor, Mary Phillips, met to compare notes on the children. Out of the total first-grade population (115), 23 children were identified who seemed by all evidence (teacher judgments, informal tests, standardized tests) to be least mature. These 23 were reassigned and all placed in one room to form a pre-first-grade group.

Intelligence quotients for the 23, as determined by SRA Tests of General Ability[1] resulted in a range of scores from 111 to 78. Scores obtained by the school psychologist with the Wechsler Intelligence Scale for Children[2] on 13 of the group ranged from 88 to 51. Lee-Clark Reading Readiness Test[3] scores ranged from mental age 3-1 to 5-1, with an average score of about 4-4. In chronological age the pupils ranged from six years, two months, to seven years, six months. One physically handicapped boy was nine years, two months old.

Patricia Derrickson, their teacher, worked with the children on a readiness program much like that described for preschoolers. She soon noted that pupils could talk more and dictate better if they were telling about something they had done or something they had directly experienced. As she put it, "The more exciting and vivid the experience and the more a child participates in an event, the better the recall for telling of a story."

Mrs. Derrickson soon discovered that even in this group there existed marked differences. In a short time she noticed that five achieved far better than the others. Their stories were longer; their sentences were better; their ideas were more related. Most significant was their rate of word learning compared with that of the rest of the class. By Thanksgiving, these five knew the following number of words: 45, 41, 38, 34, 33. These words had all been learned through dictated accounts. Most of the techniques described in this book were used. The children kept their own story notebooks, had their own word banks, wrote stories, performed word recognition skill-training activities and so on. In addition, these children, because of their special needs, received an intensive language and cognitive development program similar to that described in Chapter 2.

All the children were tested on the Monday and Tuesday before Thanksgiving. Each child was asked to identify each word in his or her word bank. On the Tuesday following the Thanksgiving break all the

[1]Published by Science Research Associates, Chicago.
[2]Published by the Psychological Corporation, New York.
[3]Published by California Test Bureau, Los Angeles.

children were retested by the reading supervisor. Post-Thanksgiving testing, in spite of the week forgetting time, yielded almost the same scores as obtained on the pre-Thanksgiving testing.

In this group of 23, the largest number of words known by any one pupil by Thanksgiving was 45, the least was 2. The average for the class was 23. Only three pupils in the class knew fewer than 16 words, the number usually introduced in a first preprimer. Notice, too, that the five top pupils possessed a recognition vocabulary that was about equal to the vocabulary total of a second preprimer, 36 words.

Table 12-1 shows the word-learning progress of the 23 pupils at different times (the end of November and January, the middle March, the end of April, and the first week in June). Word knowledge was tested by presenting words in isolation. Testing recognition this way is more demanding on recall than testing in context, so in a sense the test is a better measure of known words than are most standardized primary reading tests.

The steady progress throughout the year, along with the end-of-the-year totals, represents astounding acheivement for a specially identified

Table 12-1

	NUMBER OF WORDS KNOWN				
PUPIL	NOVEMBER	JANUARY	MARCH	APRIL	JUNE
1	33	89	129	167	257
2	45	74	101	145	202
3	41	90	130	181	246
4	38	83	126	177	233
5	34	74	120	141	187
6	24	57	108	126	166
7	23	53	75	94	129
8	22	49	85	123	171
9	17	40	62	103	133
10	21	53	76	114	149
11	30	51	70	126	157
12	23	45	71	102	138
13	22	45	72	94	123
14	18	43	60	84	110
15	21	45	90	108	138
16	26	59	—	113	136
17	23	51	73	85	118
18	12	38	62	82	105
19	20	35	62	72	75
20	7	16	28	43	62
21	9	20	23	30	36
22	2	4	13	20	25
23	25	41	65	67	97

population of this kind: the range of words known, 25 to 257; the average score, 139 words. If the five bottom scores are deducted, the average shoots up to 170 words. This represents the progress made not by a typical low group but by a low-low group.

The following stories were dictated by the top group of five in this class of 23 and are illustrative:

Cafeteria
I saw some butter. Some chicken. A great big stove. Some potatoes and gravy.

To the Fire House
I went to the fire house. I looked around. I got a hat. And I got a balloon.

Jack-O-Lantern
We made a Jack-O-Lantern. We put eyes in it, and nose, a mouth. We made him a hat.

Mother
She cooks potatoes. She washes clothes. She sets food on the table. She reads books to me.

The following were dictated by the slowest children in this room and are also illustrative:

Cafeteria
We see fried chicken. We see butter. Biscuits.

School
We went walking around school. Seen the library. Seen the kids.

Trick or Treat
We eat popcorn. We eat marshmallows. We drink tea.

Mother
My mother cooks. She cooks on the stove. We wash our hands before we get up to the table.

The following year the same teacher, Mrs. Derrickson, stayed with the group. She knew the pupils so well that she could pick up where they left off. One change occurred, though: the top six were placed in other second grades and absorbed into new classes and new groups. Interestingly enough, a visitor to the school could not identify the six pupils in the other rooms. This is evidence of how well they fitted into the new arrangement. All teachers, of course, were well posted concerning what was happening but a little skeptical about how the pupils would fit in. By the end of September, however, they, too, were convinced of the progress of the six and how well they had matured.

At the end of the second year with the same teacher, the remaining 17 pupils were assimilated into other grades. All but four went on to third-grade classes; the four remained in second-grade classrooms. The pupils were assigned in such a way that only two or three of the group were in the same room. Progress was still reported as being most favorable.

The attention spans of members of the group, particularly the first year, were short. Needed more than tolerant patience was an adjustment of expectancies. Once the teacher's experience had led her to expect according to the "spans" of such pupils, rather than like those of the rest of

the population, she was calmer and more even-patterned in her acceptance of the children. First-grade teachers are often thought of as
mother-surrogates, as indeed they often are, and in this instance the label
was most appropriate. The teacher became their "mother in school," firm
and determined, attentive and devoted, affectionate and warm.

The classroom in which these children met was a typical room. It was
in the wing with other first- and second-grade sections. The children
mixed freely with each other, shared the playground, went to the
cafeteria together, and had the same principal.

The parents and guardians of the children needed some special attention, too. At the very beginning of the program, when the pupils had been
identified, each parent was seen privately and told about the plans. Parents were asked to agree but were not coerced. In a number of instances,
there were requests to "think it over." In each instance this involved a
return visit and an unhurried interview. All the parents eventually agreed
to the plan.

During the school year all reports were made in interviews with the
parents. They were told about the word-learning process, the experience
stories, the library hour, the visits, and so on. An interview guide form
was drafted to help keep the records straight about progress and about
what was said when. End-of-the-year changes and adjustments were similarly explained.

Administrative understanding and approval were required, of
course. Luckily, the superintendent was an interested participant. On a
number of occasions he sat in with the teachers and provided help as
needed in community contacts.

The school principal was intimately involved. She lent a hand in
screening and selecting the pupils, arranging transportation, and contact-
ing parents. Trips were planned with her approval and her assistance.

The district's reading consultant was closely involved in every phase
of the program. Her constancy and knowledge were a steady source of
guidance and help. She frequently stood by when small group visits were
made. This was an all-school enterprise.

In brief, then, it is apparent that in many ways what was done here
was similar to the program of an ungraded primary school. Instruction was
geared to the level of each pupil in as many ways as possible. Some pupils
spent four years in the primary grades rather than three. Teachers
planned and worked together and literally teamed up on these pupils.

Special-Education Children

Some children are classified as in need of special education because their
genes set limits on their potential for intellectual development. Many
states provide special instruction for such children by using teachers with

special training and by placing the children in separate rooms from those attended by more typically developing children. It is of special significance that the attitudes and efforts of the teachers who work with these children favor enriched environments and varied programs that maximize potential.

J. McV. Hunt's book *Intelligence and Experience* (7), particularly Chapter 8, shows why it is advisable to realize that children change and that the process of change itself is open ended as well. Teaching according to this understanding can offset unwarranted generalizations about fixed intelligence and response. Hunt points out how parental behavior, for instance, is probably a much more important influence than such traditional indexes as parental education, socioeconomic level, and number of books in the house. Similarly, teachers' behavior is probably a much more important determinant of rates and amount of development than are traditional indexes.

Enthusiasm about results of using the cognitive wealth and potential of children has been expressed many times here. Enthusiasm was no less great in using the LEA approach with special-education children. In two schools in Cecil County, Maryland,[4] two classes of special-education children have been studied for three years with results gratifying beyond all expectation.

In each instance the teachers were previously unacquainted with the techniques of the LEA approach and were educated in it while in service. In one school the same teacher has taught the class for three years. In the other a new teacher was introduced each year. Yet in both circumstances results have been exceptional. In the second school the transition to new teachers was effected with the help of the school principal.

Most significant of all the changes that occurred in these schools was the attitude of the children and, in turn, the atmosphere in the classrooms. Children who had been withdrawn, belligerent, or extremely reticent began to share and team up, to be more thoughtful and tolerant of each other, and to talk and participate in discussions. On many occasions, Ralph Wachter, the county coordinator of special-education classes, and I visited these rooms and were astounded at what we saw. In February of the first year, on the occasion of one of our visits, the teacher suggested to us quietly that we single out a particular boy and ask him to read his latest dictated experience recording. I did so and was pleased with his oral reading, the ease and enthusiasm with which he read. Then I suggested he go to the back of the room and read to the supervisor, and, without a moment's hesitation, he did so. This was a lad who had for two years been known throughout this school as the most close-mouthed child ever to

---

[4]Holly Hall Elementary School, Elizabeth Maloney, Principal. Rising Sun Elementary School, Naomi England, Principal.

attend. This is cited as illustrative of the changes that occurred in both rooms in both schools.

What did the teachers do to effect these changes? No more than has already been described, except to adapt the technique to the children. More action experiences were engaged in that permitted seeing, feeling, and hearing over a longer period of time. For example, rather than bring in a turtle for a day or two, a turtle was kept for weeks as a pet. Of course, he was attended to. Leaves were collected and examined and mounted; this was done almost daily for a while. Each experience evoked oral language.

When the children sat down to talk with the teacher to tell about an experience, they did so privately. These children can talk, they have reactions to experiences, and they have ideas. In the privacy of a face-to-face confab, they talk. The delight they exhibit when they see "their talk" being typed and when they can hold their own materials is indeed gratifying. Pride of authorship, of doing, of constructing verbally evokes deep-seated affective responses.

These children showed special delight when they found a word in a magazine or book that they learned to recognize through a dictated and recorded account. The "look Mom, I can read" radiance is energizing as well as illuminating.

All the activities of the approach are engaged in by these children but at a slower pace and with much more repetition than with more typically developing children. Auditory and auditory-visual training occurs. Word banks are built. Word-card holders are used. Listening posts are used to listen to music as well as to oral reading. It was not at all unusual to see one of the children go to a listening post and listen over and over again to a favorite selection. The freedom to do so, to put on the record, and to listen had a calming effect.

Construction activities also proved fruitful. Moving from assembling a jig-saw puzzle, a block puzzle, a Halloween mask, Christmas tree decorations, a pen for a pet, a phonic booth, and a map to dictation and creative writing was an easy and desired step.

Much oral reading was done by the teacher, by the principal, and by other visitors. Tape recordings were sometimes made of such readings and then the children could listen again at their convenience.

Although the most significant change was in attitude and atmosphere, almost equally significant was the nature and quality of the ideas dictated and recorded. The samples that follow are indicative.

R. C., a nine-year-old boy, was placed in a special-education class at the age of seven. Stanford Binet test results showed he had an I.Q. of 75 when he was five. WISC test results when he was eight, yielded an I.Q. of 80. When he was admitted to the special education class, he could not read a word. The following is some of R.C.'s work:

The Dog

If I saw it out there in the yard, I would throw a rock at it. It was on the table trying to get at the bottle. It had its feet on the table. Then it was trying to get at the pan. You could see the shadow on the ground under the table. And it looked funny. If it was getting in the pan I would scare it. I would sneak under the table and scare it.

(Dictated September 12, 1967)

The Planetarium

We visited the Planetarium last Friday. The guy showed us the stars and the moon and the planets. We had to sit back in the seats and look up in the air.

The guy got shocked on the machine. It has holes in the top. The top looks around. The guy can make it turn around backwards and frontwards. The guy can make it face up in the air.

The Planetarium is round and big. The top is a hole. It looks funny when you look up.

We saw the moon and the stars. There were words up in the hole; the sun turned down to the ground. We saw the man and the dog. We saw the bull and the little puppy. He was standing in one place. The guy said, "Venus is the closest one to the moon."

(Dictated February 18, 1969)

The teacher described R. C. as a very clean boy and well cared for. His special interest was fire engines. He dictated, wrote creatively, and drew pictures of his experiences frequently. Much of the time he seemed to be off in a world of make-believe. At age nine he was reading at a second-grade reader level.

J. T. is a 10-year-old with a Stanford Binet I.Q. of 56. He, too, was admitted to the special-education class at the age of 8, as a nonreader. He is a friendly, easy-going fellow who gets along well with everyone. He is in a foster home. Some of his stories follow:

I Hearded Something

I make noise and I saw the star. And you tore it apart. And we do the watch the flowers in it. And we watch, we sit down. And we go outside. We send dollar. We have horse.

(Dictated September 27, 1967)

Sad

Somebody make me mad. Mrs. Williamson write on the board. We copy it down. Mom makes me sad. She spanks me

(Dictated January 11, 1968)

Robert Nov, 20 1968

The Thanksgerving Turkey

I am a Turkey. I am a pretty Turkey. I Ran after a Boy and a girl.

Bambi

Bambi like to Be a fawn
Bambi saw a man in The bushs
Bambi was scared to death.
He was to starte to run. The man
shiot Bambi in the lag.

March 13, 1969
Bobby

The Inauguration

We saw Nixon and the *White House*. We saw the *parade*. And we saw marching. We saw the daughter and his *wife*.

> (Dictated January 23, 1969)

Snow

I like snow. We make a snowman. Robin kicked our snowman down. We wear boots outside. Joe Towers and Bill Billings and Harry Towers and Bill Carter and Betty Lou Mullins and William Carter, we played in the snow. It was cold out there.

I jumped in the snow. I fell down. Lots of snow was on the ground. And Mommy likes

snow. Janie likes snow and Bud Barrett likes
snow. Bud's birthday is tomorrow.
Everybody likes snow in my room. Mrs. May
likes snow. We sat down and watched TV and I
go by the window watching it snow outside. The
snow melted.

(Dictated February 10, 1969)

J. T. has done very little writing, but he has made attempts at it. He does "I like" stories because these are two words he can write and spell.

R. M. is an eleven-year-old girl with a WISC I.Q. of 56. She is reading comfortably now at a second-grade reader level. Here is a sample of her creative writing:

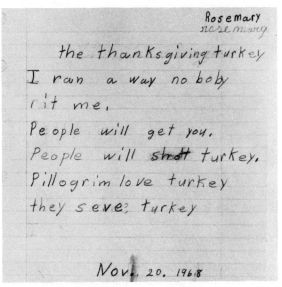

Another R. M. is an 11-year-old girl with a WISC I.Q. of 62. She, too, is reading comfortably at the second-grade reader level. The following is a story she wrote and read to me on my visit to their room:

F. J. is a 12-year-old boy with a WISC I.Q. of 73. He was known for years by his terrible temper, but in the past two years, this has changed to spells of stubbornness along with a marked effort at trying to learn. He is now reading comfortably at a third-grade reader level. The following is some of his work:

The Puppy
Mrs. Ryan brought a little puppy to school today.
And it was a German Shepherd. And it was
brown and black. And I like him very much. And
after recess we got to see him. And Mrs. Tippett
got him out of the box and untied him. Robert
asked the teacher could he pull him.

The car rake

We saw a car rake The boy
was hart he was Bleding
very very bad he had cuts
in back of his head
he was in paeen he was
harting to
                    Rose Marie
                    March 14 1967

And we all petted it and I held it. And Rose
Marie took it from me and dropped him down on
the ground.
    And Mrs. Tippett wanted to see him one
more time. And then Mrs. Tippett took the little
puppy back to his house and tied him up again.
                  (Dictated September 7, 1967)

The Planetarium
We went to the planetarium yesterday. We saw
nine planets. And there was a little arrow that
went around and pointed to the planets. It went
around the sun, too. And he said, "If you lived on
Jupiter you would only have a birthday every 12
years." You cannot throw a ball as far on Jupiter
as you can on Earth. It is about 30,000 miles long
and 7,000 miles wide. And everything looks like
real.
                  (Dictated February 2, 1968)

Examination of the items reproduced here shows how productive
such children can be. The quality of their language and the nature and
range of the experiences dealt with provide impressive evidence. These
children can talk and act and think effectively. One of the astonishing
outcomes is the self-regulation they display. Their rooms buzz with activity and with interpupil cooperation. They seem particularly sensitive to
the rights and feelings of others and display a strong *esprit de corps* for
their classmates.

In another situation J. P. Toothman, a special-education teacher working at the Charles County Learning Evaluation Center in La Plata, Maryland, has been been using LEA procedures with amazing results. In a report he prepared for the county board of education he wrote most insightfully about intellectually limited children ages 10 to 12 when he said that usually these children are "so frightened of reading and anything vaguely associated with the reading process that only a miracle would make them find reading enjoyable" (11, p.1).

He goes on to say that for the past two years he had used a LEA approach, with in-depth sight vocabulary, language, and word recognition program to develop a functional reading program for the children assigned to him. Some of the guidelines Mr. Toothman drew up for his program are as follows:

1. Reading was never confined to one period of time within the daily schedule, but was extended throughout all areas of classwork.
2. Classroom structure was flexible to allow for dictation at anytime within the daily schedule.
3. Dictation was viewed as an enjoyable experience in which both the student and the teacher actively participated.
4. Every student was allowed the opportunity to contribute to each story dictated.
5. Dictation was one of three types—student-initiated, teacher-initiated, or a combination student/teacher directed.
6. Dictation was used to reinforce (supplement) content curriculum areas, incorporating important concepts into the story formats.
7. General interest dictations for individual stories allowed students to dictate and read stories incorporating interests and background experiences.
8. Dictation for individual stories was taken whenever a student demonstrated a desire to do so [11, pp. 1–2].

If one word were used to describe Mr. Toothman's total reading program, it would be *flexibility.* "By allowing for flexibility in dictation, a greater variety, as well as a broader range of interesting topics and stories were obtained. Flexibility is the basis to the success of a reading program of this nature" (10, p. 2).

Mr. Toothman used two noteworthy procedures: (1) spontaneous dictation, and (2) teacher-structured dictations. The former were dictations resulting from spur of the moment happenings, pupil general interests, or school situations. The spontaneous dictations were largely pupil initiated. The teacher-structured situations were built around basic concepts in specific curriculum areas (arithmetic, science, social science, etc.), seasonal events, and functional reading activities. In addition, he used three types of format. A *primary format* always used pupil names, such as John said," "Mary said," and so on. This he found essential in the initial phases. The *transitional format* contained some sentences that did not use a pupil name and some that did. The *final format* was largely individual dictation and therefore did not need name indicators.

The following examples are illustrative. The reader is reminded that the children who dictated *and read* these accounts were 10 to 12 years of age and were classified as intellectually limited children.

Going to the A & P   9-3
Andre said, "Mark, come and go to the A & P with me. Mark Asked, "Is Fontella going with us?" Andre asked, "Can Jeffery and Ronnie come with us also?" Mark said, "John would like to go also with us." He needs some food to grow." Ronnie said, "I will be funny in the store." "He will jump up and down in the store." Wanda asked, "Are we going to the store or not?"

The Clock   9-23
Ronnie said, "The clock has two sides." John said, "They are the after side and the 'till side." Mark said, "There are two hands on our clock." We are working with the minute hand. Mark said, "The minute hand tells us minutes." Doris said, "There are twelve numbers on a clock." John said, "The after side has five numbers." Ronnie said, "They are one, two, three, four and five."

The Calendar   10-7
Doris said, "We have a calendar in our classroom" John said, "The calendar has numbers on it. They are the days of the month." Mark said, "The calendar tells us the days of the week." Lee Roy said, "The calendar tells us the date." Mark said, Today is October 7, 1975." Doris said, "Today is Tuesday." John said, "The month of the year is October." Mark said, "The calendar tells us the year." Jeffery said, "February has 28 days in its month." Fontella said, "October has 31 days in its month." Jeffery said, "The calendar tells us when to come to school and when to stay home." Doris said, "The calendar tells us when to go on a trip." Jeffery said, This calendar has Halloween on it. It is on the 31st. And it is on a Friday."

Fall Leaves and How We Named Them 10-27
Mark said, "When the leaves turn different colors they fall off the trees." Lee Roy said, "It is cool outside." Mark Brown said, "Yesterday we went out and found some leaves." Mark Brown said, "We looked them up in a book." Wanda said, "I found a sweet gum leaf." Lisa said, "I found two leaves—a sweet gum and a beech." Fontella said, "I found a dogwood leaf." Doris said, "We found the names of the leaves in the library."

Making Milk Shakes
We read the receipe slowly. We had to choose a
partner. After we picked our partner one of us
measured the milk. The other person put in the
ice cream. After we put the ice cream in the
container we added the milk. We put the cover
on the container. We pushed the 5 speed button
for 30 seconds until it was fluffy. Miss Smith's
class came to have milk shakes with us. Thank
you Mrs. Conley, the milk shakes were good.

How We Learned About the Stars
Mr. Arbogast called us on the intercom and told
us our bus was here. We took the bus to the
Planetarium. We hung our coats on the racks.
Mr. Williams told us to make a circle under the
sky. Then we turned around, sat down, and laid
on our backs. Then the sun started fading and
the stars came out. Mr. Williams showed us
different groups of stars with his flashlight, his
star machine, and his slide projector. He showed
us the brightest star in the sky. It is the north star.
He showed us Leo the Lion, Hercules, the
princess, the King, the little dog, the unicorn, the
big and little dipper, the whale, the hare, the
queen, and the hunter. After we saw the stars it
started to turn morning. The stars faded away
and the sun came up. Then our trip was over.

From September 3 to January 30 the class dealt with 18 different
dictations varying in length from about 78 running words and 57 different
words to 153 running words and 112 different words. The total number of
running words dealt with was 788 and the number of different words
about 600. The vocabulary varied in keeping with the nomenclature of
each topic. This brought into use such words as: *model, ambulance,
Mexico, crayfish, antenna, aquarium, electricity, asparagus, recipe*, and
the like.

As described in other instructional phases in this text, these 10- to
12-year-olds located words in newspapers, magazines, books, picture captions, and so on. They compared and contrasted words, formed word
categories, and checked on multiple uses. They prepared illustrations.

Many times these children were experiencing for the first time the
pleasure of reading on their own and enjoying it. At the same time there
existed a mutual bond between them as they worked together in the same
interest area, the same dictation, the same vocabulary, but did so at each
one's individual rate of learning.

The school library at last became a place to visit, to browse in, and to
read and was no longer a place to fear and to shun or to make trouble in.
Self-respect improved along with respect for books and reading.

Mr. Toothman's instructional feat has been matched in other schools in Charles County. A corps of special-education teachers has been developing an *esprit de corps* built around their successes in using the LEA instructional procedures.

Deaf and Partially Deaf Children

Phonics has been the harassing tyrant of reading instruction for too long a time, as Nila B. Smith once put it. If phonics is the royal road to learning to read, then all deaf people would never learn to read. But, of course, we know that deaf people do learn to read, although they are deprived of the modality of hearing or sound. So, too, we know that blind people deprived of the modality of sight learn to read. Apparently the secret to success in learning to read does not reside in either one or the other modality exclusively. This being the case, what is the secret to success? It is my conviction that as in all human communication the secret resides in meaning, intention, and expectation. These are the modalities of the mind that must be utilized and developed to the fullest. To read is to comprehend (meaning) and do so purposefully (intention) with personally determined anticipations (expectancies). In brief, if there is a royal road to reading it must be a semantic road, because to read is to comprehend.

It is a unique opportunity to work with Mrs. Marlene Harrell, reading supervisor for the faculty and staff at the Sterck School, the State of Delaware's school for the deaf. The school, which is named for Margaret E. Sterck, a pioneer in education of the deaf in Pennsylvania and Delaware, is located in the Newark, Delaware, school district. The school was opened in 1968 but until 1973 the instructional approach was devoted almost exclusively to the oralist approach. Since Roy Holcomb became the director in 1973 the pedagogical emphasis has shifted to that of total communication. Classes in sign communication were introduced for teachers, and thereafter classes were conducted within the total communication framework of sign and oral action.

Mrs. Harrell introduced the LEA approach to reading at both the lower and intermediate levels. In the beginning the primary focus was on the use of LEA procedures at the preschool for some four- and five-year-olds, kindergarten and first-grade levels.

In March a group of preschool children denied the modality of sound dictated (signed and vocalized) the following account. The stimulus was a picture of children playing in the snow.

Christine said, "Girl, boy, snowman, sled."
Ronnie said, "Four birds."
Otis said, "Boy push ball. Girl sled."
Katrina said, "Girl, man, love snow."
Ginny said, "Girl."

The children were able to read back (sign and vocalize) their names and the word *said*. Christine also read the words *girl* and *boy*. Four days after the chart had been recorded Ronnie came in from recess, went up to the chart, and read, "Ronnie said, 'Four birds.'" This four-year-old in particular seemed delighted and enthusiastic.

In April the same group dictated the following account:

Tina said, "Giant water get."
Otis said, "Luck call Father."
Tina said, "Giant grab father, mother."
Christine said, "Giant say, 'You stay! Sit here!'"
Katrina said, "Lucky smart. Mother, Daddy, boy
stay giant."
Tina said, "Lucky cry. Giant bad. Lucky mad."
Christine said, "Giant stay mad."

All the children could read each pupil's name and the words: *said, giant, father, mother, boy,* and *lucky* out of a total of 52 running words and 30 different words. Tina and Ronnie could read the entire dictation and could recognize each word in isolation.

It is apparent that the children are not using connectives and articles as is typically done by most hearing children four and five years old. This telegraphic syntactical encoding of ideas is characteristic of deaf children and tends to persist for some time. But with repeated opportunity to dictate and read back, the children did begin to insert idea connectives.

The following was dictated in late March by a group of six-year-olds:

Amy said, "The boy play with slide."
Jennifer said, "Mother, father, girl, boy eating."
Eric said, "Eric and Rusty go to lunch."
Katy said, "I saw a red and white fire."
Jennifer said, "The girls, boys watching storm."
Eric said, "The house fell."
Amy said, "The children run away house."
Eric said, "Eric and Rusty saw storm, ran from
house, tired, tired, tired. Run, run, run."
Rusty said, "Storm hurt children."

The children were responding to two picture stimuli: one a picture of a playground and the other a picture of an approaching storm. Three of the children could read the entire dictation without help and the other two could do so with some teacher pacing.

About a month later, using as a stimulus a firsthand experience that involved each pupil personally, the same children dictated the following account. It could very well be that responding to a firsthand experience in which they participated actively proved a vastly more fitting stimulus for language usage. This is the case with children who have no impairments.

What We Found Outside
Robbie said, "I found two flowers, and I saw five
leaves." Amy said, "I saw a worm. I saw a

buttercup. I found a baby buttercup. I saw a leaf
and a pinecone." Eric said, "I found a green
flower with leaves. I found one dandelion."
Jennifer said, "I saw a flower and I saw a
buttercup and I saw a soft leaf." Rusty said, "I
saw flower, I saw buttercup. White flower. I saw a
leaf."

The change in language structure is apparent. Most likely the syntactical changes reflect a better grasp of how language serves communication needs; moreover, personal involvement promotes a better-organized structure because of the participation. Again Robbie, Amy, and Eric could read all that was dictated, a total of 80 running words and 34 different words. In addition, the experience stimulus promoted the repetition of ideas and, in turn, of words. For instance, the word *found* was used 5 times; *flower*, 5 times; *saw*, 9 times; *I*, 13 times; *a*, 10 times; *and*, 4 times; *buttercup*, 4 times; and so on. These words and others were also located in places other than the chart and the children loved doing this. One child added 17 words to her word bank as a result of this one dictation.

It is to be noted, too, that the children are showing readiness for individual dictation. The spirit of group participation and sharing creates a desirable comradeship, but perhaps of even greater value is the communication that occurs as the children attend to the dictation and recording. Experience has shown teachers of preschoolers at Sterck that they obtain better responses at this age level if they obtain individual dictations. The stimulus used may be one that the children respond to in a group, but even this is not essential. This seems to be occasioned by the fact that the children are not too attentive to the signing that different ones do in response to a stimulus. The hearing child can listen to another child but the deaf child has to find the signing child in a group and then be attentive.

At grades 4 and 5, Mr. LeBuffe, the instructor, introduced the children to dictation (signed and vocalized) and met with similar success. At times he faced interesting interpretation circumstances, since signing frequently involves other body language signs, too. For instance, a child may be signing *cold* but showing by his manner of expression that he really means "freezing cold" or "extremely cold." Some of this may be clarified by questioning but if too much of this is done the spontaneity is lost and constraint sets in. Mr. LeBuffe also noted that, when reading, some of the older deaf children began attacking words by syllables and seemed to be saying or sounding them as well as signing elements in order to decode.

Illustrative of dictation by 9- and 10-year-olds as obtained by Mr. LeBuffe is the following account:

The Space Shuttle
The men say the rocket is not good. The airplane
is better. The U.S. will put the plane on a rocket.
There will be fire, then it will take off. In space, it
will land on a space platform. Three men will float
in the air. They will look down and see the earth.
It is beautiful and the stars are beautiful. Then
maybe the space shuttle will come back and land
on Earth. They will put an old flag on the moon.
by Richard and Peter

The language usage as shown here is not completely that of the children. Once the children have caught on to the dictating (signing) idea, Mr. LeBuffe begins to insert the connective words. Interestingly enough, though, when these children sign or read back recorded dictation, they accept the "fillers" and "read" them. Gradually this way the children become more familiar with the type of language structure they encounter when they turn to books, magazines, and newspapers.

Mr. LeBuffe is also having his group do creative writing. Written productions perhaps reflect more accurately the degree to which the child at this age level is learning to use the connected discourse of our hearing-speaking world.

Phils
Many people like Phils. Phils is win 7-6 than L.A.
Phils are shake L.A. Phils friend L.A. Phils are
happy, because happy about baseball. Many
people cheer to Phils, but like L.A. Many people
cheer L.A.

When Felicia read her creative writing account to Mr. LeBuffe so that he might type it for her, she read it as follows:

Phillies
Many people like the Phils. The Phils won 7-6
against L.A. The Phils are shaking L.A. The Phils
are friends of L.A. The Phils are happy because
they won the baseball game. Many people cheer
for the Phillies but like L.A. Many people cheer
for L.A.

The normally developing child's experiences are characterized by oral language (modality of sound) and sensorimotor responses (modalities of sight, touch, taste, movement). But the deaf child faces a deprivation (modality of sound) that sharply curbs and inhibits response. However, the use of total communication pedagogy permits more comprehensive participation by the deaf child. The use of LEA instructional procedures stressing active pupil participation in firsthand experiences and active use of language (sign and oral) to communicate in and about an experience helps greatly to offset the restrictive physical deficit. In addition, in working with deaf adults the children's self-respect is enhanced by the security and poise of the adults. Also, because they are urged to respond to an experience and to raise questions, they begin to approximate in their learning world the curiosity and questioning attitude of the unhandicapped.

Obviously this is an early report of instructional circumstances that appear to hold high promise. Currently closer documentation is being made of achievement and rate of progress, and much of substantial and practical value should soon be available to share with others. To help the deaf to function optimally is a considerable challenge and requires teachers who do not feel estranged from the children they teach. When teachers have insight into the positive values of the learning style, language, and modes of behavior of deaf children, they can be effective in motivating them to learn. Obviously, too, inability to use phonics and the modality of sound does not prevent deaf people from learning to communicate in and through written langauge.

CLINICAL CASES

I first began to appreciate the efficacy of the LEA approach in 1950, when I started using it clinically as a process that was in a sense an intermediate step between the Fernald technique (4) for tracing each word and the basic reader approach of most developmental classrooms. The incidence of nonreading that may cautiously be characterized as caused by visual aphasia or dyslexia is very small, but it is with people who are so affected that the V-A-K-T Fernald approach seems most effective. Some means other than tracing is needed for the larger number of children who are not dyslexic but who, for other causes, are almost nonreaders. These are the children who, because of strained circumstances at home, emotional conditions, educational practices, physiology, or slow development, have failed to learn to read. They need the equivalent to good first teaching and therapy to offset the attitudes acquired by failure.

The Reading Study Center at the University of Delaware used the LEA approach with such pupils almost exclusively by modifying the Fernald technique. This permitted a more advantageous use of Montessori methods, with their interest in the welfare of the child. The constructive effort to liberate the seriously handicapped readers from the Fernald tracing pedagogy, on the one hand, and the boring repetition of basic reader practices, on the other, has been effective. For these children both were as detrimental to their growth in ability to learn to read as a poor diet would have been to their physical growth. The language-experience approach, with its emphasis on the cognitive wealth of these readers, most of whom were bright or superior intellectually, proved functional.

Recently a colleague of mine, Dr. John Pikulski; a former student, Dr. Jules Abrams; and I prepared a professional book, *The Diagnosis, Correction and Prevention of Reading Difficulties* (9). In this text the reader will find lengthy, detailed accounts not only about instructional procedures involving an adapted version of LEA-type activities, the Fernald technique, and intensive phonics, but also about diagnosis and human adjustment.

Adult Illiterates and Semiilliterates

The LEA approach lends itself particularly well to teaching adult illiterate and semiilliterates to read and communicate more effectively orally as well as in writing. This is because the method takes advantage of the language facility that 18-year-olds and people older possess and because it uses to good advantage their experiences, interests, attitudes, and motivation.

Children in the primary grades who fail in reading become painfully aware of their failure and develop various defenses and anxieties. Adults, faced with the need to provide for themselves in a society that places increasingly high premiums on literacy, become keenly aware of their differences and disabilities. On the one hand, they seek help urgently, almost desperately, and yet, on the other, they are highly suspicious and wary. For most of them, attempts to teach them to read have been unsuccessful and, as a result, their response to "one more try" is guarded.

Conventional reading materials are not appropriate in most instances. Booklets and pamphlets with simple syntax, grammar, and semantics are readily recognized as simple. Adults resent a "Look, John Doe, look. See the gun. The gun is loaded" approach. They are quick to see the mask and its falsity.

When disadavantaged persons are given an opportunity to be producers, however, to use their own interests, to choose their own vocabulary, to articulate their own experiences, they are quick to notice that their wealth has been recognized and honored. By tapping their experience and language wealth, thinking is fostered and this, in turn, becomes stimulating to them.

If on-the-job training is given in addition to recording, typing, and using ideas to develop recognition and comprehension, then dramatic progress is shown in both educational efforts. The on-the-job training takes on additional significance and vitalizes interest, because the learners are asked to talk about what they are doing and in turn, to internalize their knowledge and experience. The ideas that they voice and the nomenclature that they use become comprehensible in print and excite further attempts at use (9).

The words can be located in print in various places, much as at the first-grade level. Words like *cocoanut, banana roll, seasoned, teaspoon, safety, railroad shop, National Bank, maternity, diploma, bureau, elastic, spark plug* can be found in brochures about different jobs, publicity materials, sales material, booklets, and books. Transfer from a typed account of dictation to other material can be immediate and effective. Word banks can be initiated, scaled, of course, to the level of the learners. Adults are just as responsive to activities that foster vocabulary growth as are children.

Newspapers and magazines can be used almost from the beginning. Known words can be located and underlined. A prize comment from one 22-year-old, after two months of training, was obtained one day when he said he had done something at breakfast he had never done before. He had bought a newspaper and read.

If adults of different age levels and different job skills are taught together, interest in what different members of the group are doing, saying, and reading can run high. A nurses' aide can read back her account of her experiences for the day and a gas-station attendant can read about happenings on his job. As skill is acquired, typed accounts can be exchanged and read silently. Such actions and interactions stimulate interest and motivation and also develop reading skill and facility in different areas.

LEA Actions Among the Navajos

This past year at an area meeting of Idaho's IRA (International Reading Association) organization in Idaho Falls, Virginia Merrill Simmons, organizer of the meeting, introduced me to one of the program participants, Mrs. Norma Heiman, from Utah State University. Mrs. Heiman, working at the Dilcon Boarding School north of Winslow, found language-experience procedures useful in the preparation of materials for and by young reservation Navajos.

Mrs. Heiman noted that surrounding the children with books about Anglo life did not solve the teaching-learning reading instruction situation. She said, "First, there is normally a language barrier, and second, the children are not usually exposed to books before they reach school age." She felt they needed materials about their own way of life and that kept the Indian style of speaking. Stories about supermarkets were replaced by stories about trading posts, prairie dogs and rabbits replaced "Dick and Jane." Stories tell about herding sheep, riding horses, getting water from a well—all things Indian children do themselves.

Not only did Mrs. Heiman have adults produce materials for the

Navajos to read through funds from the Louise E. Callister Foundation, but also students are writing and dictating stories that are being duplicated. One of the most popular student booklets is titled "How to Cook a Prairie Dog."

Luther, David, and Timothy were fifth-grade boys who could not read and were bored and distressed by repeated exposure to basic reader preprimers and primers. Their first dictations were about their families and were assembled into a 14-page illustrated booklet. The language usage is good, but the illustrations are priceless and, far more than their language, reflect their habitat.[5]

A Unique Use of LEA

Thelma R. Bullington, a first-grade teacher in Charles County, Maryland, used LEA in a most unusual instructional manner. She used to great advantage her own personal interest in the universe of knowledge and the *National Geographic* magazine to promote LEA instructional procedures in her classroom. She does this year after year with similar success each year. I have observed her in action over a three-year period and checked on her results by sitting down with her children and working with them. Each time I am all the more astounded because her classes are randomly selected and each year she achieves phenomenal success.

Mrs. Bullington is careful to choose articles that are within the children's realm of interest and ability to understand. At the same time the article is one that she can use to expand their concepts and knowledge of the world in which they live. She carefully reviews the article chosen, picking out the most interesting pictures and passages she feels the children can best understand. After assembling the group around her, she generally first discusses with them the topic of the article and has them speculate on and raise questions about it. Then as she shows the group the pictures chosen, reads the appropriate captions and passages, and paraphrases other portions, she goes through the article discussing with the children the main points and clarifying misunderstandings. There is ample time given to questioning, relating to previous experiences, discussion and reexamination of pictures, and so on. In addition, she supplements this with other reference sources from the multimedia center. These materials, which often include filmstrips, large picture books, and encyclopedias, are then placed on a special table to which the children have free access. The following accounts are ones she obtained using an article on the sea otter.

[5]Booklets can be obtained by requesting "Navajo Elementary Readers," Development Center, Utah State University, Logan, Utah, 84322.

Sea Otter

They wrap seaweed around the babies so they won't float away. They don't have sharp teeth like the beavers. [The group had previously dictated about an article on beavers.] They do down to get something to eat, then they go up and float on their back and put a rock on their stomach and use it to break open the shells. They eat a lot. They can stay underwater for four minutes. They float on their back. They have hind webbed feet. They are pretty and they are mammals. They have whiskers and they are cute. They have air in their hair so they won't get cold and die. They are one of the few animals that use a tool.

Ecosystem

Sea otters eat sea urchins and sea urchins eat seaweed. The man kills the sea otters. Then he messes up all the other animals and he doesn't have any seaweed to make paint and toothpaste. When the sea urchins cut off the seaweed at the bottom the fish don't have anyplace to hide and nothing to eat. If the sea urchin cuts off the seaweed and if the otter is wrapped up and asleep he will float away. The man had to go down and break open the sea urchins with a hammer. We feel sad and terrible.

At first one is astounded to discover that almost every child in the room can read the accounts. One might suspect memorization, but a spot check on words from the chart in isolation soon disproves this kind of skepticism. Then one thinks the concepts might be sheer verbalisms. But a random check on such words as *sea urchins, seaweed, sea otters, beavers, webbed feet,* and *mammals* proves that the children have good workable concepts.

In addition, one class wrote letters about the sea otters. One was addressed to John L. Paradise, Acting Chief, Office of Endangered Species, and another to Senator J. Glen Beall, U.S. Senator from Maryland. Through their efforts the class of 1976–1977 was influential in having the sea otter placed on the endangered species list. The children thus learned early in life that they can influence people and events.

Other dictations based on National Geographic articles include *The Sharks, Bald Eagles, The Beavers, Garden Eels, Sleeping Sharks, The Bats, The Octopus, The Sharkproof Fish, Portuguese Man-of-War, Cobra Snakes, Olive Sea Snakes, Osprey, The Polar Bear, Everglades National Park, Golden Eagles,* and *Tree Snails.* In addition, Mrs. Bullington uses items of interest in Charles County, seasonal events, and the like. Her room is a humming, industrious, active place filled with eager and excited children. The children acquire interest in the world around them and in the world far distant. In addition they are enjoying the process of discovery and rediscovery through listening, reading, and rereading. They love the challenge and respond with an insight and understanding that seem well beyond what is usually expected of six-year-olds. That these interests persist across the years is attested to by teachers in grades two and beyond and by the fact that the children make innumerable return visits to Mrs. Bullington's room.

CONCLUSION

It was a special privilege to prepare this last chapter. Every teacher who has enjoyed the genuine enthusiasm of children who have achieved will understand what it means to see their faces light up. It is a rare pleasure to see immature six-year-olds perform, to see typical first graders get excited about an article in the *National Geographic*, to see adult illiterates light up, to see clinic children pick up their spirits, to see the Navajos I worked with in New Mexico brighten and smile, and a very special treat to see deaf children flushed and exultant.

Whenever the cognitive, affective, and cultural wealth of children is used as a base for instruction, solid achievement is likely to result. Instruction, in capitalizing on this rich resource is also adapted to the level of the learner. The entire instruction-learning process utilizes an individual's thoughts, interests, and ambitions. In brief, it might be said that the LEA method resembles the Socratic method, with its painstaking and systematic development of *thought through inquiry* from early childhood to adulthood. The mind and heart of the individual are engaged in actions on things and on ideas, and this is what is vital.

Preschoolers can take a long stride forward in their acquisition of concepts and language usage as they free themselves from domination by their perceptual world. While they act and interact, see, feel, hear, smell, and taste, watch and listen to others, respond to adult guidance, and express themselves creatively, they acquire a storehouse of experiences and language that serve communication at different levels.

The immature can grow at a pace in keeping with their potential. Without their being pressured, their wealth is used and converted to serve more functionally. Instead of being shunted aside, they are helped along by steps that they can take successfully. On many occasions, paced learning based on known wealth results in unexpectedly rapid growth. But above all, it allows for steady growth rather than stagnation.

Persons in clinical situations, filled with the anxieties of failure and frustration, are encouraged to be producers and see more clearly that they possess many strengths. For them, the recognition that they have experiences and language that are useful is considerable stimulus for further effort. One more big try seems worthwhile as heads go up, shoulders go back, and new vigor is evident in every effort. Recognizing words in print is done through their own semantic trail. Word attack skills are based on their phonological wealth, syntactic power, and ability to transfer knowledge. By means of directed reading-thinking activities, a high level of motivation and interest is generated, because their thinking strategies and skills have been focused on.

Adult illiterates and semiilliterates are not stupid, only unlettered. The LEA approach capitalizes superbly on the fact that these people do not lack the power to absorb ideas and impressions. On the contrary, it builds on their ideas and impressions and the oral language facility they have acquired. As a result, a sufficient motivation to learn to read is generated and the successes that result become effective reinforcers. Their response is controlled by the consequences of their reading success. By utilizing job-oriented activities, their reading successes are immediately related to behavior needed for success in real-life situations.

The deaf are sensitive, thoughtful individuals eager to get along in a world dominated by sound. Accordingly, when total communication is used reciprocally and the children's verbal and motor exuberance activates their performance, achievement is potentially increased. Not only does total communication facilitate instruction and generate enthusiasm, but perhaps equally important, it provokes active sensorimotor involvement in the world about them. This allows their other capacities to develop, which, in turn, become a source of further growth.

The culturally different possess a source of wealth that is uniquely theirs. Wherever this is recognized and utilized they, too, blossom and produce and share with and enrich others. In a broad sense all of us are culturally different. I am Pennsylvania Dutch by birth and development. I am bilingual and can appreciate with deep awareness what it means to be honestly (not patronizingly) accepted and encouraged.

In brief, to utilize practices and procedures as described in this book is to teach so as to develop each individual to the fullest. When instruction is based on pupil actions and interactions, is projective and dynamic, and thrives on overt (first-hand experiences) and covert (reflections) manifestation, then instruction becomes highly productive. As Kant has said, when in a society of persons of good will, social peace, freedom, and cooperation are fostered, then instruction prospers.

Bibliography

1. Blake, Dathleen, *Play, Games and Sport: The Literary Works of Lewis Carroll.* Ithaca, N.Y.: Cornell University Press, 1974.
2. Davidson, Jane L., "The Quantity, Quality, and Variety of Teachers' Questions and Pupils' Responses During an Open-Communication Structured Group Directed Reading-Thinking Activity and a Closed-Communication

Structured Group Directed Reading Activity," Ph. D. dissertation, University of Michigan, 1970.

3. Division of Instruction, Maryland State Department of Education, *Guidelines, Early Identification and Instructional Programming for Learning Problems.* Baltimore: Maryland State Department of Education, 1975.

4. Fernald, Grace M., *Remedial Techniques in Basic School Subjects.* New York: McGraw-Hill, 1943.

5. Hunt, J. McV., *Intelligence and Experience.* New York: Ronald Press, 1961.

6. Petre, Richard M., "Quantity, Quality and Variety of Pupil Responses During an Open-Communication Structured Group Directed Reading-Thinking Activity and a Closed-Communication Structured Group Directed Reading Activity." Ph. D. dissertation, University of Delaware, 1970.

7. Piaget, Jean, and B. Inhelder, *The Pshchology of the Child.* New York: Basic Boosk, 1969.

8. Stauffer, Russell G., and Ronald Crammer, "Reading Specialists in an Occupational Training Program," *The Reading Teacher, 20* (March, 1967), 525–31.

9. Stauffer, Russell G., John Pikulski, and Jules Abrams, *The Diagnosis, Correction and Prevention of Reading Disabilities.* New York: Harper & Row, 1978.

10. Toothman, J. P., "Experience Reading With Twelve Special Children," unpublished Report, Learning Evaluation Center, Charles County Board of Education, La Plata, Maryland., 1976.

11. Vygotsky, L. S., *Thought and Language.* New York: Wiley, 1962.

Appendix A
A Language-Experience Film

A film entitled "The Language-Experience Approach to Teaching Reading" was produced by Professor Stauffer and the staff of the Instructional Resources Center of the University of Delaware. It is a 16-mm, color film, 45 minutes in length. It can be rented for a week for $45, or purchased for $425. The film is distributed by The Instructional Resource Center, Donald Nelson, Director, University of Delaware, Newark, DE, 19711.

Shot entirely in classrooms of a Maryland school, this film documents the language-experience approach to teaching reading as it is being used in real situations. Scenes from different classes demonstrate the application of the various techniques of the LEA Approach at different levels of reading development. As each technique is demonstrated, it is also briefly explained in narrative information added to the classroom footage.

After a brief introduction the film opens with a first-grade teacher involved in introductory reading activities with her class. The film shows her using a stimulus to gain the children's attention and interest. Once the children are involved, the film follows the variety of dictation activities used to generate student expression. The children dictate stories that the teacher transcribes and later uses as content for initial reading activities, word recognition practice, and phonics drill.

The second portion of the film demonstrates a single activity, the directed reading-thinking activity, as it is used in a second-grade class. It shows the use of speculation to gain student interest and introduce student viewpoints. It further shows how students may be stimulated to read for understanding by directing their attention to questions that need to be answered.

In another classroom the film shows second-grade children developing their skills in inquiry reading and creative writing. After presenting a starfish as a stimulus, the teacher leads a discussion in which she raises questions and gathers student views. With the introduction provided, the children readily move into the activities of inquiry reading and writing. Later they share what they have read and written.

A final portion of the film demonstrates how Inquiry Reading functions at the third-grade level. The teacher begins by gathering topics of interest from the students. The class then proceeds through steps to identify and group subinterest areas the children wish to explore; to raise specific questions; and to speculate on possible answers. The film follows the students as they search out information to answer their questions and plan and present reports of their findings.

Appendix B
Research in Language
Experience

A volume of research entitled *Action Research in Language Experience Approach Instructional Procedures* was compiled and written by Professor Stauffer. It was produced in paperback at the University of Delaware. A limited numbr of copies are available at $3.50 per copy. Copies can be obtained by writing to R. G. Stauffer, Box 83, R.D. #1, Hockessin, DE, 19707, including a check or money order or a certified purchasing order.

The publication was prepared to help teachers and others interested in improving instruction in reading through classroom research. The studies reported here are concerned primarily with comprehension as achieved by means of global LEA procedures. The interpretation of the LEA approach is not confined to initial reading instruction, since to do so would suggest naïveté about the nature and function of language and the utility of examined experiences at different age levels. In some ways the term *language arts* is more encompassing than *language experience*, but the label the *global approach* may be most descriptive.

Some of the studies are reported in considerable detail, to provide sufficient information to facilitate understanding and allow for likely replication. None of the reports provide a final truth. They do, however, report functional truths that can be implemented. This is so even though, all too often, the measuring rods used were inadequate. Even so, it may be concluded that if a trend is shown with measures of this caliber, more effective instruments would provide more convincing evidence.

First is a general position paper reflecting years of careful thought, much firsthand classroom experience, and considerable research. The paper is concerned with seven convictions about sound reading instruction. It sets the dimensions not only for instruction but also for research. The subsequent studies reported do to a good degree reflect this.

Research concerned with the improvement of instruction in the reading-thinking processes must, to be effective, be accomplished in the classroom, the primary laboratory for educational research. Instructional practices cannot be examined and improved in a laboratory vacuum. Processes must be examined, altered, and refined in the actions, interactions, and transactions of instructional dynamics.

The first four studies (R. Stauffer, et al.) are unique in many ways but especially in that the same population of children was taught and tested over a period of six years. Each reports findings impartially even though, as already stated, many of the tests used were unsuitable. Each describes in fair detail instructional practices and their implementation. Presented is a global view of an integrated LEA approach that is not truncated into an early phase but, as does the communication-learning process and the curriculum, spirals across the years.

The fifth study (M. Stauffer) is in a sense a replication study (a dire need in educational research), but it is also an extension and refinement. The major variables altered in this study as compared with the studies already reported are (1) teacher knowledge of innovative procedures, (2) the use of additional testing programs, and (3) an extended analysis of data. All other major variables such as sociocultural factors, heterogeneity of student population, and teaching procedures remained the same.

Sixth is the Petre study. He investigated the quantity, quality, and variety of pupil responses using two different reading instructional proedures. His subjects were fourth graders. His findings are encouraging indeed in that they confirm what armchair rationalization suggests—pupils can learn to read and think critically.

All of the studies reported were done at the University of Delaware except two. The seventh study, the Davidson study, was done at the University of Michigan, while I was on the doctoral committee. Her study was in many ways a replication of the Petre study but it was also an extension. Petre had found that DRTA procedures were superior when pupil responses were examined. Davidson assumed that a major factor influencing this circumstance would be the nature, quantity, and quality of teacher questions and found this to be the case.

The eighth study was done at the University of Virginia under the direction of Professor Edmund H. Henderson. The latter took his Ph.D. at the University of Delaware and taught there for seven years. He was instrumental in effecting the Petre study. The purpose of the Anderson study was to determine the effect of self-directed activity on the quantity, quality, and variety of responses in a group-directed DRTA. It was predicted that pupils would produce significantly higher-level responses than those not exhibiting the same level of self-direction.

The ninth study reported investigated the influence of method of instruction on the behavioral channeling of aggression. VanEyk Grobler postulated that in an open, multifaceted DRTA teaching-learning structure, aggression would be channeled constructively, and this is what he found. Studies of this type should be made with students at different age levels, using a variety of materials and employing increasingly more sensitive measuring instruments.

The Henderson study reported next preceded the more intense look at LEA procedures, their nature, and scope. It represented a first research-type look at directed reading-thinking procedures.

The Hammond study investigated certain aspects of syntactic structure in the creative writing performance of second-, third-, fourth-, and sixth-grade-level children. It clearly reflects the scope of an integrated global language arts approach to reading instruction. All phases of communication warrant scrutiny.

Similarly the Cramer study of spelling achievement reflects the nature and quality of achievement and its development by means of the LEA approach. Cramer investigated the spelling ability of first-grade-level children on phonologically regular and irregular words as well as spelling achievement in written composition.

The Valmont study examined another aspect of spelling performance. He investigated whether spelling consciousness and spelling achievement would be increased by requiring students to locate and correct words they had misspelled in creatively written materials.

Oehlkers examined the question of whether pupils in an LEA program make superior gains in word recognition if they start creative writing early in first grade or at a later date.

Margaret Jones's study was designed to investigate the effect of two types of purpose-setting directions on children's reading achievement. In addition, she examined intentional learning and compared it with incidental learning.

The purpose of the Lackman study was to compare the effects of four conditions of prequestioning. He used high school seniors as subjects, but, his inquiry is related to strategies that might be achieved at an earlier level, thereby implementing a vital phase of LEA procedures.

Noakes investigated the effects of using three straties for reading. Her sample consisted of 270 fifth-grade children.

The last study reported investigated the effects of two kindergarten programs on children's oral syntactical language facility. This study suggests clearly that methodology can influence children's oral langauge facility.

Needed are more and varied studies of a similar nature. If reading is taught effectively by means of LEA procedures as described here and through the medium of directed reading-thinking activities, group type and individualized, children can be taught to be more productive, efficient scholars.

Index

Abercrombie, M. L., 190, 213, 237, 259
Abrams, Jules, 321, 327
Achievement. *See* Analysis; Evaluation
Action, 23, 69, 275
  cognitive, 217, 225, 298
  learning process and, 8, 15–16, 22, 226
  preschool and, 22–24
Action centers, 48, 106, 137–138, 168–169
Action research, 230, 233, 260
Adams, Hazel, 167–168, 182
Adult illiterates, 321–322
Affective characteristics, 88, 141
Alliteration, 52, 72–74. *See also* Auditory
  discrimination
Allport, Gordon, 88, 108
Almy, Millie, 14, 15, 16, 19
Anderson, Robert, 332
Alphabet, 77, 273, 274, 287
  learning of, 116–117, 130, 273, 274, 287
  order of, 116, 273
Alphabet method, 283
Alphabetizing in word banks, 115–117
Alternating instruction, 219–220, 223, 235,
  236, 256

American Association of School Librarians,
  166, 167, 174–175, 176–177
Analysis, 55–56, 193–194, 299. *See also*
  Diagnosis; Evaluation
  of achievement, 212–213, 219, 230–232,
  234
  of phonic development, 131
  of readiness, 302
Analytic method, 3
Anticipation, 7, 12–13, 195, 225. *See also*
  Pupil purpose; Purpose
Anticipative mediators, 12
Appendixes, 329–330, 330–334
Artley, A. Sterl, 264, 281
Assimilation, 15, 16
Attitudes, of children, 195, 189, 230, 298,
  307
  teacher, 188–189, 195, 226, 237
  toward reading, 171, 173, 177, 194, 203,
  238
Attributes of concepts, 277–280
Audience interaction, 217, 227, 250–253
Auditory discrimination, 71–74
  activities to develop, 52–53, 71–74

Auditory discrimination (*continued*)
  beginning sounds, 52, 72–74
  defined, 71
  developing, 51–53, 71–74, 121, 233,
    270–271
  rhyming, 51, 71–72
  vowels, 270
Auditory-visual discrimination, 53, 68,
  74–76, 114, 122–123, 130, 234
Austin, Mary, 8, 19

Bartlett, F. C., 244, 259
Basal readers, 97, 170, 176, 198, 206, 219,
  268. *See also* Group Directed
    Reading-Thinking Activities, mate-
    rials
  research on, 161–162
  vocabulary in, 7–8, 254
Basic reading vocabulary. *See* Sight vocabu-
  lary
Bayley, Nancy, 16, 19
Beginning sounds, 72–74, 76–78, 82–83,
  114, 122–123, 269. *See also* Allitera-
    tion; Phonics
Berlyne, D. E., 244, 259
Berstein, Basin, 105, 108
Bilingual children, 41–43, 322–323
Bloom, Benjamin, 208, 213
Bond, Guy, 230, 259
Boney, C. DeWitt, 162, 163
Books, 169–170, 175–176, 221. *See also* Li-
  brary, books; Materials
  class made, 48–49
  dictated accounts and, 66, 171
  preschool, 35–36
  records of, 223–225, 254
Braine, M. S., 16, 19
Brearley, Molly, 136, 163
Britton, James, 6, 8, 9, 19, 140, 163, 195,
  213
Brown, Roger, 4, 6, 11, 12, 19
Bruner, Jerome, 14, 18, 19, 140, 163, 277,
  278, 281
Bullington, Thelma, 323–325
Bullock, Sir Alan, 4, 19, 47, 57, 108, 238,
  259
Burrows, Alvina, 160, 163, 247, 259, 283,
  285, 293

Carroll, John B., 18, 20, 57
Categorization, 115, 217, 239–241
Child development, 10–15, 38, 225
  instruction and, 7, 35, 38, 301–302
  language and, 31, 34, 275, 295
  learning and, 2, 10, 16, 34–35, 195, 296–
    297
  Piaget's views on, 10–17

Children's illustrations, 63–64, 65, 67, 85,
  86, 109, 112–113, 135, 136, 137, 150
Chomsky, Noam, 20, 57
Class dictated accounts, 89
  examples of, 32, 39, 40, 46–49, 65, 68
  recording of, 62–63
  rereading of, 39, 42, 63, 65
  underlining words in, 67, 109
  word recognition in, 65–67, 69–70
Classroom environment, 6, 23, 36, 48, 88,
  105, 106, 168–169, 178, 250
Classroom library. *See* Library, classroom
Classroom organization, 36, 79, 80, 84–86,
  87–88, 105–106, 178, 219. *See also*
    Action centers
Clinics, reading, use of Language-
  Experience Approach, 320–321
Closure, 39–55, 63–79, 81–97, 118–119,
  141, 221, 232, 244, 255, 263–264
Cognitive growth, 12–13, 31, 34–47. *See*
  also Intellectual development
  language and, 4, 5, 6, 34–37
Colman, Joseph, 27, 31, 37, 57
Communication, 2, 18, 216
  arts, 2, 228, 238
  creative writing and, 284–285, 295, 299–
    301
  language and, 104
  reading and, 226–227, 262, 263
Comprehension, 176, 202, 237, 277, 298.
  See also DRTA; Inquiry reading;
    Reading, defined
  development of, 61, 79, 115, 187, 210–
    211
Concept development, 10, 11, 12, 13, 140–
  141, 219, 277–279, 298. *See also*
    Bruner, J.; Vygotsky, L. S.
  Piaget's theories, 10–15
  role of language in, 5, 6–7, 11
  semantic triangle, 202
Concepts, 13, 140, 187, 202, 256, 277, 279,
  298
Concrete operations period, 13–15
Consonant substitution, 76–78, 82–83, 234,
  269–270, 276
Context clues to word recognition, 61,
  69–71, 87, 110, 124, 202–203, 205,
  255, 276, 280
  teaching of, 69–71
Continuity of experience. *See* Experience
Convergent thinking, 193, 211, 264
Coombs, Philip, 18, 20
Cordts, Anna, 71, 108
Cramer, Ronald, 321–322, 327, 333
Creative reader, 205
Creative word usage, 118–121, 264. *See also*
    Creative writing; Word Banks, activ-
    ities using

Creative writing, 272–273, 274, 284–287, 299, 301
  appraisal of, 50, 135–136, 158–159, 161, 231, 232
  defined, 127, 162
  editing, 121, 147, 158, 287, 300
  examples, 44–45, 50, 135, 142–144, 151–157
  first attempts, 44–45, 49–51, 152, 287
  getting started, 131–134
  illustration for, 135–137, 150
  materials, 137–138
  readiness for, 120, 127, 130–131, 132, 149–150
  sequence of ideas in, 150
  spelling in, 44–45, 50, 131–132, 145–148, 285–287, See also Encoding
  teacher's role, 131–132, 134
  topics for, 134, 138–139
  use of at different grades, 222, 227, 285, 288, 293, 299, 319
Creativity, 29, 35, 100, 160–161, 205
Critical reading, 185, 192, 298–299. See also DRTA; Inquiry reading; Reading, defined
Cue reduction, 112
Curiosity, 244
Curriculum, 15, 238, 296
Cybernetics, 297

Dale, Edgar, 252, 259
Davidson, Jane, 188, 213, 297, 326, 332
Deaf and partially deaf, 316–320
Decision making, 222, 243, 245, 252
Deighton, Lee C., 145, 163, 286, 294
Dewey John, 10, 20, 22, 23, 24, 26, 57, 108, 195, 213, 238, 242, 243, 259
Diagnosis. See Analysis; Diagnostic teaching; Evaluation
Diagnostic teaching, 65, 68, 79, 88, 91, 146, 219, 232, 302
Dialect. See Language, usage
Dictated accounts, 34, 39, 49, 79, 105, 171, 230, 299. See also Class dictated accounts; Group dictated accounts; Individual dictated accounts
  developing sight vocabulary, 42, 63, 66–67, 109–113, 193, 263
  developing word recognition skills, 65–68, 69–79, 82–83
  diagnostic use of, 65, 193, 230
  examples of, 32–33, 39–50, 62, 68, 305, 309–312, 314–319, 323–325
  grouping for, 49, 79–80, 89, 84–86
  language in, 46, 48, 85, See also Dictated accounts, examples of procedures for recording and using, 30, 39–40, 42, 62–63, 65, 66–67, 84–86

record keeping, 65, 102–103
  sources for, 34, 69, 90–103, 181
  uses at different levels, 32–33, 39–50, 299
Dictionary use, 116, 268, 273–275, 276–277, 286
Directed Listening-Thinking Activities, 194–196
Directed Reading Activity (DRA), 203–204
Directed Reading-Thinking Activity (DRTA). See Group Directed Reading-Thinking Activity; Inquiry reading
Disadvantaged, 36–37, 40
Discovery learning, 6, 13, 243. See also DRTA; Inquiry reading
Divergent thinking, 193, 205, 211
Duckworth, Eleanor, 17, 20

Early identification, 320
Editing, 121, 147, 158, 287, 300
Educated guesses. See Intent; Purposes; Speculation
Efficient reading. See Versatility
Egocentricity, 232, 251, 296
Elkind, David, 228, 301
Encoding, 50, 132, 133–134, 231, 285, 286, 296
  analysis of, 50, 135–136, 145–148, 159, 231
Encyclopedias, 66–79, 235. See also Materials
Environment. See Classroom environment
Epistemic curiosity, 244, 250, 251
Evaluation, 55–56, 230–231, 250–253. See also Analysis, Diagnostic teaching
  of first year achievement, 230–232
  of readiness for group instruction, 193–194, 219
  student, 300–301
Experience, 192
  continuity of, 26, 38, 195, 237–238
  Dewey's views of, 10, 24, 195
  dictated accounts and, 2, 33, 46, 60, 61, 62, 83–84
  education and, 10, 38, 238, 241, 243
  intellectual growth and, 7, 10, 11, 14, 35, 38, 195, 277
  language and, 2–4, 5, 7, 35–37, 38, 202, 255
  variety and wealth of, 9–10, 91
Experience-Language Approach. See Language Experience Approach
Extrapolation, 221, 232, 244. See also Closure

Fernald, Grace, 320, 327
Flavell, John, 20, 252, 259

Formal operations stage, 15
Fries, Charles, 264, 266, 267, 281

Gans, Roma, 38, 57
Gates, Arthur, 56, 57
Gaver, Mary, 167, 174-175, 183
Gifted children, 43-51
Goodenough, Florence, 63, 108
Goodlad, John, 29-30, 57, 62, 108, 293, 294
Grammar, 149, 161
Grammatical signals, 267
Grant, Barbara, 247, 259
Gray, William S., 26, 57
Grobler, C. Van Eyk, 189, 213, 333
Group dictated accounts, 79-82, 89. See
     also Dictated accounts
   examples of, 29, 32, 40, 47, 48-49, 81-82,
     314-318
   value of, 79-80
Group Directed Reading-Thinking Activi-
     ties, 218, 232, 297, 298-299
   basic principles, 185, 188-189, 196, 197,
     198, 216, 217
   example of, 198-201, 204-210
   individualized DRTA and, 216, 218, 234,
     235
   materials for, 189, 191, 196, 198, 209, 219
   oral reading in, 187, 207, 226
   plan for, 186-187, 203
   readiness for, 193-194, 212-213
   research on, 188-189, 330-334
   role of group in, 196-197
   role of teacher in, 188, 188-189, 191, 198,
     203, 204, 206, 212-213
   varying of, 193, 203-204, 210-211
Grouping, 79-80, 84-86, 89, 105, 186, 218,
     234, 288-289
Guilford, J. P., 160, 163, 205, 213

Hammond, W. Dorsey, 333
Hamp, Eric P., 104, 108
Handwriting, 127-129, 135-137
   appraisal of, 142, 152
Henderson, E. H., 188, 213, 333
Hennings, Dorothy, 34-36, 57, 247, 259
Hobson, James R., 56, 58
Holt, Robert, 91, 108
Home influences, 30, 37-38, 91-92
Horn, Ernest, 284, 294
Huey, Edmund, 37, 58, 282, 294, 283
Hunt, J. McV., 15, 17, 21, 307, 327
Hunt, Kellog, 149, 163
Hymes, James, 93, 108
Hypothesizing, 217, 232. See also Specula-
     tion

Illustrations. See Children's illustrations;
     Creative writing, illustrations; Indi-
     vidual dictated accounts

Immature six-year olds, 48-49, 302-306
Individual dictated accounts, 40, 84-102
   drawings for, 85, 86, 112, 113
   examples of, 41-45, 85-88, 90-102
   language in, 85
   organization for, 84-85
   topics for, 90-103
   underlining words in, 85, 87, 109
   value of, 89, 111
Individual differences, 6, 25, 29-30, 60, 62
   appraisal of, 65, 68, 79
   teaching for, 41, 51, 56-57, 60, 79
Individualization of instruction, 23, 41,
     56-57, 60, 79-80, 110, 128, 215, 216,
     217, 227, 292-293, 302
   in a DRTA, 216, 218, 225, 236, 245
   in inquiry reading, 227, 233
   in spelling, 288-292
Individualized reading. See Inquiry reading
Inquiry reading, 60, 178, 280, 299, 325
   distinguishing features of, 185, 216-217,
     235-236
   instructional procedures, 225-226, 239-
     253
   interest areas for, 216-217, 220-221, 223,
     227, 235, 239, 249-250
   materials for, 217, 218, 244
   pupil purposes and, 241-242
   questions in, 241-243
   record keeping, 223-225, 231, 234, 254
   skills acquired, 217, 218, 253-258
   scheduling for, 219, 220, 223, 235, 236,
     245
   sharing in, 217, 222-223, 236, 247-250,
     252
     evaluation of, 228
     planning, 247-248
     preparing, 223, 248
     scheduling, 222, 236, 249
     ways, 223, 226-227, 248, 249, 250
   teacher role, 246
   word recognition in, 221-222, 254-256
Instruction, and development, 7, 35, 38,
     296-297. See also Teacher role
   environment for, 6, 36, 48, 88
   improvement in, 59, 60
Instruction needs, 15, 18, 23, 35. See also
     Analysis; Diagnostic teaching;
     Evaluation
Intellectual development, 10, 11, 12-13, 16,
     17, 35, 37, 216, 225, 296-297
   Piaget stages, 10-15
Intent, 6, 11, 12, 60, 185, 195, 241, 243. See
     also Purposes; Speculation; DRTA;
     Inquiry reading
Interaction, 12, 24, 26, 34, 69, 219, 258. See
     also Socialization of behavior
Interests, reading, 61, 173-174, 166, 177-

178, 216, 220–221, 223, 227, 235, 239, 253
Interpolate and extrapolate. *See* Closure

Jensen, Amy, 236, 247, 250, 259
Jesperson, Otto, 71, 108
Jones, Margaret, 333

Kamii, Constance, 7, 20
Keppel, Francis, 166–167, 183
Kindergarten
  programs in, 23, 27–29, 33–37, 38
  research on effect of, 25–26
  use of LEA in, 32–33, 39–50
  word recognition in, 51–53
Klausmeier, Herbert, 13, 20, 279, 281
Kneller, George, 13, 20
Kooistra, W. H., 23

Lackman, Thomas, 333
Language, 3, 4, 25, 31–32, 37–38, 60, 104–105
  actions, 226–227
  analysis of, 7–8, 32, 161
  as communication, 2, 4, 104, 121, 226–227, 265–266
  cognitive growth and, 4, 5, 7, 15–16, 35
  concept development and, 5, 6, 11
  development of, 4–7, 8–9, 31–32, 34, 37–38, 104–105, 162, 295, 296
  in dictated accounts, 31, 33, 40, 46. *See also* Dictated accounts, examples
  intellectual growth and, 31, 35, 296
  learning and, 31–32, 35, 47, 202
  thought and, 3, 4, 296
  word recognition and, 263, 264, 265
Language-Experience Approach (LEA), 60, 130, 162, 176, 227, 275, 325
  communication and, 2, 3, 160
  environment for, 6, 36, 48, 83–84, 105
  foundations for, 2–3, 17, 39, 60, 165–166, 295–296
  in middle grades, 296–302
  principal features of, 2–3, 51, 60, 105, 129–130, 165–166, 182, 230–232, 294–295, 296
  research on, 230, 233, 332–334
Lavatelli, Celia S., 35, 58, 284, 294
Learning, 8, 18, 19, 24, 41
  conditions 61, 160, 201–202, 252, 292
  development and, 7, 15, 16
  environment, 6, 23, 36, 48, 88, 168–169, 252
  measure of, 7, 16
  rate, 160
  role of action in, 15–16, 19, 23, 24, 47
  role of group in, 196–197
Letter names. *See* Alphabet

Letter order, 130–131, 145–148. *See also* Encode: Spelling
Letter substitution, 76–78. *See also* Consonant substitution
Lexical signals, 266–267
Library, 60, 61, 175, 178, 234
  books in, 35, 169–170, 175–176, 177, 179
  classroom, 35, 105, 168–172, 182, 215
  arrangement of, 35, 168–169
  materials for, 35, 169–170, 176, 234
  use of, 66, 170–172
  public, 180, 245
  role of, 166, 167–168, 178
  school, 35, 172–179, 182, 167, 174–175, 179, 244–245
  use of, 167–168, 175, 177, 179, 181, 232, 245, 315
  standards for, 166
  teacher role and, 166, 167, 177
  usage skills, 181, 245
Librarian, 166, 167, 176, 182,
  role of, 174, 177, 179
Linguistic clues, 265, 266
Linguistic development, 5, 31–32, 104–105
Linguistic opportunities, 31–33
Listening, 208, 220, 226, 256
Listening post, 168, 170
Loban, Walter, 161, 163

McCullough, Constance, 264, 281
Materials, reading, 97, 170, 172, 176, 217, 221,323. *See also* Basal readers; Dictated Accounts; Library
  for DRTA, 185–186, 196, 209, 219
  for instruction, 174–175, 191, 239, 243–247
  locating and selecting, 253
Meaning clues, 61, 202–203, 205–206, 262, 263–268, 276, 280. *See also* Context clues
  kinds of, 264–265, 265–267
  linguistic, 265, 266
Motivation for learning, 252
Murray, Henry, 91, 108

Navajo use of LEA, 322–323
New words. *See* Sight vocabulary
Noakes, Ann Marie, 333
Note taking, 246, 247
Nursery education, 27–28

Oehlkers, William, 333
Operations, defined, 13, 16
Operation stage, 11–12
Oral language, facility, 7–8, 32
  developing, 32, 34, 34–37
Oral reading, 36, 38, 193, 194
  purpose of, 207, 226, 257, 258

Parents, 206, 207, 231
Percept, 12, 33, 34. *See also* Experience; Vocabulary
Perceptual opportunities, 31, 33–34
Personal dispositions, 88, 141
Petre, Richard, 178, 183, 188, 213, 297, 327, 332
Phonic booth, 106–107
Phonics, 61, 69, 120, 131, 276, 316
  readiness for, 51
  teaching, 51–53, 61, 71–79, 82–83, 114, 121–124, 145–146
  in context, 61, 69–70, 74, 263–264
Phonological development, 5, 8, 9, 50, 51–53, 71, 130, 132, 287–288, 272–273
Phonological encoding, 132, 134, 231, 285–287. *See also* Spelling
  analysis of, 135–136, 145
Piaget, Jean, 5, 10–17, 20, 23, 35, 37, 58, 108, 148, 160, 163, 173, 183, 195, 213, 216, 225, 228, 250, 251, 258, 259, 275, 281, 297, 301
Pictures, 226, 268. *See also* Illustrations
  use of in DRTA, 192, 209, 221
  use in word recognition, 268–269
Pikulski, John, 321, 327
Plowden report, 27–29
Preconcept period, 12
Predict-Read-Prove, 188, 192–193. *See* Group DRTA; Inquiry reading
Preoperational stage, 11, 12–13
Problem solving approach to reading, 185, 243. *See also* Group Directed Reading-Thinking Activity
Pupil purposes, 186, 187, 195–196, 204, 219, 241–243, 254. *See also* Inquiry; Purposes; Intent; Speculation
  developing, 190–192
  research on, 188–189, 330–333
  testing, 193, 207
Purpose, 219, 238. *See also* Reading purposes
  influence of, 11, 60, 195, 238

Questioning, 208–213, 241–243, 256

Readiness, 23, 25–27, 30, 31, 37–38, 116, 117
  tests, 55–56, 303
Reading, 31, 60, 103, 162, 173, 174, 194, 226, 254, 258
  appreciation for, 61, 171, 173, 177, 194, 203, 257, 258
  defined, 60, 67, 84, 185, 226, 227, 265
  efficiency. *See* Versatility
  extensive and intensive, 254, 257
  for meaning, 176, 184. *See also* Comprehension; Group Directed Reading-Thinking Activity, Inquiry reading
  problem solving, 243
  rate, 61, 186, 188, 190
Reading clinics, 320–321
Reading instruction, 2, 3, 6, 7–8, 15, 17–18, 32, 105, 146, 176, 206, 212, 226, 296
Reading maturity, 26–27, 38, 174, 184, 237, 267, 297–298
Record keeping, 254
Retention, 110, 111, 201–202
Rhyming words, 51, 71–72
Robinson, Helen, 55–56, 58
Russell, David, 279, 281

Scheduling, 179, 219, 223, 235, 236
Seashore, Robert, 20
Self-regulation, 17, 23, 24, 80, 176, 219, 220, 242, 256, 258, 297
Self-selection, 220–221, 253, 256. *See also* Inquiry reading
Semantics, 202, 277
Sensory motor period, 11, 12
Sequential order, 48
Shared learning, 34, 89, 121, 123, 180
  in creative writing, 137
  in DRTAs, 196–197
  in Inquiry reading, 217, 220, 222–223, 236, 247–250, 252, 256
    evaluation of, 228
    preparation for, 248, 252
    scheduling of, 222–223
    ways of, 223
  with books, 172, 178, 180–181, 194
Sharpe, Malda, 250, 260
Sigel, Irving, 10, 11, 20
Sight vocabulary, developing, 65–66, 75, 80–81, 82, 109–113, 171, 187, 201–202, 210. *See also* Word banks
Slobin, Dan, 6, 20
Smith, Karl, 160, 163
Smith, Madorah, 7, 21
Smith, Mary, 7, 21
Smith, Nila, B., 56, 58, 282, 283, 294, 316
Social interactions, 8, 12, 17, 24, 225, 251
Sociocentric, 232, 251
Socialization of behavior, 250–251, 301–302
Special education, 306–316
Speculation, 192, 203, 205, 217, 243–244
Speech, development of, 4–5
Spelling, consciousness, 77, 82–83, 130–131, 149, 159, 162, 288. *See also* Phonological development
  in creative writing, 50, 131–132, 145–148
  formal instruction, 288–292, 300

individualization of, 288, 289–292, 293
inventory, 289–291, 293
research on, 159, 332–333
self-correction, 288, 290–292
study procedures, 291
Stauffer, Russell G., 8, 21, 25, 56, 58, 60,
    97, 108, 116, 125, 259, 263, 167, 171,
    179, 183, 190, 204, 210, 213, 230,
    260, 327, 329, 332
Stebbing, L. Susan, 24, 58, 243, 260
Stimulus interest areas, 34, 69, 90–103
Strickland, Ruth, 21, 161, 163
Stroud, J. B., 202, 213
Structural analysis, 69, 81, 82, 115, 272–
    273, 276
Study skills, 246–247
Sullivan, Peggy, 167, 183
Summers, Andrew, 88, 108
Syntax, 120–121, 279
    in creative writing, 149
    in dictated accounts, 82
    language development and, 6–7

Teacher, attitude, 226, 237. See also Diag-
    nostic teaching
    expectations, 188–189, 195, 307
    library and, 166, 167, 176, 176–177, 179
    role in DRTAs, 188, 189–190, 191, 198,
        203–204, 206, 208–209, 212, 218
Test-study in spelling, 288, 289–291
Tests, 55–56, 303, See also Analysis; Evalu-
    ation
Thematic Apperception test, 91
Thinking, defined, 18
    language and, 4, 6, 205
    levels of, 188
Third grade instruction, 296–302
Thomas, Charles, 71, 108
Thurstone, Thelma, 161, 164
Title clues, 203, 205
Toothman, J. P., 302, 327, 313
Torrance, E. Paul, 35, 58, 205, 213
Transaction, 24–25
Transfer of knowledge, 66, 79, 81, 145,
    171–172, 194, 255

Underlining words in dictated accounts, 67,
    85, 87, 109, 111–112
Underwood, Benton, J., 140, 164, 277, 281

Valmont, William, 333
Veatch, Jeannette, 236, 260
Versatility, 61, 188, 190, 247

Visual discrimination 54, 68, 205
Vocabulary development, 15, 38, 141. See
    also Concept development; Sight vo-
    cabulary
Vowel keys, 269–272, 274, 277,
    construction of, 270–271
Vowels, 146, 159, 269
    teaching of, 234, 270–272
Vygotsky, L. S., 5, 6–7, 21, 140, 164, 277,
    278, 281, 298, 327

Walpole, Hugh, 202, 214
Waples, Douglas, 61, 108
Williams, Lois E., 247, 260
Window cards, 110, 112
Word attack skills, development of, 51–53,
    69–79, 120, 276
    sequence of, 69, 73, 205, 221–222
    teaching of, 61, 69–79, 206, 265, 269–270,
        276
    use of, 221, 254–256
Word banks, 194, 231, 273
    activities using, 66, 114–115, 116, 117,
        118, 121, 122–123, 124–125, 171–172
    alphabetizing, 115–117, 273
    creative structuring of ideas with, 118–
        121, 130
    developing word attack skills with, 121–
        124, 231
    obtaining words for, 81, 82, 109–114, 119,
        150–151
Word card holder, 118–119, 121, 264
Word cards, 113–114, 124
Word families. See Consonant substitution;
    Letter substitution
Word recognition skills, 187, 193. See also
    Auditory discrimination; Auditory
    visual discrimination; Beginning
    sounds; Consonant substitution;
    Context clues; Dictionary use; Letter
    substitution; Linguistic clues; Mean-
    ing clues; Phonics, Structural
    analysis; Visual discrimination;
    Vowel Keys; Vowels; Word Banks,
    developing word attack skills
    defined, 69, 74, 262, 263, 264
    independent use of, 203–205, 206, 221–
        222, 254–255
    purpose of, 75, 221–222, 261
    research on, 331–334
    teaching of, 61, 65–67, 69–70, 205, 265,
        267, 280
    use of word banks, 114, 120, 121–124